Sociology and Your World

How Culture Designs Power and Privilege in our Everyday Lives

FIRST EDITION

EDITED BY DAWN TAWWATER

Austin Community College

cognella®
academic publishing

Bassim Hamadeh, CEO and Publisher
Michael Simpson, Vice President of Acquisitions
Jamie Giganti, Senior Managing Editor
Miguel Macias, Graphic Designer
Zina Craft, Acquisitions Editor
Gem Rabanera, Project Editor
Elizabeth Rowe, Licensing Coordinator
Kathryn Ragudos, Interior Designer

First published in the United States of America in 2016 by Cognella, Inc.

Cover image copyright © by Depositphotos / ginosphotos1.

Printed in the United States of America

ISBN: 978-1-63189-498-5 (pbk) / 978-1-63189-499-2 (br)

www.cognella.com   800-200-3908

Contents

Acknowledgments

Developing this text was definitely a collaborative effort, and I would like to thank those most essential to the completion. A big thank you to David Embrick, who not only contributed a valued article to the text, but also introduced me to his editor at Cognella Academic Publishing and encouraged me to take on the project. David has been a good mentor and friend. Also in my corner, I have had the unyielding support and patience of contributor Jeff Torlina, whose constant upbeat and encouraging emails often reminded me why I do what I do and kept me moving forward in the face of a very difficult year. Thanks also to contributor Richard Ellefritz, whose work I greatly value and think will be a great tool for teaching introductory students.

I would like to thank the whole team who worked on the textbook at Cognella Publishing, led by my wonderful project editor Gem Rabanera. Gem showed me guidance, direction, and patience—it is so much appreciated. I would also like to thank Ethan King for being the first editor of my writing for the text. Ethan's professionalism and accuracy assisted in the earliest stages of the process of editing; the work is better for his keen eye and positive contributions.

Introduction

Education either functions as an instrument which is used to facilitate integration of the younger generation into the logic of the present system and bring about conformity or it becomes the practice of freedom, the means by which men and women deal critically and creatively with reality and discover how to participate in the transformation of their world.

Paulo Freire, *Pedagogy of the Oppressed*, (1970)

First and foremost, welcome to the academic discipline of sociology. As you begin, I want to briefly address the reasoning for this book, the approach, and my hopes for you as you get started exploring sociological perspectives. Whether you are a sociology major or find yourself in a sociology course to meet general academic requirements, I think you will find in these readings an interesting and enlightening approach to the study of our culture and the systems that drive our social world. Sociology, a contemporary of the social sciences, looks to analyze social life in terms of group, or class, interactions at a systematic and institutional level. These readings were chosen to inspire students with material that informs and excites intellectual engagement with sociological ideas in general, and issues of race, class, and gender in particular. This approach makes the text a valuable asset to introductory students as well as classes developed for discussions of inequalities in the United States, as it allows for a more in-depth approach on a few central topics.

Sociology today is an unusually ignored discipline, although it should be used as an effective approach to problems in culture. Some argue this lack of sociological focus is due to the history of the last 35–40 years; a time in the U.S. that has moved increasingly toward individualism and away from collective action as a society (see Buechler, R.2). In addition, there has been a resurgence in the assertion of human *nature* as a primary foundation of social thought and motivation, and a minimal consideration of the sociological emphasis of society as a social construction serving certain interests, discourses, and authorities. Social identities have become passive labels for political banter and social oppression rather than valued experiences used to shape a malleable culture that is often erroneously viewed as stagnant. This, in fact, is a central reason for the importance of the sociological approach. It seeks to promote and expect results from progressions in cultural knowledge; a cultural knowledge that, even in spite of the sometimes reluctant motivation to change the social world by society itself, can support those who are change makers by providing them with research and analysis of what social arrangements and systems do to interfere with or substantiate the public good.

Additionally, I have developed this text to also address some issues found in sociology's own academic house; basically that the fundamental consequences of structural inequality are also reflected in our own ranks and culture. Including in the production of our class lectures and materials. The topics I address here are obvious, but are nevertheless often overlooked in the typical sociological text. Three things dominate my critique: the use of interpreters, diversity of scholarship, and subject focus. The first thing overlooked is that we should rely on the students' intellectual abilities and expect scholarship in their approach to work. Here, you will not read all of the declared major theorists in sociology, but you will read excerpts of some of them and their work in its original form. I believe that providing original work, rather than interpretive discussions of sociological theory, gives students the privilege and the burden of forming their own analysis of those works, promoting and encouraging critical thinking, and engaging the sociological imagination. I don't mean to suggest that considering the interpretation of others shouldn't also be a part of the process of researching a topic, but that process can occur anyway, and how do we inhibit transformation through interpretation only? How is the starting point of analysis affected by the first learned values, and if it is significant then how do we shape or inhibit insight and scholarship by defining for students what can be interpreted for themselves? Another significant issue is the general state of public schools in the last three decades. As a society we have put an ever stronger emphasis on standardized testing to the point that much of the material students learn is grounded in memorization and regurgitation. This also promotes truth claims, rather than intellectual exploration. For those students, one of the biggest hurdles in higher education can be the transition from the concrete thinking of memorization to the abstract thinking of critical analysis. I find that students just starting college often read text uncritically, taking those interpretations for "truth" rather than as one perspective for consideration. It is my hope that you will feel empowered by this choice and will enjoy and value the practice of reading original works.

Secondly, this text strives to provide a more diverse perspective into the field of introductory sociology. Unfortunately, like all major academic disciplines, sociology has a tendency toward dominant voices of authority; sociology textbooks are often directed and influenced by majority group values that originate in the patriarchal systems enjoyed by European white males. This text includes readings that reflect marginalized voices not only in the topics, but also in the authors, with more than half of readings contributed by marginalized sociologists. Sociology has a unique place in incorporating the voices all too easily silenced in the history of our country. It also has the unique goal of critiquing and evaluating "truth" as a social concept and power signifier. Readings in feminist sociology, Queer sociology, Latino/Latina sociology, and African American sociology, among others, not only provide insight into the various views of seeing the world but also serve to critique the discipline itself. Again, its established roots and, all too often, modern pedagogy, remain limited to specific voices of privilege, voices that are not irrelevant as contributors, but should not limit the discipline as singular approaches, or even fundamental approaches to its progress. What's more, as with typical texts, I have not split the issues of race, class, and gender into sections; rather the topics are blended to discuss inequalities from a discourse that emphasizes the common elements of oppression in culture rather than the differences. This is a choice that is both academic and radical, although I argue that the latter shouldn't be; in fact, as I noted earlier, the retention of separatist views in discussions of inequalities is a part of the problem.

Lastly, as I said at the beginning of the introduction, this text is focused on specific issues. Rather than an attempt to address the broad discipline of sociology, the work found here focuses the student on critical sociology and its approach of questioning norms and historical context in its analysis of race, class, and gender, as well as giving students the opportunity to take an in-depth approach to the most fundamental of discussions: those of inequality, social justice, and human rights. In many introductory courses, instructors attempt to convey all the areas of society that the course seeks to explore, engaging students in a broad understanding of sociological approaches and topics of inquiry. However, this approach often results in a superficial understanding of sociology that lacks the necessary complexity and level of consideration to provide the student with a sense of what makes the sociological approach unique. A more focused approach will serve to move the introductory student into the more important and relevant sociological perspective, rather than sociological topics.

One parting thought as you begin your work: Sociology has often been seen as a liberal perspective, and while it serves its place under the banner of a liberal arts education, so do many other disciplines that are not, as often, characterized politically. While, certainly, sociological knowledge can inform us in political issues and questions when they arise, there is no homogeneity in the politics of individual sociologists. In twenty years of service to the discipline, I can attest to sociologists who represent a spectrum of political perspectives that are no more relevant to their work than the politics of a shoe salesperson has on his or her approach to selling shoes. I warn you, if you feel like you are being indoctrinated into a particular view or a political party, you do not understand the work's complexity and should consider how you can approach the topic differently using sociological methods.

To some extent, any discourse about inequalities will always be used to deconstruct the speaker, and there is a vested interest at the social level for inequalities to be maintained. However, questioning our social world, social policy, and our everyday interactions does not always result in a dismissal of *what is*. In fact, often our views support the popular understandings and our cultural approach as a society. Good sociological instruction does not seek to tell the student what to think, but rather to offer reasonable tools in how to think. To do that, sociological analysis should be a close review of the social world based in empirical research and the development of diverse academic theory. That is not to say that sociologists don't often feel strongly about social issues. As humans, how can we not? After all, we are not just studying culture, we are also living in culture. We all experience, to some extent, the way society works and the ways in which it doesn't, but that is often far from our sociological understanding of culture. Sometimes individual experiences will be represented in sociological viewpoints, and it will be validating, but sometimes they will not be. They may even be contradictory of our experience—not surprisingly, that is, when some will want to dismiss sociological thought and its relevance. In addition, sociology isn't about studying or advocating for *victimization* when looking at inequalities, but it is about studying and naming social problems that are having a negative and unjust impact on society, as well as members of oppressed groups, which can drive us to call for significant change. There should never be a move to reduce sociological observations; no matter what our beliefs or what we learn from it, we can use those observations to change the world.

How to Think Sociologically

by Steven M. Buechler

People have always tried to make sense of the world around them. Myths, fables, and religion provided traditional ways of making sense. More recently, science has provided additional ways of understanding the world. Sociology is part of the rise of science as a means of making sense of the world.

As we know in our own time, there can be tension between religious and scientific views. Contemporary disputes over evolution, sexuality, marriage, and even the age of our planet often pit religious values against scientific interpretations. More broadly speaking, both at home and abroad, religious fundamentalisms rest uneasily alongside modern, secular worldviews. These familiar tensions have a history that takes us back to the origins of sociology itself.

SOCIOLOGY AND MODERNITY

The rise of sociology is part of a much larger story about the emergence of the modern world itself. Modernity emerged in European societies through a long process of social change that unfolded from the sixteenth to the nineteenth centuries. During this time, virtually everything about organized social life in Europe was fundamentally transformed. In our day, we speak of globalization as a force that is changing the world in the most basic ways. But current patterns of globalization can be traced back to the rise of modernity itself; in many respects, they are a continuation of the changes that ushered in the modern world.

Economically, modernity transformed most people from peasants to workers in a complex division of labor. Politically, modernity created distinct nation-states with clear boundaries. Technologically, modernity applied scientific knowledge to producing everything from consumer goods to lethal weapons. Demographically, modernity triggered population growth and massive migration from small, familiar, rural communities to large, urban, anonymous cities.

When social worlds change like this, some people benefit while others are harmed. In addition, most people find rapid change and its inevitable conflict to be unsettling, and they seek to understand what is happening. It was this moment that gave rise to sociology. Explaining modernity became sociology's task at the same time that modernity was making sociology possible in the first place.

The link between modernity and sociology was the Enlightenment. This intellectual revolution accompanied other revolutionary changes occurring throughout Europe. In the broadest terms, the Enlightenment challenged religious belief, dogma, and authority. It sought to replace them with scientific reason, logic, and knowledge.

Four basic themes pervaded Enlightenment thought (Zeitlin 1987). First, human reason was the best guide to knowledge, even if it meant that scientific skepticism displaced religious certainty. Second, reason must be paired with careful, scientific observation. Third, Enlightenment thought insisted that social arrangements be rationally justified; if not, they must be changed until they could be rationally defended. Finally, Enlightenment thought assumed that with the systematic application of reason, the perfectibility of people and the progress of society were all but inevitable.

Enlightenment thought contained some potentially fatal flaws. It was a Eurocentric worldview, created by privileged white men, that made universal pronouncements about all people in all times and places. While applauding Europe's progress, it ignored the colonial domination of the rest of the world that provided the labor, goods, and wealth that underwrote that progress. Generalizations about "humanity" meant "males," to the exclusion of women, and pronouncements on the "human race" meant white Europeans, to the exclusion of darker people, who were viewed as subhuman.

The Enlightenment was much more than a justification of imperialism, sexism, and racism, but it could become that as well. More than two centuries later, the jury is still out on whether Enlightenment biases can be overcome and its promises be fulfilled. Some postmodernists see little hope for this to happen. Others, myself included, think that the critical spirit of the Enlightenment can help uproot its biases. The project is already under way as feminists, people of color, and postcolonial writers find their way into contemporary sociological discourses (Lemert 2013).

In its own day, the Enlightenment provoked a "romantic conservative reaction" (Zeitlin 1987) that rejected the elevation of reason and science over faith and tradition. It defended traditional customs, institutions, and ways of life from the new standard of critical reason. The debate between Enlightenment progress and conservative reaction set the agenda for sociology as the social science of modernity. Progress or order? Change or stability? Reason or tradition? Science or religion? Individual or group? Innovation or authority? Such dichotomies framed the subject matter of the new science of sociology.

The classical era of sociology refers to European thinkers whose ideas brought this new discipline to maturity from the late eighteenth to the early twentieth centuries. The very different sociologies of Auguste Comte, Herbert Spencer, Ferdinand Toennies, Karl Marx, Max Weber, Georg Simmel, Emile Durkheim, and others are variations on sociology's main theme: How do we understand modern society? Given these efforts, we might think of sociology as the ongoing effort of human beings to understand the worlds they are simultaneously inheriting from earlier generations and maintaining and transforming for future generations.

This approach has been described as the "sociological imagination." It arises when people realize that they can only know themselves by understanding their historical period and by examining others in the same situation as themselves. We think sociologically when we grasp how our historical moment differs from previous ones and how the situations of various groups of people differ from each other (Mills 1959).

The sociological imagination is guided by three related questions. The first concerns the social structure of society. How is it organized, what are its major institutions, and how are they linked together? The second concerns the historical location of society. How has it emerged from past social forms, what mechanisms promote change, and what futures are possible based on this historical path? The third concerns individual biography within society. What kinds of character traits are called forth by this society, and what kinds of people come to prevail? The sociological imagination is thus about grasping the relations between history and biography within society.

The sociological imagination sensitizes us to the difference between "personal troubles" and "public issues." A personal trouble is a difficulty in someone's life that is largely a result of individual circumstances. A public issue is a difficulty that is largely owing to social arrangements beyond the individual's control. The distinction is crucial because common sense often interprets events as personal troubles; we explain someone's difficulties as springing from individual shortcomings.

The sociological imagination recognizes that such difficulties are rarely unique to one person; they rather happen to many people in similar situations. The underlying causes derive more from social structures and historical developments than the individual alone. If our goal is "diagnosis," the sociological imagination locates problems in a larger social context. If our goal is "treatment," it implies changing the structure of society rather than the behavior of individuals.

This applies to success as well. Common sense often attributes success to individual qualities. The sociological imagination asks what social and historical preconditions were necessary for an individual to become a success. Many successful people, in Jim Hightower's memorable phrase, "were born on third base but thought they hit a triple." The point is that whereas common sense sees the world in individual terms, sociological thinking sees it in structural terms. Only by seeing the connections between structure, history, and biography can we understand the world in a sociological way.

This discussion implies that professional sociologists and ordinary people see the world differently. This is often true, but the issue is more complicated. Modernity has also led ordinary people to develop a practical sociology in their everyday lives. Think about it this way. Sociology sees the world as a social construction that could follow various blueprints. Indeed, social worlds *are* constructed in very different ways in different times and places.

In our time, an awareness of the socially constructed nature of social worlds is no longer the privileged insight of scholars, but has become part of everyday understanding. Whether owing to rapid change, frequent travel, cultural diffusion, or media images, many people understand that we live in socially constructed worlds. Some people are distressed by this fact, and others rejoice in it, but few can escape it. Thus, an idea that was initially associated with professional sociology has become part of the everyday consciousness of ordinary people today.

The result is that many people without formal sociological training understand social processes quite well. Put differently, the objects of sociological analysis are people who are quite capable of becoming the subjects of the sociological knowledge created by that analysis. Although few people can explain how quantum mechanics governs the physical world, many can describe sociological processes that shape the social world.

Certain circumstances prompt people to think sociologically. Perhaps the key stimulant is when familiar ways of doing and thinking no longer work. It is when people are surprised, puzzled, challenged, or damaged that they are most likely to think sociologically (Lemert 2008). People then develop sociological competence as they try to make sense out of specific, individual circumstances by linking them to broader social patterns. In this way, sociological awareness begins to understand bigger things as a by-product of wrestling with the practical challenges of everyday life.

Circumstances do not inevitably provoke sociological consciousness. Some people redouble their faith or retreat into ritualism. So perhaps we can conclude this way. Societies confront people with problems. These problems have always had the potential to promote a sociological awareness. In our times, there is a greater awareness of the socially constructed nature of the world. This makes it even more likely that when people in this society are confronted with practical challenges, they will develop sociological competence as a practical life skill. In late modernity, everyone can become a practical sociologist.

THINKING SOCIOLOGICALLY

The sociological perspective involves several themes. They overlap with one another, and some may be found in other social sciences as well as everyday consciousness. Taken together, they comprise a distinctive lens for viewing the social world. Here are some of those themes.

Society Is a Social Construction

People construct social order. Sociology does not see society as God-given, as biologically determined, or as following any predetermined plan beyond human intervention. At the same time, this does not mean that everyone plays an equal role in the process or that the final product looks like what people intended.

Social construction begins with intentions that motivate people to act in certain ways. When many people have similar goals and act in concert, larger social patterns or institutions are created. Goal-driven action is essential to the creation of institutions, and it remains equally important to their maintenance and transformation over time. Put succinctly, society is a human product (Berger and Luckmann 1966).

Basic human needs ensure some similarities in the goals that people pursue in all times and places. But these pursuits also unfold in specific historical circumstances and cultural contexts that have led to a dazzling variety of social worlds. This variety is itself the best evidence of the socially constructed nature of social worlds. If biology or genetics were the determining force behind social worlds, wouldn't they look a lot more similar than what we actually see around the globe?

Social constructionists thus insist that society arises from the goal-driven action of people. But they also recognize that the institutions created by such actions take on a life of their own. They appear to exist independently of the people who create and sustain them. They are experienced by people as a powerful external force that weighs down on them. When this external force becomes severe enough, people are likely to lose sight of the fact that society is a social product in the first place.

The value of the social constructionist premise is this dual recognition. On one hand, society is a subjective reality originating in the intentions of social actors. On the other hand, it becomes an objective reality that confronts subsequent generations as a social fact that inevitably shapes *their* intentional actions—and so it goes. Understood this way, the idea that society is a social construction is at the heart of the sociological perspective.

Society Is an Emergent Reality

Another premise of sociology is emergentism. This reveals sociology's distinctive level of analysis. For psychology, the level of analysis is the individual, even if it is acknowledged that individuals belong to groups. For sociology, the level of analysis is social ties rather than individual elements. Emergentism recognizes that certain realities only appear when individual elements are combined in particular ways. When they are, qualitatively new realities emerge through these combinations.

Take a simple example. Imagine a random pile of ten paper clips. Now imagine linking these paper clips together to form a chain. There are still ten paper clips, but a new emergent reality has appeared that is qualitatively different from the random pile because of how the elements are related to one another. Or consider human reproduction. Neither sperm nor egg is capable of producing human life on its own; in combination, qualitatively new life begins to emerge from a particular combination of elements.

Sociology specializes in the social level of analysis that emerges when elements are combined to create new, larger realities. Emergentism also implies that when we try to understand elements outside of their context, it is at best a simplification and at worst a distortion. The parts derive meaning from their relationship with other parts, and the sociological perspective is fundamentally attuned to such relationships.

Society Is a Historical Product

Thinking historically is a crucial part of the sociological imagination (Mills 1959). Classical sociologists thought historically because they lived in times of rapid social change and it was a major challenge to understand such change. Modern sociology tends to be more static, and modern people tend to be very present-oriented. Both professional and practical sociologists would benefit from a more historical perspective on the social world.

Seeing society as a historical product means recognizing that we cannot understand the present without understanding the past. Historical knowledge of past social conditions provides crucial comparisons. Without such benchmarks, it is impossible to understand what is genuinely new in the present day. Without a historical referent for comparison, sociology is clueless when it comes to understanding social change. Historical knowledge also provides the raw material for categories, comparisons, typologies, and analogies that are crucial to understanding both the present and possible future worlds.

The concept of emergentism applies here because the importance of seeing relationships between elements also works chronologically. If we look at society at only one point in time, we sever it from its past and its potential futures. Its very meaning arises from these relationships; to ignore them is to distort even the static understanding of society at one point in time. Consider the difference between a photograph and a film that presents a succession of images. We can learn something from the still photo, but its meaning often changes dramatically when we see it as one of a series of interrelated images.

Society Consists of Social Structures

Sociologists use the term *structure* to refer to the emergent products of individual elements. Structure implies that the social world has certain patterns or regularities that recur over time. Put differently, sociologists are keenly interested in social organization.

Structures are products of human purposes, but they acquire an objective reality and become a powerful influence on human action. Think about how physical structures like buildings shape action. We almost always enter buildings through doors; in rare cases we might do so through windows, but walking through walls is not an option. Social structures are less visible and more flexible than buildings, but they also channel people's actions, because they make some actions routine and expected, others possible but unlikely, and still others all but impossible.

Like buildings, social structures often have a vertical dimension. Social structures ensure that some people are better off than others and that some are not very well off at all. Some residential buildings have penthouses at the top, premium suites near the top, standard accommodations below them, and housekeeping staff in the basement. Social structures are also stratified, granting power, privilege, and opportunity to some while limiting or denying them to others. Sociologists are especially interested in the hierarchical dimension of social structures.

Sociologists traditionally thought of social structures as powerful forces weighing down upon the individual. In this image, structures constrain freedom of choice and behavior. But this is a one-sided view. Structures are constraining, but they are also enabling. These established patterns of social organization also make many actions possible in the first place or easier in the second place. Without preexisting social structures, we would have to do everything "from scratch," and the challenge of sheer survival might overwhelm us. The trick is thus to see social structures as simultaneously constraining and enabling social action (Giddens 1984).

Society Consists of Reflexive Actors

People in society are aware of themselves, of others, and of their relationships with others. As reflexive actors, we monitor our action and its effects on others. We continue, modify, or halt actions, depending on whether they are achieving their intended effects. According to one school of thought, we are literally actors, because social life is like a theatrical performance in which we try to convince others that we are a certain kind of person (Goffman 1959). To stage effective performances, we must constantly be our own critic, judging and refining our performances. Reflexivity thus means that when we act, we are conscious of our action, we monitor its course, and we make adjustments over time.

To stage such performances, we must undergo socialization. Along the way, we acquire a language that provides us with tools for reflexive thinking. We also acquire a self. Oddly enough, to have a self requires that we first have relationships with others. Through those relationships, we imaginatively see the world from their perspective, which includes seeing ourselves as we imagine we appear to them. It is this ability to see ourselves through the perspective of others—to see ourselves as an object—that defines the self. Reflexive action only becomes possible with a self.

Reflexivity makes ordinary people into practical sociologists. To be a competent person is to be a practical sociologist. We cannot help being sociologists every time we ponder a potential relationship, reconsider a hasty action, or adopt someone else's viewpoint. All such situations call upon and refine the reflexivity that is the hallmark of social action as well as a defining characteristic of the sociological perspective.

Society Is an Interaction of Agency and Structure

Social structures and reflexive actors are intimately connected. Unfortunately, much sociology emphasizes one side of this connection at the expense of the other. Agency-centered views stress the ability of people to make choices out of a range of alternatives in almost any situation. The emphasis on choice implies that people control their own destiny, at least within broad limits. Structure-centered views stress the extent to which people's choices are limited by social structures. The emphasis on structures implies that people's options—if not their lives—are essentially determined by larger social forces over which they have little control. Both approaches have merit, but the challenge is to see structure and agency in a more interconnected way.

Marx once said that people make their own history (acknowledging agency), but under circumstances they do not choose but rather inherit from the past (acknowledging structure). Here's an analogy from the game of pool. Each time you approach the table, you "inherit" a structure left by your opponent when they missed their last shot. Yet, for every layout of balls on the table, there is always a shot that you can attempt, and that action will alter the structure of the table for subsequent shots. In this analogy, structure (the position of balls on the table) both limits and creates opportunities for agency (taking a shot), which in turn alters the structure for the next round of shooting. If pool is not your game, chess is also a good analogy. The point is that agency and structure are two sides of the same coin; each conditions the possibilities of the other as we make our own history in circumstances we don't choose.

The close connection between structure and agency has led one theorist to reject the notion of structure altogether, because it implies something that exists apart from agency. Anthony Giddens (1984) talks about a *process* of structuration. In this view, actors use preexisting structures to accomplish their goals, but they also re-create them as a by-product of their actions. Consider a wedding ceremony. It is a preexisting cultural ritual people use to accomplish the goal of getting married. The by-product of all these individual marriages is the perpetuation of the cultural ritual itself. Generalize this to any situation in which we draw upon an established part of our social world to achieve a goal; in using this part we also sustain (and perhaps transform) it as a part of social structure.

Society Has Multiple Levels

Although society has multiple levels, sociologists often focus on one level at a time. Think about using Google Maps to locate a destination. You can zoom out to get the big picture at the expense of not seeing some important details. Alternatively, you can zoom in on some key details at the expense of not seeing the big picture. Combining these differing views will orient you to your destination, but we must remember it is ultimately all one interconnected landscape.

Sociologists nevertheless distinguish between macro and micro levels of society. When we look at the macro level, we typically include millions of people organized into large categories, groups, or institutions. The macro level is the "big picture" or "high altitude" perspective in which society's largest patterns are evident and individuals are invisible. When we look at the micro level, we might inspect no more than a dozen people interacting in a small group setting. Here, the role of particular individuals is very prominent, and larger social patterns fade into the background.

Some of the best sociology involves understanding not only structure-agency connections but also micro-macro links. Every macro-structure rests on micro-interaction, and every micro-interaction is shaped by macro-structures. The previous example of a wedding also illustrates this point. On the macro level, weddings are a cultural ritual that inducts people into the institution of marriage and the family. However, weddings, marriage, and the family would not exist on the macro level without countless, micro-level interactions. The macro-level institution depends on micro-level actions to sustain it. At the same time, anyone who has ever gotten married will tell you that macro-level, cultural expectations about weddings impose themselves on people as they plan for this supposedly personal event. Every micro-level wedding depends on a macro-level, cultural blueprint for its social significance. The micro and macro levels of society are one interdependent reality rather than two separate things.

Society Involves Unintended Consequences

One of the more profound insights of the sociological perspective concerns unintended and unanticipated consequences of action. Much human action is purposive or goal-directed. People act because they want to accomplish something. Despite this, they sometimes fail to achieve their goals. But whether people achieve their goals or not, their actions always create other consequences that they don't intend or even anticipate. Shakespeare made a profoundly sociological point when he had Juliet fake her own suicide to dramatize her love for Romeo. Unfortunately, the plan never reached Romeo. Juliet neither intended nor anticipated that Romeo would find her unconscious, believe that she was really dead, and take his own life in response. Nor did he intend (or even realize) that she would awaken, discover his real death, and really take her life in response. Talk about unintended consequences!

This principle acknowledges the complexity of the social world and the limits on our ability to control it. It says that despite our best efforts, the effects of social action cannot be confined to one intended path; they always spill over into unexpected areas. The principle is also a cautionary message for those seeking to solve social problems. Such efforts might succeed, but they often bring other consequences that are neither positive nor intended.

Efforts to control crime provide an example. Consider policies to "get tough" on crime through harsher treatment like capital punishment and mandatory sentencing. Because the human beings who serve as judges and juries are reflexive actors who take these facts into account, they are often less likely to convict suspects without overwhelming evidence because of the harshness of the sentence. Thus, the unintended consequence of an attempt to "get tough" on crime might be the opposite, because fewer suspects are convicted than before.

A related idea is the distinction between manifest and latent functions. A manifest function is an outcome that people intend. A latent function is an outcome that people are not aware of; it can complement, but it often contradicts, the manifest function. Crime and punishment provide yet another example. The manifest function of imprisonment is punishment or rehabilitation. The latent function is to bring criminals together where they can meet one another, exchange crime techniques, and become better criminals upon their return to society.

The concept of latent functions is crucial to sociological analysis. Sometimes we observe behavior or rituals that seem irrational, pointless, or self-defeating. This is the time to begin looking for latent functions. What we will often find is that such "irrational" behavior reinforces the identity and sustains the cohesion of the group that performs it. Thus, before we dismiss the tribal rain dance (because "rain gods" don't exist), we must explore its latent function. Even when people don't (manifestly) know what they are (latently) doing, their behavior can be crucial to group cohesion.

Recognizing unintended consequences and latent functions is not just for professional sociologists. Daily living requires managing risk, and ordinary people in everyday life recognize the tricky nature of goal-directed action. The folk wisdom that "the road to hell is paved with good intentions" acknowledges the potential disconnect between goals and outcomes. Such recognition, however, never completely prevents outcomes we neither intend nor expect. These principles give social life some of its most surprising twists, and sociology some of its most fascinating challenges.

No attempt to capture the sociological perspective in a small number of themes can be complete. Other sociologists would doubtless modify this list. But most would recognize these themes as central to thinking sociologically. As such, they provide a foundation for the more detailed investigations to follow.

SOCIOLOGY'S DOUBLE CRITIQUE

This final theme deserves special emphasis as the foundation of this book. Last but not least, thinking sociologically means looking at the social world in a critical way.

In everyday language, *critical* implies something negative. Being critical is often seen as being harsh, unfair, or judgmental. When we say someone is "critical," we often mean that their behavior is inappropriately mean-spirited. This is a perfectly reasonable use of everyday language, and the point it makes about how people should treat one another is also perfectly reasonable.

In sociological language, *critical* means something else. Doing sociology in a critical way means looking beyond appearances, understanding root causes, and asking who benefits. Being critical is what links knowledge to action and the potential of building a better society. Being critical in the sociological sense rests on the profoundly *positive* belief that we can use knowledge to understand the flaws of the social world and act to correct them.

The sociological perspective contains a double critique. First, mainstream sociology brings an inherently critical angle of vision to its subject. Second, some particular approaches in sociology carry this critique further by building on values that make sociological analysis especially critical of power and domination.

The critical dimension of mainstream sociology derives from the Enlightenment. Despite the flaws noted earlier, the Enlightenment advocated the use of reason, science, and evidence to critically examine religious truth, established doctrine, and political authority. Given its Enlightenment roots, sociology has always cast a critical eye on all types of claims, forms of knowledge, and exercises of power.

It is this quality that Peter Berger (1963) called the "debunking" tendency of sociological consciousness. Debunking means that the sociological perspective never takes the social world at face value and never assumes that it is what it appears to be. The sociological perspective rather looks at familiar phenomena in new ways to get beyond the immediately obvious, publicly approved, or officially sanctioned view. In this way, sociology sees through the facades of social structures to their unintended consequences and latent functions. Sociologically speaking, the problem might not be crime but laws, not revolution but government. Berger concludes that sociology is not compatible with totalitarianism, because the debunking quality of sociology will always be in tension with authoritarian claims to knowledge and power.

Although the world has changed since Berger wrote, the need for debunking is greater than ever. The political fundamentalisms of Cold War and rival superpowers have been replaced by other fundamentalisms that are logical targets for sociology's debunking insights. A world in which more and more people feel they know things with absolute certainty is a world that drastically needs the sociological perspective.

At the same time that some people embrace fundamentalist beliefs, others become suspicious and cynical about everything. This stance ("debunking on steroids") is too much of a good thing. For the ultra-cynical poser, all ideas, values, and beliefs are suspect, and none deserve support. Against this stance, sociology offers nuance and judgment. The sociological perspective recognizes that some ideas, values, and beliefs have more merit, logic, or evidence than others. Careful sociological thinkers make such distinctions. Indeed, the ultra-cynical mind-set itself needs debunking. Cynicism helps people avoid action or evade responsibility. A sociological perspective suggests that such inaction, or evasion, *is* action that tacitly supports dominant powers by refusing to challenge them in any way.

Mainstream sociology does not take the world for granted. Just when we think we have the answers, it poses another level of questions. For all these reasons, sociology in its most generic form has always included a critical angle of vision.

Although mainstream sociology is inherently critical, some versions of sociology take critique to another level by adopting certain values as the basis for their critique. In contrast to mainstream sociology, these approaches are devoted to a critical analysis of how social structures create relations of domination.

This fully critical sociology is best understood in contrast to mainstream sociology. Although mainstream sociology is critical because of its debunking tendency, it also adopts a scientific posture of detachment. Mainstream sociology seeks to be value-free, value-neutral, or objective. Put differently, mainstream sociology deliberately refrains from taking sides that would jeopardize its scientific neutrality. Mainstream sociology recognizes that *as citizens*, sociologists can be political actors. But it insists that in their role as scientific sociologists, they must maintain their objectivity.

Critical sociology differs from mainstream sociology on these issues. It emphasizes that in social science, humans are both the subjects and the objects of study. Notions of objectivity derived from the natural sciences don't necessarily translate into social science. But even if sociology could approximate objectivity, critical sociologists reject such a stance. It is not desirable, because the quest for objectivity diverts sociologists from asking the most important questions and from taking a more active role in the resolution of social problems.

Think of the contrast in this way. Mainstream sociology is primarily committed to one set of Enlightenment values having to do with science and objectivity. Critical sociology is primarily committed to another set of Enlightenment values having to do with freedom and equality. The latter values demand critical scrutiny of any social order that imposes unnecessary inequalities or restrictions on people's ability to organize their lives as they wish. These values require critical analysis of social arrangements that create conflicting interests between people and allow one group to benefit at the expense of another.

Critical sociologists deliberately focus on relations of domination, oppression, or exploitation, because these actions so obviously violate the values of freedom and equality. Critical sociologists are willing to advocate for groups who are victimized by such arrangements. Good critical sociologists realize they cannot speak for such groups. But they can explore how social arrangements make it difficult for some to speak for themselves, and they can underscore the importance of changing those arrangements.

Other issues distinguish mainstream from critical sociology. Mainstream sociology's commitment to science means it maintains a strict divide between scientific questions of what *is* and normative questions of what *ought* to be. Critical sociology wants to transcend this divide by linking critical analysis of how the world is organized now with normative arguments for how the world should be organized in the future. Behind such arguments are hopeful, or even utopian assumptions about alternative worlds that might be constructed. Critical sociology is simultaneously pessimistic about the current state of the world and optimistic about its possible futures. It examines our potential for living humanely, the social obstacles that block this potential, and the means to change from a problematic present to a preferable future.

The debate between mainstream and critical sociology is important and complex, and it will not be resolved by anything said here. But what can be said is that sociology is better because of the debate. Each side provides a corrective to the faults of the other. At the extreme, mainstream sociology becomes an inhumane, sterile approach that reduces human beings to objects of scientific curiosity; it needs a course correction through the humane values of critical sociology. At the extreme, critical sociology becomes an empty, ideological stance that denies the complexities of its own value commitments; it needs a course correction through the scientific caution of mainstream sociology.

Sociology's double critique thus derives from mainstream and critical sociology, respectively. My primary goal in this book is to illustrate critical sociology, but I also include the critical insights of mainstream sociology. I do so because these approaches sometimes speak to different issues, because neither seems adequate on its own, because they are often complementary, and because this best conveys the richness of our discipline itself. In the end, it is less important which side is "right" than that both sides coexist and continually provoke us to be reflexive about our role as sociologists and as actors in the world.

Sociology's double critique is also crucial to rethinking the flaws of the Enlightenment itself. Mainstream sociology's notion of debunking accepted truths grew out of the Enlightenment struggle against religion, but there is no reason it can't also foster critical examination of the Enlightenment itself. Critical sociology's challenge to domination also seems tailor-made to examining and overturning those forms of domination that the Enlightenment ignored, accepted, or promoted. Thus, for all its flaws, the Enlightenment provides tools for its own examination, critique, and transformation.

The Emergence of the Individual

by Steven M. Buechler

A popular magazine in the United States is simply titled, *Self*. It caters to young women, and contains a familiar mix of fashion, beauty, and relationship advice. But the underlying message seems to be "it's all about you." The paradox is that each reader is encouraged to cultivate a unique self, based on the same mass-marketed advice being read by millions of others. This is merely one example of the glorification of the individual in US culture. Individualism is a hallmark of modernity, but it is nowhere more pronounced than in the United States.

The pursuit of individualism can undermine bonds with others and create profound loneliness. Yet, we often seem incapable of thinking beyond ourselves. Some time ago I co-taught an experiential course based on a wilderness canoe trip. The goal of the course was to build a utopian society during our seven-day adventure. We asked our students what utopia meant to them. To a person, they said utopia would be unrestricted individual freedom to do whatever they wanted. The notion that such freedoms might clash, or that larger norms might be needed, or that utopia might mean being connected to others did not occur to these otherwise-bright students.

Critical sociology helps see beyond such taken-for-granted notions. Historical and comparative lenses are especially helpful in seeing the distinctiveness of familiar social worlds. This is why Alexis de Tocqueville's (1853) commentaries on early US society are so highly prized. As a Frenchman looking at US life, he could clearly see what was becoming invisible to Americans themselves: that their lives were increasingly organized around the principle of individualism, with both positive and negative consequences.

All this makes it hard to grasp that "individuals" did not exist until relatively recently. Nevertheless, a classic sociological argument makes exactly this claim. Although societies have always contained people, the notion that people are "individuals" with unique functions, personalities, and temperaments is historically new. In this sense, society preceded the individual, who only emerged through a long process of social evolution that eventually led to the individualism that has become a taken-for-granted part of contemporary consciousness.

FROM "WE" TO "I"

Emile Durkheim's (1893) take on individualism is part of a broader study of social evolution. It rests on a dichotomy between traditional and modern societies. For most of human history, people lived in traditional societies. People in such societies were undifferentiated; they were very similar to one another. Because of these similarities, the modern notion of the individual standing apart from or opposed to the group had no meaning. The tribe or clan was the basic social unit, and people were utterly subordinate to such units.

Some of these societies underwent technological and demographic changes that jump-started social evolution. The domestication of animals, the rise of agriculture, and the development of communication and transportation systems promoted settlement, migration, and the growth of stable and sedentary populations in villages and eventually cities. The combined effect was increasing population size, as societies accumulated the resources to support larger numbers.

Some societies also expanded geographically, allowing their increasing numbers of people to spread out over new lands and territories. Eventually, however, societies encountered limits to geographical expansion while populations continued to increase. The result of population growth and geographical limits was an increase in moral or dynamic density. More people interacted with more other people, and with greater frequency, on a daily basis.

Increasing dynamic density posed a danger that the struggle for survival would intensify and bring increasing competition and conflict. Indeed, some societies undoubtedly succumbed to these pressures and disintegrated.

In other cases, societies survived through a new social invention known as the division of labor. Rather than competing to do the same things, the division of labor allowed people to specialize in different activities. Specialization reduced competitive pressures as people sorted themselves into distinct slots in the division of labor. Such specialization also created a new interdependence among people doing different things and fulfilling different functions.

Modern societies thereby evolved with the division of labor. It solved the threats posed by increasing dynamic density, conflict, and competition by creating functional interdependence and cooperation between people's activities. With a sufficiently complex division of labor, modernizing societies could continue to expand while also reducing conflicts over scarce resources. The division of labor was thus the central survival mechanism of social evolution.

Durkheim underscored the contrast between traditional and modern societies at either end of the evolutionary process. He was especially interested in different kinds of solidarity in each society. Traditional societies had mechanical solidarity. This meant that the parts of the society were homogeneous or identical to one another; there was little interdependence between them. There was also a low degree of dynamic density. Mechanical solidarity thus linked similar units together. Think of a chain consisting of identical links. Because they are all the same, some links can be removed without destroying the chain; it simply becomes shorter than before.

Social control in traditional societies was based on punitive law and repressive sanctions. Deviance was seen as a grave threat to moral order. There was a powerful collective conscience holding the group together. It consisted of collective sentiments, emotions, norms, values, and morals. People saw themselves as group members rather than independent individuals. This collective conscience was so strong that virtually any deviance was a serious challenge to group integrity; that is why it was dealt with so harshly. The collective conscience thus sustained mechanical solidarity in traditional societies. It created solidarity based on what people thought and believed by ensuring that everyone thought and believed the same things.

There were no "individuals" in traditional society because of the functional similarities in what people did; there was simply no basis for differentiation. The collective conscience insisted that people's identities were collective and not individual; who you were was a function of your tribe or clan and not of any unique, personal characteristics. Finally, if people did "express themselves" as different, it was likely to be taken as a deviant challenge to group solidarity, for which they likely received harsh treatment. In some circles, it could get you declared a witch and burned at the stake.

If there were people but no individuals in traditional societies, and if such societies make up the vast majority of human history, then it follows that the individual is a recent social invention. It is a by-product of modern societies.

These societies have survived by organic solidarity. This means that the parts of society are heterogeneous, or different from one another. Because of these differences, there is a high degree of interdependence among the parts. There is also a high degree of dynamic density. Organic solidarity links different units together. Think of a complex molecule consisting of unique elements. Because of the differences, removing even one element jeopardizes the entire molecule, because there are no functional substitutes to play the same role.

Modern societies have a correspondingly different type of social control; with some exceptions, it is based on cooperative law and restitutive sanctions. Many forms of deviance are seen more as technical violations of rules than moral challenges to society itself. Perpetrators are more likely to pay restitution or undergo rehabilitation than to suffer harsh punishment. As before, Durkheim uses types of deviance and punishment as a lens through which to study larger questions about social solidarity.

In modern societies, the different response to deviance suggests a change in the collective conscience. It is less important, less central, and less collective than before. Indeed, in modern societies there might be multiple collective consciences coexisting alongside one another. Such plurality means that no one belief system is supreme over all others, and that none can provide a universal source of solidarity. Moreover, modern belief systems acknowledge the individual by recognizing inalienable rights, personal freedoms, and individual dignity. With social evolution, the collective conscience declines as the value of the individual increases.

This might seem to imply that modern societies have less solidarity, but they have an alternative to the collective conscience. The division of labor is modern society's functional equivalent of the collective conscience. The division of labor provides the organic solidarity that unites modern societies. Whereas traditional societies were held together by the normative integration of what people believed (and they all believed the same things), modern societies are held together by the functional integration of what people do (and they all do different things).

The fact that people do different things in the modern division of labor promotes the emergence of the individual. Individualism began when people differentiated their productive activities and occupied distinct niches in the division of labor. Once it took hold, individualism expanded its meaning from what people do to who people are. Thus was born the contemporary notion of the individual as a unique bundle of personality traits that distinguish one person from another.

Even today we can catch glimpses of the contrasts Durkheim discusses. Traces of past worlds still exist in immigrant communities, in the cultures of indigenous peoples, and in intentionally isolated communities like the Amish. Other examples can be found where religious fundamentalism provides an overriding belief system and an unambiguous moral compass for a strongly integrated community of people. Such examples illustrate Durkheim's hypothesis that traditionalism and individualism don't readily mix; when they do, look for conflict between traditional collective identities and modern individual ones. Such battles are further testimony that individualism is not "natural" but rather a product of social change and evolution.

Durkheim was a modernist who saw the emergence of the individual as a healthy development. The same individualism that would have been deviant in traditional societies is normal in modern ones. Moreover, Durkheim was a strong political supporter of individual rights and liberties. Nevertheless, he was also aware of the potential problems that arose with the new emphasis on individualism, and he detailed such problems in his subsequent work.

TOO MUCH OF A GOOD THING?

Durkheim's study of suicide (1897) is a cautionary tale about individualism in modern society. It can quickly become too much of a good thing. More broadly, Durkheim's study of suicide made the case that social facts always shape individual phenomena. For Durkheim, individual explanations of human behavior are almost always inferior to sociological explanations.

Suicide was a good example. Nothing seems more personal than the decision to take one's own life. If anything is best explained in psychological, individual terms, it would appear to be suicide. But not for Durkheim. He finds the most intriguing aspect of suicide to be variations in suicide rates across different groups, times, places, and circumstances. He proceeds to argue that suicide rates are a social fact that can only be explained by other social facts. The larger point is central to sociology itself: what appears as an individual event requiring a psychological explanation when observed "up close" is often a social reality requiring a sociological explanation when placed in a larger social context. Put differently, Durkheim puts the individual in their place by showing that even seemingly personal decisions are conditioned by social factors.

The point is that suicide rates vary inversely with the degree of integration in modern society. In other words, the less integrated a group or a society is, the higher its suicide rates. The formula was reversed in traditional societies: the more integrated the group or society, the higher its suicide rates. The seeming contradiction reflects the difference between the two societies. In traditional societies with mechanical solidarity, the potential danger is that integration becomes too strong and poses a danger to people that leads to suicide. In modern societies with organic solidarity, the potential danger is that integration is too weak and poses a danger to individuals that also manifests itself as suicide.

The link between integration and suicide has two dimensions. Cohesion refers to social bonds that link an individual to others, to larger social groups, and to a sense of belonging or membership. Regulation refers to rules, guidelines, values, and codes of conduct that help individuals orient themselves and make decisions through a strong moral compass. A low degree of integration could arise from either insufficient cohesion or inadequate regulation; both lead to higher rates of suicide.

Egoism arises with insufficient cohesion. It is "excessive individuation" in which a normal process of individual development goes too far so that the individual is no longer connected to others in a socially meaningful way. Put differently, the argument is that belonging keeps us grounded so that we avoid dangerous or self-destructive behavior. Groups with high cohesion and a sense of belonging will therefore have lower suicide rates than groups with low cohesion. Members of groups with little cohesion are especially prone to egoistic suicide.

Durkheim's evidence concerned suicide rates in different religious faiths. It was initially a puzzle that Protestant groups, regions, and countries had substantially higher suicide rates than their Catholic counterparts. The mystery dissolved with a closer look at the structure of their respective religious beliefs. Protestantism involves a direct relationship between the individual and God, with relatively little emphasis on connections among Protestants or on religious community. In Catholicism, on the other hand, there is a much stronger connection to religious community and to others who mediate one's relationship with God. Protestants were thus more prone to egoism, and correspondingly had higher rates of egoistic suicide.

Anomie describes insufficient regulation. To be anomic means to be without the norms, rules, or guidelines that normally orient people and guide decisions. When a group lacks strong normative guidelines, its members are more likely to engage in dangerous or self-destructive behaviors. Such groups will have higher rates of anomic suicide.

Durkheim's evidence here involved rapid changes in economic conditions like financial crises or unexpected prosperity. When such changes happen quickly, they create anomie because the rules, regulations, and rhythms of "normal" life no longer apply when people become suddenly poor or rich. Rapid economic fluctuations produce higher rates of anomie and higher rates of anomic suicide. The argument is especially persuasive because it works in both directions. It's not surprising that people who suddenly become impoverished are more likely to commit suicide. It *is* surprising that people who suddenly become rich are also more likely to commit suicide. The key variable is not the material fact of wealth or poverty; it is the social fact of anomie that is the better predictor of suicide rates.

In traditional societies, the dangers are reversed. Group cohesion can be so powerful that people become completely submerged in the group and offer their lives "too easily" through altruistic suicide. Alternatively, social regulation might be so overwhelmingly controlling that people succumb to fatalistic suicide. There are thus four types of suicide, but they are all related to whether social integration is too strong (in traditional societies) or too weak (in modern societies). In all cases, suicide rates are a social fact best explained by the degree of social integration.

Although suicide provided a dramatic focus, the logic applies more broadly. High rates of anomie or egoism are correlated with many different kinds of deviant, self-destructive, or anti-social behavior. After all, group cohesion and normative regulation don't just deter suicide; they minimize many undesirable behaviors. When they fail, we can expect not just higher suicide rates but higher rates of crime, delinquency, addiction, and the like. Many social problems stem from insufficient social integration.

Several theories of deviance (and its treatment) flow from these insights. To take one example, consider the importance of the group in programs like Alcoholics Anonymous. Recovery depends on attending meetings where social cohesion and bonding with others are a key element. By the same logic, people in recovery are encouraged to have a "sponsor" they can contact if they are in danger of returning to self-destructive behavior. It is connections with others that deter the problematic behavior.

Durkheim himself suggested that to combat egoism, we need small and intermediate size groups to provide people with membership and belonging. He felt this was especially important as modern society moved toward massive social institutions that dwarfed individuals. To deter anomie, Durkheim advocated moral, ethical, and civic education to balance individual freedoms with social obligations.

Durkheim's work reveals the potential dangers of (excessive) individualism. He would not have liked my students' image of utopia as a world of unrestricted freedom. To the contrary, he claimed that "it is not true . . . that human activity can be released from all restraint" (Durkheim 1897, 252). His view was that without social restraint, people become slaves to self-destructive impulses. To be without social restraints is to have no immunity against such impulses. It is society that rescues us from this fate by providing the cohesion, regulation, and integration that allow people to control their impulses and achieve relative freedom.

Durkheim really puts the individual in their place. Society precedes individuals. It existed for a long time without "individuals." And even with the emergence of the individual, social cohesion and regulation remain necessary to avoid self-destructive tendencies. In a culture that has come to glorify the self, Durkheim's work provides a healthy corrective for how to think about the individual in modern society.

A NOTE ON ADOLESCENCE

The emergence of the individual changes the life cycle in modern society. Once again, a phenomenon that seems natural and even biological—what we call adolescence—proves to be a social construction.

Indeed, childhood itself is more a social status than a biological reality. In traditional societies, "childhood" was not a distinct stage in the life cycle. Children were treated simply as small adults. They assumed adult roles and responsibilities as soon as they were physically able to do so. The transition from dependent young to adult roles was very quick.

This is true through the Middle Ages in Europe. Paintings from that era show young people dressed in the clothing of adults and involved in adult activities (Ariès 1965). Although not the conscious intention of the artists, the message in these paintings seems to be that there was no "childhood" in the Middle Ages. For all practical purposes, children were just small adults.

It was modernization in general and industrialization in particular that created "childhood." As we saw previously, industrialization transformed the family from a unit of production into a unit of consumption, and it transformed the economic roles of family members. Men became breadwinners working outside the home for someone else. Women became homemakers doing unpaid domestic labor. And little people became "children" in the modern sense. Like many women, they lost productive roles and were transformed from economic assets into economic liabilities or dependents.

Gender and childhood were altered by these developments. Masculinity became tough and competitive, and femininity became domestic and maternal. Because women and children shared the domestic sphere, similar conceptions were transposed to children. The reason we think of children as innocent, vulnerable, and needing protection derives from this historical period and the connections between childhood and domesticity. Before then, when small people functioned as adults, they were just as likely to be perceived as tough, aggressive, scheming, or vicious. In both cases, conceptions of people derived from the worlds they occupied. When the worlds changed, so did the conceptions.

The loss of children's economic role left a gap that was filled by formal education. What began as the "factory school" evolved into modern schooling dedicated to meeting the distinct needs of (newly invented) "children." The rise of this child-centered institution reinforced the ideas that children were different, they inhabited a unique world, and they needed protection, nurturance, and guidance if they were to develop into fully competent adults.

If childhood is a social construction, this is even truer of *adolescence.* The term was invented in the early twentieth century to designate a stage between childhood and adulthood. Adolescence might seem to combine the disadvantages of both, but it is here to stay. A major function of adolescence is to allow people the opportunity to explore and establish individual identities. In traditional societies, such identities would not need to be "established" as an individual achievement. Identities were rather derived from the kinship structure, and people moved quickly through initiation rites to adulthood.

Contemporary adolescence has replaced two- or three-day initiation rites with years of identity exploration. Moreover, adolescence now leads not to adulthood but to young adulthood. With extended education, delayed marriage, deferred child rearing, and later career starts, many people do not assume fully adult roles until they reach their thirties. As we saw in the previous chapter, this disaggregation of the markers of adulthood has created a new demographic among young adults who may reside in "guyland" for a decade or more (Kimmel 2008).

Many people thus ease into adulthood at biological ages that practically defined elders in traditional societies. It is not that people's biology has changed (although life expectancy and control of disease have changed). It is rather that new social constructions have arisen, dividing the life cycle into more intermediate stages in keeping with the demands and opportunities of industrial and postindustrial society.

The timing and nature of these developments are entirely consistent with Durkheim's observations about the emergence of the individual. In traditional societies, identities derived from group membership. They did not have to be "found," "explored," or "tried out." They were simply there.

In modern societies, the division of labor created social differentiation among people that in turn created the individual. Identities are now only partially fixed by birth, kinship, or geography. An increasingly large part of our identities is individually achieved rather than collectively assigned. As individualism and identity have become major life tasks, modern societies have developed more numerous stages in the life cycle to accommodate such challenges.

INDIVIDUALISM AND ITS DISCONTENTS

Although the individual is a hallmark of modern society, the greatest emphasis on individualism is in the United States. Since de Tocqueville (1853), individualism has attracted both praise and criticism. Such reactions reflect the time and place of the observers. Whereas de Tocqueville was struck by the contrast between European hierarchy and US egalitarianism, more recent sociological observers have identified other dimensions of contemporary individualism.

An example is provided by David Riesman's *The Lonely Crowd* (1950). Like William Whyte (1956) and C. Wright Mills (1956), Riesman was concerned with how large-scale organizations were turning people into anonymous, faceless cogs in the social machinery of contemporary society. In contrast to Durkheim's worries about egoism or excessive individuation, these critics were lamenting the loss of individuality and rise of overconformity in mass society.

Riesman analyzed changes in prevailing social character over time. The dominant social character in preindustrial societies, not surprisingly, was the " tradition-directed" person who conformed to social norms with little friction, because traditional people were highly subordinate to the collective.

With modern society and the emergence of the individual, the "inner-directed" person appeared. They internalize clear goals and values early in life through strong socialization by family members and authority figures. Once in place, these values firmly guide conduct, producing a highly individualized personality that stays on track. Inner-directed persons are not very susceptible to external influences that contradict their inner-direction; they tend to ignore such pressures and follow their own path.

By the 1950s, however, this inner-directed person was giving way to the "other-directed" person. They are less influenced by families and more susceptible to peer groups and the surrounding environment. They are predisposed to seek acceptance, to fit in, and to value social approval. Whereas the inner-directed person is mostly unaffected by external influences, the other-directed person seeks it out as a guide to conduct. In Riesman's metaphors, inner-directed people have psychological gyroscopes that keep them on track, and other-directed people use radar to pick up social cues and respond accordingly. To expand the metaphor, inner-directed people move in a straight line determined by their internal gyroscope. Other-directed people, by contrast, bounce around like a pinball in response to external influences.

Riesman lamented the loss of (inner-directed) individualism in the mass society of his day. Whereas Durkheim feared too much individualism in modernity, Riesman felt there was not enough. As a preferable alternative, he called for an "autonomous" individual to emerge that would overcome the drawbacks of both inner- and other-directed character types (Kivisto 1998, 109–113).

Soon after Riesman's critique of other-directedness, the political protest and counterculture of the 1960s provided a very different social backdrop for Philip Slater's take on individualism in *The Pursuit of Loneliness* (1970). The book criticized US culture's obsessions with technology, violence, competition, scarcity, and hierarchy; within this context Slater offered intriguing comments on individualism.

Three human desires are deeply frustrated by the individualism of US culture. The first is a desire for community, which has been the norm for much of human history and has only recently been overturned with the modern emphasis on individualism. The second is a desire for engagement to address social and interpersonal problems, which is frustrated by the detachment that accompanies modern individualism. The third is a desire for dependence and shared responsibility, which again is difficult to meet given the emphasis on individualism.

There is a perverse circularity built into our brand of individualism. It leads us to minimize, avoid, or deny the interdependence at the root of all human societies. It is expressed in our quest for privatized means of living by owning our own home, car, and a complete, private repertoire of technological gadgetry. The result is the pursuit of loneliness: "We seek more and more privacy, and feel more and more alienated and lonely when we get it. What accidental contacts we do have, furthermore, seem more intrusive, not only because they are unsought but also because they are unconnected with any familiar pattern of interdependence" (Slater 1970, 7).

Having constructed such traps, we can't escape them because we fall back into the "individualistic fantasy that everyone is, or should be, different—that each person could somehow build his entire life around some single, unique, eccentricity" (Slater 1970, 8). Although it might appear that we freely express our individuality, the standards are set by the larger culture so that "everyone tends, independently but monotonously, to pursue the same things in the same way" (Slater 1970, 9). In an ironic twist, the pursuit of individuality reinforces mass conformity.

Our "independence training" contrasts even with other modern societies that have a healthier balance between independence and interdependence. It also has serious emotional consequences. When independence is equated with individualism, then individualism can only be achieved through emotional detachment from others. Such detachment, in turn, breeds indifference and competitiveness toward others, accompanied by lingering guilt about these qualities. US individualism thus traps us in a snare of social and emotional difficulties.

Many of these dilemmas are evident in middle-class child-rearing techniques that prevailed in the mid-twentieth century. Dr. Spock—the pediatrician, not the Vulcan—advised permissiveness, individualism, and female domesticity. The advice built on the assumption that every individual is unique and has a positive potential that can only develop under the right circumstances.

Such assumptions place considerable burdens on children to "develop their potential" or be regarded as a failure. It also magnified the importance of proper child rearing, reinforcing women's domestic role and making child care a full-time—though individualized and privatized—activity for middle-class women. As Slater notes, "We are a product-oriented society, and she has been given the opportunity to turn out a really outstanding product" (Slater 1970, 67). The political and cultural climate of the 1960s thus illuminated numerous dilemmas arising from our brand of individualism.

A decade later, yet another critique equated individualism with narcissism (Lasch 1979). It "describes a way of life that is dying—the culture of competitive individualism, which in its decadence has carried the logic of individualism to the extreme of a war of all against all, the pursuit of happiness to the dead end of a narcissistic preoccupation with the self" (Lasch 1979, 21).

Christopher Lasch roots this malaise in post-1960s politics, when he claims Americans gave up on public, political issues in favor of purely personal preoccupations. This inward turn was accompanied by a waning of history. The past was no longer seen as a coherent model for living in the present, just as the anticipation of a predictable future also fell by the wayside. One aspect of the narcissism Lasch discusses is thus an overriding orientation to a present divorced from both past and future.

The self is now guided by a therapeutic sensibility that rejects the notion of a public or social good to pursue purely personal well-being, health, and security. Echoing Riesman's shift from inner- to other-directed personalities, Lasch sees the narcissistic personality as heavily invested in maintaining high self-esteem, while at the same time being dependent on others to validate it.

This therapeutic sensibility might identify real problems, but it offers self-defeating solutions. "Arising out of a pervasive dissatisfaction with the quality of personal relations, it advises people not to make too large an investment in love and friendship, to avoid excessive dependence on others, and to live for the moment—the very conditions that created the crisis of personal relations in the first place" (Lasch 1979, 64–65).

The narcissistic personality combines a grandiose conception of the self with an inner emptiness and loss of faith in any meaning system beyond the therapeutic sensibility. It nevertheless persists because it resonates with larger social institutions. "For all his inner suffering, the narcissist has many traits that make for success in bureaucratic institutions, which put a premium on the manipulation of interpersonal relations, discourage the formation of deep personal attachments, and at the same time provide the narcissist with the approval he needs in order to validate his self-esteem" (Lasch 1979, 91).

Rather than becoming more social and cooperative, people have simply become more adept at manipulating others for their personal benefit. In a claim that seems to describe many parents' involvement in their children's sports teams, Lasch notes that activities "ostensibly undertaken purely for enjoyment often have the real object of doing others in" (Lasch 1979, 128). Thus, the manipulation favored by the narcissistic personality is an understandable response to the degradation of social life in which pleasure and play have been taken over by self-interest, unrestrained competition, and psychic survival at all costs.

Such personality types predominate in part because of changes in the family and child rearing. In Lasch's view, traditional parental authority has been undermined by government bureaucracies, capitalist markets, and mass media. Deprived of authority, parents have become dependent on experts for advice. And the advice has shifted from clear prescriptions to vague exhortations to trusting feelings as the main guide in childhood socialization. This "cult of authenticity" allows volatile emotions to overrule traditional guidelines and reasoned judgments; it was meant to restore parental confidence but in fact has helped to undermine it.

"The decline of parental authority reflects the 'decline of the superego' in American society as a whole" (Lasch 1979, 305). Narcissistic personalities emerge because social conditions discourage the establishment of a strong super-ego with internal behavioral controls. This critique of "permissive" child rearing is most intriguing when Lasch notes, "the decline of authority does not lead to the collapse of social constraints. It merely deprives those constraints of a rational basis" (1979, 316).

Narcissistic personalities have difficulty forming attachments, while also needing recognition and affirmation. The combination puts great strains on personal relations. As much as people might desire intimacy, narcissism frustrates these desires, because narcissistic personalities are wary of commitments and more attuned to manipulating emotional states than to fully experiencing them.

In the end, Lasch traces narcissism to the new paternalism of capitalist society. It stimulates needs and dependence, but it also creates personalities that cannot fulfill those needs or escape that dependence. In Lasch's dark imagery, individuals become their own worst enemy because narcissistic personalities preclude real satisfactions.

As we saw in a previous chapter, social media provide a contemporary crucible in which these dynamics play themselves out. Despite the hyperbole about the *social* nature of such media, the technology is still trumped by the hyper-individualism of late modern culture. Thus, "the more atomized and lonely people became, the more separated from traditional community, the more they fell in love with the idea of the social. But their definition of the social was so individualized, so much a reflection of their own discrete identities that their cult of social authenticity was simultaneously a cult of the authentic self—thereby creating . . . a culture of narcissism in which the narcissist 'cannot live without an admiring audience'" (Keen 2012, 102–103).

Speaking from different historical contexts, Riesman, Slater, Lasch, and Keen demonstrate how individualism has been a battleground of conflicting social forces throughout much of the twentieth century.

HABITS OF THE HEART

Lasch's critique of narcissism is entertaining to read. He rails against contemporary culture like an old-time preacher. He has some dazzling insights. At the same time, his argument relies on isolated examples, catchy metaphors, and literary references. It lacks systematic evidence.

Such evidence can be found in *Habits of the Heart* (Bellah et al. 1985), a widely acclaimed study blending theoretical ideas with empirical research to offer fresh insights about individualism in contemporary US society. This work picks up almost a century after Durkheim to examine modern versions of old dilemmas of individualism.

Echoing Durkheim, the authors agree that individualism has grown inexorably through US history. Their concern is that this growth might have become cancerous by destroying the social bonds that moderate the harmful effects of individualism. To examine these issues, they focus on the relations between public and private life, the need for a balance between the two, and the ways in which individualism either establishes or undermines that balance.

Echoing my students cited at the beginning of this chapter, the "first language" of US individualism defines freedom as being left alone by others. However, "[w]hat it is that one might do with that freedom is much more difficult for Americans to define" (Bellah et al. 1985, 23). Moreover, this notion of freedom means "it becomes hard to forge bonds of attachment to, or cooperation with, other people, since such bonds would imply obligations that necessarily impinge on one's freedom" (Bellah et al. 1985, 23).

Their tone is more measured than Lasch's, but this is a familiar story. As people seek lives they think they want by maximizing individualism and freedom, they create conditions that make it very difficult to be connected to others in ways that are also important. This is not just a personal problem of loneliness or alienation; it also erodes the collective fabric required for social health.

Examining US character in historical context reveals two major forms of individualism. Utilitarian individualism is rooted in rational self-interest and economic calculations about success in a competitive environment with others. This form of individualism implies sturdy self-reliance on one's own skills and resources. It is the kind of individualism long associated with the entrepreneur as a social type; more recently, utilitarian individualism fits the role of the manager in a highly rationalized and bureaucratic society. Such individualism can lead to success measured by the accumulation of material resources, but it also connotes a coldly self-centered orientation to the world.

Whereas utilitarian individualism is about the rational calculation of self-interest, expressive individualism is about the exploration of emotional life. For this type, self-expression is more important than self-interest. Historically, expressive individualism has been associated with romantics, artists, musicians, poets, and others whose lives are centered on emotional aspects of self and the human condition. In the modern world, expressive individualism is symbolized by the therapist.

Both types of individualism persist, because they correspond to the functional divide in modern society between public and personal life. The utilitarian version of individualism fits well in the economic and occupational spheres of public life and their orientation to competition and success. The expressive version of individualism fits well in family roles and social relations of personal life with their emphasis on sentiment and emotional exploration. As social types, we are like instrumental managers in the public sphere and expressive therapists in the private sphere.

Whereas the utilitarian individual is explicitly self-interested, the expressive individual seeks fulfillment through relationships with others. This would appear to counteract the destructive aspects of individualism, but the picture is more complicated. With expressive individualism, "its genius is that it enables the individual to think of commitments—from marriage and work to political and religious involvement—as enhancements of the sense of individual well-being rather than as moral imperatives" (Bellah et al. 1985, 47).

Put differently, expressive individualism seeks relationships with others as long as they meet personal needs—and not a moment longer. Individualism still trumps the relationship because its rationale is fulfilling individual needs. This type of individualism treats "normative commitments as so many alternative strategies of self-fulfillment. What has dropped out are the old normative expectations of what makes life worth living" (Bellah et al. 1985, 48). In different ways, both types of individualism subordinate collective duties and social obligations to individual interests and personal needs.

Consider the iconic US quest of finding oneself. Self-reliance is often thought to arise through leaving home and community; the irony is that these are the roots of whatever self we possess in the first place. This could be why later in life many people gravitate to "lifestyle enclaves" of people with similar values and interests that provide self-validation through connections with people like them. Although radical individualism implies that we only find ourselves by leaving others, it is more accurate to say "we find ourselves not independently of other people and institutions but through them. We never get to the bottom of our selves on our own" (Bellah et al. 1985, 84).

Love and marriage offer a microcosm of the cross-pressures between individualism and commitment. Marriage traditionally has been a practical, economic arrangement between groups rather than a romantic one between individuals. The transition from one to the other has transformed marriage into a vehicle of personal fulfillment. Marriages therefore become endangered when they no longer deliver such fulfillment. Because marriage and family also remain the central social institutions for the reproduction and socialization of children, the cross-pressures between marriage as a personal satisfaction and family as a social institution symbolize the tensions between modern individualism and social commitments.

Contemporary individualism also pursues therapy as a vehicle of self-discovery. Although not as harshly critical of the therapeutic ethos as Lasch (1979), Robert Bellah and his coauthors describe how seeking self-discovery leads people away from connections with others. Self-actualization is sought as a purely personal matter, and institutional arrangements are seen as beyond one's control. In these ways, therapy unwittingly encourages accommodation to such institutions rather than a sense of agency that might change them through collective action. Finally, therapeutic advice seems to endorse expressive individualism, but it is heavily influenced by instrumental calculations of the costs and benefits of different paths to fulfillment. It is another example of modern culture's elevation of individual needs above collective engagements that might actually fulfill such needs.

Turning from private to public life, the effects of individualism are no less evident. There are many ways people get involved in larger public communities. Often, however, such involvement means associating with people like oneself; it is another version of using others to reinforce one's individuality. People do express concern about the decline of community in their interviews. However, it is difficult for them to respond effectively, because the norms that support communities and foster public involvement have withered in the face of an individualistic ethos.

Similar tensions arise around citizenship. The US ethos of individualism does not equip people to respond effectively to the macro level of society. "If the culture of individualism has difficulty coming to terms with genuine cultural or social differences, it has even more difficulty coming to terms with large impersonal organizations and institutions" (Bellah et al. 1985, 207). Social order is complex because of the interactions of many interdependent groups. Individualism keeps people from understanding this order clearly. Perhaps that is why politicians and mass media so frequently reduce complex issues to simple narratives of heroic or evil people; such narratives resonate with individualism in ways that more complex stories never could.

Religion has traditionally provided unity and integration, so it is an especially interesting arena for understanding US individualism. US history reveals a privatizing of religion, reducing it from cultural obligation to individual preference. The social fact of a religious community that precedes and imposes itself upon the individual (for better and worse) now seems quite foreign. In the individualistic United States, we choose a religion in the same way we choose lifestyles, candidates, cars, and toothpaste in a market of competing brands.

People's responses to the dilemmas of individualism are nevertheless quite complex. The very people who fiercely defend individualism also express dissatisfaction with its consequences and a desire for stronger connections with others. In other cases, people can't think "outside the box" of individualism and yet recognize that it comes with a heavy price in the deterioration of public life and community norms. As the most individualistic culture in the world, US society is thus one of the best places to examine the tensions between individualism and the longing for broader social connections.

On these issues, there is a gap between common sense and the sociological imagination. The former embraces ontological individualism, or the "idea that the individual is the only firm reality" (Bellah et al. 1985, 276). The sociological imagination, by contrast, favors ontological "relationism," or the idea that groups and individuals are interdependent so that individuals only become real in the context of the group. Even mainstream sociology is implicitly critical of common sense by debunking the surface appearance of individualism and revealing its inescapably social roots.

As a final example, consider the ideal of the "self-made man." Although the phrase resonates with US consciousness, it is sociologically nonsensical. People can only be collectively made. No one changes their diapers, invents their language, finds their food, cultivates their mind, acquires their skills, or develops their identity in isolation from others. The most basic sociological insight on this question is this: we are social before we are individual (Lemert 2008). Durkheim demonstrated this on a social evolutionary scale, but the same truth is replayed in the life of every person who emerges from a web of social ties to become an individual in modern society.

Sociology and the Social Sciences

by Emile Durkheim

When dealing with a new science such as sociology, which, born only yesterday, is merely in the process of being constituted, the best way to understand its nature, object, and method is to retrace its genesis in a summary fashion.

The word *sociology* was created by Auguste Comte to designate the science of societies.[1] If the word was new, it was because the thing itself was new; a neologism was necessary. To be sure, one could say in a very broad sense that speculation about political and social matters began before the nineteenth century: Plato's *Republic,* Aristotle's *Politics,* and the innumerable treatises for which these two works served as models—those of Campanella, of Hobbes, of Rousseau and of so many others—already dealt with these questions. But these various studies differed in one fundamental respect from those which are designated by the word *sociology.* They took as their object not the description or explanation of societies as they exist or as they have existed, but the investigation of what societies *should be, how they should be organized* in order to be as perfect as possible. The aim of the sociologist is entirely different; he studies societies simply *to know them* and to *understand them,* just as the physicist, the chemist, and the biologist do for physical, chemical, and biological phenomena. His sole task is properly to determine the facts which he undertakes to study, to discover the laws according to which they occur, leaving it to others to find, if there is need, the possible applications of the propositions which he establishes.

That is to say that sociology could not appear until men had acquired the sense that societies, like the rest of the world, are subject to laws which of necessity derive from and express their nature. Now this conception was very slow to take form. For centuries, men believed that even minerals were not ruled by definite laws but could take on all possible forms and properties if only a sufficiently powerful will applied itself to them. They believed that certain expressions or certain gestures had the ability to transform an inert mass into a living being, a man into an animal or a plant, and vice versa. This illusion, for which we have a sort of instinctive inclination, naturally persisted much longer in the realm of social phenomena.

In effect, since they are far more complex, the order which inheres in social phenomena is far more difficult to perceive and, consequently, one is led to believe that they occur in a contingent and more or less disordered way. At first sight, what a contrast exists between the simple, rigorous sequence with which the phenomena of the physical universe unfold and the chaotic, capricious, disconcerting aspect of the events which history records! From another viewpoint, the very part which we play therein disposes us to think that, since they are done by us, they depend exclusively on us and can be what we want them to be. In such circumstances, there was no reason to observe them, since they were nothing by themselves but derived any reality they had from our will alone. From this point of view, the only question which could come up was to know not what they were and according to what laws they operated but what we could and must desire them to be.

It was only at the end of the eighteenth century that people first began to perceive that the social realm, like the other realms of nature, had its own laws. When Montesquieu declared that "The laws are the necessary relationships which derive from the nature of things," he well understood that this excellent definition of natural law applied to social as well as to other phenomena; his book, *The Spirit of Laws,* attempts to show precisely how legal institutions are grounded in man's nature and his milieu. Soon thereafter, Condorcet undertook to reconstruct the order according to which mankind achieved its progress.[2] This was the best way to demonstrate that there was nothing fortuitous or capricious about it but that it depended on determinate causes. At the same time, the economists taught that the phenomena of industrial and commercial life are governed by laws, which they thought they had discovered.

Although these different thinkers had prepared the way for the conception on which sociology rests, they had as yet only a rather ambiguous and irresolute notion of what the laws of social life might be. They did not wish to say, in effect, that social facts link up according to definite and invariable relations which the scholar seeks to observe by procedures analogous to those which are employed in the natural sciences. They simply meant that, given the nature of man, a course was layed out which was the only natural one, the one mankind should follow *if it wished to be in harmony with itself and to fulfill its destiny;* but it was still possible that it had strayed from that path.

And in fact, they judged that mankind had ceaselessly strayed as the result of deplorable aberrations which, moreover, they did not take much trouble to explain. For the economists, for example, the true economic organization, the only one which science should undertake to know, has, so to speak, never existed; it is more ideal than real. For men, under the influence of their rulers and as a result of a veritable blindness, have always let themselves be led astray. That is to say that the economists far more often constructed it deductively than observed it; and in this way they returned, though in an indirect way, to the ideas which were the basis of the political theories of Plato and Aristotle.

It is only at the beginning of the nineteenth century, with Saint-Simon at first, and especially with his disciple, Auguste Comte, that a new conception was definitively brought to light.[3]

Proceeding to the synthetic view of all the constituted sciences of his time in his *Cours de philosophie positive,* Comte stated that they all rested on the axiom that the phenomena with which they dealt are linked according to necessary relationships, that is to say, on the determinist principle. From this fact, he concluded that this principle, which had thus been verified in all the other realms of nature from the realm of mathematical splendors to that of life, must be equally true of the social realm. The resistances which today are opposed to this new extension of the determinist idea must not stop the philosopher. They have arisen with regularity each time that it has been a question of extending to a new realm this fundamental postulate and they always have been overcome. There was a time when people refused to accept that this principle applied even in the world of inanimate objects; it was established there. Next it was denied for living and thinking beings; now it is undisputed there as well.

One can therefore rest assured that these same prejudices which this principle encountered in the attempt to apply it to the social world will last only for a time. Moreover, since Comte postulated as a self-evident truth—a truth which is, moreover, now undisputed— that the individual's mental life is subject to necessary laws, how could the actions and reactions which are exchanged among individual consciousnesses in association not be subjected to the same necessity?

Viewed in this way, societies ceased to appear as a sort of indefinitely malleable and plastic matter that men could mold, so to speak, at will; thenceforth, it was necessary to see them as realities whose nature is imposed upon us and which, like all natural things, can only be modified in conformity with the laws which regulate them. Human institutions could be considered

no longer as the product of the more or less enlightened will of princes, statesmen, and legislators, but as the necessary result of determinate causes that physically imply them. Given the
composition of a nation at a given moment in its history, and the state of its civilization at this
same period, a social organization results which is characterized in this or that manner, just as
the properties of a physical body result from its molecular constitution. We are thus faced with
a stable, immutable order of things, and pure science becomes at once possible and necessary
for describing and explaining it, for saying what its characteristics are and on what causes they
depend. This purely speculative science is sociology. In order better to suggest the relationship in
which it stands to the other positive sciences, Comte often calls it social physics.

It has sometimes been said that this conception implies a sort of fatalism. If the network
of social facts is so solid and so resistant a web, does it not follow that men are incapable of
modifying it and that, consequently, they cannot act upon their own history? But the example
of what has happened in the other realms of nature demonstrates to what extent this reproach
is unjustified. As we were saying a moment ago, there was a time when the human mind did
not know that the physical universe had its laws. Was it then that man held greatest sway
over things? No doubt, the sorcerer or the magician believed that he could transmute at will
various bodies one into another; but the powers which he thus attributed to himself were,
we know today, purely imaginary. On the contrary, since the positive natural sciences were
established (and they too were established by taking the determinist postulate as a foundation),
what changes we have introduced into the universe! It will be the same way in the social realm.
Until yesterday we believed that all this was arbitrary and contingent, that legislators or kings
could, just like the alchemists of yore, at their pleasure change the aspect of societies, make them
change from one type to another. In reality, these supposed miracles were illusory; and how many
grave errors have resulted from this yet too widespread illusion! On the contrary, it is sociology
which by discovering the laws of social reality will permit us to direct historical evolution with
greater reflection than in the past; for we can change nature, whether moral or physical, only by
conforming to its laws. Progress in political arts will follow those in social science, just as the
discoveries of physiology and anatomy helped perfect medical arts, just as the power of industry
has increased a hundredfold since mechanics and the physico-chemical sciences have sprung to
life. At the same time that they proclaim the necessity of things, the sciences place in our hands
the means to dominate that necessity.[4] Comte even remarks with insistence that of all the natural
phenomena, social phenomena are the most malleable, the most accessible to variations and to
changes, because they are the most complex. Therefore, sociology in no way imposes upon man
a passively conservative attitude; on the contrary, it extends the field of our action by the simple
fact that it extends the field of our science. It only turns us away from ill-conceived and sterile

enterprises inspired by the belief that we are able to change the social order as we wish, without taking into account customs, traditions, and the mental constitution of man and of societies.

But, as essential as this principle may be, it was not a sufficient basis on which to found sociology. For there to be substance to a new science called by this name, it was yet necessary that the subject matter which it undertakes to study not be confused with those which the other sciences treat. Now on first consideration, sociology might appear indistinguishable from psychology; and this thesis has in fact been maintained, by Tarde, among others.[5] Society, they say, is nothing but the individuals of whom it is composed. They are its only reality. How, then, can the science of societies be distinguished from the science of individuals, that is to say, from psychology?

If one reasons in this way, one could equally well maintain that biology is but a chapter of physics and chemistry, for the living cell is composed exclusively of atoms of carbon, nitrogen, and so on, which the physico-chemical sciences undertake to study. But that is to forget that a whole very often has very different properties from those which its constituent parts possess. Though a cell contains nothing but mineral elements, these reveal, by being combined in a certain way, properties which they do not have when they are not thus combined and which are characteristic of life (properties of sustenance and of reproduction); they thus form, through their synthesis, a reality of an entirely new sort, which is living reality and which constitutes the subject matter of biology. In the same way, individual consciousnesses, by associating themselves in a stable way, reveal, through their interrelationships, a new life very different from that which would have developed had they remained uncombined; this is social life. Religious institutions and beliefs, political, legal, moral, and economic institutions—in a word, all of what constitutes civilization—would not exist if there were no society.

In effect, civilization presupposes cooperation not only among all the members of a single society, but also among all the societies which interact with one another. Moreover, it is possible only if the results obtained by one generation are transmitted to the following generation in such a way that they can be added to the results which the latter will obtain. But for that to happen, the successive generations must not be separated from one another as they arrive at adulthood but must remain in close contact, that is to say, they must be associated in a permanent fashion. Thus, this entire, vast assembly of things exists only because there are human associations; moreover, they vary according to what these associations are, and how they are organized. These things find their immediate explanation in the nature of societies, not of individuals, and constitute, therefore, the subject matter of a new science distinct from, though related to, individual psychology: this is sociology.[6]

Comte was not content to establish these two principles theoretically; he undertook to put them into practice, and, for the first time, he attempted to create a sociological discipline. It is for this purpose that he uses the three final volumes of the *Cours de philosophie positive*. Little remains today of the details of his work. Historical and especially ethnographic knowledge was still too rudimentary in his time to offer a sufficiently solid basis for sociological inductions. Moreover, as we shall see below, Comte did not recognize the multiplicity of the problems posed by the new science: he thought that he could create it all at once, as one would create a system of metaphysics; sociology, however, like any science, can be constituted only progressively, by approaching questions one after another. But the idea was infinitely fertile and outlived the founder of positivism.

It was taken up again first by Herbert Spencer.[7] Then, in the last thirty years, a whole legion of workers arose—to some extent in all countries, but particularly in France—and applied themselves to these studies. Sociology has now left behind the heroic age. The principles on which it rests and which were originally proclaimed in a very philosophical and dialectical way have now received factual confirmation. It assumes that social phenomena are in no way contingent or arbitrary. Sociologists have shown that certain moral and legal institutions and certain religious beliefs are identical everywhere that the conditions of social life are identical. They have even been able to establish similarities in the details of the customs of countries very distant from each other and between which there has never been any sort of communication. This remarkable uniformity is the best proof that the social realm does not escape the law of universal determinism.[8]

ENDNOTES

1. The word, formed by the coupling of one Latin and one Greek root, has a hybrid quality which purists have often reproached. But despite this unfortunate derivation, it has today won acceptance in all European languages. (E. D.)

2. In the *Tableau des progrès de l'esprit humain*. (E. D.)

3. The principal works of Saint-Simon concerning sociology are: *Mémoire sur la science de l'homme*, 1813; *L'Industrie*, 1816-1817; *L'Organisateur*, 1819; *Du Système industriel*, 1821–1822; *Cathéchisme des industriels*, 1822–1824; *De la Physiologie appliquée aux améliorations sociales*. (E. D.)

4. People object that sociological determinism cannot be reconciled with free will. But if the existence of freedom truly implies the negation of any determinate law, it is an insurmountable obstacle not only for the social sciences but for all sciences. For, since human volitions are always bound to some external movements, it renders determinism just as unintelligible outside of us as within. However, no one, even among the partisans of free will, any longer disputes the possibility of physical and natural sciences. Why would it be otherwise with sociology? (E. D.)

5. See in particular his book *L'Imitation*. (E. D.)

6. The nature of societies doubtless depends in part on the nature of man in general; but the direct, immediate explanation of social facts is to be found in the nature of the society, for, otherwise, social life would not have varied more than the constituent attributes of humanity. (E. D.

7. *See his* Principles of Sociology. *(E. D.)*

8. A few examples are to be found in my *Rules of the Sociological Method*. (E. D.)

SECTION 2

SOCIOLOGICAL THEORY

Bourgeois and Proletarians

PART ONE OF THE MANIFESTO OF THE COMMUNIST PARTY

by Karl Marx

I. BOURGEOIS AND PROLETARIANS

The history of all hitherto existing society is the history of class struggles. Freeman and slave, patrician and plebeian, lord and serf, guild-master and journeyman, in a word, oppressor and oppressed, stood in constant opposition to one another, carried on an uninterrupted, now hidden, now open fight, a fight that each time ended, either in a revolutionary re-constitution of society at large, or in the common ruin of the contending classes.

In the earlier epochs of history, we find almost everywhere a complicated arrangement of society into various orders, a manifold gradation of social rank. In ancient Rome we have patricians, knights, plebeians, slaves; in the Middle Ages, feudal lords, vassals, guild-masters, journeymen, apprentices, serfs; in almost all of these classes, again, subordinate gradations.

The modern bourgeois society that has sprouted from the ruins of feudal society has not done away with clash antagonisms. It has but established new classes, new conditions of oppression, new forms of struggle in place of the old ones.

Our epoch, the epoch of the bourgeoisie, possesses, however, this distinctive feature: it has simplified the clash antagonisms: Society as a whole is more and more splitting up into two great hostile camps, into two great classes directly facing each other: Bourgeoisie and Proletariat.

From the serfs of the Middle Ages sprang the chartered burghers of the earliest towns. From these burgesses the first elements of the bourgeoisie were developed.

The discovery of America, the rounding of the Cape, opened up fresh ground for the rising bourgeoisie. The East-Indian and Chinese markets, the colonisation of America, trade with the colonies, the increase in the means of exchange and in commodities generally, gave to commerce, to navigation, to industry, an impulse never before known, and thereby, to the revolutionary element in the tottering feudal society, a rapid development.

The feudal system of industry, under which industrial production was monopolised by closed guilds, now no longer sufficed for the growing wants of the new markets. The manufacturing system took its place. The guild-masters were pushed on one side by the manufacturing middle class; division of labour between the different corporate guilds vanished in the face of division of labour in each single workshop.

Meantime the markets kept ever growing, the demand ever rising. Even manufacture no longer sufficed. Thereupon, steam and machinery revolutionised industrial production. The place of manufacture was taken by the giant, Modern Industry, the place of the industrial middle class, by industrial millionaires, the leaders of whole industrial armies, the modern bourgeois.

Modern industry has established the world-market, for which the discovery of America paved the way. This market has given an immense development to commerce, to navigation, to communication by land. This development has, in its turn, reacted on the extension of industry; and in proportion as industry, commerce, navigation, railways extended, in the same proportion the bourgeoisie developed, increased its capital, and pushed into the background every class handed down from the Middle Ages.

We see, therefore, how the modern bourgeoisie is itself the product of a long course of development, of a series of revolutions in the modes of production and of exchange.

Each step in the development of the bourgeoisie was accompanied by a corresponding political advance of that class. An oppressed class under the sway of the feudal nobility, an armed and self-governing association in the mediaeval commune; here independent urban republic (as in Italy and Germany), there taxable "third estate" of the monarchy (as in France), afterwards, in the period of manufacture proper, serving either the semi-feudal or the absolute monarchy as a counterpoise against the nobility, and, in fact, corner-stone of the great monarchies in general, the bourgeoisie has at last, since the establishment of Modern Industry and of the world-market, conquered for itself, in the modern representative State, exclusive political sway. The executive of the modern State is but a committee for managing the common affairs of the whole bourgeoisie.

The bourgeoisie, historically, has played a most revolutionary part.

The bourgeoisie, wherever it has got the upper hand, has put an end to all feudal, patriarchal, idyllic relations. It has pitilessly torn asunder the motley feudal ties that bound man to his "natural superiors," and has left remaining no other nexus between man and man than naked self-interest, than callous "cash payment." It has drowned the most heavenly ecstasies of religious fervour, of chivalrous enthusiasm, of philistine sentimentalism, in the icy water of egotistical calculation. It has resolved personal worth into exchange value, and in place of the numberless indefeasible chartered freedoms, has set up that single, unconscionable freedom—Free Trade. In one word, for exploitation, veiled by religious and political illusions, it has substituted naked, shameless, direct, brutal exploitation.

The bourgeoisie has stripped of its halo every occupation hitherto honoured and looked up to with reverent awe. It has converted the physician, the lawyer, the priest, the poet, the man of science, into its paid wage-labourers.

The bourgeoisie has torn away from the family its sentimental veil, and has reduced the family relation to a mere money relation.

The bourgeoisie has disclosed how it came to pass that the brutal display of vigour in the Middle Ages, which Reactionists so much admire, found its fitting complement in the most slothful indolence. It has been the first to show what man's activity can bring about. It has accomplished wonders far surpassing Egyptian pyramids, Roman aqueducts, and Gothic cathedrals; it has conducted expeditions that put in the shade all former Exoduses of nations and crusades.

The bourgeoisie cannot exist without constantly revolutionising the instruments of production, and thereby the relations of production, and with them the whole relations of society. Conservation of the old modes of production in unaltered form, was, on the contrary, the first condition of existence for all earlier industrial classes. Constant revolutionising of production, uninterrupted disturbance of all social conditions, everlasting uncertainty and agitation distinguish the bourgeois epoch from all earlier ones. All fixed, fast-frozen relations, with their train of ancient and venerable prejudices and opinions, are swept away, all new-formed ones become antiquated before they can ossify. All that is solid melts into air, all that is holy is profaned, and man is at last compelled to face with sober senses, his real conditions of life, and his relations with his kind.

The need of a constantly expanding market for its products chases the bourgeoisie over the whole surface of the globe. It must nestle everywhere, settle everywhere, establish connexions everywhere.

The bourgeoisie has through its exploitation of the world-market given a cosmopolitan character to production and consumption in every country. To the great chagrin of Reactionists, it has drawn from under the feet of industry the national ground on which it stood. All old-established national industries have been destroyed or are daily being destroyed. They are dislodged by new industries, whose introduction becomes a life and death question for all civilised nations, by industries that no longer work up indigenous raw material, but raw material drawn from the remotest zones; industries whose products are consumed, not only at home, but in every quarter of the globe. In place of the old wants, satisfied by the productions of the country, we find new wants, requiring for their satisfaction the products of distant lands and climes. In place of the old local and national seclusion and self-sufficiency, we have intercourse in every direction, universal interdependence of nations. And as in material, so also in intellectual production. The intellectual creations of individual nations become common property. National one-sidedness and narrow-mindedness become more and more impossible, and from the numerous national and local literatures, there arises a world literature.

The bourgeoisie, by the rapid improvement of all instruments of production, by the immensely facilitated means of communication, draws all, even the most barbarian, nations into civilisation. The cheap prices of its commodities are the heavy artillery with which it batters down all Chinese walls, with which it forces the barbarians' intensely obstinate hatred of foreigners to capitulate. It compels all nations, on pain of extinction, to adopt the bourgeois mode of production; it compels them to introduce what it calls civilisation into their midst, *i.e.,* to become bourgeois themselves. In one word, it creates a world after its own image.

The bourgeoisie has subjected the country to the rule of the towns. It has created enormous cities, has greatly increased the urban population as compared with the rural, and has thus rescued a considerable part of the population from the idiocy of rural life, just as it has made the country dependent on the towns, so it has made barbarian and semi-barbarian countries dependent on the civilised ones, nations and peasants on nations of bourgeois, the East on the West.

The bourgeoisie keeps more and more doing away with the scattered state of the population, of the means of production, and of property. It has agglomerated population, centralised means of production, and has concentrated property in a few hands. The necessary consequence of this was political centralisation. Independent, or but loosely connected provinces, with separate interests, laws, governments and systems of taxation, became lumped together into one nation, with one government, one code of laws, one national class-interest, one frontier and one customs-tariff. The bourgeoisie, during its rule of scarce one hundred years, has created more massive and more colossal productive forces than have all preceding generations together. Subjection of Nature's forces to man, machinery, application of chemistry to industry and agriculture, steam-navigation, railways, electric telegraphs, clearing of whole continents for cultivation, canalisation of rivers, whole populations conjured out of the ground—what earlier century had even a presentiment that such productive forces slumbered in the lap of social labour?

We see then: the means of production and of exchange, on whose foundation the bourgeoisie built itself up, were generated in feudal society. At a certain stage in the development of these means of production and of exchange, the conditions under which feudal society produced and exchanged, the feudal organisation of agriculture and manufacturing industry, in one word, the feudal relations of property became no longer compatible with the already developed productive forces; they became so many fetters. They had to be burst asunder; they were burst asunder.

Into their place stepped free competition, accompanied by a social and political constitution adapted to it, and by the economical and political sway of the bourgeois class.

A similar movement is going on before our own eyes. Modern bourgeois society with its relations of production, of exchange and of property, a society that has conjured up such gigantic means of production and of exchange, is like the sorcerer, who is no longer able to control the powers of the nether world whom he has called up by his spells. For many a decade past the history of industry and commerce is but the history of the revolt of modern productive forces against modern conditions of production, against the property relations that are the conditions for the existence of the bourgeoisie and of its rule. It is enough to mention the commercial crises that by their periodical return put on its trial, each time more threateningly, the existence of the entire bourgeois society. In these crises a great part not only of the existing products, but also of the previously created productive forces, are periodically destroyed. In these crises there breaks out an epidemic that, in all earlier epochs, would have seemed an absurdity—the epidemic of over-production. Society suddenly finds itself put back into a state of momentary barbarism; it appears as if a famine, a universal war of devastation had cut off the supply of every means of subsistence; industry and commerce seem to be destroyed; and why? Because there is too much civilisation, too much means of subsistence, too much industry, too much commerce. The productive forces at the disposal of society no longer tend to further the development of the conditions of bourgeois property; on the contrary, they have become too powerful for these conditions, by which they are fettered, and so soon as they overcome these fetters, they bring disorder into the whole of bourgeois society, endanger the existence of bourgeois property. The conditions of bourgeois society are too narrow to comprise the wealth created by them. And how does the bourgeoisie get over these crises? On the one hand by enforced destruction of a mass of productive forces; on the other, by the conquest of new markets, and by the more thorough exploitation of the old ones. That is to say, by paving the way for more extensive and more destructive crises, and by diminishing the means whereby crises are prevented.

The weapons with which the bourgeoisie felled feudalism to the ground are now turned against the bourgeoisie itself.

But not only has the bourgeoisie forged the weapons that bring death to itself; it has also called into existence the men who are to wield these weapons—the modern working class—the proletarians.

In proportion as the bourgeoisie, *i.e.,* capital, is developed, in the same proportion is the proletariat, the modern working class, developed—a class of labourers, who live only so long as they find work, and who find work only so long as their labour increases capital. These labourers, who must sell themselves piece-meal, are a commodity, like every other article of commerce, and are consequently exposed to all the vicissitudes of competition, to all the fluctuations of the market.

Owing to the extensive use of machinery and to division of labour, the work of the proletarians has lost all individual character, and consequently, all charm for the workman. He becomes an appendage of the machine, and it is only the most simple, most monotonous, and most easily acquired knack, that is required of him. Hence, the cost of production of a workman is restricted, almost entirely, to the means of subsistence that he requires for his maintenance, and for the propagation of his race. But the price of a commodity, and therefore also of labour, is equal to its cost of production. In proportion, therefore, as the repulsiveness of the work increases, the wage decreases. Nay more, in proportion as the use of machinery and division of labour increases, in the same proportion the burden of toil also increases, whether by prolongation of the working hours, by increase of the work exacted in a given time or by increased speed of the machinery, etc.

Modern industry has converted the little workshop of the patriarchal master into the great factory of the industrial capitalist. Masses of labourers, crowded into the factory, are organised like soldiers. As privates of the industrial army they are placed under the command of a perfect hierarchy of officers and sergeants. Not only are they slaves of the bourgeois class, and of the bourgeois State; they are daily and hourly enslaved by the machine, by the over-looker, and, above all, by the individual bourgeois manufacturer himself. The more openly this despotism proclaims gain to be its end and aim, the more petty, the more hateful and the more embittering it is.

The less the skill and exertion of strength implied in manual labour, in other words, the more modern industry becomes developed, the more is the labour of men superseded by that of women. Differences of age and sex have no longer any distinctive social validity for the working class. All are instruments of labour, more or less expensive to use, according to their age and sex.

No sooner is the exploitation of the labourer by the manufacturer, so far, at an end, that he receives his wages in cash, than he is set upon by the other portions of the bourgeoisie, the landlord, the shopkeeper, the pawnbroker, etc.

The lower strata of the middle class—the small tradespeople, shopkeepers, and retired tradesmen generally, the handicraftsmen and peasants—all these sink gradually into the proletariat, partly because their diminutive capital does not suffice for the scale on which Modern Industry is carried on, and is swamped in the competition with the large capitalists, partly because their specialised skill is rendered worthless by new methods of production. Thus the proletariat is recruited from all classes of the population.

The proletariat goes through various stages of development. With its birth begins its struggle with the bourgeoisie. At first the contest is carried on by individual labourers, then by the workpeople of a factory, then by the operatives of one trade, in one locality, against the individual bourgeois who directly exploits them. They direct their attacks not against the bourgeois conditions of production, but against the instruments of production themselves; they destroy imported wares that compete with their labour, they smash to pieces machinery, they set factories ablaze, they seek to restore by force the vanished status of the workman of the Middle Ages.

At this stage the labourers still form an incoherent mass scattered over the whole country, and broken up by their mutual competition. If anywhere they unite to form more compact bodies, this is not yet the consequence of their own active union, but of the union of the bourgeoisie, which class, in order to attain its own political ends, is compelled to set the whole proletariat in motion, and is moreover yet, for a time, able to do so. At this stage, therefore, the proletarians do not fight their enemies, but the enemies of their enemies, the remnants of absolute monarchy, the landowners, the non-industrial bourgeois, the petty bourgeoisie. Thus the whole historical movement is concentrated in the hands of the bourgeoisie; every victory so obtained is a victory for the bourgeoisie.

But with the development of industry the proletariat not only increases in number; it becomes concentrated in greater masses, its strength grows, and it feels that strength more. The various interests and conditions of life within the ranks of the proletariat are more and more equalised, in proportion as machinery obliterates all distinctions of labour, and nearly everywhere reduces wages to the same low level. The growing competition among the bourgeois, and the resulting commercial crises, make the wages of the workers ever more fluctuating. The unceasing improvement of machinery, ever more rapidly developing, makes their livelihood more and more precarious; the collisions between individual workmen and individual bourgeois take more and more the character of collisions between two classes. Thereupon the workers begin to form combinations (Trades Unions) against the bourgeois; they club together in order to keep up the rate of wages; they found permanent associations in order to make provision beforehand for these occasional revolts. Here and there the contest breaks out into riots.

Now and then the workers are victorious, but only for a time. The real fruit of their battles lies, not in the immediate result, but in the ever-expanding union of the workers. This union is helped on by the improved means of communication that are created by modern industry and that place the workers of different localities in contact with one another. It was just this contact that was needed to centralise the numerous local struggles, all of the same character, into one national struggle between classes. But every class struggle is a political struggle. And that union, to attain which the burghers of the Middle Ages, with their miserable highways, required centuries, the modern proletarians, thanks to railways, achieve in a few years.

This organisation of the proletarians into a class, and consequently into a political party, is continually being upset again by the competition between the workers themselves. But it ever rises up again, stronger, firmer, mightier. It compels legislative recognition of particular interests of the workers, by taking advantage of the divisions among the bourgeoisie itself. Thus the ten-hours' bill in England was carried.

Altogether collisions between the classes of the old society further, in many ways, the course of development of the proletariat. The bourgeoisie finds itself involved in a constant battle. At first with the aristocracy; later on, with those portions of the bourgeoisie itself, whose interests have become antagonistic to the progress of industry; at all times, with the bourgeoisie of foreign countries. In all these battles it sees itself compelled to appeal to the proletariat, to ask for its help, and thus, to drag it into the political arena. The bourgeoisie itself, therefore, supplies the proletariat with its own elements of political and general education, in other words, it furnishes the proletariat with weapons for fighting the bourgeoisie.

Further, as we have already seen, entire sections of the ruling classes are, by the advance of industry, precipitated into the proletariat, or are at least threatened in their conditions of existence. These also supply the proletariat with fresh elements of enlightenment and progress.

Finally, in times when the class struggle nears the decisive hour, the process of dissolution going on within the ruling class, in fact within the whole range of society, assumes such a violent, glaring character, that a small section of the ruling class cuts itself adrift, and joins the revolutionary class, the class that holds the future in its hands. Just as, therefore, at an earlier period, a section of the nobility went over to the bourgeoisie, so now a portion of the bourgeoisie goes over to the proletariat, and in particular, a portion of the bourgeois ideologists, who have raised themselves to the level of comprehending theoretically the historical movement as a whole.

Of all the classes that stand face to face with the bourgeoisie today, the proletariat alone is a really revolutionary class. The other classes decay and finally disappear in the face of Modern Industry; the proletariat is its special and essential product.

The lower middle class, the small manufacturer, the shopkeeper, the artisan, the peasant, all these fight against the bourgeoisie, to save from extinction their existence as fractions of the middle class. They are therefore not revolutionary, but conservative. Nay more, they are reactionary, for they try to roll back the wheel of history. If by chance they are revolutionary, they are so only in view of their impending transfer into the proletariat, they thus defend not their present, but their future interests, they desert their own standpoint to place themselves at that of the proletariat.

The "dangerous class," the social scum, that passively rotting mass thrown off by the lowest layers of old society, may, here and there, be swept into the movement by a proletarian revolution; its conditions of life, however, prepare it far more for the part of a bribed tool of reactionary intrigue.

In the conditions of the proletariat, those of old society at large are already virtually swamped. The proletarian is without property; his relation to his wife and children has no longer anything in common with the bourgeois family-relations; modern industrial labour, modern subjection to capital, the same in England as in France, in America as in Germany, has stripped him of every trace of national character. Law, morality, religion, are to him so many bourgeois prejudices, behind which lurk in ambush just as many bourgeois interests.

All the preceding classes that got the upper hand, sought to fortify their already acquired status by subjecting society at large to their conditions of appropriation. The proletarians cannot become masters of the productive forces of society, except by abolishing their own previous mode of appropriation, and thereby also every other previous mode of appropriation. They have nothing of their own to secure and to fortify; their mission is to destroy all previous securities for, and insurances of, individual property.

All previous historical movements were movements of minorities, or in the interests of minorities. The proletarian movement is the self-conscious, independent movement of the immense majority, in the interests of the immense majority. The proletariat, the lowest stratum of our present society, cannot stir, cannot raise itself up, without the whole superincumbent strata of official society being sprung into the air.

Though not in substance, yet in form, the struggle of the proletariat with the bourgeoisie is at first a national struggle. The proletariat of each country must, of course, first of all settle matters with its own bourgeoisie.

In depicting the most general phases of the development of the proletariat, we traced the more or less veiled civil war, raging within existing society, up to the point where that war breaks out into open revolution, and where the violent overthrow of the bourgeoisie lays the foundation for the sway of the proletariat.

Hitherto, every form of society has been based, as we have already seen, on the antagonism of oppressing and oppressed classes. But in order to oppress a class, certain conditions must be assured to it under which it can, at least, continue its slavish existence. The serf, in the period of serfdom, raised himself to membership in the commune, just as the petty bourgeois, under the yoke of feudal absolutism, managed to develop into a bourgeois. The modern labourer, on the contrary, instead of rising with the progress of industry, sinks deeper and deeper below the conditions of existence of his own class. He becomes a pauper, and pauperism develops more rapidly than population and wealth. And here it becomes evident, that the bourgeoisie is unfit any longer to be the ruling class in society, and to impose its conditions of existence upon society as an over-riding law. It is unfit to rule because it is incompetent to assure an existence to its slave within his slavery, because it cannot help letting him sink into such a state, that it has to feed him, instead of being fed by him. Society can no longer live under this bourgeoisie, in other words, its existence is no longer compatible with society.

The essential condition for the existence, and for the sway of the bourgeois class, is the formation and augmentation of capital; the condition for capital is wage-labour. Wage-labour rests exclusively on competition between the labourers. The advance of industry, whose involuntary promoter is the bourgeoisie, replaces the isolation of the labourers, due to competition, by their revolutionary combination, due to association. The development of Modern Industry, therefore, cuts from under its feet the very foundation on which the bourgeoisie produces and appropriates products. What the bourgeoisie, therefore, produces, above all, is its own grave-diggers. Its fall and the victory of the proletariat are equally inevitable.

Introduction to Symbolic Interaction and Cultural Studies

by Howard S. Becker and
Michal M. McCall

WHAT IS SYMBOLIC INTERACTION?

Symbolic interaction is a sociological tradition that traces its lineage to the Pragmatists—John Dewey and George Herbert Mead, particularly—and to sociologists of the "Chicago School"—Robert E. Park, Herbert Blumer, Everett C. Hughes, and their students and successors. We can summarize its chief ideas, perhaps oversimply, this way:

> Any human event can be understood as the result of the people involved (keeping in mind that that might be a very large number) continually adjusting what they do in the light of what others do, so that each individual's line of action "fits" into what the others do. That can only happen if human beings typically act in a non-automatic fashion, and instead construct a line of action by taking account of the meaning of what others do in response to their earlier actions. Human beings can only act in this way if they can incorporate the responses of others into their own act and thus anticipate what will probably happen, in the process creating a "self" in the Meadian sense. (This emphasis on the way people construct the meaning of others' acts is where the '"symbolic" in "symbolic interaction" comes from.) If everyone can and does do that, complex joint acts can occur. (Adapted from Becker 1988:18; see also Blumer 1969:10.)

These ideas have furnished the basis of thousands of fieldwork (ethnographic) studies in such areas as community, race, class, work, family, and the sociologies of art, science, and deviance. Symbolic interaction is an empirical research tradition as much or more than a theoretical position, and its strength derives in large part from the enormous body of research that embodies and gives meaning to its abstract propositions.

WHAT IS CULTURAL STUDIES?

We use the term *cultural studies* to refer to the classically humanistic disciplines which have lately come to use their philosophical, literary, and historical approaches to study the social construction of meaning and other topics traditionally of interest to symbolic interactionists, disciplines to which, in turn, social scientists have lately turned for "explanatory analogies" (Geertz 1983:23) as they "have turned away from a laws and instances ideal of explanation toward a cases and interpretations one" (ibid.: 19). The term is most closely identified with work carried on, since 1964, at the Centre for Contemporary Cultural Studies at the University of Birmingham in England. The main features of cultural studies, according to scholars associated with the center, are "its openness and theoretical versatility, its reflexive even self-conscious mood" (Johnson 1986-87:38), and its critical (or "engaged") approach to its primary objects of study: working class and youth subcultures, the media, language, and the social relations of education, the family and the state (S. Hall 1980).

Perhaps because cultural studies is self-consciously non-disciplinary, and has resisted theoretical orthodoxy (ibid., 1980) and methodological codification (Johnson 1986-87), it has engaged many of the important intellectual currents of the last twenty-five years, in a way that symbolic interaction has not. Among them: the revolution in literary criticism; the "new social history" movement; the "complex Marxism" of Lukács, Goldman, Walter Benjamin, and the "Frankfurt School"; the structuralisms, both the structural linguistics of Lévi-Strauss and Barthes and the Marxist structuralism of Althusser and Gramsci; the feminisms (Weedon 1987; S. Hall 1980); and the poststructuralisms, developed in and from the work of Derrida, Lacan, Kristeva, Althusser, and Foucault (Weedon 1987:19; S. Hall 1980; Johnson 1986–87).

Symbolic interactionists, like many other social scientists, have for the most part not been very attentive to these major intellectual currents represented in cultural studies. But, as the humanities and social sciences have approached one another in recent years, a lively discourse has grown up along the border. The intention of this volume is to bring symbolic interactionists into that conversation, both as listeners and speakers.

THE BORDER: TOPICS AND METHODS OF MUTUAL INTEREST

A number of major topics are addressed by workers in both traditions. Their interests converge most generally on the problem of meaning. Under that broad heading they find much of mutual interest in such topics as the nature of knowledge, our experience of our own lives and the lives of others, the relation between individual experience and action and the workings of social structures, the self and subjectivity, language and discourse. Both groups are interested, as well, in such concrete subject matters as art, science, education, and religion.

Empiricism

The great strength of the symbolic interaction approach to meaning is that it is empirical. The ultimate interactionist test of concepts is whether they make sense of particular situations known in great detail through detailed observation. You answer questions by going to see for yourself, studying the real world, and evaluating the evidence so gathered. Symbolic interaction takes the concrete, empirical world of lived experience as its problematic and treats theory as something that must be brought into line with that empirical world (Blumer 1969:151).

Addelson argues, on just these grounds, that philosophers must become sociologists (by which she means symbolic interactionist sociologists) because symbolic interactionism is empirical and, therefore, gives better accounts of human nature, human action, and of human group life than traditional philosophy does. She applies this reasoning in a nice example of how the interactionist emphasis on process helps solve the traditional philosophical problem of rules and rulebreaking. She quotes Blumer: "It is the social process in group life that creates and upholds the rules, not the rules that create and uphold group life," and goes on to say that if this is true, it is the social process and not the rules that must be understood and conceptually analyzed and clarified to answer the question, "What is morality?"

Symbolic interactionists typically find that meaning is constructed in the process *of interaction,* and have always insisted that process is not a neutral medium in which social forces play out their game, but the actual stuff of social organization and social forces (Blumer 1969). Society, for them, *is* the process of symbolic interaction, and this view allows them to steer the middle course between structuralism and idealism John Hall recommends in his paper.

For symbolic interactionists, process is not just a word. It's shorthand for an insistence that social events don't happen all at once, but rather happen in steps: first one thing, then another, with each succeeding step creating new conditions under which all the people and organizations involved must now negotiate the next step. This is more than a theoretical nicety. It makes theoretical room for contingency, another point many workers in cultural studies want to emphasize (Turner 1986). Nothing *has* to happen. Nothing is fully determined. At every step of every unfolding event, something else *might* happen. To be sure, the balance of constraints and opportunities available to the actors, individual and collective, in a situation will lead many, perhaps most, of them to do the same thing. Contingency doesn't mean people behave randomly, but it does recognize that they can behave in surprising and unconventional ways. The interactionist emphasis on process stands, as Blumer insisted, as a corrective to any view that insists that culture or social structure determines what people do.

Neitz's discussion of religious conversion shows the utility of such a view for a variety of problems of interest to cultural theorists. Earlier analyses looked for the conditions that led people to be converted, but had no language to describe the back-and-forth, shifting character of what went on when they did. Such "instantaneous" theories of conversion failed to see the importance of the events that lead up to conversion and, perhaps more important, the events that follow conversion, reinforcing and solidifying what might otherwise be a momentary whim. The new research, according to Neitz, sees conversion as a process and, for that reason, can turn to symbolic interaction and its concern with process for help in understanding the fluid relationships between religious and social structures today.

Although much of the work in cultural studies, and particularly at the Centre for Contemporary Cultural Studies, has been accused of being too theoretical, it has also been empirical, right from the start. Unlike symbolic interactionism, though, cultural studies has not been willing, or able, to privilege empirical work over theory: "we had no alternative but to undertake a labour of theoretical definition and clarification at the same time as we attempted to do concrete work in the field" (S. Hall 1980:25).

Nor have empirical workers in cultural studies identified themselves as fieldworkers as thoroughly as symbolic interactionists have. Indeed, in Stuart Hall's words, "the tension between experiential accounts and a larger account of structural and historical determinations has been a pivotal site of Centre theorizing and debate ever since" Paul Willis's ground-breaking ethnographic work in *Learning to Labour* (ibid.:24). "While sharing an emphasis on people's ability to make meaning, critical theorists concerned with cultural production" differ in important ways from symbolic interactionists: their ethnographies are more "openly ideological" and they are more overtly concerned with locating human agency in social structure:

> Both approaches emphasize human agency and the production of meaning and culture, but the critical production theorists ground their work on a moral imperative, [on a] "political commitment to human betterment." Moreover, the critical production theorists recognize the power of structural determinants in the sense of material

practices, modes of power, and economic and political institutions. Unlike the more voluntaristic [symbolic interactionists and ethnomethodologists], the critical . . . theorists remain acutely aware that, as Marx notes, "while men |sic] make their own history, they do not make it just as they please." Their recent work has focused in different ways on the need for a theory that will recognize both human agency and the production of knowledge and culture and will at the same time take into account the power of material and ideological structures. This dialectic between individual consciousness and structural determinants has led them to seek more developed theories of ideology, hegemony, and resistance, and to the development of what has been called "critical ethnography." (Weiler 1988:12-13)

Willis himself recognizes the "profoundly important methodological possibility" in fieldwork—"that of *being surprised,* of reaching knowledge not prefigured in one's starting paradigm" (1980:90), but argues there is "no truly untheoretical way in which to 'see' an 'object.'" To "remove the hidden tendency towards positivism" in fieldwork research, he suggests that the "theoretical organization of the startingout position should be outlined and acknowledged in any piece of research"; that fieldworkers "add to the received notion of the 'quality' of the data an ability to watch for inconsistencies, contradictions and misunderstandings" and "make theoretical interpretations of them"; and that they recognize their "reflective relationship to their subjects" (ibid.:90-92).

McCall and Wittner also address these issues, emphasizing how studies in the social sciences have tended to take the point of view of dominant social groups and thus have failed to create knowledge about matters considered important to less powerful people. Aware of the "key insight of advanced semiology," that "narratives or images always imply or construct a position or positions from which they are to be read or viewed" and that "realist" texts "naturalise the means by which positioning is achieved" (Johnson 1986-87:66), they challenge other fieldworkers to ask, Where have we positioned ourselves as researchers? From what position have we viewed the subjects of our research? How has our realistic, documentary style of representing social life naturalized our own authority?

Culture Production and Reproduction

Cultural studies is, in important ways, the result of Marxist critiques of economism and of the realization that "cultural practice and cultural production are not simply derived from an otherwise constituted social order but are themselves major elements in its constitution" (Williams 1981:12). Much of their best work has focused on the production of knowledge in educational institutions. Early work concerned social and cultural *reproduction*—that is, the reproduction of class structures and of class cultures, knowledge, and power relationships in schools. However, much of this work on reproduction "did not get inside the school to find out how reproduction went on" (Apple 1985:20). According to Weiler, furthermore, it was based on "the underlying view that students are shaped by their experiences in schools to internalize or accept a subjectivity and a class position that leads to the reproduction of existing power relationships and social and economic structures" (Weiler 1988:6).

Later work, by critical ethnographers like Paul Willis, "demonstrated that rather than being places where culture and ideologies are imposed on students, schools are the sites where these things are produced" (Apple 1985: 26). By opening up the black box of education, critical ethnographers revealed that education is a system of production as well as reproduction. Furthermore, they discovered that students aren't simply shaped by their experiences, but actively "assert their own experience and contest or resist the ideological and material forces imposed upon them" (Weiler 198811).

The importance of these critical ethnographies to symbolic interaction is the suggestion, carried forward in education, that ethnography must be consciously ideological and can be both "transformative/' that is, can "help create the possibility of transforming such institutions as schools—through a process of negative critique" (Brodkey 1987:67), and "empowering" so long as it rests upon the assumption that "each person [has the] ability to understand and critique his or her own experience and the social reality 'out there'" (Weiler 1988:23).

Recent work in the sociology of science, reported on in the paper by Clarke and Gerson, makes related points, demonstrating that the organization of scientific work creates and shapes the knowledge we accept as "scientific." Treating science as the work people do, rather than as a privileged window on reality, lets us see science as continuous with the rest of human experience. This empirical approach coincides with the philosophical critique of scientism made in the name of pragmatism by Rorty (1979) and others.

Social Worlds and institutional Ethnography

Many sociologists have criticized symbolic interaction theory for being too focused on the "micro" aspect of society, on face-to-face interaction as opposed to the "macro" structural level of society. Gilmore, basing his argument on empirical work in the sociology of art, shows how the idea of social worlds helps bridge the micro-macro gap, making the insights of interactionism more useful to workers in cultural studies.

Symbolic interaction emphasizes collective action. One special version of this has proved useful: the idea of a "world," a more or less stable organization of collective activity. This idea has been used extensively in the sociologies of art and science (Kling and Gerson, 1977, 1978; Shibutani 1955; Becker 1982; and P. Hall 1987) but it can, in principle, come into use anywhere people are connected through their joint involvement in a task or event of a repetitive kind. Wherever social events happen routinely, we can expect to find a world.

Gilmore argues that the concept of social world, as developed and used by symbolic interactionists, allows for the kind of movement back and forth between "micro" and "macro" levels, between structure and culture and individuals, which has come to seem more important in cultural studies. Gilmore suggests that the idea of social worlds offers a solution to Marxists who want to stop talking about the reflections of the economic base in the cultural superstructure and instead look at how human agents produce culture. "World" does the work of a good concept. It tells you what to look for, what ought to be there to find in the phenomena we study. Then you can either find what you were told would be there or know that you have a new and interesting theoretical problem, because something that ought to be there wasn't there after all.

Dorothy E. Smith has recently proposed an alternative way of bridging the micro-macro gap, which she calls institutional ethnography. A feminist methodology, Smith's is compatible with the concerns of the critical ethnographers. Specifically, although it is careful to try to understand the everyday world from the point of view of the people who live in it, institutional ethnography also recognizes that knowledge of "the extralocal determinations of our experience does not lie within the scope of everyday practices" and must, therefore, "be the sociologist's special business" (1987:161).

> Our point of entry was women's experience of the work they did in relation to their children's schooling. We would begin by asking women to talk to us about this work. The resulting accounts would provide a wealth of descriptive material about particular women's local practices. There is nothing new sociologically about this procedure. While feminism has brought new sensitivities and a new scrupulousness to open-ended interviewing, it is our uses of material that have been distinctive. And here we are trying something different again. Standard sociological analysis uses some method of coding and interpreting such accounts to order the interview materials in relation to the relevances of the sociological and/or feminist discourses. These enable the interviews to be sorted into topics typical of the study population. In such a process, the standpoint of women themselves is suppressed. The standpoint becomes that of the discourse reflecting upon properties of the study population. Characteristics of the study population become the object of the knower's gaze.

We sought a method that would preserve throughout the standpoint of the women interviewed. To do so we worked with a sequence of stages in the research. We were concerned to locate women's work practices in the actual relations by which they are organized and which they organize. This meant talking to women first. Women's accounts of the work they did in relation to their children's schooling would then be examined for the ways in which they were articulated to the social organization of the school. That scrutiny would establish the questions and issues for the second stage of research, interviewing teachers and administrators in the schools. Our strategy would move from particular experiences to their embedding in the generalizing social organization of the school. It would preserve a perspective in which we could look out from where we are, from where our respondents are, onto the larger landscape organizing and containing their daily practices. (Ibid.: 182—183)

Self, Body, and Subjectivity

The idea of *the self* in the simple symbolic interaction version emphasizes the existence and profound consequences of the interior dialogue through which society is incorporated into the individual. Blumer explained this idea through an exegesis of George Herbert Mead's thought:

> In declaring that the human being has a self, Mead had in mind chiefly that the human being can be the object of his own actions. He can act toward himself as he might act toward others . . . . This mechanism enables the human being to make indications to himself of things in his surroundings and thus to guide his actions by what he notes . . . . The second important implication of the fact that the human being makes indications to himself is that his action is constructed or built up instead of being a mere release. Whatever the action in which he is engaged, the human individual proceeds by pointing out to himself the various conditions which may be instrumental to his action and those which may obstruct his action; he has to take account of the demands, the expectations, the prohibitions, and the threats as they may arise in the situation in which he is acting. His action is built up step by step through a process of such self-indication. The human individual pieces together and guides his action by taking account of different things and interpreting their significance for his prospective action. (Blumer 1969:79-81)

This stripped-down notion of the self builds society into every empirical analysis, in the form of all those others present in the situation of action to whom the actor pays attention. Most importantly, it recognizes people's ability to check their activity and reorient it on the basis of what's going on around them, rather than responding automatically to stimuli, impulses, or the dictates of a culture or social organization. A classic example of the utility of such a view of the self is Lindesmith's (1948) study of opiate addiction, which emphasizes the crucial importance of the self-process in understanding how addicts learn to see themselves as needing opiates to function normally.

Feminist theorists have criticized the dualism of Western culture and thought, especially the classic dualisms of nature/nurture and mind/body, and this criticism can reasonably be leveled at symbolic interactionists who often (though not always, see Becker 1986:47-66) leave out bodies, the biological component of human experience. Addelson criticizes Mead for this, and the fault is there to criticize. Interactionists have largely left the body and physical experience out of the self. Glassner now shows us one way to avoid this dualistic error and deal with bodies as well as minds when we talk about the self. He takes advantage of the insights of feminists and postmodernist thinkers to import a cultural-economy argument into the interactionist concept of the self. (See, also, Yonnet, 1985.)

Another critique of the symbolic interactionist self is implicit in Boden's paper on discourse analysis. Following Althusser (1971), cultural studies has replaced the "conscious, knowing, unified rational" *self* with the *subject* of discourse. In this account, "[t]he 'I,' the seat of consciousness and the foundation of ideological discourses, [is] not the integral Cartesian centre of thought but a contradictory discursive category constituted by ideological discourse itself" (S. Hall 1980:33).

> The political significance of decentering the subject and abandoning the belief in essential subjectivity is that it opens up subjectivity to change . . . . As we acquire language we learn to give voice—meaning—to our experience and to understand it according to particular ways of thinking, particular discourses, which pre-date our entry into language. These ways of thinking constitute our consciousness, and the positions with which we identify structure our sense of ourselves, our subjectivity. Having grown up within a particular system of meanings and values, which may well be contradictory, we may find ourselves resisting alternatives. Or, as we move out of familiar circles, through education or politics, for example, we may be exposed to alternative ways of constituting the meaning of our experience which seem to address our interests more directly . . . . This process of discovery can lead to a rewriting of personal experience in terms which give it social, changeable causes. (Weedon 1987:33)

Discourses

The various critical, feminist, and poststructuralist theories that have so profoundly influenced cultural studies have made discourse— talk and text—the site of meaning, social organization, power, and subjectivity. In this view, social structures and social processes are organized by institutions and cultural practices such as the law, the political system, the church, the family, education, and the media, each of which is "located in and structured by a particular discursive field" or discourse. Following Foucault, discourses are defined as "ways of constituting knowledge, together with the social practices, forms of subjectivity and power relations which inhere in such knowledges and the relations between them" (ibid.: 108). A discourse both constitutes the "nature" of the "subjects" it "seeks to govern" and subjects its speakers to its own power and regulation (ibid.: 108, 119). Powerful discourses are based in institutions and realized in institutional practices. "Yet these institutional locations are themselves sites of contest, and the dominant discourses governing the organization and practices of social institutions are under constant challenge" (ibid: 109).

> Much feminist discourse is, for example, either marginal to or in direct conflict with dominant definitions of femininity and its social constitution and regulation. Yet even where feminist discourses lack the social power to realize their versions of knowledge in institutional practices, they can offer the discursive space from which the individual can resist dominant subject positions . . . [and] resistance to the dominant at the level of the individual subject is the first stage in the production of alternative forms of knowledge or where such alternatives already exist, of winning individuals over to these discourses and gradually increasing their social power, [ibid: 110—11]

In this volume, Boden introduces symbolic interactionists to discourse analysis, suggesting studies of the social production of culture and cultural products, especially science but also social science itself, as discourse: talk and text. Her analysis shows that the details of ordinary conversation, analyzed with the tools of conversational analysis, constitute the process of mutual adjustment of lines of action called for in Blumer's theory, and thus are integral to the understanding of organizational activity at every level. McCall and Wittner suggest that symbolic interactionist might well imitate other social scientists, especially anthropologists, who have begun to pay attention to their own discourse, looking critically at their own "central task, in the field and thereafter"—that is, writing—and at the contextual, rhetorical, institutional, genre, political and historical contexts which "govern the inscription" of cultural accounts (Clifford 1986:2, 6).

CONCLUSION

The above thoughts suggest the variety of uses to which the audiences these papers address can put these materials. We hope that interactionists will learn from each other to cross subject matter boundaries in search of ideas and examples. We hope that noninteractionist sociologists will see how the symbolic interaction tradition, consisting of both theoretical ideas and detailed research findings, can contribute to their own work. And we hope that workers in cultural studies will find, in the ideas and results of this sociological tradition, as yet a largely unused resource, much to use and integrate into their own traditions.

REFERENCES

Althusser, Louis. 1971. "Ideology and Ideological State Apparatuses," in Althusser, *Lenin and Philosophy, and Other Essays,* translated by Ben Brewster (London: New Left Books), pp. 121–173.

Apple, Michael. 1985. *Education and Power.* Boston: Ark Paperbacks.

Becker, Howard S. 1982. "Culture: A Sociological View," in Becker, *Doing Things Together* (Evanston: Northwestern University Press), pp. 11–24.

------. 1986. "Consciousness, Power, and Drug Effects," in Becker, *Doing Things Together* (Evanston: Northwestern University Press), pp. 47–66.

------. 1988. "Herbert Blumer's Conceptual Impact." *Symbolic Interaction* 11 (Spring, 1988): 13–21.

Blumer, Herbert. 1969. *Symbolic Interactionism: Perspective and Method.* Englewood Cliffs, N. J.: Prentice Hall.

Brodkey, Linda. 1987. "Writing Critical Ethnographic Narratives." *Anthropology and Education Quarterly* 18 (June): 67–76.

Clifford, fames. 1986. "Introduction: Partial Truths," in James Clifford and George E. Marcus, editors, *Writing Culture* (Berkeley: University of California Press), pp. 1–26.

Geertz, Clifford. 1983. *Local Knowledge.* New York: Basic Books.

Hall, Peter. 1987. "Interactionism and the Study of Social Organization," *Sociological Quarterly* 28: 1–22.

Hall, Stuart. 1980. "Cultural Studies and the Centre: some problematics and problems," in *Culture, Media, Language: Working Papers in Cultural Studiesr, 1972–79* (London: Hutchinson in association with the Centre for Contemporary Cultural Studies, University of Birmingham) pp. 15–47.

Johnson, Richard. 1986–87. "What is Cultural Studies Anyway?" *Social Text* 16: 38–80.

Kling, Rob, and Elihu M. Gerson. 1977. "The Social Dynamics of Technical Innovation in the Computing World." *Symbolic Interaction* 1:132–46.

------. 1978. "Patterns of Segmentation and Interaction in the Computing World." *Symbolic Interaction* 2: 24–33.

Lindesmith, Alfred. 1948. *Opiate Addiction.* Bloomington, Ind.: Principia Press.

Rorty, Richard. 1979. *Philosophy and the Mirror of Nature.* Princeton: Princeton University Press.

Shibutani, Tomatsu. 1955. "Reference Groups as Perspectives." *American Journal of Sociology* 60: 562–69.

Smith, Dorothy E. 1987. *The Everyday World as Problematic: A Feminist Sociology.* Boston: Northeastern University Press.

Turner, Victor. 1986. *The Anthropology of Performance.* New York: PAJ Publications.

Weedon, Chris. 1987. *Feminist Practice and Poststructuralist Theory.* London: Basil Blackwell.

Weiler, Kathleen. 1988. *Women Teaching for Change: Gender, Class, and Power.* Granby, Mass.: Bergin and Garvey.

Williams, Raymond. 1981. *The Sociology of Culture.* New York: Schocken Books.

Willis, Paul. 1977. *Learning to Labour.* Westmead, England: Saxon House.

------. 1980. "Notes on Method," in *Culture, Media, Language: Working Papers in Cultural Studies, 1972–79* (London: Hutchinson in association with the Centre for Contemporary Cultural Studies, University of Birmingham), pp. 88–95.

Yonnet, Paul. 1985. "Joggers et marathoniens," in Yonnet, *Jeux, modes et masses* (Paris: Gallimard) pp. 91–140.

The Tasks of Sociology

by W.E.B. DuBois, Dan S. Green, and Edwin D. Driver

This section presents Du Bois' conception of sociology and why he believed that the study of the Afro-American was especially valuable to the development of a science of sociology. To Du Bois, sociology was "the science that seeks to measure the limits of chance in human action." While recognizing that sociologists seek laws which are historically and universally true for the human group, Du Bois felt that sociology's best possibility of generating laws was through the exhaustive study of the small, isolated group. For this purpose, the Afro-American was ideally suited. Here, by virtue of historical social forces, was a group diverse enough in cultural forms to mirror the stages of evolution experienced at one time or another by most other social groups.

The purpose of the program outlined in "The Atlanta Conferences" (1904) was the systematic and scientific study of the Afro-American. The aspects of his condition were to be divided into ten large subjects, and each year one subject was to be studied until the cycle was completed. Then the cycle would begin again. The plan was that in a course of a century "we shall have a continuous record on the condition and development of a group of 10 to 20 millions of men—a body of sociological material unsurpassed in human annals."

As the second paper, "The Laboratory in Sociology at Atlanta University" (1903), makes clear, Atlanta University was important to the implementation of this plan. It was located near the geographical center of the black population of the nation and was therefore near the center of the congeries of human problems which cluster around the black Americans. Upper classmen at Atlanta University were therefore trained to systematically study conditions of living around the university and, when possible, to compare these with conditions elsewhere. At the graduate level, students were to collect and analyze primary source data obtained through interviews and schedules, discuss the findings, and prepare written reports. While the "social study," or intensive study of a local community proved successful and had its unique advantages, Du Bois recognized that it was geographically limited and could not provide the kind of national statistics needed for discussions about the status of the Afro-American.

In the third paper, "The Twelfth Census and the Negro Problems" (1900), he proposed that the United States Census schedules be extended to incorporate questions specifically addressed to the status of the Afro-American and that these parts of the schedules later be turned over to an unpaid committee of twenty-five distinguished persons, from the North and South and both black and white, for an unbiased analysis and reporting of the findings.

The fourth paper, "The Study of the Negro Problems" (1898), presents Du Bois' conception of a social problem. It is "the failure of an organized social group to realize its group ideals through the inability to adapt a certain desired line of action to given conditions of life." He offered four considerations for the study of the social problems of black Americans: the historical development of the problems; the necessity for their diligent, systematic study; the results of scientific analyses of the Negro; and the scope and method to be used by future analysis. He deplored the fact that so much of the work done on the Negro question had been "uncritical from lack of discrimination in the selection and weighing of evidence; uncritical in choosing the proper point of view from which to study these problems; and, finally, uncritical from the distinct bias in the minds of so many writers." In the future, the proper scientific study of the Negro would have to make explicit the premises from which it began and would, for the sake of logical clarity, have to separately investigate the Negro as a social group, and his peculiar social environment. The study of the Negro as a social group would have to combine the approaches of history, statistics, anthropology, and sociology.

The final paper, "The Negro Race in the United States of America" (1911), demonstrates Du Bois' careful, early use of these various disciplines in providing us with a general portrait.

The Problem of the Twentieth Century is the Problem of the Color Line

by W.E.B. DuBois

We are just finishing the first half of the Twentieth Century. I remember its birth in 1901. There was the usual discussion as to whether the century began in 1900 or 1901; but, of course, 1901 was correct. We expected great things . . . peace; the season of war among nations had passed; progress was the order . . . everything going forward to bigger and better things. And then, not so openly expressed, but even more firmly believed, the rule of white Europe and America over black, brown and yellow peoples.

I was 32 years of age in 1901, married, and a father, and teaching at Atlanta University with a program covering a hundred years of study and investigation into the condition of American Negroes. Our subject of study at that time was education: the college-bred Negro in 1900, the Negro common school in 1901. My own attitude toward the Twentieth Century was expressed in an article which I wrote in the Atlantic Monthly in 1901. It said:

> The problem of the Twentieth Century is the problem of the color-line . . . I have seen a land right merry with the sun, where children sing, and rolling hills lie like passioned women wanton with harvest. And there in the King's Highway sat, and sits, a figure veiled and bowed, by which the Traveler's footsteps hasten as they go. On the tainted air broods fair. Three centuries' thought have been the raising and unveiling of that bowed human soul; and now behold, my fellows, a century now for the duty and the deed! The problem of the Twentieth Century is the problem of the color-line.

This is what we hoped, to this we Negroes looked forward; peace, progress and the breaking of the color line. What has been the result? We know it all too well . . . war, hate, the revolt of the colored peoples and the fear of more war.

In the meantime, where are we; those 15,000,000 citizens of the United States who are descended from the slaves, brought here between 1600 and 1900? We formed in 1901, a separate group because of legal enslavement and emancipation into caste conditions, with the attendant poverty, ignorance, disease and crime. We were an inner group and not an integral part of the American nation; but we were exerting ourselves to fight for integration.

The burden of our fight was in seven different lines. We wanted education; we wanted particularly the right to vote and civil rights; we wanted work with adequate wage; housing, without segregation or slums; a free press to fight our battles, and (although in those days we dare not say it) social equality.

In 1901 our education was in perilous condition, despite what we and our white friends had done for thirty years. The Atlanta University Conference said in its resolutions of 1901:

> We call the attention of the nation to the fact that less than one million of the three million Negro children of school age are at present regularly attending school, and these attend a session which lasts only a few months. We are today deliberately rearing millions of our citizens in ignorance and at the same time limiting the rights of citizenship by educational qualifications. This is unjust.

More particularly in civil rights, we were oppressed. We not only did not get justice in the courts, but we were subject to peculiar and galling sorts of injustice in daily life. In the latter half of the Ninteenth Century, where we first get something like statistics, no less than 3,000 Negroes were lynched without trial. And in addition to that we were subject continuously to mob violence and judicial lynching.

In political life we had, for twenty-five years, been disfranchised by violence, law and public opinion. The 14th and 15th amendments were deliberately violated and the literature of the day in book, pamphlet and daily press, was widely of opinion that the Negro was not ready for the ballot, could not use it intelligently, and that no action was called for to stop his political power from being exercised by Southern whites like Tillman and Vardaman.

We did not have the right or opportunity to work at an income which would sustain a decent and modern standard of life. Because of a past of chattel slavery, we were for the most part common laborers and servants, and a very considerable proportion were still unable to leave the plantations where they worked all their lives for next to nothing.

There were a few who were educated for the professions and we had many good artisans; that number was not increasing as it should have been, nor were new artisans being adequately trained. Industrial training was popular, but funds to implement it were too limited, and we were excluded from unions and the new mass industry.

We were housed in slums and segregated districts where crime and disease multiplied, and when we tried to move to better and healthier quarters we were met by segregation ordinance if not by mobs. We not only had no social equality, but we did not openly ask for it. It seemed a shameful thing to beg people to receive us as equals and as human beings; that was something we argued "that came and could not be fetched." And that meant not simply that we could not marry white women or legitimize mulatto bastards, but we could not stop in a decent hotel, nor eat in a public restaurant nor attend the theatre, nor accept an invitation to a private white home, nor travel in a decent railway coach. When the "public" was invited, this did not include us and admission to colleges often involved special consideration if not blunt refusal.

Finally we had poor press . . . a few struggling papers with little news and inadequately expressed opinion, with small circulation or influence and almost no advertising.

This was our plight in 1901. It was discouraging, but not hopeless. There is no question but that we had made progress, and there also was no doubt but what that progress was not enough to satisfy us or to settle our problems.

We could look back on a quarter century of struggle which had its results. We had schools; we had teachers; a few had forced themselves into the leading colleges and were tolerated if not welcomed. We voted in Northern cities, owned many decent homes and were fighting for further progress. Leaders like Booker Washington had received wide popular approval and a Negro literature had begun to appear.

But what we needed was organized effort along the whole front, based on broad lines of complete emancipation. This came with the Niagara Movement in 1906 and the NAACP in 1909. In 1910 came the Crisis magazine and the real battle was on.

What have we gained and accomplished? The advance has not been equal on all fronts, nor complete on any. We have not progressed with closed ranks like a trained army, but rather with serried and broken ranks, with wide gaps and even temporary retreats. But we have advanced. Of that there can be no atom of doubt.

First of all in education; most Negro children today are in school and most adults can read and write. Unfortunately this literacy is not as great as the census says. The draft showed that at least a third of our youth are illiterate. But education is steadily rising. Six thousand Bachelor degrees are awarded to Negroes each year and Doctorates in philosophy and medicine are not uncommon. Nevertheless as a group, American Negroes are still in the lower ranks of learning and adaptability to modern conditions. They do not read widely, their travel is limited and their experience through contact with the modern world is curtailed by law and custom.

Secondly, in civil rights, the Negro has perhaps made his greatest advance. Mob violence and lynching have markedly decreased. Three thousand Negroes were lynched in the last half of the Nineteenth Century and five hundred in the first half of the Twentieth. Today lynching is comparatively rare. Mob violence also has decreased, but is still in evidence, and summary and unjust court proceedings have taken the place of open and illegal acts. But the Negro has established, in the courts, his legal citizenship and his right to be included in the Bill of Rights. The question still remains of "equal but separate" public accommodations, and that is being attacked. Even the institution of "jim-crow" in travel is tottering. The infraction of the marriage situation by law and custom is yet to be brought before the courts and public opinion in a forcible way.

Third, the right to vote on the part of the Negro is being gradually established under the 14th and 15th amendments. It was not really until 1915 that the Supreme Court upheld this right of Negro citizens and even today the penalties of the 14th amendment have never been enforced. There are 7,000,000 possible voters among American Negroes and of these it is a question if more than 2,000,000 actually cast their votes. This is partly from the national inertia, which keeps half of all American voters away from the polls; but even more from the question as to what practical ends the Negro shall cast his vote.

He is thinking usually in terms of what he can do by voting to better his condition and he seldom gets a chance to vote on this matter. On the wider implications of political democracy he has not yet entered; particularly he does not see the economic foundations of present civilization and the necessity of his attacking the rule of corporate wealth in order to free the labor group to which he belongs.

Fourth, there is the question of occupation. There are our submerged classes of farm labor and tenants: our city laborers, washerwomen and scrubwomen and the mass of lower-paid servants. These classes still form a majority of American Negroes and they are on the edge of poverty, with the ignorance, disease and crime that always accompany such poverty.

If we measure the median income of Americans, it is $3,000 for whites and $2,000 for Negroes. In Southern cities, 7 percent of the white families and 30 percent of the colored families receive less than $1,000 a year. On the other hand the class differentiation by income among Negroes is notable: the number of semi-skilled and skilled artisans has increased or will as membership in labor unions. Professional men have increased, especially teachers and less notably, physicians, dentists and lawyers.

The number of Negroes in business has increased; mostly in small retail businesses, but to a considerable extent in enterprises like insurance, real estate and small banking, where the color line gives Negroes certain advantages and where, too, there is a certain element of gambling. Also beyond the line of gambling, numbers of Negroes have made small fortunes in anti-social enterprises. All this means that there has arisen in the Negro group a distinct stratification from poor to rich. Recently I polled 450 Negro families belonging to a select organization forty-five years old. Of these families 127 received over $10,000 a year and a score of these over $25,000; 200 families received from $5,000 to $10,000 a year and eighty-six less than $5,000.

This is the start of a tendency which will grow; we are beginning to follow the American pattern of accumulating individual wealth and of considering that this will eventually settle the race problem. On the other hand, the whole trend of the thought of our age is toward social welfare; the prevention of poverty by more equitable distribution of wealth, and business for general welfare rather than private profit. There are few signs that these ideals are guiding Negro development today. We seem to be adopting increasingly the ideal of American culture.

Housing, has, of course, been a point of bitter pressure among Negroes, because the attempt to segregate the race in its living conditions has not only kept the more fortunate ones from progress, but it has confined vast numbers of Negro people to the very parts of cities and country districts where they have fewest opportunities and least social contacts. They must live largely in slums, in contact with criminals and with fewest of the social advantages of government and human contact. The fight against segregation has been carried on in the courts and shows much progress against city ordinances, against covenants which make segregation hereditary.

Literature and art have made progress among Negroes, but with curious handicaps. An art expression is normally evoked by the conscious and unconscious demand of people for portrayal of their own emotion and experience. But in the case of the American Negroes, the audience, which embodies the demand and which pays sometimes enormous price for satisfaction, is not the Negro group, but the white group. And the pattern of what the white group wants does not necessarily agree with the natural desire of Negroes.

The whole of Negro literature is therefore curiously divided. We have writers who have written, not really about Negroes, but about the things which white people, and not the highest class of whites, like to hear about Negroes. And those who have expressed what the Negro himself thinks and feels, are those whose books sell to few, even of their own people; and whom most folk do not know. This has not made for the authentic literature which the early part of this century seemed to promise. To be sure, it can be said that American literature to-day has a considerable amount of Negro expression and influence, although not as much as once we hoped.

Despite all this we have an increasing number of excellent Negro writers who make the promise for the future great by their real accomplishment. We have done something in sculpture and painting, but in drama and music we have markedly advanced. All the world listens to our singers, sings our music and dances to our rhythms.

In science, our handicaps are still great. Turner, a great entomologist, was worked to death for lack of laboratory; just never had the recognition he richly deserved, and Carver was prisoner of his inferiority complex. Notwithstanding this, our real accomplishment in biology and medicine; in history and law; and in the social sciences has been notable and widely acclaimed. To this in no little degree is due our physical survival, our falling death rate and our increased confidence in our selves and in our destiny.

The expression of Negro wish and desire through a free press has greatly improved as compared with 1900. We have a half dozen large weekly papers with circulations of a hundred thousand or more. Their news coverage is immense, even if not discriminating. But here again, the influence of the American press on us has been devastating. The predominance of advertising over opinion, the desire for income rather than literary excellence and the use of deliberate propaganda, had made our press less of a power than it could be, and leaves wide chance for improvement in the future.

In comparison with other institutions, the Negro church during the Twentieth Century has lost ground. It is no longer the dominating influence that it used to be, the center of social activity and of economic experiment. Nevertheless, it is still a powerful institution in the lives of numerical majority of American Negroes if not upon the dominant intellectual classes. There has been a considerable increase in organized work for social progress through the church, but there has also been a large increase of expenditure for buildings, furnishings, and salaries; and it is not easy to find any increase in moral stamina or conscientious discrimination within church circles.

The scandal of deliberate bribery in election of Bishops and in the holding of positions in the churches without a hierarchy has been widespread. It is a critical problem now as to just what part in the future the church among Negroes is going to hold.

Finally there comes the question of social equality, which, despite efforts on the part of thinkers, white and black, is after all the main and fundamental problem of race in the United States. Unless a human being is going to have all human rights, including not only work, but friendship, and if mutually desired, marriage and children, unless these avenues are open and free, there can be no real equality and no cultural integration.

It has hitherto seemed utterly impossible that any such solution of the Negro problem in America could take place. The situation was quite similar to the problem of the lower classes of laborers, serfs and servants in European nations during the Sixteenth, Seventeenth and Eighteenth centuries. All nations had to consist of two separate parts and the only relations between them was employment and philanthropy.

That problem has been partly solved by modern democracy, but modern democracy cannot succeed unless the peoples of different races and religions are also integrated into the democratic whole. Against this large numbers of Americans have always fought and are still fighting, but the progress despite this has been notable. There are places in the United States, especially in large cities like New York and Chicago, where the social differences between the races has, to a large extent, been nullified and there is a meeting on terms of equality which would have been thought impossible a half century ago.

On the other hand, in the South, despite religion, education and reason, the color line, although perhaps shaken, still stands, stark and unbending, and to the minds of most good people, eternal. Here lies the area of the last battle for the complete rights of American Negroes.

Within the race itself today there are disquieting signs. The effort of Negroes to become Americans of equal status with other Americans is leading them to a state of mind by which they not only accept what is good in America, but what is bad and threatening so long as the Negro can share equally. This is peculiarly dangerous at this epoch in the development of world culture.

After two world wars of unprecedented loss of life, cruelty and destruction, we are faced by the fact that the industrial organization of our present civilization has in it something fundamentally wrong. It went to pieces in the first world war because of the determination of certain great powers excluded from world rule to share in that rule, by acquisition of the labor and materials of colonial peoples. The attempt to recover from the cataclysm resulted in the collapse of our industrial system, and a second world war.

In spite of the propaganda which has gone on, which represents America as the leading democratic state, we Negroes know perfectly well, and ought to know even better than most, that America is not a successful democracy and that until it is, it is going to drag down the world. This nation is ruled by corporate wealth to a degree which is frightening. One thousand persons own the United States and their power outweighs the voice of the mass of American citizens. This must be cured, not by revolution, not by war and violence, but by reason and knowledge.

Most of the world is today turning toward the welfare state; turning against the idea of production for individual profit toward the idea of production for use and for the welfare of the mass of citizen. No matter how difficult such a course is, it is the only course that is going to save the world and this we American Negroes have got to realize.

We may find it easy now to get publicity, reward, and attention by going along with the reactionary propaganda and war hysteria which is convulsing this nation, but in the long run America will not thank its black children if they help it go the wrong way, or retard its progress.

Women's Perspective as a Radical Critique of Sociology

by Dorothy E. Smith

1.

The women's movement has given us a sense of our right to have women's interests represented in sociology, rather than just receiving as authoritative the interests traditionally represented in a sociology put together by men. What can we make of this access to a social reality that was previously unavailable, was indeed repressed? What happens as we begin to relate to it in the terms of our discipline? We can of course think, as many do, merely of the addition of courses to the existing repertoire—courses on sex roles, on the women's movement, on women at work, on the social psychology of women and perhaps somewhat different versions of the sociology of the family. But thinking more boldly or perhaps just thinking the whole thing through a little further might bring us to ask first how a sociology might look if it began from the point of view of women's traditional place in it and what happens to a sociology which attempts to deal seriously with that. Following this line of thought, I have found, has consequences larger than they seem at first.

From the point of view of "women's place" the values assigned to different aspects of the world are changed. Some come into prominence while other standard sociological enterprises diminish. We might take as a model the world as it appears from the point of view of the afternoon soap opera. This is defined by (though not restricted to) domestic events, interests, and activities. Men appear in this world as necessary and vital presences. It is not a women's world in the sense of excluding men. But it is a women's world in the sense that it is the relevances of the women's place that govern. Men appear only in their domestic or private aspects or at points of intersection between public and private as doctors in hospitals, lawyers in their offices discussing wills and divorces. Their occupational and political world is barely present. They are posited here as complete persons, and they are but partial—as women appear in sociology predicated on the universe occupied by men.

But it is not enough to supplement an established sociology by addressing ourselves to what has been left out, overlooked, or by making sociological issues of the relevances of the world of women. That merely extends the authority of the existing sociological procedures and makes of a women's sociology an addendum. We cannot rest at that because it does not account for the separation between the two worlds and it does not account for or analyze for us the relation between them. (Attempts to work on that in terms of biology operate within the existing structure as a fundamental assumption and are therefore straightforwardly ideological in character.)

The first difficulty is that how sociology is thought—its methods, conceptual schemes, and theories— has been based on and built up within the male social universe (even when women have participated in its doing). It has taken for granted not just that scheme of relevances as an itemized inventory of issues or subject matters (industrial sociology, political sociology, social stratification, etc.) but the fundamental social and political structures under which these become relevant and are ordered. There is a difficulty first then of a disjunction between how women find and experience the world beginning (though not neces- sarily ending up) from their place and the concepts and theoretical schemes available to think about it in. Thus in a graduate seminar last year, we discussed on one occasion the possibility of a women's sociology and two graduate students told us that in their view and their experience of functioning in experimental group situations, theories of the emergence of leadership in small groups, etc., just did not apply to what was happening as they experienced it. They could not find the correlates of the theory in their experiences.

A second difficulty is that the two worlds and the two bases of knowledge and experience don't stand in an equal relation. The world as it is constituted by men stands in authority over that of women. It is that part of the world from which our land of society is governed and from which what happens to us begins. The domestic world stands in a dependent relation to that other and its whole character is subordinate to it.

The two difficulties are related to one another in a special way. The effect of the second interacting with the first is to impose the concepts and terms in which the world of men is thought as the concepts and terms in which women must think their world. Hence in these terms women are alienated from their experience.

The profession of sociology is predicated on a universe which is occupied by men and is itself still largely appropriated by men as their "territory." Sociology is part of the practice by which we are all governed and that practice establishes its relevances. Thus the institutions which lock sociology into the structures occupied by men are the same institutions which lock women into the situations in which they find themselves oppressed. To unlock the latter leads logically to an unlocking of the former. What follows then, or rather what then becomes possible—for it is of course by no means inevitable—is less a shift in the subject matter than a different conception of how it is or might become relevant as a means to understand our experience and the conditions of our experience (both women's and men's) in corporate capitalist society.

2.

When I speak here of governing or ruling I mean something more general than the notion of government as political organization. I refer rather to that total complex of activities differentiated into many spheres, by which our kind of society is ruled, managed, administered. It includes that whole section which in the business world is called "management." It includes the professions. It includes of course government more conventionally defined and also the activities of those who are selecting, training, and indoctrinating those who will be its governors. The last includes those who provide and elaborate the procedures in which it is governed and develop methods for accounting for how it is done and predicting and analyzing its characteristic consequences and sequences of events, namely the business schools, the sociologists, the economists, etc. These are the institutions through which we are ruled and through which we, and I emphasize this we, participate in ruling.

Sociology then I conceive as much more than ideology, much more than a gloss on the enterprise which justifies and rationalizes it, and, at the same time as much less than "science." The governing of our kind of society is done in concepts and symbols. The contribution of sociology to this is that of working up the conceptual procedures, models, and methods by which the immediate and concrete features of experience can be read into the conceptual mode in which the governing is done. What is actually observed or what is systematically recovered by the sociologist from the actualities of what people say and do, must be transposed into the abstract mode. Sociology thus participates in and contributes to the formation and facilitation of this mode of action and plays a distinctive part in the work of transposing the actualities of people's lives and experiences into the conceptual currency in which it is and can be governed.

Thus the relevances of sociology are organized in terms of a perspective on the world which is a view from the top and which takes for granted the pragmatic procedures of governing as those which frame and identify its subject matter. Issues are formulated as issues which have become administratively relevant not as they are significant first in the experience of those who live them. The kinds of facts and events which are facts for us have already been shaped up and given their character and substance as facts, as relations, etc., by the methods and practice of governing. Mental illness, crimes, riots, violence, work satisfaction, neighbors and neighborhoods, motivation, etc., these are the constructs of the practice of government. In many instances, such as mental illness, crimes, neighborhoods, etc., they are constituted as discrete phenomena primarily by administrative procedures and others arise as problems in relation to the actual practice of government, as for example concepts of motivation, work satisfaction, etc.

The governing processes of our society are organized as social entities constituted externally to those persons who participate in and perform them. The managers, the bureaucrats, the administrators, are employees, are people who are *used*. They do not own the enterprises or otherwise appropriate them. Sociologists study these entities under the heading of formal organization. They are put together as objective structures with goals, activities, obligations, etc., other than those which its employees can have as individuals. The academic professions are also set up in a mode which externalizes them as entities vis-à-vis their practitioners. The body of knowledge which its members accumulate is appropriated by the discipline as its body. The work of members aims at contributing to that body of knowledge.

As graduate students learning to become sociologists, we learn to think sociology as it is thought and to practice it as it is practiced. We learn that some topics are relevant and some are not. We learn to discard our experienced world as a source of reliable information or suggestions about the character of the world; to confine and focus our insights within the conceptual frameworks and relevances which are given in the discipline. Should we think other kinds of thoughts or experience the world in a different way or with edges and horizons that pass beyond the conceptual, we must practice a discipline which discards them or find some procedure which makes it possible to sneak them in. We learn a way of thinking about the world which is recognizable to its practitioners as the sociological way of thinking.

We learn to practice the sociological subsumption of the actualities of ourselves and of other people. We find out how to treat the world as instances of a sociological body of knowledge. The procedure operates as a sort of conceptual imperialism. When we write a thesis or a paper, we learn that the first thing to do is to latch it on to the discipline at some point. This may be by showing how it is a problem within an existing theoretical and conceptual framework. The boundaries of inquiry are thus set within the framework of what is already established. Even when this becomes, as it happily often does, a ceremonial authorization of a project which has little to do with the theory used to authorize it, we still work within the vocabularies and within the conceptual boundaries of what we have come to know as "the sociological perspective."

An important set of procedures which serve to constitute the body of knowledge of the discipline as something which is separated from its practitioners are those known as "objectivity." The ethic of objectivity and the methods used in its practice are concerned primarily with the separation of the knower from what he knows and in particular with the separation of what is known from any interests, "biases," etc., which he may have which are not the interests and concerns authorized by the discipline. I must emphasize that being interested in knowing something doesn't invalidate what is known. In the social sciences the pursuit of objectivity makes it possible for people to be paid to pursue a knowledge to which they are otherwise indifferent. What they feel and think about society can be taken apart from and kept out of what they are professionally or academically interested in.

3.

The sociologist enters the conceptually ordered society when he goes to work. He enters it as a member and he enters it also as the mode in which he investigates it. He observes, analyzes, explains, and examines as if there were no problem in how that world becomes observable to him. He moves among the doings of organizations, governmental processes, bureaucracies, etc., as a person who is at home in that medium. The nature of that world itself, how it is known to him and the conditions of its existence or his relation to it are not called into question. His methods of observation and inquiry extend into it as procedures which are essentially of the same order as those which bring about the phenomena with which he is concerned, or which he is concerned to bring under the jurisdiction of that order. His perspectives and interests may differ, but the substance is the same. He works with facts and information which have been worked up from actualities and appear in the form of documents which are themselves the product of organizational processes, whether his own or administered by him, or of some other agency. He fits that information back into a framework of entities and organizational processes which he takes for granted as known, without asking how it is that he knows them or what are the social processes by which the phenomena which correspond to or provide the empirical events, acts, decisions, etc., of that world, may be recognized. He passes beyond the particular and immediate setting in which he is always located in the body (the office he writes in, the libraries he consults, the streets he travels, the home he returns to) without any sense of having made a transition. He works in the same medium as he studies.

But like everyone else he also exists in the body in the place in which it is. This is also then the place of his sensory organization of immediate experience, the place where his coordinates of here and now before and after are organized around himself as center; the place where he confronts people face to face in the physical mode in which he expresses himself to them and they to him as more and other than either can speak. It is in this place that things smell. The irrelevant birds fly away in front of the window. Here he has indigestion. It is a place he dies in. Into this space must come as actual material events, whether as the sounds of speech, the scratchings on the surface of paper which he constitutes as document, or directly, anything he knows of the world. It has to happen here somehow if he is to experience it at all.

Entering the governing mode of our kind of society lifts the actor out of the immediate local and particular place in which he is in the body. He uses what becomes present to him in this place as a means to pass beyond it to the conceptual order. This mode of action creates then a bifurcation of consciousness, a bifurcation of course which is there for all those who participate in this mode of action. It establishes two modes of knowing and experiencing and doing, one located in the body and in the space which it occupies and moves into, the other which passes beyond it. Sociology is written in and aims at this second mode. Vide Bierstedt:

> Sociology can liberate the mind from time and space themselves and remove it to a new and transcendental realm where it no longer depends upon these Aristotelian categories. (1966)

Even observational work aims at its description in the categories and hence conceptual forms of the "transcendental realm."

4.

Women are outside and subservient to this structure. They have a very specific relation to it which anchors them into the local and particular phase of the bifurcated world. For both traditionally and as a matter of occupational practices in our society, the governing conceptual mode is appropriated by men and the world organized in the natural attitude, the home, is appropriated by (or assigned to) women (Smith, 1973).

It is a condition of a man's being able to enter and become absorbed in the conceptual mode that he does not have to focus his activities and interests upon his bodily existence. If he is to participate fully in the abstract mode of action, then he must be liberated also from having to attend to his needs, etc., in the concrete and particular. The organization of work and expectations in managerial and professional circles both constitutes and depends upon the alienation of man from his bodily and local existence. The structure of work and the structure of career take for granted that these matters are provided for in such a way that they will not interfere with his action and participation in that world. Providing for the liberation from the Aristotelian categories of which Bierstedt speaks, is a woman who keeps house for him, bears and cares for his children, washes his clothes, looks after him when he is sick, and generally provides for the logistics of his bodily existence.

The place of women then in relation to this mode of action is that where the work is done to create conditions which facilitate his occupation of the conceptual mode of consciousness. The meeting of a man's physical needs, the organization of his daily life, even the consistency of expressive background, are made maximally congruent with his commitment. A similar relation exists for women who work in and around the professional and managerial scene. They do those things which give concrete form to the conceptual activities. They do the clerical work, the computer programming, the interviewing for the survey, the nursing, the secretarial work. At almost every point women mediate for men the relation between the conceptual mode of action and the actual concrete forms in which it is and must be realized, and the actual material conditions upon which it depends.

Marx's concept of alienation is applicable here in a modified form. The simplest formulation of alienation posits a relation between the work an individual does and an external order which oppresses her, such that the harder she works the more she strengthens the order which oppresses her. This is the situation of women in this relation. The more successful women are in mediating the world of concrete particulars so that men do not have to become engaged with (and therefore conscious of) that world as a condition to their abstract activities, the more complete man's absorption in it, the more effective the authority of that world and the more total women's subservience to it. And also the more complete the dichotomy between the two worlds, and the estrangement between them.

5.

Women sociologists stand at the center of a contradiction in the relation of our discipline to our experience of the world. Transcending that contradiction means setting up a different land of relation than that which we discover in the routine practice of our worlds.

The theories, concepts, and methods of our discipline claim to account for, or to be capable of accounting for and analyzing the same world as that which we experience directly. But these theories, concepts, and methods have been organized around and built up out of a way of knowing the world which takes for granted the boundaries of an experience in the same medium in which it is constituted. It therefore takes for granted and subsumes without examining the conditions of its existence. It is not capable of analyzing its own relation to its conditions because the sociologist as an actual person in an actual concrete setting has been cancelled in the procedures which objectify and separate him from his knowledge. Thus the linkage which points back to its conditions is lacking.

For women those conditions are central as a direct practical matter, to be somehow solved in the decision to take up a sociological career. The relation between ourselves as practicing sociologists and ourselves as working women is continually visible to us, a central feature of experience of the world, so that the bifurcation of consciousness becomes for us a daily chasm which is to be crossed, on the one side of which is this special conceptual activity of thought, research, teaching, administration, and on the other the world of concrete practical activities in keeping things clean, managing somehow the house and household and the children, a world in which the particularities of persons in their full organic immediacy (cleaning up the vomit, changing the diapers, as well as feeding) are inescapable. Even if we don't have that as a direct contingency in our lives, we are aware of that as something that our becoming may be inserted into as a possible predicate.

It is also present for us to discover that the discipline is not one which we enter and occupy on the same terms as men enter and occupy it. We do not fully appropriate its authority, i.e., the right to author and authorize the acts and knowing and thinking which are the acts and knowing and thinking of the discipline as it is thought. We cannot therefore command the inner principles of our action. That remains lodged outside us. The frames of reference which order the terms upon which inquiry and discussion are conducted originate with men. The subjects of sociological sentences (if they have a subject) are male. The sociologist is "he." And even before we become conscious of our sex as the basis of an exclusion (*they* are not talking about *us*), we nonetheless do not fully enter ourselves as the subjects of its statements, since we must suspend our sex, and suspend our knowledge of who we are as well as who it is that in fact is speaking and of whom. Therefore we do not fully participate in the declarations and formulations of its mode of consciousness. The externalization of sociology as a profession which I have described above becomes for women a double estrangement.

There is then for women a basic organization of their experience which displays for them the structure of the bifurcated consciousness. At the same time it attenuates their commitment to a sociology which aims at an externalized body of knowledge based on an organization of experience which excludes theirs and excludes them except in a subordinate relation.

6.

An alternative approach must somehow transcend this contradiction without reentering Bierstedt's "transcendental realm" (1966). Women's perspective, as I have analyzed it here, discredits sociology's claim to constitute an objective knowledge independent of the sociologist's situation. Its conceptual procedures, methods, and relevances are seen to organize its subject matter from a determinate position in society. This critical disclosure becomes, then, the basis for an alternative way of thinking sociology. If sociology cannot avoid being situated, then sociology should take that as its beginning and build it into its methodological and theoretical strategies. As it is now, these separate a sociologically constructed world from that which is known in direct experience and it is precisely that separation which must be undone.

I am not proposing an immediate and radical transformation of the subject matter and methods of the discipline nor the junking of everything that has gone before. What I am suggesting is more in the nature of a re-organization which changes the relation of the sociologist to the object of her knowledge and changes also her problematic. This reorganization involves first placing the sociologist where she is actually situated, namely at the beginning of those acts by which she knows or will come to know; and second, making her direct experience of the everyday world the primary ground of her knowledge.

We would reject, it seems to me, a sociology aimed primarily at itself. We would not be interested in contributing to a body of knowledge the uses of which are not ours and the knowers of whom are who knows whom, but generally male—particularly when it is not at all clear what it is that is constituted as knowledge in that relation. The professional sociologist's practice of thinking it as it is thought would have to be discarded. She would be constrained by the actualities of how it happens in her direct experience. Sociology would aim at offering to anyone a knowledge of the social organization and determinations of the properties and events of their directly experienced world. Its analyses would become part of our ordinary interpretations of the experienced world, just as our experience of the sun's sinking below the horizon is transformed by our knowledge that the world turns. (Yet from where we are it seems to sink and that must be accounted for.)

The only way of knowing a socially constructed world is knowing it from within. We can never stand outside it. A relation in which sociological phenomena are objectified and presented as external to and independent of the observer is itself a special social practice also known from within. The relation of observer and object of observation, of sociologist to "subject" is a specialized social relationship. Even to be a stranger is to enter a world constituted from within as strange. The strangeness itself is the mode in which it is experienced.

When Jean Briggs (1970) made her ethnographic study of the ways in which an Eskimo people structure and express emotion, what she learned and observed emerged for her in the context of the actual developing relations between her and the family with whom she lived and other members of the group. Her account situates her knowledge in the context of those relationships. Affections, tensions, and quarrels were the living texture in which she learnt what she describes. She makes it clear how this context structured her learning and how what she learnt and can speak of became observable to her. Briggs tells us what is normally discarded in the anthropological or sociological telling. Although sociological inquiry is necessarily a social relation, we have learned to disattend our own part in it. We recover only the object of its knowledge as if that stood all by itself and of itself. Sociology does not provide for seeing that there are always two terms to this relation. An alternative sociology must be reflexive (Gouldner, 1971), i.e., one that preserves in it the presence, concerns, and experience of the sociologist as knower and discover.

To begin from direct experience and to return to it as a constraint or "test" of the adequacy of a systematic knowledge is to begin from where we are located bodily. The actualities of our everyday world are already socially organized. Settings, equipment, "environment," schedules, occasions, etc., as well as the enterprises and routines of actors are socially produced and concretely and symbolically organized prior to our practice. By beginning from her original and immediate knowledge of her world, sociology offers a way of making its socially organized properties first observable and then problematic.

Let me make it clear that when I speak of "experience" I do not use the term as a synonym for "perspective." Nor in proposing a sociology grounded in the sociologist's actual experience, am I recommending the self-indulgence of inner exploration or any other enterprise with self as sole focus and object. Such subjectivist interpretations of "experience" are themselves an aspect of that organization of consciousness which bifurcates it and transports us into mind country while stashing away the concrete conditions and practices upon which it depends. We can never escape the circles of our own heads if we accept that as our territory. Rather the sociologist's investigation of our directly experienced world as a problem is a mode of discovering or rediscovering the society from within. She begins from her own original but tacit knowledge and from within the acts by which she brings it into her grasp in making it observable and in understanding how it works. She aims not at a reiteration of what she already (tacitly) knows, but at an exploration through that of what passes beyond it and is deeply implicated in how it is.

7.

Our knowledge of the world is given to us in the modes in which we enter into relations with the object of knowledge. But in this case the object of our knowledge is or originates in a "subject." The constitution of an objective sociology as an authoritative version of how things are is done from a position and as part of the practices of ruling in our kind of society. It has depended upon class and sex bases which make it possible for sociology to evade the problem that our kind of society is known and experienced rather differently from different positions within it. Our training teaches us to ignore the uneasiness at the junctures where transitional work is done—for example, the ordinary problems respondents have of fitting their experience of the world to the questions in the interview schedule. It is this exclusion which the sociologist who is a woman cannot so easily preserve, for she discovers, if she will, precisely that uneasiness in her relation to her discipline as a whole. The persistence of the privileged sociological version (or versions) relies upon a substructure which has already discredited and deprived of authority to speak, the voices of those who know the society differently. The objectivity of a sociological version depends upon a special relation with others which makes it easy for the sociologist to remain outside the other's experience and does not require her to recognize that experience as a valid contention.

Riding a train not long ago in Ontario I saw a family of Indians, woman, man, and three children standing together on a spur above a river watching the train go by. There was (for me) that moment—the train, those five people seen on the other side of the glass. I saw first that I could tell this incident as it was, but that telling as a description built in my position and my interpretations. I have called them a family; I have said they were watching the train. My understanding has already subsumed theirs. Everything may have been quite other for them. My description is privileged to stand as what actually happened, because theirs is not heard in the contexts in which I may speak. If we begin from the world as we actually experience it, it is at least possible to see that we are located and that what we know of the other is conditional upon that location as part of a relation comprehending the other's location also. There are and must be different experiences of the world and different bases of experience. We must not do away with them by taking advantage of our privileged speaking to construct a sociological version which we then impose upon them as their reality. We may not rewrite the other's world or impose upon it a conceptual framework which extracts from it what fits with ours. Our conceptual procedures should be capable of explicating and analyzing the properties of their experienced world rather than administering it. Their reality, their varieties of experience must be an unconditional datum.

8.

My experience on the train epitomizes a sociological relation. The observer is already separated from the world as it is experienced by those she observes. That separation is fundamental to the character of that experience. Once she becomes aware of how her world is put together as a practical everyday matter and of how her relations are shaped by its concrete conditions (even in so simple a matter as that she is sitting in the train and it travels, but those people standing on the spur do not) the sociologist is led into the discovery that she cannot understand the nature of her experienced world by staying within its ordinary boundaries of assumption and knowledge. To account for that moment on the train and for the relation between the two experiences (or more) and the two positions from which those experiences begin involves positing a total socio-economic order "in back" of that moment. The coming together which makes the observation possible as well as how we were separated and drawn apart as well as how I now make use of that here—these properties are determined elsewhere than in that relation itself.

Further, how our knowledge of the world is mediated to us becomes a problem. It is a problem in knowing how that world is organized for us prior to our participation as knowers in that process. As intellectuals we ordinarily receive it as a media world, of documents, images, journals, books, talk, as well as in other symbolic modes. We discard as an essential focus of our practice other ways of knowing. Accounting for that mode of knowing and the social organization which sets it up for us again leads us back into an analysis of the total socio-economic order of which it is part. It is not possible to account for one's directly experienced world or how it is related to the worlds which others directly experience who are differently placed by remaining within the boundaries of the former.

If we address the problem of the conditions as well as the perceived forms and organization of immediate experience, we should include in it the events as they actually happen or the ordinary material world which we encounter as a matter of fact—the urban renewal project which uproots 400 families; how it is to live on welfare as an ordinary daily practice; cities as the actual physical structures in which we move; the organization of academic occasions such as that in which this paper originated. When we examine them, we find that there are many aspects of how these things come about of which we have little as sociologists to say. We have a sense that the events which enter our experience originate somewhere in a human intention, but we are unable to track back to find it and to find out how it got from there to here. Or take this room in which I work or that room in which you are reading and treat that as a problem. If we think about the conditions of our activity here, we could track back to how it is that there are chairs, table, walls, our clothing, our presence; how these places (yours and mine) are cleaned and maintained, etc. There are human activities, intentions, and relations which are not apparent as such in the actual material conditions of our work. The social organization of the setting is not wholly available to us in its appearance. We bypass in the immediacy of the specific practical activity, a complex division of labor which is an essential precondition to it. Such preconditions are fundamentally mysterious to us and present us with problems in grasping social relations in our land of society with which sociology is ill equipped to deal. Our experience of the world is of one which is largely incomprehensible beyond the limits of what is known in a common sense. No amount of observation of face-to-face relations, no amounts of analysis of commonsense knowledge of everyday life, will take us beyond our essential ignorance of how it is put together. Our direct experience of it constitutes it (if we will) as a problem, but it does not offer any answers. The matrix of direct experience as that from which sociology might begin discloses that beginning as an "appearance" the determinations of which lie beyond it.

We might think of the "appearances" of our direct experience as a multiplicity of surfaces, the properties and relations among which are generated by a social organization which is not observable in its effects. The structures which underlie and generate the characteristics of our own directly experienced world are social structures and bring us into unseen relations with others. Their experience is necessarily different from ours. Beginning from our experienced world and attempting to analyze and account for how it is, necessitates positing others whose experience is different.

Women's situation in sociology discloses to her a typical bifurcate structure with the abstracted conceptual practices on the one hand and the concrete realizations, the maintenance routines, etc., on the other. Taking each for granted depends upon being fully situated in one or the other so that the other does not appear in contradiction to it. Women's direct experience places her a step back where we can recognize the uneasiness that comes in sociology from its claim to be about the world we live in and its failure to account for or even describe its actual features as we find them in living them. The aim of an alternative sociology would be to develop precisely that capacity from that beginning so that it might be a means to anyone of understanding how the world comes about for her and how it is organized so that it happens to her as it does in her experience.

9.

Though such a sociology would not be exclusively for or done by women it does begin from the analysis and critique originating in their situation. Its elaboration therefore depends upon a grasp of that which is prior to and fuller than its formulation. It is a little like the problem of making a formal description of the grammar of a language. The linguist depends and always refers back to the competent speakers' sense, etc. In her own language she depends to a large extent upon her own competence. Women are native speakers of this situation and in explicating it or its implications and realizing them conceptually, they have that relation to it of knowing it before it has been said.

The incomprehensibility of the determinations of our immediate local world is for women a particularly striking metaphor. It recovers an inner organization in common with their typical relation to the world. For women's activities and existence are determined outside them and beyond the world which is their "place." They are oriented by their training and by the daily practices which confirm it, toward the demands and initiations and authority of others. But more than that, the very organization of the world which has been assigned to them as the primary locus of their being is determined by and subordinate to the corporate organization of society (Smith, 1973). Thus, as I have expressed her relation to sociology, its logic lies elsewhere. She lacks the inner principle of her own activity. She does not grasp how it is put together because it is determined elsewhere than where she is. As a sociologist then the grasp and exploration of her own experience as a method of discovering society restores to her a center which in this enterprise at least is wholly hers.

REFERENCES

Bierstedt, Robert. 1966. "Sociology and general education." In Charles H. Page (ed.), *Sociology and Contemporary Education.* New York: Random House.

Briggs, Jean L. 1970. *Never in Anger.* Cambridge, Mass.: Harvard University Press.

Gouldner, Alvin. 1971. *The Coming Crisis in Western Sociology.* London: Heinemann Educational Books.

Smith, Dorothy E. 1973. "Women, the family and corporate capitalism." In M. L. Stephenson (ed.), *Women in Canada.* Toronto: Newpress.

SECTION 3

EPISTEMOLOGIES

The American Dream of Meritocracy

by Heather Beth Johnson

The American Dream has been continually re-invented over time, so that for each generation of Americans it has held different meanings. And since the phrase "the American Dream" could mean different things to every one of us, it might be more accurate to call it "the American Dreams." At its core, however, some aspects of the Dream (or Dreams) are consistently fundamental. Simply, the American Dream explains the logic of our country's social system. *It is a way (or perhaps the way) we are to understand how American society operates.* It is how we make sense of our particular social structure. The American Dream rests on the idea that, with hard work and personal determination anyone, regardless of background, has an equal opportunity to achieve his or her aspirations. The American Dream promises that our system functions as a meritocracy. *Within a meritocracy people get ahead or behind based on what they earn and deserve, rather than what circumstances they were born into.* This notion of is central to the American Dream, and is the central logic of how our system is supposed to operate. The American Dream, in many ways, defines us and sets our system apart from others.

Given the importance of the American Dream to our national identity, and the enormity of it in shaping our core ideologies, it is curious how little attention the idea has received in academe, especially in the social sciences. Until relatively recently, no one had traced the history of its origins, meanings, or cultural impacts. In the past decade, however, groundbreaking scholarship on the American Dream has yielded important understandings. We know, for example, that the principles of the American Dream were promoted by even the very first settlers to arrive from Britain. Later, the American Dream was central to the charter of the United States when the Declaration of Independence was created. And although the phrase "the American Dream" does not appear to have been coined until around 1931, it has quickly become recognizable the world over. The American Dream is, for better or for worse, the central creed of our nation.

As a creed, the American Dream represents a basic belief in the power and capacity of the individual. Deeply embedded in this belief is a particular notion of individual agency—the idea that over the course of our own lives we are each accountable for whatever position we find ourselves in. Full collective potential for this agency, though, depends on exactly that which the dream promises: A system of opportunity, so that regardless of background each individual has an equal chance to prosper. The American Dream promises that an egalitarian system will allow individuals to advance based on their own merit. This promise resonates throughout contemporary American society telling us—through multiple variations on a theme, through school assignments and television advertisements, through song lyrics and newspaper stories—that in a meritocratic process we rise or fall self-reliantly. So, despite differences across generations and regardless we each have unique hopes and dreams, we share the American Dream of meritocracy in common: That is, we are each subject—in one way or another—to our nationalist ideology of meritocracy.

Meritocracy explains not only how our society works but how inequality exists. The idea is that what we reap—good or bad—is merited; whatever we have, whatever our status, whatever our place in the social world, we earn. A system of meritocracy does not assert equality *per se*—within any social hierarchy some individuals will inevitably be positioned higher and some lower—rather, it justifies inequality of social positioning by the meritocratic process itself. Inequality of outcomes is justified and legitimized by equality of opportunity. This meritocratic idea has roots dating back to the British colonialists' aspirations for a society founded in a "natural aristocracy." In their vision upward mobility and prominence would be merited and achieved, rather than ascribed. For those first families settling from Europe, this vision was a defiant rebellion from other forms of social structure where social rank was inherited based on such distinctions as family lineage, royalty, and caste. Although they never precisely defined how merit should be measured, it was always clear how it should not be: achievement based on individual merit is not unearned advantage; it is not inherited privilege. A meritocratic system is contingent upon a societal commitment to fair competition so that no individual or group is advantaged or disadvantaged by the positions or predicaments of their ancestors.

The American Dream of meritocracy is at once a simple idea and a complex national ethos. For some people the American Dream may simply represent owning a home, while for others it might represent striking it rich. Although those may be part of what the American Dream means for many people, as a foundational ideology it is about more than material abundance or a place with streets-paved-with-gold. It is about opportunity—not just an opportunity, but equal opportunity. It is about not just a chance, but equal chances. In her landmark book, *Facing Up to the American Dream: Race, Class, and the Soul of a Nation*, political scientist Jennifer Hochschild explicates the American Dream and identifies its main tenets. She distinguishes key premises which interlock to form its philosophical foundation. These premises include meritocracy, the notion that in our social system upward and downward mobility is based on personal achievement so that people get ahead or behind based on merit; equal opportunity, the notion that all members of society are given equal opportunity for social mobility; individualism, the notion that each individual makes it on his or her own; and the open society, the notion that the United States is a free country, the melting pot of the world, the land of opportunity for all people. As Hochschild outlines, the American Dream is a set of deeply held beliefs, a particular mindset. It is a particular way of viewing the world, and it is a particular way in which we want the world to view us. For many Americans, the American Dream is a great source of pride. But even many who question it as an accurate portrayal of social life believe strongly in the egalitarian and inclusive principles for which it stands.

As a dominant ideology the American Dream echoes throughout our nation, it carries on through generations, and can cement in crystal form in our minds. But it can also be easily taken for granted. For as central the American Dream is to our national identity, we don't consciously reflect on it often. As historian Jim Cullen has noted, the American Dream is "an idea that seems to envelop us as unmistakably as the air we breathe." We can be reminded of it, without even being aware, every time we are told that we will achieve if we work hard enough, or that we could have achieved if we had only worked harder. The American Dream can inspire great aspirations and explain great achievements, and it can depress us as we ponder our regrets. It is malleable enough to fit in almost any social situation. We can use it to justify our accomplishments: I earned it on my own. This is the result of my hard work. I deserve this. And we can feel the sting of it as we question ourselves: Should I have worked harder? Could I have gone farther? Why am I not where he is? And, we can use it to question others' social standing: Why doesn't she try harder? Doesn't he want more? Why don't they make better choices? The American Dream is all around us, and, in many ways it is in us.

Ultimately, the American Dream is an explanation for the hierarchical ordering of our class positions in our social world. It explains our relative rank as the result of solely our own doing, not as the result of social forces or the circumstances we find ourselves in. It is not surprising, then, that Americans might genuinely believe that they independently earn and deserve their class positions—the dominant ideology of our culture tells them so. This internalized sense of class positioning has been the subject of scholarly research, especially in regards to working-class and poor families. In Richard Sennett and Jonathan Cobb's pivotal book *The Hidden Injuries of Class*, for example, they discuss the "hidden injury" of the internal class conflict experienced among working-class men. They wrote that "Every question of identity as an image of social place in a hierarchy is also a question of social value. . . . This is the context in which all questions of personal and social legitimacy occur." The American Dream helps to sustain these "hidden injuries" by bombarding people with the message that their social place—and their social value, their self-worth—is directly and exclusively the result of their own actions.

In their interviews for this book, people spoke in depth and at length about the American Dream, despite the fact that in the first 182 interviews the families were not even asked about it. Those parents were told that the project was to study assets and inequality, and during the interviews they were asked to speak about the communities they lived in, their children's schools, and their families' financial histories. Over and over, however, the focus of the interviews turned to beliefs in meritocracy as families repeatedly brought up the subject and wove it into the conversations. I must admit that I myself was surprised with the extent to which the interview findings were so ideological in nature. And I was even more surprised when interviews—including those interviews from the second phase which did directly ask people about their thoughts on the American Dream—revealed the depths of people's commitment to, and belief in, meritocracy as a real and valid explanation for how contemporary American society operates. People from all walks of life spoke forthrightly of their belief in meritocracy, not just as rhetoric, but as an accurate explanation of our social system.

Trying to confirm these findings has been frustrating due to the lack of qualitative studies that have asked people in-depth about their perspectives on the American Dream. Curiously, even in terms of quantitative studies, surprisingly few public opinion polls have been conducted on the subject of the American Dream. However, related social survey data that do exist reflect that Americans overwhelmingly believe that their country operates as a meritocracy. Indeed, after his review of the data political scientist Everett Carl Ladd concluded that survey research "shows Americans holding tenaciously and distinctively to the central elements of their founding ideology." He found Americans' belief in the American Dream to be more intense, pervasive, and firmly entrenched than generally recognized. Very recent qualitative research on post-civil rights views also finds that in in-depth interviews people are remarkably insistent in their beliefs that the playing field is level, that meritocracy is real. While these findings are definitely in line with my own, perhaps the most compelling affirmation for me has been to discover that other sociologists doing in-depth interviewing on subjects not explicitly focused on the American Dream are finding, as I have, that respondents consistently evoke the American Dream—specifically the notion of meritocracy—as their own theme in interviews. In the 200 interviews conducted for this study, what families said, their views, their decisions, and their experiences, were explicitly framed by their belief in meritocracy. These families' perspectives give a vivid account of the place and significance of the American Dream in contemporary life.

The reality of wealth in America though—the way it is acquired, distributed, and the way it is used—is a direct contradiction to these fundamental ideas. In interviews with American families we have seen a way how that plays out. Examining school decision-making (just one arena wherein families potentially experience the ramifications of wealth inequality), those parents from backgrounds of even moderate wealth had a significant advantage over parents with family histories of wealth poverty. Disproportionately white, wealth-holding parents used the financial assistance, intergenerational transfers, and security of their family wealth to help access schools for their own children that were viewed as advantageous by all of the parents. Meanwhile, parents without family wealth to rely upon, who were disproportionately black, were navigating the same arena unaided, with relatively limited resources and constrained capacities. *A central incongruity surfaces when families' school decisions are considered in the context of the American Dream: the assets that the wealth-holding families had owned, relied upon, and utilized in choosing schools had most often originated from non-merit sources.* Inherited wealth and the security of family wealth were critical advantages being passed along to the next generation—advantages often unearned by the parents themselves, and always unearned by their children.

A foundational conflict exists between the meritocratic values of the American Dream and the structure of intergenerational wealth inequality. Simply, advantageous resources inherited and passed along in families are not attained through individual achievement. Although wealth can, of course, be earned by an individual entirely independently, in the case of the families we spoke with it had not. This is the aspect of family wealth that concerns us here. Family wealth generates unearned advantages for those who have it. It is a form of privilege. In light of their beliefs in the American Dream, how do those families who present the most transparent contradiction to the idea of meritocracy—families with wealth privilege—understand their positioning and the unearned advantages they pass along to their children?

We could presume that as with other forms of privilege (such as race privilege or gender privilege) wealth privilege would generally appear invisible and be taken for granted by those who have it. However, one of the most striking aspects of the interviews was the acknowledgement of wealth privilege on the part of wealth-holding families. The parents who had benefited from family wealth acknowledged a structure of wealth inequality that grants privilege to some families and disadvantage to others, and they acknowledged the advantages they were passing along to the next generation through the schools that they chose.

Acknowledging Advantage: A Structure of Wealth Inequality

Given the fact that these families had so vehemently expressed their beliefs in the legitimacy of the American Dream, it was startling to hear them so openly discuss the reality of structured wealth inequality in American society. Not only did parents talk openly about this, they expressed specific views concerning the advantages conferred by wealth. Wealth-holding families thought of wealth as a distinctive resource to be used in particular ways, and even asset-poor families had concrete opinions about how they would use wealth—as opposed to income—if they had it. *Regardless of whether a family had a lot, a little, or none, wealth was thought of as a special form of money, different from income.* Wealth was perceived as a vehicle to provide opportunities, experiences, and material things, as well as a source to provide other less tangible advantages that were harder to articulate but no less important (a sense of security, or confidence about the future, for example). *As a whole, families' perspectives on the advantages of family wealth centered around two notions: wealth as a push and wealth as a safety net.* While families across the board alluded to these ideas, they were especially prevalent among the wealthier families, who emphasized them repeatedly. The first notion—a "push"—or an "edge" as some referred to it, was used by parents to explain how family wealth put some people "ahead" of others right from the start and "paved the way" for them over time.

> Int: Do you believe that you would have achieved the same social and economic situation that you have today if you weren't given the same financial support from your parents?
>
> James: I would say no, because I feel what it has given me is the edge today. But for us today—for what I am, where I work, my abilities as well as my level of education—I feel

without that I don't think I would be where I am today. Because the son would not have been successful without his father doing this—

Pamela: Paving the way for him—

James: [Nods] So, his father paved the way for him to start off and climb up the ladder to be what he is right now. Each kid has the potential, aspiration, a dream. And with wealth you can guide them, you can steer them that way. And you can help them, smooth the way for them, open up doors which they had never seen before.

Pamela and James Gordon, just as the other parents from backgrounds of family wealth, had experienced how that wealth had given them a push and believed it had made a positive difference in the trajectory of their life course. And they believed that this same push they were now giving their own children would make a difference for them too down the road.

Some of the wealth-holding families interviewed were more resistant than others to explicitly conceptualize that "push" they referred to, or those "difference down the road," as concrete "advantage." Joel, for example, asserted right away that wealth passed on to children is "not advantage." He did, however, believe that "it helps." While he described the wealth passed along in families as "a pushing factor," he was careful to not suggest that this translated into actual advantage.

Int: Does the financial help in terms of wealth that some people receive from their families give them certain advantages?

Joel: Not advantage, but it helps. It will help.

Int: Do you think it's significant?

Joel: Depends on what kind of financial help you're talking about.

Int: I'm not talking about billionaires. I'm talking, like, giving a kid after he graduates a $45,000 car. Or giving him, like, $30,000 for his wedding gift. Joel: That helps, yeah, that does help. Yeah, the normal help that the parents give to the children, that is a pushing factor. Just puts you ahead a little bit.

Int: Do you believe those without stable economic situations have a harder time achieving success?

Joel: Yes, I do. That's the rule of life. I mean if you have the money you have peace of mind. So you probably can make better decisions. If you're under pressure for lack of money you could go wrong, you could make wrong decisions, definitely.

Here we see a tension between the ideology of meritocracy and the reality of structured wealth inequality in the nuances of how Joel Conrad talked about, perceived, and made sense of family wealth. While a few other parents expressed similar resistance to acknowledging that the "push" of family wealth was a form of privilege, most families did not. Victoria and Abraham Keenan, for example, conceptualized what they were doing for their own children as "absolutely" giving them advantages. While they were careful to point out that they were not "multi-millionaires" like other people they knew, they did fully believe, and acknowledge, that their family wealth was giving their children "a better chance of becoming successful." Implicit in the way they discussed the passing along of their wealth was their acknowledgement that by doing so they were passing along advantage.

Family wealth was believed to give children a push that, as Abraham said, "gives them a better chance of becoming successful." Some families, of course, can give bigger pushes than others, but even small pushes are clearly advantageous. Children who get the pushes of family wealth benefit from advantages they did nothing to individually earn. The acknowledgement of this on the part of the families who were passing advantages along is an important part of their perspectives on wealth privilege and an important insight to how they think about inequality. The second major way that parents depicted the advantages of family wealth was that it acted as a "safety net" for them in important decisions and throughout their lives. Parents from wealth-holding families repeatedly articulated their sense that family wealth was a "safety net" that gave them tremendous "peace of mind." The Barrys, a white couple whose families on both sides had given them significant financial assets over the years, described their wealth-holdings, and the family wealth they believed they could rely upon in the future, as "a sense of economic security." When asked what that sense of security provides for them, Briggette answered:

> Briggette: Sleep at night. It's very non-tangible things. Being able to give my children a sense of peace. Being able to live worry free. It's really non-tangible things. Knowing that I will probably never have the income that my parents had, but still being comfortable with that and being able to provide for my children what they need.

Another parent who explicitly described her family's wealth as a "safety net," went on to explain, "Well, I think just having, um, the assets, just gives us a certain freedom. . . . You know? You're more freer and more comfortable." The sense of security parents felt from the safety net of family wealth, their desire to re-establish that safety net for their own children, and their ability to rely on it and expand on it in investing in their children's futures cannot be overemphasized.

This was a major way that individuals we interviewed—for example Cynthia and Paul Perkins, a white middle-class couple with three children in Boston—acknowledged the power of wealth and wealth's associated privileges.

When a "safety net" of wealth—or, "a cushion for the future"—could not be relied upon, families without it felt the insecurity of having nothing on which to fall back. This is where the difference between wealth and income is perhaps the clearest. As Lenore Meehan, a young black mother from Boston explained it: "You know, if you look on paper, I make a lot of money, but it doesn't feel like it. . . . I mean, I don't feel like I'm economically secure at all." While she was up-front about the fact that she felt she made quite a lot of money working as a dispatcher for the police force, Lenore's income simply could not provide the sense of security that family wealth was granting to other parents who had it. The families interviewed from all race and class backgrounds made a clear distinction between wealth and income and had concrete understandings of the kinds of advantages that family wealth can provide. Their conceptualization of the "push" and the "safety net" that wealth affords for families and children (and that lack-of-wealth prohibits) reveals their intrinsic awareness and understanding of the power of wealth. *Their acknowledgement of the role of wealth in shaping opportunities, life trajectories, and future chances reveals their awareness and understanding of a structure of wealth inequality.*

As Abigail Connor said, "for someone like her" (someone from a wealthy white family with accumulated, historically rooted race and class advantages), intergenerational transfers of wealth along the way had created a real form of contemporary privilege: family wealth advantage that is not earned entirely independently but which make opportunities relatively easier to attain, aspirations relatively more achievable, and life chances relatively more optimistic. When asked to reflect on the way this had played out in their own lives Abigail and others "like her" (others from families of relative wealth privilege) were quite aware of the essential role that their family wealth had played in their lives. Here Emily Mitchel explains:

> Int: Do you believe that you would have achieved the same social and economic situation that you have today if you weren't given the same financial support from your parents growing up?
> Emily: No.
> Int: [silent pause] How essential, if at all, do you believe family wealth is in attaining success?
> Emily: I think it certainly helps. I think more people who have money tend to excel than people who have no money. It gives you the education, it gives you the contacts,

it gives you the clothes, the way of talking. The things that make life easier. Can you do it without it? Yes. Is it as easy? I don't think so. . . . I think early in our history hard work was really important. But I think money—you can work really hard and be the best foreman on a construction job, but it's not gonna get you a villa in France or a villa in Tuscany. It's just gonna get you whatever kind of advance you want, and a place to live. So I really think that wealth or family money is one of the essential ingredients.

Parents who had benefited from the advantages of family wealth consistently expressed their beliefs that they would not have achieved their same level of success without the financial support that they had received. Of the families who had benefited from family wealth, in only two cases did a parent insist without any compromise that they would have ended up in exactly the same position without any of the financial support that they had received from their family. And in the two exceptions it is possible, of course, that they are correct. It is also the case that we have no way to really know.

In addition to talking about how it had impacted them, parents with family wealth also discussed how they were using that wealth to shape their own children's lives. They were consciously aware that their own relatively privileged positions were enabling them to pass advantage along to the next generation. From these parents' perspectives, family wealth provided specific advantages such as educational opportunities that without it their children would not have. Elizabeth Cummings, a white mother from a wealthy St. Louis family, explained her perspective:

Elizabeth: No question about it! I mean, if my parents hadn't had the money to send my kids to *The Hills School*, we couldn't have considered it. We would have had to really do belt tightening, and financial aid, and many more loans, more mortgages. It would have been very difficult and a real strain on us, especially with two. And we probably would have felt like we just couldn't swing it as a family. So, I don't know, I would have had to gone out and gotten a job that would pay enough to justify two kids in private school. With that, it would have meant not being able to mother them as much myself. Or my husband having to change work, and all the soul searching that would have meant for him. It's unimaginable. I can't envision a path that we would have been able to so comfortably just sail on over to *The Hills School*.

The idea that "you have to have wealth to get it" (or, at least, that having wealth makes it relatively easier to get more) and the idea that "wealthier people have better life chances" (or, at least, that wealth confers relatively better chances for success), stood at the heart of the matter in the interviews.

And these concepts stand at the heart of the matter here: If family wealth makes the next generation's wealth relatively easier to acquire, and if wealth makes success (however defined) relatively easier to attain, then people born into families with wealth are born with a distinct, unearned advantage. They are born with privilege that others do not have.

Conviction in Meritocracy: Hard Work or Lack Thereof

Carter: The fact of the matter is because you get some assistance from your parents doesn't mean that you haven't primarily achieved anything on your own. The fact of the matter is getting a down payment on a house means you were able to get a house sooner, but you still have to make the payments on the house, you still have to do everything necessary to maintain that house. So yeah, it's a help, but it's not the overriding factor.

Int: You think the overriding factor is your own—

Carter: Your own psyche. . . . At the end of the day, hard work is the most important ingredient—in anybody's success.

Int: Think so?

Carter: Yes. The determination to be successful is like the tide, you know? You can't stop it.

Faith & Carter Martin, Homemaker &
Attorney, White, Washington, D.C.

Tracei Diamond, a black single mother from St. Louis, spent much of her interview answering "no" to every question regarding any financial assistance she might have received and explaining the lack of any family financial resources available to her. As a full time banquet waitress at a private country club, Tracei's annual income was $24,000, she had zero net financial assets, and held only a high school degree. Tracei talked about how she sees the members of the country club at functions and events and thinks about how they and their children had advantages that she and her three children simply did not have. She spoke at length, for example, about how the schools "out there" (where the country club was located) were "good schools," how the teachers "really work with them" (the students), and how overall "the education is better." In Tracei's view, for as much as she would like to be able to give her kids those same kinds of opportunities, she simply cannot afford the move to such an area. On top of supporting her three children on her own (she was receiving no child support), Tracei also was doing whatever she could to financially support her younger sister and their mother.

Tracei's interview was typical in that she articulated clear recognition of a structured inequality amongst families that blatantly and categorically translates into unequal educational opportunities for children of different family wealth backgrounds. Yet also typical was Tracei's outright rejection of this inequality and of unequal opportunity. Tracei recognized it and rejected it at the same time. After Tracei had talked about how "wealthy families" get the "better schools," she was asked about how a family's wealth plays a factor in their children's access to quality education. She replied: "It really doesn't have an impact on it. I guess pretty much it depends on you, as far as what kind of life you will have for your child." When she was asked if wealth has any impact, she said "I don't really look at it like that. So, like I say, money definitely doesn't have anything to do with it." When asked to explain further, Tracei did: "It's basically what the parents want or whatever, that's the only thing I really can see. It just depends on how they raise them really." Despite their perspectives that class inequality structures life chances, Tracei and the other families maintained their belief that merit—not money—is what matters; they maintained with conviction their belief in meritocracy.

It was striking to hear disadvantaged parents talk so vehemently about meritocracy, to hear them assert repeatedly that positions in society are earned entirely through hard work and personal achievement, and to hear them deny family wealth inequality as a legitimate explanation. But considering that many of these parents had no direct experience with wealth privilege, that they had no awareness of the extent to which wealthy families are using and extending intergenerational transfers of assets, that they did not know for sure how much others are advantaged by unearned resources, then it makes sense how they clung so resolutely to the dominant ideology. What was most remarkable, however, is that those parents with family wealth who had spoken openly of their unearned advantages, who had so plainly seen and felt and known wealth privilege in motion in their own lives, were, at the same time, insistent that meritocracy is an accurate and realistic explanation for social stratification in America. In an interview in St. Louis, Briggette and Joe Barry spoke in detail of the financial help they had received from their parents. *They openly declared that these resources had allowed for a lifestyle they would not otherwise have had. After listing extensive financial assistance, the security of family wealth, and the many advantages they have had, the Barrys insisted that the way they had earned their assets was through hard work.*

The Barrys were not atypical of the white middle-class families interviewed; on the contrary, they portrayed the sentiments of families like them in the sample. Their socioeconomic positions were due, in large part, to the inheritance and accumulative advantages of family wealth, yet at the same time they were adamant that they single-handedly earned and deserved their places in society. These families' insistence that they had, "worked their butts off" for what they had was astonishing. They listed in detail the help they had received from their families: Financial assistance with major purchases, down payments on houses, school tuition for children, "loans" that were later forgiven, etc. They catalogued the gifts they had received from family members for birthdays, graduations, weddings, and births of children. They discussed the numerous ways their extended families had been financially generous over the years by providing used cars, old furniture, flight tickets home for holidays, family vacations, dining out, kids' back-to-school clothes, and groceries, to name a few. They described the "push" and the "safety net" that comes with family wealth: Feeling that they have had "a head start" or "an edge" over others, knowing they would have something to fall back on in a financial pinch, and the expectation of future inheritances. While they talked about, listed, and described these things when asked, they repeatedly emphasized how hard they had worked for all that they owned and how much they deserved their stations in life.

Regardless of background, families used the American Dream of meritocracy to explain their assertion that anyone can be anything and do anything and get anywhere with hard work. They stressed that hard work or lack thereof was the determinant of each individual's position in society. But for those with family wealth, what was most notable was how they implied, implicitly and explicitly, that their own advantages as well as the advantages they were passing along to their children were earned and deserved autonomously—through hard work, perseverance, and determination alone.

Another example comes from our interview with Chris and Peter Ackerman, a white couple in their early thirties who lived in a white suburb of St. Louis. They had three kids, ages six, three, and two. They had been married for ten years and both worked in management positions on the staff of a local university. Their combined annual income was $83,000, their net worth $210,000, and their net financial assets totaled $91,500. This couple owned savings accounts, savings bonds, small trust funds for each child, and a boat worth $12,500. They had received significant financial assistance from their families, including help with a down payment on their first home, which they bought when they married. The equity from that house was later used as a down payment for an upgraded home when they had their children. Chris and Peter's parents financed their college educations; they never had to take out student loans; their children regularly received cash gifts and savings bonds from their grandparents on holidays and birthdays; Chris's parents had often paid for the family to vacation with them; Peter's parents had bought many of their major household appliances for them, as well as their car; and so on. They talked about how appreciative they were of all this help, about how they would not be in the position that they are without it. Despite this acknowledgement, Chris and Peter continually insisted that their wealth had been achieved single-handedly:

Int: How did you acquire the assets you own?
Chris: By working.
Peter: Saving, working.
Chris: Working and saving, working and saving. That's basically how we do it.

The Ackermans and many of their peers simultaneously acknowledged the power of their wealth privilege and avowed that it does not really matter. They were resolute in their explanation that hard work and determination had gotten them to where they are. For as much as they were upfront about the structure of wealth, they also depicted social positioning as independently earned and deserved. As one young mother from just outside of New York City put it, "You know—and I'm not bragging, I'm not saying anything—but it just comes from setting your priorities straight, and taking care of business!" In discussing hard work and individual achievement people often spoke louder, quicker, and sometimes at a higher pitch. People leaned forward or moved in toward the tape recorder's microphone as if to want to be sure they were heard clearly on this. They spoke with fervor and conviction when crediting themselves with their own success. For example, in talking with Lily and Jonathan Boothe, a white wealthy family from the New York City area, Jonathan had been quite serene throughout the interview. However, when we began talking about the Boothes' perspectives on success and achievement, Jonathan became noticeably more vivacious.

Just as people with wealth credited themselves for their success, conversely, those who lacked family wealth blamed themselves. Conviction in meritocracy worked both ways, and meritocracy could justify both positions. The themes of "sticking to one's ideals," "being focused," "motivated," and "willing to work hard" were as consistent in interviews with working-class and impoverished families as they were in affluent families. People blamed themselves for their inability to attain what they wished for and wanted for themselves and their children, even when they were starting from the most disadvantaged backgrounds. One parent from Boston explained that, compared to others, she comes up short because "I did a lot of fooling around." A mother from St. Louis said, "I would say that I am a little bit limited. But it's nobody's fault but my own. So I can't complain." And still another parent lamented, "If I was to make more, better, wiser decisions along the way, I wouldn't have the debt that I have now."

Most people have regrets in life, and maybe if the families who were struggling to make ends meet had made "more, better, wiser decisions along the way," things would have turned out differently for them. Maybe not. But one of the things that stood out the most about this explanation was that many of these families had in fact done extraordinarily well for themselves. More often than not, however, the fruits of unaided self-achievement simply paled in comparison to the results of self-achievement combined with the advantages of family wealth. Still, throughout the interviews, parents from poor and working-class family backgrounds compared themselves to more "well-off" others, blamed themselves, and legitimized their situations by saying they should have worked harder. While to some extent they understood that a structure of wealth inequality existed, and while they recognized the real advantages for those with family wealth, they simultaneously blamed themselves for not having worked harder and done better than they had.

The interviews also show the power of hope. For these families the American Dream was hope. It held out hope that what is wanted will happen, and that what is wanted can be expected. It held out hope that children's life chances were all equally unconstrained. It held out hope that the world is just. To think otherwise (to think that the world is not just) would be heartbreaking to any parent. And, I believe, many parents fear that to think otherwise (to think that the world is not just) could potentially—if conveyed to children—break the spirit of any child. So they hold on to the American Dream, they hold on to their hope. This hope was reflected in the parents' perspectives regarding themselves, the social system they are acting on and within, and—most importantly—their children.

REFERENCES

Hochschild, Jennifer. 1995. *Facing Up to the American Dream: Race, Class, and the Soul of a Nation.* Princeton, NJ: Princeton University Press.

------. 1981. *What's Fair? American Beliefs about Distributive Justice.* Cambridge, MA: Harvard University Press.

Schwartz, John E. 1997. *Illusions of Opportunity: the American Dream in Question.* New York: W. W. Norton.

Sennett, Richard & Cobb, Jonathan. 1972. *The Hidden Injuries of Class.* New York: W. W. Norton.

The Power of Self-Definition

by Patricia Hill Collins

"In order to survive, those of us for whom oppression is as American as apple pie have always had to be watchers," asserts Black feminist poet Audre Lorde (1984, 114). This "watching" generates a dual consciousness in African-American women, one in which Black women "become familiar with the language and manners of the oppressor, even sometimes adopting them for some illusion of protection" (p. 114), while hiding a self-defined standpoint from the prying eyes of dominant groups. Ella Surrey, an elderly Black woman domestic, eloquently summarizes the energy needed to maintain independent self-definitions: "We have always been the best actors in the world . . . . I think that we are much more clever than they are because we know that we have to play the game. We've always had to live two lives—one for them and one for ourselves" (Gwaltney 1980, 238, 240).[1]

Behind the mask of behavioral conformity imposed on African-American women, acts of resistance, both organized and anonymous, have long existed (Davis 1981, 1989; Terborg-Penn 1986; Hine 1989; Barnett 1993). Despite the strains connected with domestic work, Judith Rollins (1985) asserts that the domestic workers she interviewed appeared to have retained a "remarkable sense of self-worth." They "skillfully deflect these psychological attacks on their personhood, their adulthood, their dignity, these attempts to lure them into accepting employers' definitions of them as inferior"

(p. 212). Bonnie Thornton Dill (1988a) found that the domestic workers in her study refused to let their employers push them around. As one respondent declared: "When I went out to work . . . my mother told me, 'Don't let anybody take advantage of you. Speak up for your rights, but do the work right. If they don't give you your rights, you demand that they treat you right. And if they don't, then you quit'" (p. 41). Jacqueline Bobo (1995) reports that the U.S. Black women in her study who viewed the film *The Color Purple* were not passive consumers of controlling images of Black womanhood. Instead, these women crafted identities designed to empower them. In 1905, a period of heightened racial repression, educator Fannie Barrier Williams viewed the African-American woman not as a defenseless victim but as a strong-willed resister: "As meanly as she is thought of, hindered as she is in all directions, she is always doing something of merit and credit that is not expected of her" (Williams 1987, 151). Williams saw the Black woman as "irrepressible. She is insulted, but she holds up her head; she is scorned, but she proudly demands respect . . . . The most interesting girl of this country is the colored girl" (p. 151).

Resisting by doing something that "is not expected" could not have occurred without Black women's long-standing rejection of mammies, matriarchs, and other controlling images. When combined, these individual acts of resistance suggest that a distinctive, collective Black women's consciousness exists. Such a consciousness was present in Maria Stewart's 1831 speech advising the "daughters of Africa" to "Awake! Arise! No longer sleep nor slumber, but distinguish yourselves. Show forth to the world that ye are endowed with noble and exalted faculties" (Richardson 1987, 30). Such a consciousness is present in the worldview of Johnny Mae Fields, a mill worker from North Carolina possessing few opportunities to resist. Ms. Fields wryly announces, "If they tell me something and I know I ain't going to do it, I don't tell them. I just go on and don't do it" (Byerly 1986, 141).

Silence is not to be interpreted as submission in this collective, self-defined Black women's consciousness. In 1925 author Marita Bonner cogently described how consciousness remained the one sphere of freedom available to her in the stifling confines of both her Black middle-class world and a racist White society:

> So—being a woman—you can wait. You must sit quietly without a chip. Not sodden—and weighted as if your feet were cast in the iron of your soul. Not wasting strength in enervating gestures as if two hundred years of bonds and whips had really tricked you into nervous un-certainty. But quiet; quiet. Like Buddha—who brown like I am—sat entirely at ease, entirely sure of himself; motionless and knowing . . . . Motionless on the outside. But inside?
>
> (Bonner 1987, 7)

U.S. Black women intellectuals have long explored this private, hidden space of Black women's consciousness, the "inside" ideas that allow Black women to cope with and, in many cases, transcend the confines of intersecting oppressions of race, class, gender, and sexuality. How have African-American women as a group found the strength to oppose our objectification as "de mule uh de world"? How do we account for the voices of resistance of Audre Lorde, Ella Surrey, Maria Stewart, Fannie Barrier Williams, and Marita Bonner? What foundation sustained Sojourner Truth so that she could ask, "Ain't I a woman?" The voices of these African-American women are not those of victims but of survivors. Their ideas and actions suggest that not only does a self-defined, group-derived Black women's standpoint exist, but that its presence has been essential to U.S. Black women's survival.

"A system of oppression," claims Black feminist activist Pauli Murray, "draws much of its strength from the acquiescence of its victims, who have accepted the dominant image of themselves and are paralyzed by a sense of helplessness" (1987, 106). U.S. Black women's ideas and actions force a rethinking of the concept of hegemony, the notion that Black women's objectification as the Other is so complete that we become willing participants in our own oppression. Most African-American women simply do not define themselves as mammies, matriarchs, welfare mothers, mules, or sexually denigrated women. The matrix of domination in which these controlling images are embedded is much less cohesive or uniform than imagined.

African-American women encounter these controlling images, not as disembodied symbolic messages but as ideas designed to provide meaning in our daily lives (Scott 1985). Black women's work and family experiences create the conditions whereby the contradictions between everyday experiences and the controlling images of Black womanhood become visible. Seeing the contradictions in the ideologies opens them up for demystification. Just as Sojourner Truth deconstructed the term *woman* by using her own lived experiences to challenge it, so in a variety of ways do everyday African-American women do the same thing. That fewer Maria Stewarts, Sojourner Truths, Ella Surreys, or Johnny Mae Fieldses are heard from may be less a statement about the existence of Black women's ideas than it is a reflection of the suppression of their ideas. As Nancy White, an inner-city resident points out, "I like to say what I think. But I don't do that much because most people don't care what I think" (Gwaltney 1980, 156). Like Marita Bonner, far too many Black women remain motionless on the outside . . . but inside?

FINDING A VOICE: COMING TO TERMS WITH CONTRADICTIONS

"To be able to use the range of one's voice, to attempt to express the totality of self, is a recurring struggle in the tradition of [Black women] writers," maintains Black feminist literary critic

Barbara Christian (1985, 172). African-American women have certainly expressed our individual voices. U.S. Black women have been described as generally outspoken and self-assertive speakers, a consequence of expectations that men and women both participate in Black civil society. But despite this tradition, the overarching theme of finding a voice to express a collective, self-defined Black women's standpoint remains a core theme in Black feminist thought.

Why this theme of self-definition should preoccupy African-American women is not surprising. Black women's lives are a series of negotiations that aim to reconcile the contradictions separating our own internally defined images of self as African-American women with our objectification as the Other. The struggle of living two lives, one for "them and one for ourselves" (Gwaltney 1980, 240) creates a peculiar tension to construct independent self-definitions within a context where Black womanhood remains routinely derogated. As Karla Holloway points out, "the reality of racism and sexism means that we must configure our private realities to include an awareness of what our public image might mean to others. This is not paranoia. It is preparedness" (Holloway 1995, 36).

Much of the best of Black feminist thought reflects this effort to find a collective, self-defined voice and express a fully articulated womanist standpoint (Collins 1998, 61–65). Audre Lorde observes that "within this country where racial difference creates a constant, if unspoken, distortion of vision, Black women have on the one hand always been highly visible, and so, on the other hand, have been rendered invisible through the depersonalization of racism" (1984, 42). Lorde also points out that the "visibility which makes us most vulnerable"—that which accompanies being Black—"is also the source of our greatest strength" (p. 42). The category of "Black woman" makes all U.S. Black women especially visible and open to the objectification of Black women as a category. This group treatment potentially renders each individual African-American woman invisible as fully human. But paradoxically, being treated as an invisible Other places U.S. Black women in an outsider-within position that has stimulated creativity in many.

For individual women, resolving contradictions of this magnitude takes considerable inner strength. In describing the development of her own racial identity, Pauli Murray remembers: "My own self-esteem was elusive and difficult to sustain. I was not entirely free from the prevalent idea that I must prove myself worthy of the rights that white individuals took for granted. This psychological conditioning along with fear had reduced my capacity for resistance to racial injustice" (1987, 106). Murray's quest was for constructed knowledge (Belenky et al. 1986), a type of knowledge essential to resolving contradictions. To learn to speak in a "unique and authentic voice, women must 'jump outside' the frames and systems authorities provide and create their own frame" (p. 134). Unlike the controlling images developed for middle-class

White women, the controlling images applied to Black women are so uniformly negative that they almost necessitate resistance. For U.S. Black women, constructed knowledge of self emerges from the struggle to replace controlling images with self-defined knowledge deemed personally important, usually knowledge essential to Black women's survival.[2]

SAFE SPACES AND COMING TO VOICE

While domination may be inevitable as a social fact, it is unlikely to be hegemonic as an ideology within social spaces where Black women speak freely. This realm of relatively safe discourse, however narrow, is a necessary condition for Black women's resistance. Extended families, churches, and African-American community organizations are important locations where safe discourse potentially can occur. Sondra O'Neale describes the workings of these Black women's spaces: "Beyond the mask, in the ghetto of the black women's community, in her family, and, more important, in her psyche, is and has always been another world, a world in which she functions— sometimes in sorrow but more often in genuine joy . . . —by doing the things that 'normal' black women do" (1986, 139). These spaces are not only safe—they form prime locations for resisting objectification as the Other. In these spaces Black women "observe the feminine images of the 'larger' culture, realize that these models are at best unsuitable and at worst destructive to them, and go about the business of fashioning themselves after the prevalent, historical black female role models in their own community" (O'Neale 1986, 139). By advancing Black women's empowerment through self-definition, these safe spaces help Black women resist the dominant ideology promulgated not only outside Black civil society but within African-American institutions.

These institutional sites where Black women construct independent self-definitions reflect the dialectical nature of oppression and activism. Schools, print and broadcast media, government agencies, and other institutions in the information business reproduce the controlling images of Black womanhood. In response, African-American women have traditionally used family networks and Black community institutions as sites for countering these images. On the one hand, these Black community institutions have been vitally important in developing strategies of resistance. In the context of deep-seated U.S. racial segregation that persisted through the 1960s, the vast majority of U.S. Black women lacked access to other forms of political organization.

On the other hand, many of these same institutions of Black civil society have also perpetuated racist, sexist, elitist, and homophobic ideologies. This same period of desegregation of U.S. society overall spurred a parallel desegregation *within* Black civil society where women, working-class folks, lesbians, gays, bisexuals and transgendered individuals, and other formerly subjugated subpopulations within Black civil society began to speak out.

As a result of this changing political context, the reality is much more complex than one of an all-powerful White majority objectifying Black women with a unified U.S. Black community staunchly challenging these external assaults. No uniform, homogeneous culture of resistance ever existed among U.S. Blacks, and such a culture does not exist now. One can say, however, that U.S. Blacks have shared a common political agenda and culture, one that has been differently experienced and expressed by U.S. Blacks as a heterogeneous collectivity. Historically, survival depended on sticking together and in many ways aiming to minimize differences among African-Americans. More recently, in a changing political economy where survival for many U.S. Blacks seems less of an issue, space to express these differences now exists. Black feminism itself has been central in creating that space, in large part, via Black women's claims for self-definition. Overall, African-American women find ourselves in a web of crosscutting relationships, each presenting varying combinations of controlling images and Black women's self-definitions.

Thus, the historical complexity of these institutional arrangements of racial segregation and heterogeneous Black community politics profoundly affected Black women's consciousness and its articulation in a self-defined standpoint. Given this context, what have been some important safe spaces where Black women's consciousness has been nurtured? Where have individual African-American women spoken freely in contributing to a collective, self-defined standpoint? Moreover, how "safe" are these spaces now?

Black women's relationships with one another

Traditionally, U.S. Black women's efforts to construct individual and collective voices have occurred in at least three safe spaces. One location involves Black women's relationships with one another. In some cases, such as friendships and family interactions, these relationships are informal, private dealings among individuals. In others, as was the case during slavery (D. White 1985), in Black churches (Gilkes 1985; Higginbotham 1993), or in Black women's organizations (Giddings 1988; Cole 1993; Guy-Sheftall 1993), more formal organizational ties have nurtured powerful Black women's communities. As mothers, daughters, sisters, and friends to one another, many African-American women affirm one another (Myers 1980).

The mother/daughter relationship is one fundamental relationship among Black women. Countless Black mothers have empowered their daughters by passing on the everyday knowledge essential to survival as African-American women (Joseph 1981; Collins 1987). Black daughters identify the profound influence that their mothers have had upon their lives (Bell-Scott et al. 1991). Mothers and mother figures emerge as central figures in autobiographies such as Maya Angelou's *I Know Why the Caged Bird Sings* (1969), Bebe Moore Campbell's *Sweet Summer* (1989), Mamie Garvin Fields and Karen Fields's *Lemon Swamp and Other Places* (1983), and Elaine Brown's *A Taste of Power* (1992). Alice Walker attributes the trust she has in herself to her mother. In describing this relationship, Mary Helen Washington points out that Walker "never doubted her powers of judgment because her mother assumed that they were sound; she never questioned her right to follow her intellectual bent, because her mother implicitly entitled her to it" (Washington 1984, 145). By giving her daughter a library card, Walker's mother showed she knew the value of a free mind.

In the comfort of daily conversations, through serious conversation and humor, African-American women as sisters and friends affirm one another's humanity, specialness, and right to exist. Black women's fiction, such as Toni Cade Bambara's short story "The Johnson Girls" (1981) and Toni Morrison's novels *Sula* (1974), *The Bluest Eye* (1970), and *Beloved* (1987), as well as Terry McMillan's blockbuster novel *Waiting to Exhale* (1992), is one important location where Black women's friendships are taken seriously. In a dialogue with four other Black women, Evelynn Hammonds describes this special relationship that Black women can have with one another: "I think most of the time you have to be there to experience it. When I am with other black women I always laugh. I think our humor comes from a shared recognition of who we all are in the world" (Clarke et al. 1983, 114).

This shared recognition often operates among African-American women who do not know one another but who see the need to value Black womanhood. Marita Golden describes her efforts in 1968 to attend a college which was "nestled . . . in the comfortable upper reaches of northwest Washington, surrounded by . . . the manicured, sprawling lawns of the city's upper class." To enter this world, Golden caught the bus downtown with "black women domestic workers who rode to the end of the line to clean house for young and middle-aged white matrons." Golden describes her fellow travelers' reaction to her acquiring a college education:

> They gazed proudly at me, nodding at the books in my lap . . . . I accepted their encouragement and hated America for never allowing them to be selfish or greedy, to feel the steel-hard bite of ambition . . . . They had parlayed their anger, brilliantly shaped it into a soft armor of survival. The spirit of those women sat with me in every class I took.

> (Golden 1983, 21)

My decision to pursue my doctorate was stimulated by a similar experience. In 1978 I offered a seminar as part of a national summer institute for teachers and other school personnel. After my Chicago workshop, an older Black woman participant whispered to me, "Honey, I'm real proud of you. Some folks don't want to see you up there [in the front of the classroom], but you belong there. Go back to school and get your Ph.D., and then they won't be able to tell you nothing!" To this day, I thank her and try to do the same for others. In talking with other African-American women, I have discovered that many of us have had similar experiences.

This issue of Black women being the ones who really listen to one another is significant, particularly given the importance of voice in Black women's lives. Identifying the value of Black women's friendships, Karla Holloway describes how the women in her book club supported one another: "The events we shared among ourselves all had a similar trigger—it was when someone, a child's school principal or teacher, a store clerk, medical personnel, had treated us as if we had no sense of our own, no ability to filter through whatever nonsense they were feeding us, or no earned, adult power to make choices in our children's lives" (Holloway 1995, 31). These women described cathartic moments when, in creative ways, they responded to these assaults by "turning it out." Each knew that only another Black woman could fully understand how it felt to be treated that way and to respond in kind.

Audre Lorde describes the importance that the expression of individual voice within collective context of Black women's communities can have for self-affirmation: "Of course I am afraid, because the transformation of silence into language and action is an act of self-revelation, and that always seems fraught with danger" (1984, 42). One can write for a nameless, faceless audience, but the act of using one's voice requires a listener and thus establishes a connection. For African-American women the listener most able to pierce the invisibility created by Black women's objectification is another Black woman. This process of trusting one another can seem dangerous because only Black women know what it means to be Black women. But if we will not listen to one another, then who will?

Black women writers have led the way in recognizing the importance of Black women's relationships with one another. Mary Helen Washington points out that one distinguishing feature of Black women's literature is that it is about African-American women. Women talk to one another, and "their friendships with other women—mothers, sisters, grandmothers, friends, lovers—are vital to their growth and well-being" (1987, xxi). The significance placed on relationships among Black women transcends U.S. Black women's writings. For example, Ghanian author Ama Ata Aidoo's novel *Changes* (1991) uses the friendship between two African professional women to explore the challenges facing professional women in contemporary African societies. Within U.S. Black women's fiction, this emphasis on Black women's relationships has been so striking that novelist Gayl Jones suggests that women writers select different themes from those of their male counterparts. In the work of many Black male writers, the significant relationships are those that involve confrontation with individuals outside the family and community. But among Black women writers, relationships within family and community, between men and women, and among women are treated as complex and significant (Tate 1983, 92).

U.S. Black women writers and filmmakers have explored many themes affecting Black women's relationships. One concerns the difficulties that African-American women can have in affirming one another in a society that derogates Black women as a group. Albeit for different reasons, the inability of mothers to help their daughters come to understandings of Black womanhood characterize mother–daughter relationships in Toni Morrison's novel *The Bluest Eye* and in the film *Just Another Girl on the IRT*. Another theme concerns how Black women's relationships can support and renew. Relationships such as those between Celie and Shug in Alice Walker's novel *The Color Purple*, among sisters in the film *Soul Food*, among the four women in *Waiting to Exhale*, and among women in an extended family in the film *Daughters of the Dust* all provide cases where Black women helped one another grow in some fashion. Another theme involves how relationships among Black women can control and repress. Audre Lorde's relationship with her mother in her autobiography *Zami* (1982) and Black adolescent Alma's relationship with her overbearing mother in the film *Alma's Rainbow* both illustrate ways in which Black women with some sort of power, in these examples that of the authority of motherhood, can suppress other women. Perhaps Ntozake Shange best summarizes the importance that Black women can have for one another in resisting oppressive conditions. Shange gives the following reason for why she writes: "When I die, I will not be guilty of having left a generation of girls behind thinking that anyone can tend to their emotional health other than themselves" (in Tate 1983, 162).

The Black women's blues tradition

African-American music as art has provided a second location where Black women have come to voice (Jackson 1981). "Art is special because of its ability to influence feelings as well as knowledge," suggests Angela Davis (1989, 200). Davis contends that the dominant group failed to grasp the social function of music in general and particularly the central role music played in all aspects of life in West African society. As a result, "Black people were able to create with their music an aesthetic community of resistance, which in turn encouraged and nurtured a political community of active struggle for freedom" (1989, 201). Spirituals, blues, jazz, rhythm and blues, and progressive hip-hop all form part of a "continuum of struggle which is at once aesthetic and political" (p. 201).

African-derived communication patterns maintain the integrity of the individual and his or her personal voice, but do so in the context of group activity (Smitherman 1977; Kochman 1981; Asante 1987; Cannon 1988). In music one effect of this oral mode of discourse is that individuality, rather than being stifled by group activity or being equated with specialization, actually flourishes in a group context (Sidran 1971).[3] "There's something about music that is so penetrating that your soul gets the message. No matter what trouble comes to a person, music can help him face it," claims Mahalia Jackson (1985, 454). "A song must do something for me as well as for the people that hear it. I can't sing a song that doesn't have a message. If it doesn't have the strength it can't lift you" (p. 446).

The blues tradition is an essential part of African-American music.[4] Blues singer Alberta Hunter explains the importance of the blues as a way of dealing with pain: "To me, the blues are almost religious . . . almost sacred—when we sing the blues, we're singing out of our own hearts . . . our feelings" (Harrison 1978, 63). Black people's ability to cope with and even transcend trouble without ignoring it means that it will not destroy us (Cone 1972).

Traditionally, blues assumed a similar function in African-American oral culture to that played by print media for White, visually based culture. Blues was not just entertainment—it was a way of solidifying community and commenting on the social fabric of working-class Black life in America. Sherley Anne Williams contends that "the blues records of each decade explain something about the philosophical basis of our lives as black people. If we don't understand that as so-called intellectuals, then we don't really understand anything about ourselves" (in Tate 1983, 208). For African-American women, blues seemed to be everywhere. Mahalia Jackson describes its pervasiveness during her childhood in New Orleans: "The famous white singers like Caruso—you might hear them when you went by a white folk's house, but in a colored house you heard blues. You couldn't help but hear blues—all through the thin partitions of the houses—through the open windows—up and down the street in the colored neighborhoods—everybody played it real loud" (1985, 447).

Black women have been central in maintaining, transforming, and recreating the blues traditions of African-American culture (Harrison 1978, 1988; Russell 1982; Davis 1998). Michele Russell asserts, "Blues, first and last, are a familiar idiom for Black women, even a staple of life" (1982, 130). Blues has occupied a special place in Black women's music as a site of the expression of Black women's self-definitions. The blues singer strives to create an atmosphere in which analysis can take place, and yet this atmosphere is intensely personal and individualistic.

When Black women sing the blues, we sing our own personalized, individualistic blues while simultaneously expressing the collective blues of African-American women.

Michele Russell's (1982) analysis of five Black women blues singers' music demonstrates how the texts of blues singers can be seen as expressions of a Black women's standpoint. Russell claims that the works of Bessie Smith, Bessie Jackson, Billie Holiday, Nina Simone, and Esther Phillips help Black women "own their past, present, and future." To Russell, these women are primary because "the content of their message, combined with the form of their delivery, make them so" (p. 130).

The music of the classic blues singers of the 1920s—almost exclusively women—marks the early written record of this dimension of U.S. Black oral culture. The songs themselves were originally sung in small communities, where boundaries distinguishing singer from audience, call from response, and thought from action were fluid and permeable. Despite the control of White-run record companies, these records were made exclusively for the "race market" of African-Americans and thus targeted Black consumers. Because literacy was not possible for large numbers of Black women, these recordings represented the first permanent documents exploring a working-class Black women's standpoint that until then had been accessible to Black women in local settings. The songs can be seen as poetry, as expressions of ordinary Black women rearticulated through Black oral traditions.

The lyrics sung by many of the Black women blues singers challenge the externally defined controlling images used to justify Black women's objectification as the Other. The songs of Ma Rainey, dubbed "Queen of the Blues" and the first major female blues singer to be extensively recorded, validate Black feminist intellectual traditions expressed by working-class Black women. In contrast to the ingenues of most White popular music of the same period, Ma Rainey and her contemporaries sing of mature, sexual women. For example, Sara Martin's "Mean Tight Mama" rejects the cult of true womanhood and its confining images of beauty:

> Now my hair is nappy and I don't wear no clothes of silk
> Now my hair is nappy and I don't wear no clothes of silk
> But the cow that's black and ugly has often got the sweetest milk.
>
> (Harrison 1978, 69)

Bessie Smith's "Get It, Bring It, and Put It Right Here"—like the words of Maria Stewart—advises Black women to possess the spirit of independence. She sings of her man:

> I've had a man for fifteen years, give him his room and his board
> Once he was like a Cadillac, now he's like an old worn-out Ford.
> He never brought me a lousy dime, and put it in my hand
> Oh, there'll be some changes from now on, according to my plan.

He's got to get it, bring it, and put it right here
Or else he's gonna keep it out there.
If he must steal it, beg it, or borrow it somewhere
Long as he gets it, I don't care.

(Russell 1982, 133)

Sometimes the texts of Black women blues singers take overtly political forms. Billie Holiday recorded "Strange Fruit" in 1939 at the end of a decade rife with racial unrest:

Southern trees bear a strange fruit, blood on the leaves and blood at the root
Black body swinging in the Southern breeze, strange fruit hanging from the poplar trees.
Pastoral scene of the gallant South, the bulging eyes and the twisted mouth,
Scent of magnolia sweet and fresh, and the sudden smell of burning flesh!
Here is a fruit for the crows to pluck, for the rain to gather, for the wind to suck, for the sun to rot, for a tree to drop,
Here is a strange and bitter crop.

(*Billie Holiday Anthology* 1976, 111)

Through her powerful rendition of these lyrics, Billie Holiday demonstrated a direct connection to the antilynching political activism of Ida B. Wells-Barnett and other better-known Black feminists. Holiday's music reaches from the past to express themes that shed light on the present.

Despite the contributions of Black women's blues as one location where ordinary Black women found voice, Ann duCille (1993) cautions against a trend in contemporary Black cultural criticism of viewing the blues through idealized lenses. DuCille contends that while Black blues queens like Bessie Smith and Ma Rainey sang of sex and sexuality with a startling frankness for their times, they rarely could do so on their own terms. Despite the fact that at the peak of the classic blues era hundreds of women had the opportunity to record their work, they did so for White-male-controlled record companies. At the same time, middle-class Blacks who were engaged in a cultural Renaissance during the 1920s typically saw such music as antithetical to the aims of their cultural movement. Black women's blues was often designated as "low" culture (Davis 1998, xii-xiii). Thus, while it appears that the Black women blues singers of the 1920s sang freely of sexually explicit themes, they did so in a complicated context of race, class, and gender politics.

Moreover, duCille points out that identifying the blues as the "authentic" location for Black women's voice splits Black experience into two seemingly opposed groups, middle-class Black women "literati" and working-class Black women blues singers. Deeming the blues singers to be more "authentic" relegates Black women writers, and those who study them, to the category of a less authentic Blackness. DuCille explores how the fiction of two middle-class Black women writers, Jessie Fauset and Nella Lawson, offered a more complex critique of society than that forwarded by the blues singers. DuCille's argument is not with the singers themselves, but primarily with how such seemingly safe spaces of Black women's blues are viewed within contemporary Black cultural criticism. However, keeping her caveats in mind, it is important to remember that despite their contemporary appropriations, for the vast majority of Black working-class women, Black women's blues spaces have long been important and remain so today (Davis 1998). Where else could working-class Black women say in public the things they had long shared among one another in private?

The voices of Black women writers

During the summer of 1944, recent law school graduate Pauli Murray returned to her California apartment and found the following anonymous note from the "South Crocker Street Property Owner's Association" tacked to her door: "We . . . wish to inform you the flat you now occupy . . . is restricted to the white or Caucasian race only . . . . We intend to uphold these restrictions, therefore we ask that you vacate the above mentioned flat . . . within seven days" (1987, 253). Murray's response was to write. She remembers: "I was learning that creative expression is an integral part of the equipment needed in the service of a compelling cause; it is another form of activism. Words poured from my typewriter" (p. 255).

Though a Black women's written tradition existed (Christian 1985; Carby 1987), it was available primarily to educated women. Denied the literacy that enabled them to read books and novels, as well as the time to do so, working-class Black women struggled to find a public voice. Hence the significance of the blues and other dimensions of Black oral traditions in their lives. In this class-segmented context, finding Black women's writing that transcends these divisions among written and oral traditions is noteworthy. In this regard, because it fits neither solely within the Black women's blues tradition nor within equally important traditions of Black women's writers, the work of Alice Childress (1956) remains exemplary. Childress created the character of Mildred, a fictional working-class, Black woman domestic worker. Through short monologues to her friend Marge, Mildred, a domestic worker, speaks out on a range of topics. Mildred's 62 monologues, each two or three pages in length, constitute provocative statements of Childress's Black feminist theory (Harris 1986). Take, for example, Mildred's rendition to Marge of what she said to her boss in response to hearing herself described to her boss's luncheon friends as a quasi-family member:

> I am *not* just like one of the family at all! The family eats in the dining room and I eat in the kitchen. Your mama borrows your lace tablecloth for her company and your son

entertains his friends in your parlour, your daughter takes her afternoon nap on the living room couch and the puppy sleeps on your satin spread . . . so you can see I am not *just* like one of the family.

(Childress 1956, 2)

In this passage, Childress creates a fictional version of what many Black women domestic workers have wanted to say at one time or another. She also advances a biting critique of how the mammy image has been used to justify Black women's bad treatment.

Foreshadowing Barbara Neely's creation of the character of Blanche, Mildred's ideas certainly ring true. But Childress's Mildred also illustrates a creative use of Black women's writing that is targeted not just to educated Black women, but to a wider Black women's community. The character of Mildred first appeared in a series of conversations that were originally published in Paul Robeson's newspaper, *Freedom*, under the title "Conversations from Life." They continued in the *Baltimore Afro-American* as "Here's Mildred." Since many of Childress's readers were themselves domestic workers, Mildred's bold assertions resonated with the silenced voices of many of these readers. Moreover, Mildred's identity as a Black working-class domestic and the form of publication of these fictionalized accounts illustrates an increasingly rare practice in Black intellectual production—a Black author writing to an African-American, working-class audience, using a medium controlled by Black people (Harris 1986).[5]

Since the 1970s, increased literacy among African-Americans has provided new opportunities for U.S. Black women to expand the use of scholarship and literature into more visible institutional sites of resistance. A community of Black women writers has emerged since 1970, one in which African-American women engage in dialogue among one another in order to explore formerly taboo subjects. Black feminist literary criticism has documented the intellectual and personal space created for African-American women in this emerging body of ideas (Washington 1980, 1982; Tate 1983; Evans 1984; Christian 1985; O'Neale 1986). Especially noteworthy are the ways in which many Black women writers build on former themes and approaches of the Black women's blues tradition (Williams 1979) and of earlier Black women writers (Cannon 1988).

How "safe" are safe spaces?

Historically, safe spaces were "safe" because they represented places where Black women could freely examine issues that concerned us. By definition, such spaces become less "safe" if shared with those who were not Black and female. Black women's safe spaces were never meant to be a way of life. Instead, they constitute one mechanism among many designed to foster Black women's empowerment and enhance our ability to participate in social justice projects. As strategies, safe spaces rely on exclusionary practices, but their overall purpose most certainly aims for a more inclusionary, just society. As the work of Black women blues singers and Black women writers suggests, many of the ideas generated in such spaces found a welcome reception outside Black women's communities. But how could Black women generate these understandings of Black women's realities without first talking to one another?

Since the 1970s, U.S. Black women have been unevenly incorporated into schools, jobs, neighborhoods, and other U.S. social institutions that historically have excluded us. As a result, African-American women have become more class stratified than at any period in the past. In these newly desegregated settings, one new challenge consists of building "safe spaces" that do not become stigmatized as "separatist." U.S. Black women who find ourselves integrating corporations and colleges encounter new forms of racism and sexism that require equally innovative responses. A new rhetoric of color-blindness that reproduces social inequalities by treating people the same (Crenshaw 1997) makes it more difficult to maintain safe spaces at all. Any group that organizes around its own self-interests runs the risk of being labeled "separatist," "essentialist," and antidemocratic. This protracted attack on so-called identity politics works to suppress historically oppressed groups that aim to craft independent political agendas around identities of race, gender, class, and/or sexuality.

Within this climate, African-American women are increasingly asked why we want to "separate" ourselves from Black men and why feminism cannot speak for all women, including us. In essence, these queries challenge the need for distinctive Black women's communities as *political* entities. Black women's organizations devoted to cooking, nails, where to find a good babysitter, and other apolitical topics garner little attention. But how do Black women as a collectivity resist intersecting oppressions as they affect us without organizing as a group? How do U.S. Black women identify the specific issues associated with controlling images of Black womanhood without safe spaces where we can talk freely?

One reason that safe spaces are so threatening to those who feel excluded, and so routinely castigated by them, is that safe spaces are free of surveillance by more powerful groups. Such spaces simultaneously remove Black women from surveillance and foster the conditions for Black women's independent self-definitions. When institutionalized, these self-definitions become foundational to politicized Black feminist standpoints. Thus, much more is at stake here than the simple expression of voice.

A broader climate that aims to suppress political speech among African-American women, among others, has affected the organization of historically safe spaces within Black civil society.

Relationships among Black women, within families, and within Black community organizations all must contend with the new realities and rhetoric that characterize an unfulfilled racial and gender desegregation in the context of increasingly antagonistic class relationships.

The blues tradition in Black women's music also remains under assault under these new social conditions. Traditionally, Black women blues singers drew upon traditions of struggle in order to produce "progressive art." Such art was emancipatory because it fused thought, feeling, and action and helped Black women among others to see their world differently and act to change it. More recently, commodification of the blues and its transformation into marketable crossover music have virtually stripped it of its close ties to African-American oral traditions. Considerable controversy surrounds the issue of how to assess the diverse genres of contemporary Black music. As Angela Davis observes, "Some of the superstars of popular-musical culture today are unquestionably musical geniuses, but they have distorted the Black music tradition by brilliantly developing its form while ignoring its content of struggle and freedom" (1989, 208). Black literary critic Sondra O'Neale suggests that similar processes of depoliticization may be affecting Black women's writing. "Where are the Angela Davises, Ida B. Wellses, and Daisy Bateses of black feminist literature?" she asks (1986, 144).

Contemporary African-American musicians, writers, cultural critics, and intellectuals function in a dramatically different political economy than that of any prior generation. It remains to be seen whether the specialized thought generated by contemporary Black feminist thinkers in very different institutional locations is capable of creating safe spaces that will carry African-American women even further.

CONSCIOUSNESS AS A SPHERE OF FREEDOM

Traditionally, when taken together, Black women's relationships with one another, the Black women's blues tradition, and the work of Black women writers provided the context for crafting alternatives to prevailing images of Black womanhood. These sites offered safe spaces that nurtured the everyday and specialized thought of African-American women. In them Black women intellectuals could construct ideas and experiences that infused daily life with new meaning. These new meanings offered African-American women potentially powerful tools to resist the controlling images of Black womanhood. Far from being a secondary concern in bringing about social change, challenging controlling images and replacing them with a Black women's standpoint constituted an essential component in resisting intersecting oppressions (Thompson-Cager 1989). What have been some of the important ideas that developed in these safe spaces? Moreover, how useful are these ideas in responding to the greatly changed social context that confronts U.S. Black women?

The importance of self-definition

"Black groups digging on white philosophies ought to consider the source. Know who's playing the music before you dance," cautions poet Nikki Giovanni (1971, 126). Her advice is especially germane for African-American women. Giovanni suggests: "We Black women are the single group in the West intact. And anybody can see we're pretty shaky. We are . . . the only group that derives its identity from itself. I think it's been rather unconscious but we measure ourselves by ourselves, and I think that's a practice we can ill afford to lose" (1971, 144). When Black women's very survival is at stake, creating independent self-definitions becomes essential to that survival.

The issue of the journey from internalized oppression to the "free mind" of a self-defined, womanist consciousness has been a prominent theme in the works of U.S. Black women writers. Author Alexis DeVeaux notes that there is a "great exploration of the self in women's work. It's the self in relationship with an intimate other, with the community, the nation and the world" (in Tate 1983, 54). Far from being a narcissistic or trivial concern, this placement of self at the center of analysis is critical for understanding a host of other relationships. DeVeaux continues, "you have to understand what your place as an individual is and the place of the person who is close to you. You have to understand the space between you before you can understand more complex or larger groups" (p. 54).

Black women have also stressed the importance of self-definition as part of the journey from victimization to a free mind in their blues. Sherley Anne Williams's analysis of the affirmation of self in the blues makes a critical contribution in understanding the blues as a Black women's text. In discussing the blues roots of Black literature, Williams notes, "The assertion of individuality and the implied assertion—as action, not mere verbal statement—of self is an important dimension of the blues" (1979, 130).

The assertion of self usually comes at the end of a song, after the description or analysis of the troublesome situation. This affirmation of self is often the only solution to that problem or situation. Nina Simone's (1985) classic blues song "Four Women" illustrates this use of the blues to affirm self. Simone sings of three Black women whose experiences typify controlling images: Aunt Sarah, the mule, whose back is bent from a lifetime of hard work; Sweet Thing, the Black prostitute who will belong to anyone who has money to buy; and Saphronia, the mulatto whose Black mother was raped late one night. Simone explores Black women's objectification as the Other by invoking the pain these three women actually feel. But Peaches, the fourth woman, is an especially powerful figure, because Peaches is angry. "I'm awfully bitter these days," Peaches cries out, "because my parents were slaves." These words and the feelings they invoke demonstrate her growing awareness and self-definition of the situation she encountered.

They offer to the listener not sadness and remorse, but an anger that leads to action. This is the type of individuality Williams means—not that of talk but self-definitions that foster action.

While the theme of the journey also appears in the work of Black men, African-American women writers and musicians explore this journey toward freedom in ways that are characteristically female (Thompson-Cager 1989). Black women's journeys, though at times embracing political and social issues, basically take personal and psychological forms and rarely reflect the freedom of movement of Black men who hop "trains," "hit the road," or in other ways physically travel in order to find that elusive sphere of freedom from racial oppression. Instead, Black women's journeys often involve "the transformation of silence into language and action" (Lorde 1984, 40). Typically tied to children and/or community, fictional Black women characters, especially those created prior to the 1990s, search for self-definition within close geographical boundaries. Even though physical limitations confine the Black heroine's quest to a specific area, "forming complex personal relationships adds depth to her identity quest in lieu of geographical breadth" (Tate 1983, xxi). In their search for self-definition and the power of a free mind, Black heroines may remain "motionless on the outside . . . but inside?"

Given the physical limitations on Black women's mobility, the conceptualization of self that has been part of Black women's self-definitions is distinctive. Self is not defined as the increased autonomy gained by separating oneself from others. Instead, self is found in the context of family and community—as Paule Marshall describes it, "the ability to recognize one's continuity with the larger community" (Washington 1984, 159). By being accountable to others, African-American women develop more fully human, less objectified selves. Sonia Sanchez points to this version of self by stating, "We must move past always focusing on the 'personal self' because there's a larger self. There's a 'self' of black people" (Tate 1983, 134). Rather than defining self in opposition to others, the connectedness among individuals provides Black women deeper, more meaningful self-definitions.[6]

This journey toward self-definition has political significance. As Mary Helen Washington observes, Black women who struggle to "forge an identity larger than the one society would force upon them . . . are aware and conscious, and that very consciousness is potent" (1980, xv). Identity is not the goal but rather the point of departure in the process of self-definition. In this process Black women journey toward an understanding of how our personal lives have been fundamentally shaped by intersecting oppressions of race, gender, sexuality, and class. Peaches's statement, "I'm awfully bitter these days because my parents were slaves," illustrates this transformation.

This particular expression of the journey toward self-definition offers a powerful challenge to the externally defined, controlling images of African-American women. Replacing negative images with positive ones can be equally problematic if the function of stereotypes as controlling images remains unrecognized. John Gwaltney's (1980) interview with Nancy White, a 73-year-old Black woman, suggests that ordinary Black women can be acutely aware of the power of these controlling images. To Nancy White the difference between the controlling images applied to African-American and White women is one of degree, not of kind:

> My mother used to say that the black woman is the white man's mule and the white woman is his dog. Now, she said that to say this: we do the heavy work and get beat whether we do it well or not. But the white woman is closer to the master and he pats them on the head and lets them sleep in the house, but he ain't gon' treat neither one like he was dealing with a person.

(p. 148)

Although both groups are objectified, albeit in different ways, the images function to dehumanize and control both groups. Seen in this light, it makes little sense in the long run for Black women to exchange one set of controlling images for another even if positive stereotypes bring better treatment in the short run.

The insistence on Black women's self-definitions reframes the entire dialogue from one of protesting the technical accuracy of an image—namely, refuting the Black matriarchy thesis—to one stressing the power dynamics underlying the very process of definition itself. By insisting on self-definition, Black women question not only what has been said about African-American women but the credibility and the intentions of those possessing the power to define. When Black women define ourselves, we clearly reject the assumption that those in positions granting them the authority to interpret our reality are entitled to do so. Regardless of the actual content of Black women's self-definitions, the act of insisting on Black female self-definition validates Black women's power as human subjects.

Self-valuation and respect

Self-definition speaks to the power dynamics involved in rejecting externally defined, controlling images of Black womanhood. In contrast, the theme of Black women's self-valuation addresses the actual content of these self-definitions. Many of the controlling images applied to African-American women are actually distorted renderings of those aspects of our behavior that threaten existing power arrangements (Gilkes 1983a; D. White 1985). For example, strong mothers are threatening because they contradict prevailing definitions of femininity. To ridicule strong, assertive Black mothers by labeling them matriarchs reflects an effort to control a dimension of Black women's behavior that threatens the status quo. African-American women who value those aspects of Black womanhood that are stereotyped, ridiculed, and maligned in scholarship and the popular media challenge some of the basic ideas inherent in an ideology of domination.

The emphasis that Black feminist thinkers have placed on respect illustrates the significance of self-valuation. In a society in which no one is obligated to respect African-American women, we have long admonished one another to have self-respect and to demand the respect of others. Black women's voices from a variety of sources reflect this demand for respect. Katie G. Cannon (1988) suggests that Black womanist ethics embraces three basic dimensions: "invisible dignity," "quiet grace," and "unstated courage," all qualities essential for self-valuation and self-respect. Black feminist critic Claudia Tate (1983) reports that the issue of self-esteem is so primary in the writing of Black women that it deserves special attention. Tate claims that what the writers seem to be saying is, "Women must assume responsibility for strengthening their self-esteem by learning to love and appreciate themselves" (p. xxiii). Her analysis is certainly borne out in Alice Walker's comments to an audience of women. Walker cautioned, "Please remember, especially in these times of group-think and the right-on chorus, that no person is your friend (or kin) who demands your silence, or denies your right to grow and be perceived as fully blossomed as you were intended. Or who belittles in any fashion the gifts you labor so to bring into the world" (Walker 1983, 36). The right to be Black *and* female *and* respected pervades everyday conversations among African-American women. In describing the importance self-respect has for her, elderly domestic worker Sara Brooks notes, "I may not have as much as you, I may not have the education you got, but still, if I conduct myself as a decent person, I'm just as good as anybody" (Simonsen 1986, 132).

Respect from others—especially from Black men—has been a recurring theme in Black women's writing. In describing the things a woman wants out of life, middle-class Marita Bonner lists "a career as fixed and as calmly brilliant as the North Star. The one real thing that money buys. Time . . . . And of course, a husband you can look up to without looking down on yourself" (Bonner 1987, 3). Black women's belief in respect also emerges in the works of a variety of Black women blues singers. One of the best-known popular statements of Black women's demand for self-respect and the respect of others is found in Aretha Franklin's (1967) rendition of the Otis Redding song "Respect." Aretha sings to her man:

> What you want? Baby I got it.
> What you need? You know I got it.
> All I'm asking for is a little respect when you come home.

Even though the lyrics can be sung by anyone, they take on special meaning when sung by Aretha in the way that she sings them. On one level the song functions as a metaphor for the condition of African-Americans in a racist society. But Aretha's being a Black *woman* enables the song to tap a deeper meaning. Within the blues tradition, the listening audience of African-American women assumes "we" Black women, even though Aretha as the blues singer sings "I." Sherley Anne Williams describes the power of Aretha's blues: "Aretha was right on time, but there was also something about the way Aretha characterized respect as something given with force and great effort and cost. And when she even went so far as to spell the word 'respect,' we just knew that this sister wasn't playing around about getting Respect and keeping it" (Williams 1979, 124).

June Jordan suggests that this emphasis on respect is tied to a distinctive Black feminist politic. For Jordan, a "morally defensible Black feminism" is verified in the ways U.S. Black women present ourselves to others, and in the ways Black women treat people different from ourselves. While self-respect is essential, respect for others is key. "As a Black feminist," claims Jordan, "I cannot be expected to respect what somebody else calls self-love if that concept of self-love requires my suicide to any degree" (1981, 144).

Self-reliance and independence

In her 1831 essay Black feminist thinker Maria Stewart not only encouraged Black women's self-definition and self-valuations but linked Black women's self-reliance with issues of survival:

> We have never had an opportunity of displaying our talents; therefore the world thinks we know nothing . . . . Possess the spirit of independence. The Americans do, and why should not you? Possess the spirit of men, bold and enterprising, fearless and undaunted: Sue for your rights and privileges . . . . You can but die if you make the attempt; and we shall certainly die if you do not.
>
> (Richardson 1987, 38)

Whether by choice or circumstance, African-American women have "possessed the spirit of independence," have been self-reliant, and have encouraged one another to value this vision of womanhood that clearly challenges prevailing notions of femininity (Steady 1987). These beliefs have found wide support among African-American women. For example, when asked what they admired about their mothers, the women in Gloria Joseph's (1981) study of Black mother/daughter relationships recounted their mothers' independence and ability to provide in the face of difficulties. Participants in Lena Wright Myers's (1980) study of Black women's coping skills respected women who were resourceful and self-reliant. Black women's autobiographies, such as Shirley Chisholm's *Unbought and Unbossed* (1970) and Maya Angelou's *I Know Why the Caged Bird Sings* (1969), typify Black women's self-valuation of self-reliance. As elderly domestic worker Nancy White cogently explains, "Most black women can be their own boss, so that's what they be" (Gwaltney 1980, 149).

The works of prominent Black women blues singers also counsel the importance of self-reliance and independence for African-American women. In her classic ballad "God Bless the Child That Got His Own," Billie Holiday sings:

> The strong gets more, while the weak ones fade,
> Empty pockets don't ever make the grade;
> Mama may have, Papa may have,
> But God bless the child that got his own!
>
> (*Billie Holiday Anthology* 1976, 12)

In this mournful song Billie Holiday offers an insightful analysis of the need for autonomy and self-reliance. "Money, you got lots of friends, crowdin' 'round the door," she proclaims. But "when you're gone and spendin' ends they don't come no more." In these passages Holiday admonishes Black women to become financially independent because having one's "own" allows women to choose their relationships.

The linking of economic self-sufficiency as one critical dimension of self-reliance with the demand for respect permeates Black feminist thought. For example, in "Respect" when Aretha sings, "Your kisses sweeter than honey, but guess what, so is my money," she demands respect on the basis of her economic self-reliance. Perhaps this connection between respect, self-reliance, and assertiveness is best summarized by Nancy White, who declares, "There is a very few black women that their husbands can pocketbook to death because we can do for ourselves and will do so in a minute!" (Gwaltney 1980, 149).

Self, change, and personal empowerment

"The master's tools will never dismantle the master's house. They may allow us temporarily to beat him at his own game, but they will never enable us to bring about genuine change" (Lorde 1984, 112). In this passage Audre Lorde explores how independent self-definitions empower Black women to bring about social change. By struggling for self-defined womanist perspectives that reject the "master's" images, African-American women change ourselves. A critical mass of individuals with a changed consciousness can in turn foster Black women's collective empowerment. A changed consciousness encourages people to change the conditions of their lives.

Nikki Giovanni illuminates these connections among self, change, and personal empowerment. She admonishes that people are rarely powerless, no matter how stringent the restrictions on our lives: "We've got to live in the real world. If we don't like the world we're living in, change it. And if we can't change it, we change ourselves. We can do something" (in Tate 1983, 68). Giovanni recognizes that effective change occurs through action. The multiple strategies of resistance that Black women have employed, such as withdrawing from postemancipation agricultural work in order to return their labor to their families, ostensibly conforming to the deference rituals of domestic work, protesting male bias in African-American organizations, or creating the progressive art of Black women's blues all represent actions designed to bring about change. Here is the connected self and the individual empowerment that comes from change in the context of community.

But change can also occur in the private, personal space of an individual woman's consciousness. Equally fundamental, this type of change is also personally empowering. Any individual Black woman who is forced to remain "motionless on the outside," can develop the "inside" of a changed consciousness as a sphere of freedom. Becoming personally empowered through self-knowledge, even within conditions that severely limit one's ability to act, is essential. In Black women's literature

> this type of change . . . occurs because the heroine recognizes, and more importantly respects her inability to alter a situation . . . . This is not to imply that she is completely circumscribed by her limitations. On the contrary, she learns to exceed former boundaries but only as a direct result of knowing where they lie. In this regard, she teaches her readers a great deal about constructing a meaningful life in the midst of chaos and contingencies, armed with nothing more than her intellect and emotions.
>
> (Tate 1983, xxiv)

In this passage Claudia Tate demonstrates the significance of rearticulation, namely, redefining social realities by combining familiar ideas in new ways (Omi and Winant 1994, 163). But rearticulation does not mean reconciling womanist ethics with typically opposed Eurocentric masculinist ones. Instead, as Chezia Thompson-Cager contends, rearticulation "confronts them in the tradition of 'naming as power' by revealing them very carefully" (1989, 590). Naming daily life by applying language to everyday experience infuses it with the new meaning of a womanist consciousness. Naming becomes a way of transcending the limitations of intersecting oppressions.

Black women's literature contains many examples of how individual Black women become personally empowered by a changed consciousness. Barbara Christian maintains that the heroines of 1940s Black women's literature, such as Lutie Johnson in Ann Petry's *The Street* (1946) and Cleo Judson in Dorothy West's *The Living Is Easy* (1948), are defeated not only by social reality but by their "lack of self-knowledge." In contrast, the heroines from the 1950s to the present represent a significant shift toward self-knowledge as a sphere of freedom. Christian dates the shift from Gwendolyn Brooks's *Maud Martha* (1953) and claims, "Because Maud Martha constructs her own standards, she manages to transform that 'little life' into so much more despite the limits set on her . . . . [She] emerges neither crushed nor triumphant" (1985, 176).

According to many African-American women writers, no matter how oppressed an individual woman may be, the power to save the self lies within the self. Other Black women may assist a Black woman in this journey toward personal empowerment, but the ultimate responsibility for self-definitions and self-valuations lies within the individual woman herself. An individual woman may use multiple strategies in her quest for the constructed knowledge of an independent voice. Like Celie in Alice Walker's *The Color Purple*, some women write themselves free. Sexually, physically, and emotionally abused, Celie writes letters to God when no one else will listen. The act of acquiring a voice through writing, of breaking silence with language, eventually moves her to the action of talking with others. Other women talk themselves free. In *Their Eyes Were Watching God*, Janie tells her story to a good friend, a prime example of the rearticulation process essential for Black feminist thought (Hurston 1937). Ntozake Shange's *For Colored Girls* (1975) also captures this journey toward self-definition, self-valuation, and an empowered self. At the end of the play the women gather around one woman who speaks of the pain she experienced at seeing her children killed. They listen until she says, "I found God in myself and I loved her fiercely." These words, expressing her ability to define herself as worthwhile, draw them together. They touch one another as part of a Black women's community that heals the member in pain, but only after she has taken the first step of wanting to be healed, of wanting to make the journey toward finding the voice of empowerment.

Does Black women's consciousness still matter?

Despite the persistence of these four ideas about consciousness—the importance of self-definition, the significance of self-valuation and respect, the necessity of self-reliance and independence, and the centrality of a changed self to personal empowerment—these themes do not find a prominent place in much U.S. Black feminist thought within academia. Sadly, Black women intellectuals in the academy find themselves pressured to write for academic audiences, most of which remain resistant to including U.S. Black women as students, faculty, and administrators. However interested highly educated, middle-class, White male and female academic audiences may be in Black women's intellectual production, their concerns differ markedly from those of the majority of U.S. Black women.

Despite this context, many Black women intellectuals within academia still explore this theme of consciousness, but do so in new and often highly important ways. Take, for example, criminologist Beth Richie's (1996) book *Compelled to Crime: The Gender Entrapment of Battered Black Women*. Through interviews with women who were being detained in jail, Richie advances the innovative thesis that those Black women who had been self-reliant and independent as children and thus imagined themselves as strong Black women were *more* likely to be battered than those who did not. Upon first glance, this is a curious combination—the more self-reliant simultaneously value themselves less. Richie's explanation is revealing. The strong Black women saw themselves as personal failures if they sought help. In contrast, those women who did not carry the burden of this seemingly positive image of Black womanhood found it easier to ask for help. Richie's study points to the significance of external definitions of all types. By attending to heterogeneity among Black women, her work creates space for new self-valuations to appear that need not be attached to images of strong Black women.

The increased scholarly attention to Black adolescent girls should reveal new reactions to intersecting oppressions among a population that has come of age under new social conditions. Within this tradition, *Sugar in the Raw* (1997), Rebecca Carroll's 15 published interviews from more than 50 that she conducted among U.S. Black girls provides a glimpse into the consciousness of contemporary Black girls. Despite elements of Black popular culture that bombard them with images of sexualized women and the plethora of "hoochies" populating music videos, many of the girls display an impressive maturity. Take, for example, 18-year-old Kristen's reflections on her struggles for self-valuation brought on by her crush on a Black boy who seemed unaware that she existed:

> It was obvious and evident that most if not all of the black boys in my school wanted nothing to do with black girls, which was sort of traumatizing. You can't really come away from an experience like that without feeling like there is something wrong with you. In the final analysis, I ended up feeling that there was something wrong with him, but it was hell getting there.

(Carroll 1997, 131–32)

The increased attention in Black feminist-influenced scholarship paid to Black women's pain in abusive relationships of all sorts, and to the special concerns of Black adolescent girls both seem designed to create new intellectual and political space for the "hellish" journeys that many Black women still encounter. At least at this historic moment, the need to put up a united front seems less important than exploring the various ways that individual Black women are personally empowered and disempowered, even within allegedly safe spaces. Consciousness still matters, but it becomes one that acknowledges the complexities of crosscutting relations of race, gender, class, and sexuality.

Weaving throughout these historic and contemporary efforts at self-definition is the quest to move from silence to language to individual and group action. In this quest, persistence is a fundamental requirement for this journey. Black women's persistence is fostered by the strong belief that to be Black and female is valuable and worthy of respect. In the song "A Change Is Gonna Come," Aretha Franklin (1967) expresses this feeling of enduring despite the odds. She sings that there were times that she thought that she would not last for long. She sings of how it has been an "uphill journey all the way" to find the strength to carry on. But despite the difficulties, Aretha "knows" that "a change is gonna come."

Whether individual struggles to develop a changed consciousness or the group persistence needed to transform social institutions, actions that bring about changes empower African-American women. By persisting in the journey toward self-definition, as individuals, we are changed. When linked to group action, our individual struggles gain new meaning. Because our actions as individuals change the world from one in which we merely exist to one over which we have some control, they enable us to see everyday life as being in process and therefore amenable to change. Perhaps that is why so many African-American women have managed to persist and "make a way out of no way." Perhaps they knew the power of self-definition.

Making Sense of Race, Class, Gender

THE DISCURSIVE CONSTRUCTION OF CLASS

by Celine-Marie Pascale

Celine-Marie Pascale, "Making Sense of Race, Class, Gender: The Discursive Construction of Class," Excerpted and Adapted from *Making Sense of Race, Class and Gender: Commonsense Power and Privilege in the U.S.*, pp. 79-108. Copyright © 2008 by Taylor & Francis Group. Reprinted with permission.

The gap between rich and poor in the United States has arguably exceeded the capacity to sustain meaningful democracy. Congressional Budget Office data show that, after adjusting for inflation, the average after-tax income of the top one percent of the population rose by $576,000—or 201 percent—between 1979 and 2000; the average income of the middle fifth of households rose $5,500, or 15 percent; and the average income of the bottom fifth rose $1,100, or 9 percent (Center on Budget and Policy Priorities 2003).[1] In daily, life this disparity is embodied in the struggles of African American, Native American, Native Alaskan, and Hispanic families that, according to the U.S. Census, have *median* household incomes $10–20,000 below government-based calculations for self-sufficiency. The disparity also is embodied in the struggles faced by 40 percent of poor single-parent working mothers who paid at least half of their income for child care in 2001(Center on Budget and Policy Priorities 2003); in the struggles of 4.9 million families who paid half of their income in rent in 2002 (National Alliance to End Homelessness 2002); and, in the struggles of more than 3.7 million adults with disabilities living on federal Supplemental Security Income (SSI), which now provides less than one-third the income needed for one-bedroom apartment (O'Hara and Cooper 2003:11). Minimum-wage workers, in 2002, were unable to afford a one-bedroom apartment in any city in the nation. If the increase in poverty is apparent, the tremendous increase in wealth accruing to the top 1% of the population is more extremely hard to track. While conditions of poverty may make the evening news, thorough reports on conditions of affluence are more unusual. The affluence and poverty that variously shape life in the United States are not part of a sustained or routine public conversation. In the United States, economic inequality—arguably one of the most *material* sites of 'difference'—is often one of the least visible.

If commonsense leads people to believe that we can recognize race and gender on sight, even if we might sometimes find ourselves confused or mistaken, commonsense about class operates quite differently. While people living in the extreme poverty of homeless make class visually recognizable, generally class is not apparent "just by looking" at a person, or in passing encounters. The presence of people who are homeless is arguably the most consistently clear display of class in daily life. If the observable presence of race and gender means that each can be made relevant at potentially any moment, the relative invisibility of class renders it far less likely to be made relevant.

I do not mean to suggest that wealth and poverty are simply a matter of language and representation but rather, I argue that because material conditions and discursive practices are not distinct, understandings of class need to be rooted to language, as well as economics. All objects and events are made meaningful through language. An earthquake may be understood as a geological phenomenon or an act of god; a stone may be a marker, a sculpture, or geological evidence, depending on the meaning we give to it (Hall 1997). We must interpret experience in order for it to become meaningful. The cultural discourses that enable people in the U.S. to make sense of wealth and poverty cannot be separated from the material conditions of that production. While the word "discourse" often is used as a synonym for "talk," here it has a more specialized meaning. Discourses are cultural frameworks for understanding what knowledge is useful, relevant or true in a specific context. For example, a scientific discourse enables scientists to 'recognize' a stone as a kind of geological evidence.

In my initial analysis of interviews, talk about class appeared to be so completely dislocated from economics as to lack *any* concrete mooring. Indeed, everyday assumptions about class appeared to be idiosyncratic. Scholars have often raised the specter of "false consciousness" to describe a lack of class-consciousness. Yet it is important to recall there was a time in U.S. history when cogent class analyses shaped public discourse. The disappearance of public discourse cannot be separated from a class history shaped by the U.S. government's consistent willingness to use deadly violence against workers and unions through deployment of the National Guard and federal troops between 1870 and 1930. Although we 'forget' it, we begin talking about wealth and poverty within a pre-existing discourse shaped by class struggle.

We live in a country that appears to be devoted to the ideal of democratic equality, yet is divided by disparities that are produced through a commitment to competitive prosperity. I begin by focusing my analysis on the simple questions: In what ways, and on what terms, does commonsense knowledge make class positions (our own and others) recognizable? In order for class differences to be generally invisible, there must be a systematic detachment between the social displays and economic productions of class. How is that people recognize, or fail to recognize, themselves and others as members of socio-economic classes? I examine how commonsense knowledge about class in the United States leads people to engage in practices that systematically disorganize the presence of social and economic capital. By analyzing commonsense understandings of class, I unsettle economic determinism and move toward more complex, fluid conceptualizations that incorporate discursive aspects of class.

Belonging to the Middle Class

Most people I interviewed characterized themselves as middle-class—regardless of whether they were multimillionaires or blue-collar workers. While this might strike readers as itself a matter of commonsense, rather than as a point of analytic interest, it is possible to understand this information as something more than a cliché. Toward that end, let me begin by saying that four of the five multimillionaires I interviewed characterized themselves as middle class and asserted that perceptions of them as wealthy were mistaken. (I will come back to this exception a bit later.) For example, Brady, a white attorney specializing in estate planning explained: "I guess we define class by wealth since we don't have nobility here. So [. . .] I guess I'm in the middle, based our tests, our society, probably middle class."[2] I found it difficult to think of Brady, with assets of nearly $5 million dollars, as "in the middle" of the economic spectrum. As Brady continued, he described upper-class people as "pretentious" and added: "I don't feel class is that important and I don't care for folks who think it is." Brady's dismissal of class is not so much a denial of his wealth but a dismissal of the "folks" who make wealth the measure of a person. Similarly, Polard, a white commercial real estate developer, distinguished his wealth from his personality. He talked about himself as "middle class" and called himself "an average kinda joe" who "eats hamburgers at McDonalds." Polard did not just call himself 'average' but invoked a discourse that links him to a certain kind of masculinity. Polard elaborated: "I don't feel a connection to I guess what one would consider upper class. I don't feel connected to that. You know, my friends—my relationships—and that, are middle America." Throughout the interview

Polard, reinforced a distinction between the kind of person he is and the wealth that he has. For instance, Polard said:

> When uh you live in this house [. . .] the average person driving down the street will view the big house with all the land sitting on an expensive street, [and think] he must be very rich. But I mean that's not me, it isn't my personality. [. . .] I'm just an ordinary kinda guy.

Polard is not denying his wealth; on the exit interview form, he valued his assets at over $100 million. Yet Polard displaces economic considerations of class by centering personal values. From eating at McDonald's to his personal relationships, Polard lays claim to a *class* identity that stands apart, or is made to stand apart, from his wealth.

Polard and Brady talk about "being middle-class" as being *a particular kind of person*—rather than as being a particular level of income or assets. Certainly, the routine nature of daily life leads most people to think of themselves as average (Sacks 1992). While it would be quite easy to press the claim that Polard is deluding himself (or me) by characterizing himself as "middle class," such a claim would foreclose important questions. In particular, on what terms, or in what contexts, do people characterize themselves by a *class* category that is independent of their economic resources? How might such misrecognition of class (willful or not) create a cultural quarantine that prevents critical questions, and opposing interpretations, from arising, or being seriously engaged?

While the rhetoric people invoke when talking about class may be race and/or gender specific (eg., "an average joe"), I sought and examined patterns of commonsense about class that transcended boundaries of race and gender. So, it is important to note that white men were not the only multimillionaires to characterize themselves as middle class. Two women, one Latina and one American Indian, who were self-made multimillionaires expressed similar sentiments. Marisol Alegria owned two burger franchises at the time of our interview. Marisol explained:

> In the community here, um, I find that there's a lotta respect for that [owning and operating fast food franchises]. Sometimes it's a misconceived respect, I think, an' especially in my case, because the perception is, "Oh my gosh, there's a lady that must be a multimillionaire." Or, you know, "That lady's just making beaucoup bucks," you know, and—and that kind of a thing. But it really, um—and there ARE some out there. I mean, because most of my counterparts throughout, are REALLY in the big buck category.

Marisol talks about herself as the object of "misconceived respect" based on a false perception. Yet, she is a self-made multimillionaire with assets just under $10 million. It seems possible that Marisol can argue that perceptions of her as wealthy are "misconceived" by comparing herself to even wealthier peers. Certainly, "beaucoup bucks" and "big bucks" are relative terms that avoid any fixed notion of wealth. However, Marisol also resists being perceived by others as a multimillionaire—a very specific category and one that is consistent with her own characterization of her assets. It seems unlikely then that Marisol is invoking a purely relative notion of wealth, or that she is trying to conceal her wealth in the interview. Since Marisol objects to the *perception* of her as a multimillionaire, it seems possible that she does not believe that she is *recognizable* as a multimillionaire—that in social environments she does not stand out as different. It is not just that class, seen from within, can be imagined to be invisible but that *markers of class can be disorganized in such a way as to make class unintelligible*. Indeed, Marisol later talked about the care that she takes with her appearance so that she does not stand out.

> Marisol: I have a wonderful, and I really feel very good about this, I have a wonderful experience at mixing very well. I could be with the richest of the rich and not drop the beat, not feel intimidated, or uncomfortable. Celine-Marie: Mmhm
> Marisol: You know, I know that I have an outfit or two that would wear just as well. And if were going to . . . uh, one of my employee's baptismals, out in Las Viejas I know that I could wear, you know, something there to not intimidate or feel . . . you know, as though I'm out of . . . out of class there Celine-Marie: Mmhmm
> Marisol: or would intimidate the guests or anything else.
> Celine-Marie: Mmhmm
> Marisol: I think I can do that very well. So . . . for that reason, I think I . . . I just kinda . . . mesh very well.

Here one can better see why Marisol might object to the *perception* that she is a multimillionaire. Marisol talks about herself as someone in the middle. She can socialize with the "richest of the rich" and not "feel intimidated" and can attend a social gathering hosted by one of her fast food employees without intimidating the other guests. Marisol talks about class as a social category based on interaction; to intimidate or be intimidated is "to be out of class."

Lorraine Doe, an American Indian who worked as a tribal administrator, also talked about herself as being middle class based on being an "average" person. At the time of our interview, she held assets of over $500 million dollars. It is not just that Marisol, Lorraine, Polard, and Brady think of class in purely personal terms but that in order to maintain their 'ordinariness,' they *must* think of class in this way. And in this sense their personal identity as ordinary people is in conflict with a class location based on extraordinary wealth.

In order to produce and maintain the appearance of a class identity, people must understand and manipulate complex meanings attached to work, wealth, consumer goods and other commodified cultural forms. Recall, for instance, that Polard described himself as "an average joe who eats hamburgers at McDonalds" and Brady referred to "folks" rather than to "people."

Outside of the Middle Class

Among the five multimillionaires I interviewed, Charlie Chin, a land and business developer, stood as the exception. Charlie identified himself as a first-generation Chinese-American and talked about himself as anything BUT ordinary. Charlie, with assets over $10 million, was the only multimillionaire to categorize himself as "around the top" in terms of class. He described himself as a person who enjoys socializing among university presidents, hospital administrators, and government officials. Whereas other multimillionaires articulated a gap between the way others might perceive them based on wealth, and the kind of person they really are, Charlie made no such distinction. Charlie was also the only multimillionaire to talk about wealth as a means to overcome the vulnerabilities racism, immigration, and poverty. For instance, Charlie explained:

> I think that if you were a Mexican or Chinese immigrant and you don't have a great command of the language or let's say you have a command of the language but you slip up a little bit with your words or your tenses, things like that and you go to a hospital . . . you're treated differently than if I go in there. [. . .]

> So I'll go into the hospital and I'll KNOW the doctor. Ok? Or, I'll know the other doctors there. I'll know the HEAD of the HOSPITAL. Ok? [. . .] Whereas if you go in and you look like you don't belong or you can't pay your bill or um or you're not going to cause them a problem if they leave an instrument in your stomach or something like that . . . it's just, it's just COMPLETELY different. [. . .] I think you will live longer. [. . .] I think you will be cheated less, you will be treated with more respect, you will get faster service and they will make sure that YOU don't die. [. . .] That's why I work hard so I can take care of myself and my family and my extended family [big inhale] in that, in that manner. Also I KNOW that that's rotten and so I like to do things so that everybody gets a certain type of respect and care and consideration, too. Because what kind of society do you live in if it's too, too far that way?

Charlie Chin's strong identification with the experiences of immigrants, racism and poverty produces *disidentification* with dominant class discourse, even as he celebrates the benefits of wealth. Disidentification is more than a lack of identification; it is a process of challenging a dominant (i.e., hegemonic) discourse in ways that expose what the hegemonic discourse conceals. Indeed it is the work of disidentification that makes Charlie Chin's class privilege visible. His celebratory success emerges from a history of legal exclusions in the U.S. that once prevented his parents, aunts, and uncles from the rights of citizenship, property ownership, and fair employment. In addition, Charlie's family was consistently vulnerable to the physical, emotional, and economic violence of racists. While, one might say Charlie Chin is a poster child for the American Dream, in his talk about class, he does not identify with the notions of equality and fairness that permeate the mythology of the American Dream. Nor does he identify with the mythic middle class. Rather, Charlie effectively resists hegemonic class discourses and resituates the competitive prosperity of the American Dream within historical processes of racism and economic oppression. This particular practice of disidentification is possible because class identification is constituted within various, often competing, systems of representation that carry forward different parts of histories.

Excepting Charlie Chin, people who did not identify themselves as middle-class resisted characterizing themselves by class at all—regardless of whether they eventually categorized themselves as above or below 'middle class.' For example, Lana Jacobs, a highly successful artist who held assets of nearly a million dollars at the time of our interview, illustrates this point. Lana continued to make her home and studio in the working-class community of color, where she had lived before her success as an artist. While, she freely characterized herself as an artist, as black, and as a woman, Lana refused to characterize herself by class. Lana explained:

> I guess I am a universal person. I don't see myself fitting into a group. I am not a group-minded kind of person. [. . .] I feel stifled by groups because I have my own . . . my own attitude about uh what I feel what I know I lived. [. . .] I try not to judge. I work on my judgments about people.

Lana talked about class as a voluntary social category—something she could refuse to join. If Lana experiences being a woman, an artist, or black, as a social *fact,* she talks about class as a social *judgment.* However, the unwillingness of the people I interviewed to characterize themselves as wealthy or poor should not be confused with their willingness to characterize others as such. Lana had no difficulty characterizing her grandparents as "a little below middle class." Yet being *a little* above or below the middle is an assessment comparatively free of judgment since to be 'in the middle' is to be like most other people. By contrast, if Lana were to characterize herself by assets and wealth, she would be far more than "a little above" her family and community. By resisting class categorization, Lana implicitly asserts her long-standing connections to family, neighbors, and friends.

Similarly, when I asked Cuauhtemoc, a part-time stock clerk, if he had a class identity, he explained:

> I consider myself a full-blooded Mexican but as far as a class . . . money's not a big thing to me, yeah we need it and everything but you know if it wasn't around or whatever, things would be a lot better. You know uhm . . . I think, I don't really consider myself a class, I think I'm more, I think I'm really . . . how would you say it, privilege who I am and what I have you know, because no, I don't have a lot of money but I have what I need.

Cuauhtemoc advances his identity as "full-blooded Mexican" yet, like Lana, dismisses the importance of class identification. Interestingly he explains that he "privileges" who he is and what he has *because* he doesn't have a lot of money. If "not having a lot of money" conjures images of need or poverty, Cuauhtemoc also quickly dispels those images by saying "I have what I need." The class identifications most readily available to him through U.S. hegemonic discourse would be poor or lower class—identifications more likely to diminish, than enhance, a sense of self.

All of the people I interviewed who experienced daily economic hardship resisted hegemonic class categories, sometimes by inventing new categories. Emerson Piscopo, was unemployed at the time of our interview. He offered a surprising response to my question about class.

> Celine-Marie: Uh-huh. Do you have a class identity?
> Emerson: Uh, meaning where, where I fit in to society?
> Celine-Marie: Mhmm
> Emerson: Um, I guess fore . . . forefront, I'm a transsexual,
> Celine-Marie: Mhmm
> Emerson: transgender, transgender um, I'm since I'm still, I'm it just using hormones right now, and I have had surgery though, a hysterectomy, I guess I'm PART of the way there.

Initially, I was flummoxed by his answer. Had he misunderstood the question? Was he subverting a question he didn't want to answer? Was he refocusing the conversation to a topic more important to him? I came back to the issue later in the interview and reintroduced a question about his class identity. Emerson explained his family's economic circumstances this way:

> I'm starting out, I just, I had that major surgery so I'm not backed by a year's worth of work and it affected us [short pause] financially greatly, and we are both trying to catch up. We're, we're doin' it, but we're struggling, basically. We're in the struggling class. Not, not POOR but somewhere in between poor and okay.

Emerson introduces his family's economic difficulties through news of his surgery and his loss of work; he offers an *explanation* even before mentioning the economic hardship. Emerson talks about "trying to catch up"—indicating that ordinarily, his family had more resources and then frames their efforts to "catch up" as successful, if incomplete. In this way, Emerson is able to describe economic hardship while resisting identification with poverty. He underscores this resistance by saying "Not POOR but somewhere in between poor and okay." Thus Emerson not only defines the conceptual space between being poor and okay as one of personal struggle, he constitutes the meaning of his experience in a broader economic and social context.

If Emerson's response appears to be an anomaly, or a strategy that might adopted only by people in economic transition, consider this exchange with Captain Ahab, a senior partner in a successful law firm:

> Celine-Marie: Uh-huh. Where would you place yourself in terms of class? Captain Ahab: I am first of all an immigrant. I moved to the United States at age six from Canada but um moved from Canada to Florida so it was a fairly long move. And so I arrived in Florida, again you know as an immigrant, and with an accent and so went through that type of displacement. Was exposed to discrimination issues at that age. I can remember very clearly driving through the southern United States and having my parents explain to me uh about the situation involving segregation in the South. This would have been in 1952. [. . .]
> Celine-Marie: That's interesting. Where do you put yourself today in terms of class?
> Ahab: Uh . . . upper-middle class.

Captain Ahab, like Emerson, responded to my question in a way that deferred or deflected a discussion of class. Both men also displaced my question about class identity by responding with features of their identity that each felt to be more central than class: Captain Ahab as an immigrant and Emerson as a transsexual. If class is important to either man, they seem anxious to privilege a representation of self that is not class-based.

When I pursued the conversation about class, Captain Ahab described his class identity this way:

> My wife is superintendent and principal of a school district, a one-school school district. She has a master's degree. I have a BA, an MA and a JD. And probably we're more upper-middle class by education, than by finances. Uh but uh still I think in the overall scale, we'd probably be considered upper-middle class

Ahab underscores education as the determining factor in his assessment of class and then seems to capitulate to an unwanted characterization as upper-middle class. While one might argue that hegemonic notions of class can be produced through education, in Captain Ahab's talk about class, educational attainments are made to eclipse economic ones.

Overall, the people I interviewed understood class as a social judgment, not just an evaluation of someone's economic resources, but of their 'self'. When talking about their own *class* identities, everyone (except Charlie Chin) used discursive practices invoking social criteria that masked, distorted, or rendered invisible, their economic circumstances—even though they each volunteered their income and assets on the interview form. Class—construed in very personal terms, as something social—depends upon corresponding discourses of free will, personal values, and individual choices. In asserting the *primary importance* of a 'me' that stands apart from one's economic conditions, talk about class systematically hid from view the cultural, social, and economic conditions that structure access to jobs, income, and wealth.

Concluding Remarks

At stake in class identities is the capacity for self-recognition (the source of agency) and the capacity of *others* to recognize us—the capacity for collective identities. So it is especially important to note that very discourses through which people articulated class identities disorganized the presence and meaning of social and economic capital. To the extent that people can and do talk about class *as if* it is unrelated to power and wealth, they shrouded the political dimensions of daily life with commonsense knowledge. The discursive production of class obscured the networks of power that emerge through wealth. These networks of power extend beyond resources that are owned to the *potential* to control resources and people. And, in this sense the everyday "doing of class" (West and Fenstermaker 1995), and the discursive formations upon which such doing relies, occluded not only visible displays of wealth and poverty but also the history and politics of class and class struggle.

The discursive practices regarding class constituted that which they purported to describe: the relative irrelevance of class. Hegemonic discourse effectively subverts the capacity for collective identity based on class interests because class subjects are produced through discourses that conceal class positions, interests, and relationships. Class functions as it does in the United States, not because people are engaged in fictional performances of passing or because they are beset by false consciousness. Rather, class must be understood as performative precisely because discourse—as a kind of societal speech—is a practical part of what people think and feel—how we see the world.

The language of class is performative (i.e., constitutive) in that discursive practices produce the appearance of "classlessness" that they purport to describe. The relationship between material economic circumstances and the social meanings of those circumstances are not completely distinct. While capitalism has always relied on global and local relations of production, it also has produced—and required—particular forms of consciousness. Because relations of exploitation are never lived in economic terms alone, understandings of language in general—and discursive practices in particular—are critical to understanding class struggle. As mentioned at the start, we *begin* talking about class within a pre-existing discourse shaped by class struggle. Like all hegemonic discursive practices, the discursive production of class secures institutionalized relations of power. One of the most important goals of power is to prevail in determining the agenda of the struggle, to determine which questions can be raised and on what terms. Class conflict is pre-empted by the hegemonic discursive practices through which class is constituted.

Hegemonic discourse—not material circumstances—shaped class categorizations and subverted the capacity for collective identity/agency based on economic interests. While theories of class offer insight into important aspects of capitalism, within sociology much of this theory is used to reify categories of class and center debates on the adequacy and limitations of various categorization efforts. However, even if one thinks of class in purely economic terms, it exceeds existing frameworks for understanding class. Is it reasonable to think of someone with $450,000 in assets as wealthy? What if those assets are equity accrued through 40 years of real estate inflation on a small house owned by someone who works in a small factory making jewelry? How is one to understand the class position of a person who earns $70,000 a year as an independent contractor in the technology industry and who is unable to afford to buy a home because of inflated housing prices? If working-class jobs once provided workers and others with the ability to buy not only homes and cars but also boats and vacation property, this is no longer the case. Today, even people with upper-income professional careers do not necessarily experience the benefits of what was once considered wealth; rather, many now refer to themselves as "house poor" because all of their income is tied up in homeownership. This is not to equate those who are "house poor" with those who are living on minimum wage in a rented apartment, but to argue that historical categories of class are inadequate for understanding the contemporary distribution of wealth, the kinds of work and remuneration available, and the potential for social justice organizing. We are in need of new ways of conceptualizing class.

Understanding how identity and subjectivity are constituted within language provides an opportunity to re-theorize economic inequalities and the possibilities for social change. The imagined communities of class are not distinguished by truth or falsity but by the styles in which they are imagined which allow us to recognize different parts of our histories, and to construct points of identification.

The work of disindentification requires resituating the politics that personalize poverty and wealth into the historical conditions that make each possible and apparently natural. This would require the remembering of self and others by calling into question the identities we have come to inhabit as members of a "classless" nation. As scholars, one means through which we can advance an agenda of social justice is by working at the constitutive frontiers of language to imagine new socialities, new subjectivities. In the beginning of the 21st century, resistance to hegemonic economic forces in the United States requires an understanding of the performativity of language in relation to material conditions lived experience.

ENDNOTES

1. The Census Bureau does not publish data on the incomes of the top one percent; the Congressional Budget Office supplements Census data with IRS data to capture gains and losses among the top one percent of the population.

2. My racial characterization of interviewees comes from self-identifications on the interview exit form. All names a pseudonyms chosen by the interviewees.

REFERENCES

Hall, Stuart. 1997. "The Work of Representation." Pp. 1–74 in *Representation: Cultural representations and signifying practices*, edited by S. Hall. Thousand Oaks: Sage Publications, Inc.

Homelessness, National Alliance to End. 2002, Retrieved 2005 http://www.endhome-lessness. org/).

O'Hara, Ann and Emily Cooper. 2003, "Priced Out", May. Retrieved July 7, 2005 (http://www. tacinc.org/).

Priorities, Center on Budget and Policy. 2003, "Poverty Increases and Median Income Declines for Second Consecutive Year", Retrieved Fall 2005, 2006 (http://www.cbpp.org/9-26-03pov.htm).

Sacks, Harvey. 1992. "On Doing "Being Ordinary"." Pp. 413–440 in *Structures of Social Action: Studies in conversation analysis*, edited by J. M. Atkinson and J. Heritage. Cambridge: Cambridge University Press.

West, Candace and Sarah Fenstermaker. 1995. "Doing Difference." *Gender and Society* 9:8–37.

Social Class

by Jeff Torlina

A social class is a large group of individuals who share a similar social position based on a set of economic and related resources, and therefore have, in common general living standards, lifestyles, values, and life chances. There are several classes, each with overlapping boundaries, in which people share relatively similar patterns of living along with a similar subculture. This definition begins with such economic concerns as income level and associated resources—such as access to quality education, housing, and rewarding work—and leads into cultural concerns such as tastes in food, music, recreation, consumption, and social ties. It then acknowledges the life chances that differ across class lines, such as the likelihood of divorce, occupational security, mental and physical illness, incarceration, and a host of other structural variables that generally determine the quality of life and the ability to improve one's circumstances.

Social class is most often assigned at birth because children are shaped by the cultural and material standards of their parents and their surrounding communities. Class boundaries are not closed, and people often experience their lives in multiple settings that expose themselves in varying degrees to conflicting class values and tastes. This makes it impossible to clearly distinguish the sets of different class experiences into specific categories that are mutually exclusive and explicitly divided. Even though class boundaries are relatively open and people may live in contradictory class positions that have qualities of classes on either side of the line, the lives of most people are clustered around a set of similar class circumstances that lead to patterned ways of behaving, thinking, and interacting.

Society is divided into classes that make social life a different experience for members of one group or another. It has been that way since civilization began in western societies, and the classes have changed over time to reflect the kind of economy that dominated society in each historical period. Until recently social classes were typically distinguished by the type of occupation a person had along with the education and the economic standing of class members. The most common understanding of class differences regard the upper class as the upper 1% of society who live off investments and wealth, and who occupy the most powerful positions in business and finance. The middle class includes white-collar positions, especially those that require college educations. People with blue-collar jobs and lower-level non-production jobs are in the working class. Those who are chronically unemployed and have little money reside in poverty, or the lower class.

The differences between classes are becoming less obvious in contemporary United States society. As mass media becomes an ever greater part of our daily lives, as our economy becomes increasingly dominated by powerful corporations that supplant locally owned businesses and industries with global franchises and products, as college enrollment becomes more common, and as advertisers look for more creative strategies to inspire us to buy their mass-produced products, citizens appear more homogeneous than ever. The divisions between classes were more apparent in generations past because people of comparable economic means were more likely to live close to one another, to interact with others who had similar living standards, and to have a similar quantity and quality of material things. Differences between classes were more obvious because people lived in homes that identified their class membership in terms of location, size, and decor. They wore clothes that indicated their class identity in terms of cost and function. People's hobbies and leisure activities were limited to those that were shared by others with similar resources and tastes. The kind of food one ate, the stores one patronized, the shoes one wore, the newspapers one read, the church one attended, and the political party one supported were all closely related to the social class that one inhabited. Political values, speech patterns, musical preferences, and consumption patterns were divided along class lines so that class membership was relatively clear.

Mass-produced consumer goods have lowered the relative cost of items to make it easier now for less affluent people to buy the products that used to be inaccessible for everyone except the wealthier classes.

Even those with low incomes are encouraged with easy credit to own the latest product innovations. People no longer have to live in neighborhoods that are close to their employer, allowing those of different class backgrounds to inhabit communities where they may intermingle in the stores and schools and parks that surround their homes. Industrial agriculture has lowered the cost to feed ourselves, freeing up resources to purchase consumer goods that used to be out of reach for most citizens. The news outlets and the television stations are owned by a decreasing number of global corporations, reducing the diversity of information that people are exposed to. Advertisers present images of normalcy to which people of wide-ranging backgrounds should all aspire, creating a uniform standard of style and "must-have" items. We now expect nearly everyone to go to college and, assumedly, attain a white-collar profession. As society becomes more homogeneous in its popular culture and standards of achievement, it may appear that class has lost some of its importance as a descriptive characteristic of contemporary life. That appearance is only on the surface, however. The categories have shifted, but social class remains one of the most influential aspects of our lives.

Consider the values that you hold dear to your heart. They are probably reflective of your class position. The cultures of each different class have alternative expectations for raising children, what to expect from a spouse, our commitment to others in our community, notions of dignity and honor, standards for prestige and respect, definitions of fairness, admiration for certain skills, and many other values that shape our conception of right and wrong. Our tastes in music, food, sports, and recreation also vary by class. It is still a class marker that we like country or classical music, hip-hop or rock and roll, or opera or chamber music. Do you prefer grits and bacon over eggs benedict? Hamburger and french fries over tartare and caviar? Fried chicken over roasted lamb? Do you prefer to go to a baseball game or a polo match? Chances are, knowing the winner of last year's Super Bowl means that you don't know the winner of last year's Masters Tournament. There is a different type of crowd at the bowling league than you will find at the yacht club. These surface-level preferences are listed to illustrate differences in class cultures, but more significant class-based cultural differences will be addressed in this chapter (and by Jensen, 2012; Lareau, 2011; Lindquist, 2002; Lamont, 2000). First we must consider the formal definitions of social class in the social science literature so that we have a standard for comparison and critique of the concept.

Conceptualizing Social Class

Social class is one of several important identity categories that determine our lives. Gender and race are two of the variables that intersect with class to shape life chances and interaction patterns. Scholars have added categories such as nationality and sexuality to the mix of identities that collectively influence people's experiences, but sociologists used to single out class as its primary concern without recognizing the complexity of factors that combine with social class. This reveals the improvements made by recent scholarship over the flawed, narrow perspective of social science in earlier times. For all its recognition and application, social class is still the most misunderstood and misused variable in social research. The concept is essential for understanding social interaction, identity, and individual behavior. At the same time, the way *social class* is defined—like the concepts *race* and *gender*—imbues the term with associations of positive or negative traits. We have to be careful when placing a specific definition on the term "class" because the biases that are inherent in our thinking may alter the way we understand the concept. The way we define *class* makes a tremendous difference in how inequality between the social classes is reproduced across generations. With that in mind, we examine the way class is defined by society and by social science.

Class has traditionally been understood as a multidimensional concept that included the array of cultural influences on behavior, speech patterns, value judgments, identity constructions, tastes, and standards of living, along with the societal limitations of income, education, autonomy, and other relative allotments of resources and life chances. Both the abstract and subjective aspects of the concept made it incompatible with social researchers' need for discrete categories and precise standards of measurement. The development of computers made sophisticated statistical analysis of large-scale survey research possible, but it needed variables whose measurement is compatible with the linear equation models used to examine the data. Quantitative statistical analysis of survey research data made it possible to generalize precise results from a sample to the broader population, and it opened opportunities to draw conclusions about a vast array of social circumstances and their consequences on individuals and groups. To take advantage of the new possibilities for social research, a scale was developed that used objective criteria to define the specific rank of a person on a spectrum of high and low positions. It was reasoned that one's social position is a function of income and educational achievement, and by adding together the scores for those variables, researchers could create a composite score that determined where on the social hierarchy a person was positioned. This simple solution to the problem of measuring class status in survey research led to a transformation in the thinking of scholars about the *meaning* of social class.

Social class was once considered the cultural context for people's view of the world—their social relationships that organized, and even defined, their way of life. People of different classes behaved in ways that reflected alternative cultural expressions that were based in unequal material circumstances. The new method of analysis altered the conceptualization of class by pushing researchers to measure class in a way that fit their mathematical formulas. The new research methods made the complex conception of class obsolete, and class identity became expressed as an index that defined each person's place on a continuum of high or low rank in the social system by the basic determinants of income level and amount of formal education. This limited the depth of understanding about the people of various social classes, and it also classified each position in terms of its relative place on a hierarchy. What mattered about class identity became the status rung of the social ladder on which a person sat, not how a person actively views the world or reacts to its forces. Positions were now clearly categorized as above and beneath each other. Each person could be classified as high or low on the stratified social scale, superior or inferior to others. Social class had always been regarded as a general grouping of people with more or less access to certain resources, and there had always been a recognition that each class position had greater or lesser ability to control political outcomes and acquire assets, but now those broad categories of people who collectively live generally similar lifestyles are regarded as superior or inferior according to very narrow and limited bases for measurement. The mathematical precision by which statistical analysis could be applied to the numerical index hid the biases that determined the hierarchical order of class positions.

The index of income level coupled with median educational attainment allowed Peter Blau and Otis Dudley Duncan to rank occupations on a continuum that determined where each job stood in the occupational structure. Their influential book from 1967, *The American Occupational Structure,* established the questionable criteria of income and education levels as *the* standard for defining which jobs were above or below each other, but that was not all they did to reinforce a biased conception of superiority and inferiority between occupational categories. The book compiles the set of occupational titles into a conceptual model that places farm workers at the bottom of the scale, with blue-collar positions above them in the categories of unskilled manual, semi-skilled manual, and blue-collar craftsmen. Further up the scale, superior to all blue-collar occupations, Blau and Duncan placed the white-collar occupations. This is curious, because up until this point Blau and Duncan had used precise mathematical indicators to determine the relative level at which an occupation was ranked as high or low. There are many reasons to question their use of income and education as the measures of class standing because working-class people value those things in different ways than do people in the white-collar professional class, but even with this standard, Blau and Duncan's formula placed skilled blue-collar workers above retail salesmen on the occupational hierarchy. Blau and Duncan gave no justification, but they decided that blue-collar craftsmen belong below white-collar salesmen in their theoretical model of the occupational structure: they simply switched around those two categories to maintain consistency in the model with their value judgment that white-collar jobs are superior to blue-collar jobs, regardless of what their formula indicated. They describe their depiction of the occupational structure, which they claim to be "the foundation of the stratification system of contemporary industrial society," as an objective representation of the class system. In an obscure passage in a footnote on page 26, however, they acknowledge: "The one exception is the placement of retail salesmen above craftsmen, which has been made to maintain the nonmanualmanual distinction."

The theoretical model of the social class system that was created by Blau and Duncan was precedent setting. For years their index was used as the standard depiction of social status by the United States Census Bureau, and other researchers bought into the popularity of the scale because of its ease and consistency of results. It institutionalized the conception of social class in terms of an index that positioned the blue-collar working class beneath the white-collar middle class, even though the determining formula actually arranged some blue-collar jobs above some white-collar occupations. This is where the prevailing conceptualization of social class became an ideological construction that reinforces the unequal allotment of resources among the classes. From here on, social class would be defined according to just a few narrow structural indicators that are part of a hierarchical system in which some classes are perceived as inherently inferior to others. The many advantages and disadvantages of each class position, along with the unique cultural experiences that differed across class boundaries, were ignored in order to reinforce a vision of class differences that looked down on the people who had not attended college, who don't have an office job, and who prefer not to buy into the competitive consumer culture and suburban normalcy of the white-collar professional class. When the concept of social class is no longer associated with the different subcultures that are reflective of the different class experiences as it was before quantitative research forced a narrow operationalization of the concept, the positive features of the less-affluent class cultures become invisible. Now those classes toward the bottom of the income distribution are simply regarded as "lower" or "less" than, or "beneath" the class experiences that are advantaged by higher paying jobs and greater inclusion in the bureaucratic structures of contemporary organizations. In this way, the concept of class became an ideological tool that reinforces the norms, the values, and the worldview of white-collar professionals.

The point of the discussion thus far is that the basic definition of social class, however it has been specified, has imbued the concept with specific limitations and assumptions that have positive and negative outcomes for various groups in the social system. When a social class is regarded as lower, its alternative ways are ridiculed rather than appreciated. When blue-collar jobs are defined as beneath white-collar jobs, it justifies a lower share of the profits for blue-collar workers. Defining the working class as inferior creates an acceptance in the wider society of declining living standards for working-class people. The conception of variables is a political process, and the way the concepts are understood affects the identities and living conditions for large segments of the population. Since Blau and Duncan published *The American Occupational Structure* in 1967, the measurement of the occupational structure has gotten a little more sophisticated, but it is no less biased against the majority of people whose work does not rate highly on the index of education and income. The conventional measure of class standing now includes an occupational status score along with the levels of income and formal education. *Socio-economic status,* so the index is called, still "reflects the traditional distinction between mental and manual labor" (Ainley, 1993, p. 53) with manual labor at the bottom and nonmanual labor at the top. "The blue-collar/white-collar distinction is highly collinear with occupational status," sociologists Mary and Robert Jackman explain; "the correlation between the two variables is 0.80" (1983, p. 91). Moreover, they claim that the manual–nonmanual distinction is a "rough proxy for socioeconomic status" (p. 95). The index appears to be an objective continuum, but it conceals the traditional hierarchy that separates classes into the superior white-collar categories and the inferior blue-collar categories.

Class in the Bigger Picture ~ Culture of Class

Sociologists traditionally speak of class as an all-encompassing variable that determines not only living standards because of occupational opportunities and the related level of income that allows different access to resources, but also a related worldview and culture. Measuring social class through an index that emphasizes narrow economic variables while downplaying the cultural dimensions limits the explanatory power of the concept while it imposes a ranking system of "higher or lower" that easily translates into "better or worse." That is a big mistake, and the consequences are enormous. This limited conception of class has permeated popular culture and it became the standard way of thinking and speaking about class. This "standard way of thinking" reflects the culture of the white-collar professional class. The working class, for example, has a different way of understanding the meaning of class. Variables such as income and formal education are not necessarily the indicators that working-class people use to determine which people are superior or inferior. They also may challenge the notion that white-collar occupations are above blue-collar occupations.

The devalued placement of working-class occupations allowed researchers to regard blue-collar work as meaningless—devoid of intrinsic rewards. In the theoretical model of the class system as a vertical hierarchy, the working class is at the bottom of the ladder. For example, the prominent stratification scholar Harold Kerbo explains, "The working class usually occupies positions toward the bottom of all authority structures. Its members receive orders from many layers above and are seldom in a position to give orders to others. Typically, they are told what work to do, how it should be done, when, and how fast" (2006, p. 209). One of the chapters in a widely read text on work stated,

> Generations of the working class . . . have made a "realistic adaptation". . . by relinquishing, or by never bothering to take seriously, aspirations towards intrinsic satisfactions. Much evidence . . . points to there having always been a tendency for major sections of lower-level employees to see their work in purely instrumental or "extrinsic" terms, meaning by this that they see it only as a means to the consumption of goods and services outside work (or some other extrinsic reward) and that the work itself has no intrinsic meaning and satisfaction for them. (Fox, 1980, p. 151)

This statement was about the working class in general.

Data from my book *Working Class: Challenging the Myths About Blue-Collar Labor* (2011) show the sweeping generalization that all working-class jobs are meaningless is inaccurate. I found a large number of different categories of jobs within two different industries—in construction and factories—that were regarded by the men in those jobs to be rewarding, intrinsically meaningful, and desirable. They find dignity, honor, reward, and meaning in blue-collar work. That was true for all occupational categories in the sample, whether they were filled by young or old men, if they were union members or not, if they were company owners or recently hired hands, and if they held the highest authority or if they were at the bottom of the job ladder, and it was true across industries at opposite ends of the spectrum. Blue-collar work was universally described—even by the lowest skilled assembly-line workers, material handlers, and laborers in my sample—as meaningful, rewarding, desirable, and preferable to white-collar work. Workers also recognized the many informal ways that their experiential knowledge and their control at the point of production were essential to the final product.

There are three important things about this conclusion. The first is that it is inaccurate to make sweeping statements that the working class is stationed at the bottom of the social hierarchy. Academics have defined blue-collar work as subordinate, alienating, and meaningless, but blue-collar workers themselves do not support that depiction. The devalued identity of working-class people in social theory represents the values of the white-collar professionals who created the categories, but that does not reflect the standpoint of the working class. The second important thing is that the positive experience of blue-collar work exists alongside several dreadful aspects of the work. None of the blue-collar workers who claimed to enjoy their work were so positive about their jobs that they did not also express lengthy lists of the negative dimensions. In fact, it was often the workers who had the most positive appraisals of their own work, those who praised their jobs as "perfect" or "the best," who also gave the longest list of terrible aspects of their occupations. The experience of work was not good or bad, but rather it was good *and* bad. Those two extremes could not be disentangled. The third important thing was that the workmen's complex experiences and attitudes had been misrepresented in the research literature. Research that had previously claimed to represent working-class viewpoints was shown to capture only a small part of the blue-collar experience, and much of what that research said about blue-collar workers was inaccurate.

When Blau and Duncan presented their theoretical model of the class system in *The American Occupational Structure,* they imposed their own class biases onto the model. By their own measure, blue-collar and white-collar workers do not fall neatly onto a continuum where white-collar positions are above blue-collar positions. Even more damaging to the theoretical depiction of the stratification system as a vertical hierarchy is the finding from my research that explains how workers recognize occupational prestige. Occupational prestige studies (e.g., Hodge, Siegel, & Rossi, 1963) conducted with survey data from the National Opinion Research Center presume that working-class responses reflect their own personal understanding of the relative rank of occupations, but my interviews show that the workers do not identify the prestige of white-collar professions as superior to their own occupations. The working-class respondents give their *personal opinion* of the *general standing* of occupations, as the survey questionnaire directs them to do, but they are not reporting their opinion on the standing of jobs *generally;* they are reporting the societal conditions in which those jobs have a *general standing* as high or low, regardless of how they themselves regard prestige in occupational categories. The workers I interviewed had great respect for their own jobs and for others who perform productive labor—much more, in fact, than they had for white-collar jobs. They gave logical explanations for their preference for blue-collar work, and they justified their enjoyment of their blue-collar work, in spite of its distasteful aspects, with clear evidence and sound reasoning. Several men actually left white-collar employment for blue-collar work because of the advantages they saw in blue-collar jobs. From their perspective, working-class experiences are not inferior, subordinate, or subjugated compared to middle-class experiences. They did not want to be middle class, and they did not want a white-collar job. Working-class values are not the same as those of white-collar professionals, and my sample of blue-collar men were proud of that.

How Do We Define Class Membership?

I am one of several scholars who challenge the traditional depiction of class identity according to the ranked difference between white- and blue-collar labor. Those categories are too simplistic (see Gilbert, 2008; Hurst, 2003; Wright, 1997; Halle, 1984; Braverman, 1974). Recent attempts to overcome the limitations of the old mental/manual dichotomy of occupational categories have proven equally problematic, however. For example, Michael Zweig has provided an important alternative conception of class identity that situates class positions according to the power a worker has on the job. Zweig (2004, p. 4) defines the working class as made up of those who work under close supervision, "who have little control over the pace or the content of their work, who aren't the boss of anyone." As many researchers have shown (Roy, 1954 and 1952; Kornblum, 1974; Kusterer, 1978; Juravich, 1985; Noble, 1987; Finlay, 1988; Hamper, 1992; Applebaum, 1993; Ouellet, 1994; Zetka, 1995; Meztgar, 2000; Papp, 2006), the amount of power that a worker has is not always clearly apparent. In fact, when looking at the informal, unofficial channels of authority, workers have a tremendous amount of control over how their work is performed. We find that defining any job as "powerless" is a mistake and that those positions that hold authority over others are often incapable of giving explicit instructions because of a lack of understanding of how "lower" jobs are done. It is problematic to define blue-collar jobs as powerless because so many studies, including my own, have shown that management has exclusive control in theory only. Everyday reality on the job clearly places much discretion and authority in the hands of workers, even if that power is not formally recognized in the organizational power structure. Not only is it inaccurate to say that production workers have no power, but that claim also reinforces the devalued, subordinate definition of working-class positions.

Others have tried to create a workable conception of the class system, especially since globalization and the outsourcing of productive industries have transformed the economic system and threaten to make the old categories from the industrial economy obsolete. In response, Robert Perucci and Earl Wysong (2008, p. 24) define the class structure as ranked according to income and power. Their model contains five classes with five subcategories (p. 29), but they contend that "The New Class Society" can be simplified into two basic classes of "privileged" and "non-privileged" (2008, pp. 30–38). Attempts by Perucci and Wysong, Zweig, and others to redefine the class structure do little to overcome the premise that defines the class system as a vertical hierarchy in which some classes are advantaged over others according to a narrow set of indicators. As with traditional ways of measuring social class divisions, every recent attempt to measure class inequality has selected a particular set of indicators by which to establish where various class positions lay on the scale. Each attempt to define particular groups as higher or lower in the stratified social order makes the mistake of singling out specific variables by which judgment can be made about which group is superior or inferior to other groups in the hierarchy. In every case, highlighting some attribute or set of resources over others reflects a value judgment about what is most important in identifying which group is at the top and which is at the bottom. For some issues, variables such as income inequality might be of central importance. For other questions about class differences, the unequal distribution of income may be unimportant for understanding the lived experience of various class circumstances.

Each theory of class inequality raises important points about the class system. They share a theme of pointing out the imbalance of resources between class categories, and their data generally affirm their conclusions. The differences between each model of stratification highlight subtle distinctions that have real consequences for the distribution of life chances, justice, exploitation, discrimination, and a host of rewards and disadvantages for real people. Those inequalities must be acknowledged if our society is to be understood and made more just, egalitarian, peaceful, and democratic. At the same time, there is a danger in defining the social order rigidly in those terms because each class then becomes associated with a specific rank relative to others in the social system. When depiction of the class structure recognizes only those variables of which some classes (particularly the working and poverty classes) are limited compared to others (usually the "middle" or "upper-middle" classes) that are relatively advantaged, the identity of the "lower" class is mistakenly seen across the board as limited. The working class in general is stigmatized as the lower end of the spectrum and deserving of its inferior status based upon limited, albeit important, variables. Highly paid white-collar professionals are recognized as upper-middle class, yet the negative dimensions of living and working in those circumstances— those dimensions in which their lives may be disadvantaged relative to the working class—are ignored. When theory singles out a limited set of variables as determining the distribution of class positions in a rigid hierarchy, even if that variable set is crucial to understanding the relative possession of certain social resources like income, benefits, or power on the job, entire classes are defined in sweeping terms as inferior. That stigmatized identity becomes the standard perception of members of particular social classes, which then creates an ideological justification for maintaining and enhancing advantages and disadvantages across the class system.

Variables such as power, income, type of job, educational attainment, and/or prestige are important parts of the picture, but social class is far more complex than those concerns. Again, scholars apply a logic that reflects a particular worldview when they set specific variables as the indicator for class membership. Some working-class groups may even de-emphasize such issues in order to seek out rewards in other dimensions that are regarded as more important, such as personal relationships in their communities, meaningful connections to the physical world, traditional skills, and the creation of important products. Theory may identify income level as a primary measure of class membership, for example, and define those with high incomes as upper or upper-middle class, but citizens in lower classes may regard how much money they earn as less important than what they would have to give up in order to make large sums of money. For example, a highly credentialed corporate lawyer who is paid huge amounts of money to defend a corporation's degradation of the environment and the displacement of indigenous peoples may be at the top of the class structure according to the standard measurement of socio-economic status, but working-class values may regard that job as an unacceptable violation of moral standards. Because the meanings of work and status, honor and respect, prosperity and wealth, identity and dignity, personal rewards and sense of importance all vary across social classes, there is no consistent measure of the relative rank of social positions. Social class is too complex to fit into a hierarchical conceptual framework without imposing value judgments that promote attributes of some class memberships and discount others.

The definition of class identity and the understanding of social stratification have important outcomes for the way categories of people are regarded. In many instances, the sweepingly inferior identity of working-class people could actually be a greater disadvantage than that caused by the exploitation on the job that theorists use to determine their inferior identity in the first place. The stigmatized identity has become an impediment to social change by suggesting that working-class and lower-class people deserve the stigma and the limited share of resources that they receive. When theories of social class define large categories of people by name as "lower," they participate in the stigmatization of those people by legitimating the classification scheme that regards them as such. Classes are different from each other, and class membership does shape people's lives and life chances, but it is inaccurate to say that some classes are inherently above other classes in any general sense. In income level, educational attainment, or political power, some classes are obviously advantaged over others. In other areas, such as intrinsic reward from producing tangible and important products or from providing services that nurture and heal needy people, those classes that are disadvantaged by income may have advantages in other ways. The class system should be seen as horizontally situated rather than vertically structured. Classes need to be compared to each other on each issue rather than simply defined in sweeping terms as "lower," "middle," or "upper." Such a static hierarchy is inconsistent with reality, and it reinforces notions that reward particular class experiences while denigrating other classes.

Class Inequality

Inequality in the United States is difficult to explain because mass marketing has created an expectation in popular culture for the achievement of a particular style and a certain (ever-expanding) level of consumption. Now that media dominates our lives in new and complex ways, and especially because advertising drives so many of the images we see on television, in movies, in magazines, and on the Internet, people have been taught to consider media images—wholly artificially constructed identities—as the standard of normalcy. Commercials entice people to purchase stuff by presenting high levels of conspicuous consumption as normal. Media images tend to reflect stereotypes, or idealized representations of reality, so that people today often compare their own circumstances to an image that does not reflect their own experience. Fictitious media images of normalcy have come to replace popular conceptions of inequality and they misrepresent the growing reality of expanding poverty and misfortune in society.

Low-wage, mass-production industry in the global economy has corresponded with declining prices for commodities that used to be beyond the reach of all but the high-income earners. Even as wages fell for most U.S. citizens in recent decades, public demand for cheap, foreign-made goods remained high as long as credit was cheap and widely available (until the sub-prime real estate market collapsed in 2008). Even today, shoppers scour the Internet, discount stores, and estate sales searching for deals on regularly high-priced, and high-status, items that otherwise would be slightly beyond their ability to afford. Advertisements entice people to accumulate the kinds of goods that the highly paid professionals can afford to buy. Falling prices, rising expectations, and easy access to credit cards have made class divisions less obvious because so many people wear the latest style of clothing, or at least a cheap knock-off, and give the impression that they can conform to the standard of respectability as illustrated by role-model celebrities. This homogenization of taste and style as a result of ubiquitous media marketing hides the true class inequality simmering just out of sight. At the bottom end of the spectrum, having the latest clothing styles and brand-named shoes is often compensated for by consuming cheap food of low nutritional value. The stylish new car masks the stress of the owner who must work a second job to make the payment and struggles to stay ahead of the repossession notices. The top end of the class ladder is also distorted, because "making it" is measured by a standard of consumption that is attainable for the upper-income brackets, but the very small percentage of the public who actually have most of the financial resources are not even on the chart. The truly rich "upper class" is not even visible to most Americans.

No other western nation has as great a gap between the haves and the have-nots as the United States. Thomas Piketty, author of *Capital in the Twenty-First Century* (2014, p. 256), indicates that the top 10% of income earners take home 35% of total income while the bottom half of workers get 25% of the national income. Wealth inequality is even more askew. Piketty reports that the top 10% of the population owns 72% of U.S. wealth while the bottom half holds just 2% (p. 258). Even among the top 10% of wealth holders in society, "the 9%" and the top 1% encompass very different worlds" (Piketty, 2014, p. 280) where half of all the wealth in the country goes to those in the top 1% of society alone.

The entire bottom half of society must share a paltry 2% of the total wealth in the country. Piketty explains how exclusive it is to possess wealth by describing what wealth means to the lower half of society:

> For this half of the population, the very notions of wealth and capital are relatively abstract. For millions of people, "wealth" amounts to little more than a few weeks' wages in a checking account or low-interest savings account, a car, and a few pieces of furniture. The inescapable reality is this: wealth is so concentrated that a large segment of society is virtually unaware of its existence. (2014, p. 259)

Wealth is the net worth of one's possessions and assets, which is different from their earned income from wages, rent, or salaries. It is real estate, stock holdings, valuable works of art and other precious possessions, and other property. Without wealth, the bottom half of society has little insulation from downturns or misfortune. There is also little value to transfer between generations in the form of inheritance or financial support for children.

Income is not as unequal as wealth, but things are changing in that direction. According to Piketty, if the trend of the last 30–40 years continues, by the year 2030 the bottom half of society could be earning just half as much in total compensation as those in the top 10% (2014, p. 256). Incomes were much less unequal in the 1970s than they are today. Back then the top 1% of income earners took in 8–9% of the total, but the top incomes climbed to above 20% of the total in the first decade of the 21st century (Piketty, 2014, p. 292). In 1980, as *The Wall Street Journal* reported in 1999, the ratio between the income of the average corporate executive and the average worker in U.S. factories was 42:1. Stock options, along with the outsourcing of manufacturing and stagnant or falling wages, increased that ratio to 419:1 by 1998 (Philips, 2004, p. 66). Incomes for those at the top skyrocketed while the incomes for most citizens fell in constant dollars (controlling for inflation). Those at the bottom of the income ladder have seen the minimum wage drop in constant value. Piketty documents a rising gap between the bottom 10% of income earners and the overall average. He says the gap "widened significantly in the 1980s, then narrowed in the 1990s, and finally increased again in the 2000s" (p. 310). During the 2000s the top 10% of income earners increased their share dramatically while the incomes of the bottom 90% fell. Since the Great Recession that followed the real estate market collapse in 2008, the incomes of the bottom 90% actually shrank (Piketty, & Saez, 2013).

Income is unequal, and occupations are shifting in ways that enhance the inequality. Productive industries such as manufacturing and agriculture have been largely sent offshore. Jobs that can be sent to countries where costs of living, and thus wages, are lower have been outsourced, and that goes far beyond employment in manufacturing. Still-greater numbers of jobs have been displaced by automation. Millions of white-collar and clerical jobs have been replaced by computers (see Rifkin, 1995). There is a widening gap in compensation between those occupations with highly specialized skills in growing industries and the remaining workforce whose training no longer matches the available positions in today's labor market. Even when industries are stable and employment rates are steady, the competitive market has transformed many workers from company employees with secure wages and benefits to contracted labor in which workers are now hired as independent contractors. That way a business is not responsible for the workers' health insurance, retirement savings, or contributions to programs like social security, unemployment insurance, and workers' compensation. That also lowers the company's commitment to retain employees when they are no longer needed. The squeeze of more lower-end workers competing for fewer lower-end jobs puts downward pressure on wages, making it even harder for growing numbers of Americans to make ends meet. Businesses have reduced the number of employees and pushed the remaining workers to take up the slack through greater efficiency. In order to remain competitive in today's labor market, most workers are forced to attain a college degree. This adds to the financial and time pressures on members of less affluent classes, especially those for whom college attendance is not a family tradition.

The pressure to earn a college degree in order to compete in the changing economic climate has exacerbated the class divide. The professional white-collar class has long depended upon college credentials as a primary component of its identity. Children from this class are taught the communication skills and the individualistic demeanor that are rewarded in the college environment. They are also advantaged by having college-educated parents whose reading skills and habits promote those skills and habits in their kids. The knowledge and values that are priorities in the education institution are instilled by this class culture to create what Pierre Bourdieu called "social capital" (1984), which is the set of valuable cultural attributes that are rewarded in particular settings, schools and colleges in this case. Children from the professional white-collar class enjoy the benefit of financial resources to pay for college, and for the living expenses while students are enrolled in classes, but they also benefit from being taught the necessary knowledge and skills of the academic environment. On the other hand, children from working-class backgrounds do not always learn the values and knowledge that are prized in universities and colleges.

Sociologists have identified a definite link between social class and success in school (Ballantine, & Hammack, 2012, p. 70). This is due to more than the cultural values and skills for success that students learn from their families, but these are still the most significant factors. Among the structural factors that shape the distribution of resources according to class membership, the funding for public education is most often the product of local property taxes. This gives advantages in resources to students in more affluent communities. According to Ballantine and Hammack (2012, p. 86), "School spending per student can be up to four times greater in wealthy districts than in poor ones." Moreover, schools that serve working-class and less-affluent communities may be structured with an emphasis on controlling students and teaching them rudimentary skill sets as opposed to schools of more-affluent classes where students learn college-prep skills of critical thinking, written communication, and independent creativity.

Education is expected to be the vehicle through which individuals can overcome their disadvantaged circumstances of birth and improve their living conditions. Unequal educational opportunities undermine the value of education as an equalizing force, often reinforcing class inequality rather than altering it. Now that college is such an important factor for determining occupational success, the benefits of class membership are especially important. Students from low-performing primary and secondary schools are disadvantaged from the start, but they often lack other resources that are important for success. The cost of tuition is enough to keep many underprivileged students away, and those who must work long hours to pay their living expenses while in college suffer from their lack of time. Working students have little time to complete reading assignments or to study course material, and their jobs often conflict with their course schedules. There is little time for extracurricular learning from campus events and activities when students are juggling work, class, and home responsibilities. Chances of completing college go down for students who work long hours, and they often emerge from college without a degree and with extensive debt. For-profit colleges, especially those that offer online degrees, are frequently the only option for busy, low-income students, but lower outcome standards at those colleges make their degrees less marketable than public and other not-for-profit colleges and universities.

The three most commonly used indicators of class membership (type of occupation and its accompanying prestige score, income, and education) are marked by dramatic inequality in the United States. This creates a cycle that reproduces itself, from living in low-income neighborhoods to attending low-resource schools that lead to low-paying jobs that keep people in low-income neighborhoods with poor-performing schools. There are many other ways that social class also impacts people's life chances. Income is positively correlated with stable occupations and marriages, with access to health care and chances for physical and mental health, safety on the job, positive encounters with the criminal justice system, and freedom from violence. The benefits of living in the upper class, the upper-middle class, and even the middle-middle class are obvious. The majority of people who are members of the lower-middle class, the working class, or the poverty class are disadvantaged on each of these measures. By all these indicators, their lives are harder, less secure, and underprivileged. Their lives are deprived, not only in terms of financial resources, but also in terms of life chances. That is why social classes are labeled by their position on the stratified class hierarchy: upper, upper-middle, middle, lower-middle, skilled working, unskilled working, and lower. Each class is defined by its relative place on the social ladder.

But this narrow understanding of class identity that dominates the popular as well as the academic understanding of social class inequality is deeply flawed. The heavy dependence on economic variables to identify class membership is useful when classes are compared on the basis of economic resources, but there are many other important dimensions of life that ought to be part of the equation. The reliance upon economic indicators of class membership disregards the many aspects of life that do not relate to income or occupation. A big reason for disregarding other dimensions of class identity is that they are difficult to measure in a way that fits with statistical analysis. When the things that are predominantly possessed by the upper classes are the exact and only things that are identified as the indicators of class position in the hierarchical class system, it is no wonder that those classes are regarded as "upper." From that logical premise, it follows that those classes with lower incomes and "lower" occupations and lower formal educational attainment are defined as the lower classes. There may be an abundance of positive things about life in the working class, for instance, but as long as those attributes are ignored and the rank of the entire working class is defined according to a few economic indicators on which the class is undersupplied relative to more wealthy classes, all working-class people are regarded in theory as inferior human beings.

It is poor logic to sweep every working-class experience into the inferior category with the broad, comprehensive, wholesale conclusion that simply having fewer economic resources makes a group of people inherently lower than other groups, but that is the way classes are typically defined. That is incorrect, and it reduces the value of people and their lifestyles in those classes labeled as below the classes at the top of the scale. In fact, working-class people may disregard income and wealth as important concerns relative to the dignity and honor of taking care of others and making positive contributions to the community. The concept of social class is more complex than a simple calculation of occupation plus income plus years of formal education. When the alternative class cultures are acknowledged, it allows an appreciation for the different ways of living and for the different definitions of what is important and honorable.

Class is such a complex, multidimensional concept that it must be measured in a variety of ways. It may be appropriate to rank some class experiences below others when specific issues are addressed, such as formal educational attainment. In that case, the professional white-collar class is clearly situated above the working and poverty classes. When other issues are addressed, however, such as the pride a person has from making direct, tangible contributions to society through the creation of important products, or in the confidence that one's work improves the lives of others, the scales may actually be reversed. If the discussion were focused on individuals' connection to a larger community and integration into a supportive, helpful group of friends and close relationships, the classes with the least amount of income may rank above the high-income professionals who are more independent and isolated. There are many other factors than income and formal education attainment on which to compare classes, and several of them would place the high-income earners at the bottom of the scale. No class has things so good across all the dimensions of its experience that it should be labeled as above the others in general. Likewise, even those in poverty have aspects of their lives that make it incorrect to define the entire class as the bottom of the barrel as its identity. Social class is the last remaining identity construct for which categories are defined as superior or inferior. It is finally time to change the way class is understood and measured so that people are no longer ranked in a hierarchy that legitimates an unequal distribution of resources.

The New Economic Reality and a New Understanding of Class Identity

Those same technological advancements that created the capacity for computer assisted quantitative analysis of survey research data also spawned telecommunications technologies and GPS integration, which allowed for globalized industry and commerce at a new level of efficiency. Computers replaced workers, especially those in clerical occupations and middle-level management, while satellite communication allowed the offshoring of entire production industries along with other white-collar jobs. The class system is in flux, and we are unsure how the outsourcing of the industrial economy will create new class identities and relationships in Western society. There is a breakdown in the seemingly neat division between white-collar and blue-collar labor that was created in the early days of the 20th century. The old relationship between one's work and its product has been severed. Consumerism has blurred the differences in lifestyle and consumer goods of the different class positions. The working-class and middle-class values of the past no longer match the realities of life in the new "service economy," the "information economy," the "post-industrial" economy," or the "global economy," or however we choose to label the economic system that now shapes our lives in ways that do not seem to make sense.

What does it mean to working-class people, whose identities are defined by the skills and the products of their labor, to have a job defined by what they serve, guard, clean, or monitor? A manager cannot manage when the things that need managing have been sent overseas. The old industrial economy that manufactures goods and transports them from the points of production to distribution centers and to retail outlets is still alive, much as there are a few farmers whose practices stem from the old agrarian economic model, but the industries and occupations of the 20th century no longer dominate our social system. It is essential that we re-envision how our social class system operates. Not only have the old class identities been transformed by the changing tides of economic development, but these changes have also altered the social contract that determined a fair day's pay for a fair day's work, what dignified and meaningful work is, and what the appropriate expectations are for living standards and hopes for the future. The old categories no longer apply, so we must make new ones. So far the circumstances have created instability, reduced compensation, and other hardships for millions of workers (see Sweet, & Meiksins, 2012), but it is too soon to tell how the new economic reality will take shape, or what it will mean for workers in the various class positions.

The presumption of a hierarchical arrangement of classes in a stratified social order actually enabled the destruction of the old identities that kept the industrial economy relatively stable. In that system the blue-collar working class was taught to value productive skills and identities, and the white-collar class was taught to identify with managing and facilitating the productive economy. There was a logic to the system, and people assumed that meeting the expectations of their respective class positions would bring them rewarding and successful lives according to the cultural standards in their particular class environments. The notion that the class system is a hierarchy, such as a ladder on which specific classes occupy rungs that are organized in a descending or ascending order, one on top of the other, made it possible to think that some classes are less important than the others. Some work is defined as less desirable, less skilled, and less valuable than other work, so eliminating those jobs or shipping them overseas was reasonable and even seen as preferable. The dismantling of the industrial-class system, much like the agricultural system before it, extended from the belief that some classes are less deserving of a living wage, and they can be sacrificed to the competitive global market.

The class system does not have to be defined that way. In fact, the evidence shows that it is invalid to define social stratification as a vertical hierarchy. My interviews with factory and construction workers (Torlina, 2011) show that working-class values do not identify office work as superior as the stratification research literature claims. The blue-collar workers regarded desk work as "constricting" and "confining," and they likened it to imprisonment. In fact, several of the interviewees questioned whether white-collar work was *real* work at all. They considered much of office work to be a "scam." The anthropologist Julie Lindquist discovered that working-class individuals in her ethnography preferred not to join the white-collar professional class because "they did not want to reposition themselves in another cultural milieu, one that might demand different habits and manners" (2002, p. 75). The working-class people Lindquist studied, like the blue-collar workers in my research, disapproved of many of the ways of life in the professional middle class and they had no desire to join it.

It was common for the working-class men in my research to value their blue-collar jobs because they produce tangible things of importance. The blue-collar workers did not want office jobs for a variety of reasons, but chief among them is the inability to create tangible, useful results that extend from their skill, effort, and knowledge. They also preferred their working-class communities to the individualistic, competitive personalities of the professional middle class. The working-class men did not want to be middle class, they did not want a white-collar job, and they did not respect middle-class people. My interviews with blue-collar workers indicate that they see the hierarchical order of classes differently than do the "upper-middle class" scholars who created the theories about the class system. The social scientists who defined the stratified class system did so according to the cultural assumptions of their own class background, and to them it was logical to rank the working class beneath their own class of white-collar professionals. Through the logic of their class standpoint, they recognized themselves as superior, but those of the working class prefer their own class circumstances. Once we recognize that any depiction of the social class system in hierarchical terms reflects the biases of the person who creates the theoretical model, then it becomes possible to see that there is value and dignity in each class position. Social classes, by definition, present their members with alternative lifestyles, worldviews, values, and preferences. In some ways one class or another may have more of some resources, but in other ways that class may have disadvantages. It is a fallacy to claim that any one class is broadly and consistently above or below others, because class is such a complicated subject. Class experiences are different, but they do not fit on a hierarchical continuum from higher to lower. That realization holds the key for improving the difficult situation faced by most U.S. workers in the new economic climate.

Human societies have always been organized around the need for people to satisfy their needs and earn a living. Economic systems reflect each society's way of meeting its needs in its particular environment. As the story goes, when hunting-and-gathering economies were replaced by settled agriculture, human societies gained the capacity to produce surplus and support larger populations. As the population grew and societies became complex, some groups gained privileges that were accompanied by cultural beliefs that justified the differential allotment of resources. All societies that produce surplus have a belief system that explains and justifies the unequal distribution of things. The idea that our modern industrial society is (was) structured in a hierarchically stratified order (with an upper class at the top and a descending list of ranked positions from upper-white-collar to middle-white-collar to lower-white-collar to skilled blue-collar to low-skilled blue-collar to the poverty class) reflects the ideology that legitimates the inequality of our society. There is injustice in that belief system because of the economic hardships faced by those who inhabit the lower-paid positions. As with all other inequality systems in societies past and present, the foundation for the class structure was connected to the means of production and to the need for human labor to create the valuable and essential things of life. What makes the current economic system different, at least in the "advanced" or "developed" economies like those of the United States, is that the system has disconnected the actual production of commodities and, therefore, value from the human labor of society in much of the economy. It is a new economic model that expects the creation of value to be outsourced to foreign societies and machinery while the work for most of our own country's citizens is unrelated to extracting/cultivating valuable resources or creating value-added goods. It is unheard of that a society's economy can function with the majority of its members working in service occupations that do not produce things of value. The math for figuring out how that system works does not add up.

That system of outsourcing the productive capacity of the economy may serve the interests of the top investor class and some members of the top professional class, but it is a disaster for the rest of society. Our economic system is based on the assumption of classical economics that goods and services will be produced on a relatively small scale and distributed locally, and the logic of the system breaks down when resources and commodities are produced elsewhere by giant multinational corporations. It is the devalued identity of the "lower" productive classes that justified the offshoring of those industries, but we need to recognize that those industries and jobs are necessary for our society. All societies need productive economies and work that satisfies people's needs. The way that social class is understood is a key factor in the changes needed to rebuild the economic system and reverse the recent trends of expanding inequality, declining standards of living, and growing instability. Transforming the negative identity associated with working-class lifestyles and with working in productive industries will incentivize investment in smaller-scale production businesses (agriculture, manufacturing, etc.) while also removing the justification for compensating productive work with such a small share of the profits from their labor. Perhaps the most important outcome from redefining the class system so that classes are not ranked in a vertical hierarchy is that individual members of the working and low-income classes will no longer be regarded as inherently inferior. The way classes are currently understood in most social science research defines the majority of the population as beneath the more highly paid positions. As long as broad categories of people are labeled by name as lower than others, it will be legitimate to treat those individuals unfairly. In the history of western civilization there has always been an underlying belief that some groups of people are inherently below the privileged groups. We finally know better.

References

Ainley, Pat. (1993). *Class and skill: Changing divisions of knowledge and labour.* London: Cassell.

Applebaum, Herbert. (1999). *Construction workers, U.S.A.* Westport, CT: Greenwood Press.

Ballantine, Jeanne H., & Floyd M. Hammack. (2012). *The sociology of education: A systematic analysis* (7th ed.). Boston: Pearson.

Blau, Peter M., & Otis Dudley Duncan. (1967). *The American occupational structure.* New York: John Wiley and Sons, Inc.

Bourdieu, Pierre. (1984). *Distinction: A social critique of the judgement of taste.* Translated by Richard Nice. Cambridge, MA: Harvard University Press.

Braverman, Harry. (1974). *Labor and monopoly capital: The degradation of work in the twentieth century.* New York: Monthly Review Press.

Finlay, William. (1988). *Work on the waterfront: Worker power and technological change in a West Coast port.* Philadelphia: Temple University Press.

Fox, Alan. (1980). The meaning of work. In Esland, Geoff, & Grame Salaman (Eds.), *The politics of work and occupations.* Milton Kenes: The Open University Press.

Gilbert, Dennis. (2008). *The American class structure in an age of growing inequality* (7th ed.). Los Angeles: Pine Forge Press.

Halle, David. (1984). *America's working man.* Chicago: University of Chicago Press.

Hamper, Ben. (1992). *Rivethead: Tales from the assembly line.* New York: Time-Life Books.

Hodge, Robert W., P. M. Siegel, & Peter H. Rossi. (1964). Occupational prestige in the United States, 1925–1963. *American Journal of Sociology, 70,* 286–302.

Hurst, Charles E. (2001). *Social inequality: Forms, causes and consequences* (4th ed.). Boston: Allyn and Bacon.

Jackman, Mary R., & Robert W. Jackman. (1983). *Class awareness in the United States*. Berkeley: University of California Press.

Jensen, Barbara. (2012). *Reading classes: On culture and classism in America*. Ithaca, NY: Cornell University Press.

Juravich, Tom. (1985). *Chaos on the shop floor: A worker's view of quality, productivity, and management*. Philadelphia: Temple University Press.

Kerbo, Harold R. (2006). *Social stratification and inequality: Class conflict in historical and comparative perspective* (6th ed.). New York: McGraw-Hill, Inc.

Kornblum, William. (1974). *Blue collar community*. Chicago: University of Chicago Press.

Kusterer, Kenneth C. (1978). *Know how on the job: The important working knowledge of "unskilled" workers*. Boulder, CO: Westview Press.

Lamont, Michele. (2000). *The dignity of working men: Morality and the boundaries of race, class, and immigration*. New York: Russell Sage Foundation.

Lareau, Annette. (2011). *Unequal childhoods: Class, race, and family life* (2nd ed.). Berkeley: University of California Press.

Lindquist, Julie. (2002). *A place to stand: Politics and persuasion in a working class bar*. New York: Oxford University Press.

Metzgar, Jack. (2000). *Striking steel: Solidarity remembered*. Philadelphia: Temple University Press.

Noble, David F. (1987). *Forces of production: Social history of industrial automation*. New York: Oxford University Press.

Ouellet, Lawrence J. (1994). *Pedal to the metal: The work lives of truckers*. Philadelphia: Temple University Press.

Paap, Kris. (2006). *Working construction: Why white working-class men put themselves—and the labor movement—in harm's way*. Ithaca, NY: Cornell University Press.

Perrucci, Robert, & Earl Wysong. (2008). *The new class society: Goodbye American dream?* (3rd ed.). Lanham, MD: Rowman & Littlefield.

Phillips, Kevin. (2004). *American dynasty: Aristocracy, fortune, and the politics of deceit in the house of Bush*. New York: Penguin Books.

Piketty, Thomas. (2014). *Capital in the twenty-first century*. Translated by Arthur Goldhammer. Cambridge, MA: Belknap/Harvard University Press.

Piketty, Thomas, & Emmanuel Saez. (2013). Top incomes and the great recession: Recent evolutions and policy implications. *IMF Economic Review, 61*, 456–478.

Rifkin, Jeremy. (1996). *The end of work: The decline of the global labor force and the dawn of the post-market era.* New York: Tarcher/Putnam Books.

Roy, Donald. (1954). Efficiency and "the fix": Informal intergroup relations in a piecework machine shop. *American Journal of Sociology, 6*(3), 255–266.

_____. (1952). Quota restriction and goldbricking in a machine shop. *American Journal of Sociology, 67*(2), 427–42.

Sweet, Stephen A., & Peter F. Meiksins. (2012). *Changing contours of work: Jobs and opportunities in the new economy* (2nd ed.). Thousand Oaks, CA: Sage.

Torlina, Jeff. (2011). *Working class: Challenging myths about blue-collar labor.* Boulder, CO: Lynne Rienner.

Wright, Erik Olin. (1998). *Classes* (2nd ed.). London: Verso.

Zetka, James R. Jr. (1995). *Militancy, market dynamics, and workplace authority: The struggle over labor process outcomes in the U.S. automobile industry, 1946 to 1973.* Albany, NY: SUNY Press.

Zweig, Michael. (2004). *What's class got to do with it? American society in the twenty-first century.* Ithaca, NY: Cornell University Press.

Patriarchal Prosumerism on Web 2.0

THE SOCIOLOGICAL VECTORS OF THE PATHOGENIC INTERNET MEME, "GET BACK TO THE KITCHEN"

by Richard G. Ellefritz

When you plant a fertile meme in my mind you literally parasitize my brain, turning it into a vehicle for the meme's propagation in just the way that a virus may parasitize the genetic mechanism of a host cell.

—Richard Dawkins (1989, p. 192), The Selfish Gene

"Everything," to be sure, may be said always to have "come out of the past," but the meaning of that phrase—"to come out of the past"—is what is at issue. Sometimes there are quite new things in the world, which is to say that "history" does and "history" does not "repeat itself"; it depends upon the social structure and upon the period with whose history we are concerned."

—C. Wright Mills (1959, p. 156), The Sociological Imagination

The Internet meme has arisen as a vast meaning network on Web 2.0. Some Internet memes are benign, banal, and even benevolent, such as the LOLcats meme or #TheDress, but others carry an imbedded semiotic code that, like a virus, injects itself into new hosts, infecting them/us with the raw material that fuels (hetero)sexism, racism, classism, militarism, nationalism, imperialism, and many other ideologies that continue to separate and divide us humans against ourselves. How is it that some Internet memes reinforce, replicate, and reproduce millennia-old social structures designed and used for domination and oppression?

The Internet hosts a bastion of websites through which take place social interactions, socialization, personal and social development, cultural production and consumption, commerce, and political struggle, but it also provides key sites of research for social scientists. The Internet, and the World Wide Web (or just Web) that it facilitates, make available at once virtual locations to test classical and contemporary social theories as well as a chance for observing novel behaviors and explaining them accordingly (Beer & Burrows, 2007; DiMaggio, Hargittai, Neuman, & Robinson, 2001). Web 2.0 is among the newest developments on the Internet, familiar to many of us who use websites like Instagram, Pinterest, Twitter, and YouTube, and it is one of the most recently constructed social locations where sociologists can carry out our practices (Beer & Burrows, 2007).

The Internet meme (or just meme as it is colloquially known) is the particular unit of analysis in this chapter, and, more specifically, the "Get Back to the Kitchen" meme (Dahlen, 2011) is held under the lenses of prosumerism (Ritzer, Dean, & Jurgenson, 2012; Ritzer & Jurgenson, 2010) in terms of the feminist presumption of a pervasive and oppressive social structure known as the patriarchy (or just patriarchy, or patriarchies) (Bryson, 1999; hooks, 2000; Hunnicutt, 2009; Walby, 1989). More specifically yet, I argue that it is a specific ideological social structure patriarchal militarism (Kaplan, 1994) that is in operation when prosumers on Web 2.0 construct, consume, and share the Get Back to the Kitchen meme. My overall thesis is that the Internet meme serves as a clear example of how social forces influence, shape, or lead to ideology and social action: The Get Back to the Kitchen meme, and especially its more pathogenic expression in terms of images depicting male violence against women, demonstrates how social structures impact human consciousness and behavior.[1]

Of MEMES and Internet MEMES

The following section presents a disambiguation of memes and Internet memes. "Meme" refers to a unit of cultural transmission, whereas "Internet meme" refers to user-generated digital content that typically takes the form of images and text shared on Web 2.0. Memes are replete in society, and Internet memes are ubiquitous across Web 2.0. Memes are a social force behind many beliefs and behaviors, and the social forces behind Internet memes include the daily prosumption that takes place on Web 2.0 in the context of social structures like capitalism, prosumerism, patriarchy, and militarism.

Internet memes are common to stumble upon while surfing the Web (Shifman, 2014), and their popularity creates and necessitates new literacies in their production and consumption (Knobel & Lankshear, 2007; Lewis, 2007). The people who construct successful and/or popular Internet memes communicate easily understandable or quickly consumable ideas to receptive audiences, and the audiences who consume, share, and replicate such memes must be able to "read" or comprehend these cultural artifacts in order for the production-consumption process to proceed. Internet memes communicate complex ideas by (re)creating, (re)combining, mashing up, and/or remixing images and text in such a way that the whole of the message is greater than the sum of its parts (Lankshear & Knobel, 2007). Memes, as a more general form of the Internet meme, are units of cultural transmission, or, put another way, memes are all those ways that humans emulate other humans' beliefs and behaviors. So, *the* Internet meme is a genus or family of the kingdom or domain of memes more generally. *The* Internet meme takes the form of tens of thousands of *specific* variants or species of Internet memes, and each one of those can be considered a meme as well.

Internet memes, like memes in general (Dawkins, 1989), can take on a life of their own, such as the case of Tardar Sauce, a domestic shorthair cat born April 4, 2012. Like actors who become recognized for the beloved characters they create—think Leonard Nimoy and Mr. Spock, or Daniel Radcliffe and Harry Potter—Tardar Sauce, only shortly into her feline life, spawned Grumpy Cat, who spontaneously "became an Internet sensation after her photo was posted on Reddit on September 22, 2012" (Grumpy Cat®, 2015a). Grumpy Cat is an Internet meme in the sense that it (i.e., the meme known as "Grumpy Cat") is a series of images of an apparently frowning cat often accompanied with text expressing pessimism, doubt, frustration, worry, depression, and other negative sentiments. However, Tardar Sauce, the biophysical specimen of *Felis catus*, and Grumpy Cat, the Internet meme, have morphed into Grumpy Cat™, which is a trademarked brand used to sell human and pet toys, stuffed animals, clothing, books, a Christmas-themed movie, coffee mugs, and even a beverage line called "Grumpuccino™," which "is a delicious and creamy blend of premium Arabica coffee and milk, with just the right amount of rich mocha flavor to satisfy your sweet tooth! It's Awfully Good™" (Grumpy Cat®, 2015b).

Memes are popular ways of doing and thinking, behaving and believing, acting and knowing. Drinking coffee is a meme, drinking coffee out of a mug is a meme, going to movies is a meme, and it is also mimetic to wear fashionable clothes or play with stuffed animals. Mimetic behavior ranges from singing "Happy Birthday," a copyrighted song that is sung without compensation to its copyright holders thousands of times on any particular day; to using drugs, like caffeine, marijuana, and insulin; to praying, (complaining about) paying one's taxes, and on and on like this. The sheer variety of beliefs and behaviors that can be defined as memes is part of the problematic nature of this particular term (Aunger, 2002), and so too is the colloquial use of "meme" to refer to Internet memes. We should keep in mind that memes are units of cultural transmission, or imitative behavior, and that when they spread from person to person, group to group, they oftentimes mutate and evolve, sometimes even taking on a life of their own.

The Mutagenic Nature of (Internet) Memes

As distinguished from the term's original definition as "a unit of cultural transmission, or a unit of *imitation*" [italicized in original] (Dawkins, 1989, p. 192), "meme" is currently used in popular vernacular to refer to images with text overlays, or what are more specifically known as Internet memes (Bauckhage, 2011; Shifman, 2014). The term "meme," however, was originally coined by Richard Dawkins (1989), and here is his original conceptualization:

> Examples of memes are tunes, ideas, catch-phrases, clothes fashions [sic], ways of making pots or of building arches. Just as genes propagate themselves in the gene pool by leaping from body to body via sperms or eggs, so memes propagate themselves in the meme pool by leaping from brain to brain via a process which, in the broad sense, can be called imitation. (p. 192)

For sociologists, the symbolic interactions that individuals engage in are understood to be much more complex and open to creativity and spontaneity than mere *imitation* (Blumer, 1969), even if much of our social behavior is guided by and reproduces social structural regularities, routines, rituals, and other forms of highly predictable social behavior (Knottnerus, 2011; Stryker, 1980). The main point of Dawkins' (1989) concept has been taken up by sociologists as a way to talk about how culture is transmitted between people and reproduced and altered across space and time, i.e., sociocultural evolution (Blute, 2005; Situngkir, 2004). Rumors, gossip, myths, dogma, fads, fashions, trends, stereotypes, and other types of mass belief (e.g., taboos and the various isms of ideological thought—capitalism, militarism, imperialism, racism, sexism, etc.) and collective behavior spread throughout society like communicable diseases, passing from one viable host to another. In this way of thinking, people do not catch (onto) ideas so much as ideas find and infect people, affecting their/our attitudes, values, beliefs, and ways of knowing the world; this is what is known as "thought contagion" (Lynch, 1996).

Due in part to social and technological changes brought about by modernization (Misa, Brey, & Feenberg, 2003; Volti, 2009), at no other point in human history have ideas so easily spread from mind to mind: "People have more communication partners from whom to catch communicable ideas, and more potential retransmitting contacts as well. Modern technology also fosters thought contagion," Lynch (1996, p. 25) goes on to say, "by putting those potential recipients only a phone call or a broadcast away." Nearly twenty years after Lynch (1996) published his aptly titled book on memetics, *Thought Contagion: How Beliefs Spread Through Society*, and at the time of this writing (early spring of 2015), the Internet has taken over many of the functions of telephone lines, and the Web has replaced broadcasts with webcasts and instant access to streaming video. The product of modernity, and housed within the Internet, the Web serves as a daily site of virtual social interactions, information consumption, and production of digital media and other web-based content, such as *the* Internet meme (Beer & Burrows, 2007).

As stated above, the Internet meme is a specific type or example of a meme, and it has been defined thusly:

> (a) A group of digital content units sharing common characteristics of content, form, and/or stance. For instance—photos featuring funny cats with captions share a topic (cats), form (photo + caption), and stance (humor). (b) These units are created with awareness of each other—the person posting the "cat with caption" image builds on the previous cats in the series. (c) These units are circulated, imitated, and/or transformed via the Internet by many users. Internet memes are multiparticipant creative expressions through which cultural and political identities are communicated and negotiated. (Shifman, 2014, p. 177)

From this definition, we can understand that Internet memes, like all memes, are (a) structured (b) meaning units (c) produced by people for other people to consume and share (i.e., replicate), but Internet memes, as a more specific variant of memes generally, also serve to facilitate and generate social (as well as cultural and political) identities and interactions that necessitate *communication and negotiation*. For sociologists who analyze society, social behavior, and the self, especially those of us who make our observations through the lenses of social constructionism (Berger & Luckmann, 1966) and symbolic interactionism (Blumer, 1969; Styker, 1980), communication and negotiation are primary components of how people come to share definitions of the situations they/we navigate every day during social encounters. Communication and negotiation move us past thinking of memes as imitative behaviors. People are not mindless automatons, passively consuming information and thoughtlessly transmitting it to others (i.e., the monkey-see-monkey-do style of imitation); rather, we—albeit, some more than others (Reicher, Haslam, & Hopkins, 2005)—communicate with intent and motivation: We negotiate, argue, agree to disagree, dispute, ignore, critique, criticize, and critically challenge other people, groups, and social structures in our daily lives, especially when their interests do not align with our own, or vice versa.

As one example of how people communicate and negotiate via memes, we can analyze the evolution of a popular Internet meme, namely Demotivational Posters (Kimball, 2010) and, earlier still, Demotivators (Despair, Inc., 2015). As is the case with most memes (Bauckhage, 2011), Demotivators and Demotivational Posters each developed as a commentary, imitation, and parody of other memes found offline and online, respectively. In this particular case, the product design team at Despair.com creatively challenged and redefined the black framed motivational posters that are sometimes found hanging on walls of offices and institutions, and their final product was the Demotivator meme. "Motivational products are *anything but*," [emphasis mine] says the team at Despair, Inc. (2015):

> While they briefly raise hopes with induced delusions about the untapped potential greatness within, sooner or later reality intrudes, and you realize the only people made rich and successful by motivational products are the ones selling them to gullible chumps (i.e. you). Stop the inanity! [sic]

Despair, Inc. redefined motivational posters in terms of contextualizing modernity as a pitfall rather than a playground. Therein, the meaning or purpose of motivational posters was parodied by Demotivators; whereas the former were intended to inspire, the latter were designed to dishearten. The structure of motivational posters became mimetic when it was imitated by Demotivators; both exhibit thick black borders, a large image above a capitalized word or short phrase, and an explanatory or expository passage or quote written in smaller typeface below. And, like most memes, the Demotivator meme itself eventually produced imitations and parodies.

While the original parody (Demotivators) of the authentic meme (motivational posters) involved the use of banal optimism and comical pessimism in tandem with a scenic vision of an atmospheric picture, Demotivational Posters (the imitator meme of Demotivators) eventually

> became increasingly popular across the web, the joke was no longer bound within corporate/educational themes and became a signature meme involving "crude but funny" comments. Today, the white-on-black format of demotivators is a staple in Internet memescape and it's fairly common to find demotivational posters *sans* cynicism. [sic, italicized in original] (Kimball, 2010)

The eventual perversion of Demotivators produced a style of Internet memes known as Demotivational Posters, and these are used to construct, modify, and promote a wide variety of meanings via the *memetic structure* of the original motivational poster meme.

Memes can spontaneously emerge out of the creative and dynamic improvisations humans sometimes produce during social interactions, but memes also evolve from other memes, mutating and emerging as entirely new entities, and Internet memes are no different. When the thought contagion of a meme reaches critical mass, which in our common parlance means to "go viral" (Guadagno, Rempala, Murphy, & Okdie, 2013), it begins to take on a life of its own, making possible new ways of thinking and acting, but they can also legitimate and reify the existing or ideologically preferred social structures, i.e., the status quo. As a prime example of this, the Demotivational Poster meme has been used to produce a version of this chapter's unit of analysis, which is the Get Back to the Kitchen meme (see Figure 1). Below, I show how the development of the Demotivational Poster meme conjoined with the Get Back to the Kitchen meme, but I do this in a way that sets up the rest of this chapter, and this is accomplished with an analysis of the subtext of the image in Figure 1, which is that which is known as patriarchal militarism.

Patriarchal Militarism as an Embedded Mimetic Structure

Motivational posters, products hallowing the optimism of modernity, were mimicked and satirized by Demotivators, an Internet meme designed to highlight the harrowing features of a *contrite* modernity (see Habermas, 2008). In our contemporary age, the Digital Age of Web 2.0 and prosumerism, dilemmas of the self (Giddens, 1991) now include whether or not to click the "like" or "share" buttons on such Internet memes as that in Figure 1; whether or not to pass over them with little notice or thought; or whether or not to critically assess them as vectors of virus-like units of cultural imperialism, infecting us with ideologies like (hetero)sexism and militarism that justify and legitimate oppressive social structures as natural orders in the social hierarchy.

With regard to the Internet meme reproduced in Figure 1, we are presented with a scene of a father and son socializing over a simulated war game in the form of Battleship, a two-player war game that simulates maritime military combat. Military, war, and combat

FIGURE 13.1 ▷

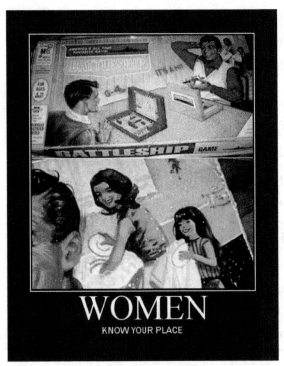

toys and games are common consumer items gifted or given to young boys (and increasingly more common with girls), and they tend to glorify enacting violence upon others while mystifying the many detriments of combat and war (Varney, 2000). While the adventurism, heroism, and patriotism of war, military, and combat are lionized, the many pervasive costs are downplayed and hidden. These costs include being maimed or killed on the battlefield, killing and maiming others, the resulting post-traumatic stress disorder that afflicted (circa 2008) 15–20% of returning combat veterans from Iraq and Afghanistan (Tanielian, 2008), the increasing rates and disproportionate ratio of homelessness among veterans—2010 estimates were that 16% of homeless adults in the United States were veterans, whereas veterans made up only 8% of the total U.S. population (Perl, 2012), and, finally, that 21% of all suicides in 2010 were committed by veterans (Bossarte, 2013). It is not that all little boys who play with toys that promote militarism will one day grow up to join the military—although, this might be a dream or desire of military recruiters. Rather, "many might grow up to approve of brutal military measures if their toys and other socializing apparati [e.g., Battleship] encourage them to associate violence with political decisiveness, necessity and natural manhood" (Varney, 2000, p. 390).

While the board game, Battleship, itself is not the central aspect of the Internet meme in Figure 13.1, it is important to recognize the types of social structures that undergird the production of such memes as military/war/combat toys and games. It has long been recognized that "militarism has been a significant aspect of the socialization and education of boys and largely determines what comprises socially desirable masculine attributes" (Reardon, 1996, p. 144). Within militarized societies, strength, stoicism, phallocentricity, patriotism, heroic achievement, risk taking, competitiveness, aggressiveness, and the willingness and ability to dominate the weak characterize "a form of masculine identity (hegemonic masculinity) to which boys and men are generally encouraged to aspire" (Higate & Hopton, 2005, p. 433). Militarism is the belief system that supports the allocation of physical (e.g., raw materials) and social (e.g., money, labor power, leisure activities, and community support of "the troops" and returning veterans) resources to the waging of war, and there are numerous individuals, organizations, and institutions that benefit from the militarization of civilian psychology, which is "aimed at the organization of civil society for the production of *violence*" [emphasis mine] (Orr, 2004, p. 456). Militarism, then, has an elective affinity with hegemonic masculinity because if aggressive males who buy into the naturalness of social hierarchies cannot themselves be persuaded or motivated to directly engage in combat or military service otherwise, they can at least indirectly engage in it during the vicarious acts of consuming military-themed mass media products, such as the billion-dollar industry of digital combat simulations in the form of video games (Dyer-Witheford & de Peuter, 2009; Huntemann & Payne, 2010).

Militarism is closely related to another social structure, patriarchy, which is understood by many feminists to be a way of organizing societies around the interests of and benefits for males, men, and masculinities. In militarized societies, domination over weaker bodies and minds is valorized, and in patriarchal societies, the devaluation of females, women, and femininities is a means toward the maintenance and expansion of power by dominating members of society, whether male or female, heterosexual or not. With the recognition that gender inequality under patriarchy privileges and advantages males, men, and masculinities over and at the expense of females, women, and femininities, we should note that militarism contributes to perpetration and justifications of domestic violence, typically expressed in the form of male violence against women (Adelman, 2003). Now, keeping in mind the particular Internet meme represented in Figure 1, "the archetype of 'woman as caretaker' supports patriarchal militarism because it is used by [the archetype of] male warriors in the service of the war effort and because it builds on a gender opposition created by patriarchy to contain women" (Kaplan, 1994, p. 124). Thus, constructing and consuming cover art and Internet memes as shown in Figure 1 are processes that support and are supported by patriarchal militarism. This particular argument is central to my overall thesis, which I continue to expand upon below.

Motivating Women to Get Back to the Kitchen

With reference to Figure 1, the cover art for this particular board game represents a traditional nuclear family setting, which is the hallmark of the white middle-class family structure of the 1950s in the United States. The artist(s) and production staff who produced the cover art either took for granted or intentionally promoted these traditional gender roles; the difference matters not for this analysis. The existence of the board game's cover art provided the opportunity for a patron of Web 2.0 to highlight or exaggerate the traditional gender roles of the 1950s by focusing the audience's attention on the background in the image, which shows a mother and daughter washing the dishes, ostensibly, from that evening's meal—to note, the terms "dinner" and "supper" are also memes, just as are the social practices they signify. Bringing this background image into focus with the written title, "WOMEN," and the explanatory subtitle, "KNOW YOUR PLACE," indicates that the author of this meme understood (a) the patriarchal order, even if he (or, less likely, she) was operating by its logic as opposed to criticizing it with irony or satire; and (b) the meme construction or production process, which includes appropriating images and general Internet meme forms (i.e., Demotivational Posters) in order to create a new Internet meme. The question is, *why?* Why use the Demotivational Poster meme and the cover art of this particular version of Battleship to denigrate women?

As compared to the end of the 1950s, when 65% of U.S. children experienced growing up in the traditional nuclear family style, the fourteenth year of the new millennium hosted a wide diversity of family structures, including only 22% of children who lived with their married parents (Cohen, 2014). Presumably, the authors of such Web 2.0 content look back to a time in U.S. history when clearly defined gender roles were lauded as admirable and desirable, and interpret it as a desirable and achievable social order, even if this involves women's loss of full autonomy and a diminished capacity for agency. A critical sociological perspective looks upon such images as perpetuations and examples of dominant ideologies, such as (hetero)sexism, hegemonic masculinity, and/or patriarchal militarism, which should be replaced with egalitarianism, at the least (Feagin & Vera, 2001). This type of division in interpretative styles can be seen in cultural conflicts whereby some nostalgically look back to the 1950s as *the* golden era in U.S. American history, but others see it as a time in need of the social progress and change ushered in by the following decade's many social movements (Hunter, 1992).

The 1950s model of the domestic nuclear family is an aberration in the entire history of the United States (Coontz, 1992). During that era, though, some very prominent and highly esteemed sociologists optimistically theorized that the status differentials between men (the supposed breadwinners) and women (the supposed homemakers) produced and sustained positive functions for a society that depended on the stability of the traditional nuclear family (Parsons & Bales, 1955). The rise of social movements in the 1960s that challenged the existing sociocultural and politico-economic inequalities showed that the social structure of the period did not produce positive consequences equally and for all people alike (Tarrow, 1994). Social theorists who supported the status quo of the 1950s were criticized for their uncritical attention toward the status of oppressed social categories within U.S. society, and similar criticisms apply to the prosumers who constructed, "Like," and uncritically "Share" the species of the Internet meme presented in Figure 13.1.

The Internet meme in Figure 1 can be considered to be a Demotivational Poster, and certainly it is intended to demotivate women from moving too far beyond traditional gender roles. However, while this form or class of Internet memes is known as Demotivational posters, this image also falls into the order of Internet memes known as the Get Back to the Kitchen meme, which currently (March 8, 2015—incidentally this is International Women's Day) produces 26,963 results on MemeCenter.com, an online community where users construct, consume, rate, and share Internet memes. At this point, I can only surmise that the proliferation of this particular meme indicates that many people do not only *not* critically evaluate it in terms of its repressive (Ferree, 2005) and oppressive nature (Young, 1990), but they also revel in their ability to consume and produce more and more of these types of (Internet) memes. What we shall see in the following section(s) of this chapter is that the Get Back to the Kitchen meme (hereafter referred to as the GB2K meme) mutated over time from promoting the patriarchal belief that "women, and men alike, should know that the female's natural place is in the kitchen" to using images of male violence against women as an expression of patriarchal militarism in the form of a more virulent version of GB2K.

PROSUMERISM AND PATRIARCHY ON WEB 2.0

The following section addresses how Internet memes are contextualized by two social structures: prosumerism and patriarchal militarism. Prosumerism is the belief system behind the drive toward melding production and consumption practices, such as filling one's own cup with soda at a fast food restaurant or filling out one's own order information on shopping websites (Ritzer, 2013; Ritzer, Dean, & Jurgenson, 2012; Ritzer & Jurgenson, 2010). Much like the ideological foundation of prosumption, (hetero)sexism is the belief system that drives patriarchy, a social structure defined by the dominance of males, men, and masculinities (hooks, 2000), and domination and violence—two qualities of hegemonic masculinity—are at the heart of militarism, an ideology that legitimates conflict and warfare as justifiable solutions to interpersonal and international disagreements alike (Higate & Hopton, 2005; Orr, 2004). The GB2K meme is the product of both prosumerism and patriarchy, and the prosumption of this particular meme illustrates several aspects of how memes and Internet memes evolve and mutate. This is highlighted by the use of images that depict male violence against women, which, among many other factors, is an expression of hegemonic masculinity, the mechanism that sustains patriarchal militarism. Taken together, these modes of oppression normalize and legitimate male violence against women (Johnson, 1995; Kaplan, 1994; Koss et al., 1994; White & Kowalski, 1998; Young, 1990).

Social Structures, Internet Memes, and Web 2.0

Internet memes are typically posted on blogs, sent via email, or, more popularly, shared through social networking sites like Twitter or Facebook. Internet memes tend to spread rapidly, peak, and then die out quickly, or, less often, they morph into a dominant force in the Internet meme pool by generating thousands of imitations, spinoffs, parodies, and entire subcultures (Bauckhage, 2011; Knobel & Lankshear, 2007). The most recent example of an Internet meme that has gone viral or produced a quick rise in mass appeal has been #TheDress, which "refers to a Tumblr post in which viewers were asked to identify the color of a dress, which appeared to be either white and gold or black and blue" (amanda b., 2015). #TheDress is only one of thousands of Internet memes that people create and share with each other to engage in social bonding, social critique, political commentary, or sometimes to simply express a personal sentiment or opinion on a forum or thread (Shifman, 2014). While Internet memes like #TheDress are rather benign in their content, others, like the GB2K meme, are produced and consumed, i.e., prosumed, with potentially harmful consequences, such as normalizing male violence against women.

Not only do Internet memes require for their existence the Internet and the Web (2.0), nor do they require only symbols, images, text, and systems of meaning be used that are negotiated through communicative processes in order to be comprehensible or understandable (Lewis, 2007), but Internet memes also depend upon the many ways that human societies produce and reproduce ordered or regular patterns of social behavior, which are referred to as *social structures* (see Bernardi, Gonzalez, & Requena, 2007; Giddens, 1979; Knottnerus, 1996). Social structures can take macro, objective forms, such as entities like nation-states and practices like global commerce, but social structure also exists in micro, subjective forms, such as ideologies that sustain and legitimate micro-level social interactions and macro-level social systems in turn. This is why prosumerism, a micro-level ideology, and patriarchy, a macro-level pattern of societal organization, can both be considered social structures, and the GB2K meme depends upon both social structures, among others (i.e., patriarchal militarism), for its existence.

The participatory web cultures that prosume Internet memes are themselves stable or orderly patterns of human behavior (Beer & Burrows, 2010; Knobel & Lankshear, 2007); this is to say, a regular series of social interactions are behind the production-consumption cycles of Internet memes, and this cycle depends upon a mass community, however large or small it might be, who share a definition of the situation. If the central message or intended meaning of an Internet meme is about something too idiosyncratic or particular, it will not have the requisite inclusivity or readability necessary to garner mass appeal (Lewis, 2007; Shifman, 2014). In light of all this, we should expect prosumers on Web 2.0 to use Internet memes to comment on, at the very least, dominant or pervasive social structures. This is because widely shared social practices and mass belief systems would be more likely to generate readability than Internet memes that focus on too narrow of a given subject or a subject that is too far outside of the purview of society writ large. In light of the fact that Internet memes are prosumed on Web 2.0, subcultures can easily form through social networking sites, like MemeCenter.com and KnowYourMeme.com, and these subcultures can share in a definition of social reality that is not widely recognized or appreciated throughout society. So, what might be considered offensive within the standards of the dominant culture might be considered hilarious or amusing within a subculture, which is far from saying that dominant social structures would not have an influence over the subcultural groups that coalesce on Web 2.0.

Web 2.0 and (Non-)Random Acts of Patriarchy

Web 2.0 is a collection of websites familiar to the hundreds of millions of people who use YouTube, Wikipedia, Twitter, Pinterest, WordPress, Craigslist, Tumblr, IMDB, Yelp, Instagram, and dozens of other popular social networking sites that facilitate user-generated content (eBizMBA Guide, 2015). As compared to the static, read-only webpages constructed by web coders and designers and viewed via web browsers on Web 1.0 (1993–2003), Web 2.0 (2004–present) is based upon networks of applications that allow and encourage users to generate and share content via their/our social networking profiles (Beer & Burrows, 2006; Cormode & Krishnamurthy, 2008). "Perhaps the key-defining feature of Web 2.0," say Beer & Burrows (2006, para. 3.2), "is that users are involved in processes of production and consumption as they generate and browse online content, as they tag and blog, post and share." Web 2.0 allows prosumption to go digital, which opens up new possibilities of what can be created and shared; unlike prosumption in the offline world, which typically entails a business that generates profits from consumers laboring to consume physical resources, the online world offers low-cost access to a nearly limitless source of information, including images, audio, video, and text (Ritzer & Jurgenson, 2010).

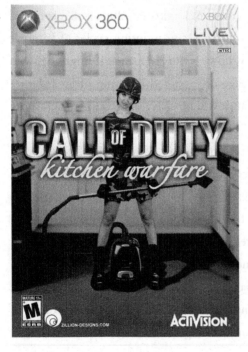

FIGURE 13.2 ▷

This project's genesis lies in an experience with StumbleUpon.com, a Web 2.0 website where, like Pinterest.com, users contribute Web pages for other "stumblers" so that they/we can "easily discover new and interesting stuff on the Web" (StumbleUpon.com, 2015). A webpage had been contributed to the networking site that was dedicated to a domestically oriented sexist Internet meme called Get Back to the Kitchen.[3] Its having piqued my curiosity, I investigated this particular Internet meme further, and I discovered an interesting pattern and uncovered a startling phenomenon: *Many of the GB2K memes contained content that directly linked women to the kitchen, but many more did not reference anything resembling a domestic situation at all except for the use of the meme's title to contextualize how the audience was to interpret the image.* Like the examples in Figure 13.1 and Figure 13.2, many of the GB2K memes directly depict a female in a kitchen, with one particularly telling set having parodied a popular videogame franchise. Whereas the examples in Figures 1 and 2 represent the location described in this Internet meme's namesake, many others depict one or more females only in a domestic context, such as in a laundry room, cleaning, or standing next to a house, but not necessarily in a kitchen per se (see Figure 3).

FIGURE 13.3

The GB2K meme in Figure 13.2, much more explicitly than that in Figure 13.1, relies upon patriarchal militarism (Kaplan, 1994), and so it demands a similar discussion of the role of military and war games in the socialization process as that given above. Military game franchises are targeted predominantly to males, and they typically place the player in control of a male character that itself is continuously placed in situations where they are designated to simulate killing (typically) other males. These games more and more are produced with insight and direction from the military itself (i.e., military personnel co-construct some of these games), and they are even sometimes used to socialize and train military recruits (see Dyer-Witheford & de Peuter, 2009; Huntemann & Payne, 2010). Millions of boys and men (and fewer, yet many, girls and women) engage daily in hours-long simulations of combat in virtual wartime scenarios, and these practices "help normalize ongoing exceptional states of war" (Smicker, 2010, p. 118). Video games act as agents of socialization, with many transmitting values of competitiveness, heroism, adventurism, risk taking, domination, aggression, violence, and other aspects of hegemonic masculinity and militarism (Hearn, 2004; Higate & Hopton, 2005), and so too does the Internet meme act as an agent of socialization. The particular Internet meme in Figure 2 not only normalizes military/war games like Call of Duty, but it also normalizes the patriarchal standard that women's roles are tied to domesticity; in this situation, particularly within the kitchen, but now, and unlike the image in Figure 13.1, "women's place" is expanded beyond the kitchen vis-à-vis the "weaponry" of the weaponized vacuum cleaner.

Memes mutate when any given infected host modifies the belief or practice in terms of their social interactions, whether face to face or facilitated virtually, and so too it is not uncommon

FIGURE 13.4 ▷

IF YOU WATCH CINDERELLA BACKWARDS

IT'S ABOUT A WOMAN WHO LEARNS HER PLACE

for prosumers on Web 2.0 to incubate a mutagenic variant of any given Internet meme. With prosumerism on Web 2.0, this is actualized when prosumers appropriate or redeploy copyrighted material in their construction and sharing of Internet memes (Collins, 2010). This aspect of prosumerism is known as the cyber-libertarian ethic (Kelemen & Smith, 2001) or digital socialism (Kelly, 2009). The prosumers who used the Battleship board game cover art and the Call of Duty franchise, complete with corporate logos from Activision and Xbox 360, to express their patriarchal standards rely upon the ability to use free of charge the images and text that others might own. This same ethic or ideal is also a component of *how* Internet memes mutate and evolve. Demonstrating how memes will sometimes cross-pollinate or cross-fertilize, such as the case with the GB2K Demotivational Poster in Figure 1, the form or structure of other popular Internet memes are used to reproduce the central logics of the GB2K meme. "If a woman's place is in the kitchen," reads one that uses the Philosoraptor meme[6] (see kikinak, 2010), "who is doing the laundry?" The prosumer of this particular Internet meme used the logics of Philosoraptor, which are to pose paradoxes, issue Zen koans, and state rhetorical questions. The function of the Philosoraptor meme used in Figure 13.3 was to challenge the basic logic of the GB2K meme, which originally was developed to specifically promote the kitchen as the domain of women in the cult of domesticity. In line with this, Figure 13.4 depicts the digital socialism or cyber-libertarianism of prosumerism as well as the mutation in the GB2K meme that eventually moved from a focus on patriarchal standards for women's labor in the kitchen, specifically, to domestic labor, generally.

When an Internet meme is constructed with direct reference to dominant and pervasive social structures (in the cases of Figures 13.1 and 13.2, these would be the military, patriarchy, and mass media), the prosumer is presented with the associated values (e.g., aggression, competitiveness, dominance, male superiority, and entertainment or leisure). Likewise, the particular Internet meme in Figure 4 relies upon a similar social structural element as does Figure 13.2 vis-à-vis the entertainment industry, in this case the Disney Corporation's appropriation and popularization of the German brothers Jacob and Wilhelm Grimm's fairytale "Cinderella." Somewhat like the Disney Corporation's appropriation of fairytales that are in the public domain, prosumers on Web 2.0 operate under the ethics of digital socialism or cyber-libertarianism (Ritzer &

Jurgenson, 2010), but their repurposing of copyrighted material under the fair-use provisions of copyright law (Collins, 2010) is not the analogy I am making here.

The logics of the GB2K meme eventually shifted from kitchen-centricity to the inclusivity of domesticity generally. This can be observed with reference to the images and statements in Figure 13.1 (i.e., "KNOW YOUR PLACE") and Figure 13.2 ("CALL OF DUTY"), both of which clearly indicate a kitchen. Somewhat like the use of the Philosoraptor meme in Figure 13.3, which challenged the central logics of the GB2K meme as a way to demotivate women from straying too far from the kitchen to motivating them/you to concentrate on domestic duties generally, the Cinderella version of the GB2K meme blatantly replicates patriarchal values in terms of traditional gender roles related to domestic labor, but in this case women are expected to mobilize outside of the kitchen, if only to scrub a floor on their/your hands and knees. Somewhat like how the princess characters in Disney films typically act as role models in the socialization process for girls (and boys), displaying the dominant cultural standards of femininity in terms of coyness and other attributes, like a standard hourglass body type and an attraction toward qualities in male characters defined by hegemonic masculinity (Do Rozario, 2004), a similarly narrow representation of females, women, and femininity is presented in the GB2K Internet memes displayed above. The prosumers who generated them, knowingly or not, appropriated not only copyrighted or trademarked material, but they also latched onto and employed the logics of patriarchy to present a narrow scope of appropriate behaviors and identities for females, not for the pleasure of women, but as a spectacle for the male gaze (Snow, 1989).

PROSUMERISM, A VECTOR FOR PATRIARCHAL MILITARISM

The following sections conclude this chapter with a discussion that makes an analogy between pathogens (i.e., disease-causing agents) and social structures that promote or reinforce injustice, oppression, and domination. I discuss the GB2K meme in terms of anti-feminist backlash, and I present two final examples of the GB2K meme that highlight how memes evolve in context of social structural forces. The first highlights a direct connection between patriarchy and militarism, and the second demonstrates the insidious nature of pathogenic (Internet) memes. The final example of the GB2K meme is actually a variant, which I use GB2Kv to signify. The key factor that makes GB2Kv the most caustic version of GB2K is that it depicts through imagery only male violence against women; no other signifier was used in its association with patriarchal standards for gender roles other than a male assaulting a woman. This shows that patriarchal militarism is part of a systemic, structural system of domination and oppression that influences the consciousness of (some) prosumers on Web 2.0.

Of Mimetic Pathogens and Patriarchy

Pathogens are infectious agents that disrupt the normal physiological functions of plants and animals, and they typically require a medium or unit of transmission to spread to a new host, which is known in epidemiology as a vector. Patriarchy, a term used to talk about social systems dominated by and/or that privilege males, men, and/or masculinities (Connell, 2005), is interconnected with other systems of power and domination, such as (hetero)-sexism, imperialism, militarism, capitalism, and white privilege (Bryson, 1999; hooks, 2000; Walby, 1989). Therefore, patriarchal militarism is a breed of militarism just as patriarchal prosumerism is a breed of prosumerism. The fact that GB2K is but one of hundreds, possibly thousands, of Internet memes more generally (e.g., LOLcats and Grumpy Cat) that do not have as their guiding logic the standards of patriarchy means that prosumerism is the guiding factor behind the creation and prosumption of Internet memes generally. Thus, while militarism harnesses and honors hegemonic masculinity, prosumerism facilitates the spread of (hetero)sexism, and thus prosumerism on Web 2.0 is a vector for patriarchy and patriarchal militarism.

The user-generated content of Web 2.0 does not represent the standpoint of all social categories (class, race, gender, etc.) equally, but rather a digital production gap exists whereby advantaged or privileged categories tend to produce the most content (Schradie, 2011). Privileged categories in society benefit from or are advantaged by most of the existing social structures, and so they/we (i.e., white, heterosexual, educated males) have an interest in maintaining those social structures that advantage or privilege them/us the most, even if this interest is expressed unreflexively or without conscious intention. Even though prosuming Internet memes allows individuals to express themselves/ourselves in ways never practiced before the development of Web 2.0 (Chen, 2012), "the practice of prosumption. . .tends to entrench status quo relations and structures and, in so doing, as an institutional mediator of social-economic relations, generally it frames and contains prospectively radical imaginations" (Comor, 2010, p. 314). Therefore, privileged categories have a way to express, promote, and reify their/our advantaged positions vis-à-vis prosumerism on Web 2.0, in this case specifically through prosuming GB2K.

There exists much user-generated content on Web 2.0 that promotes stereotypical gender roles, (hetero)sexism, and the disempowerment of females, women, and non-heterosexuals, and this content can be considered to be part of the backlash against feminism (Shifman &

Lemish, 2010). And, as one feminist scholar has pointed out, "[a]nti-feminist backlash exists because the movement was successful at showing everyone the threat patriarchy poses to the well-being of females and males" (hooks, 2000, p. 116). Established symptoms of anti-feminist backlash—i.e., sexism and assaults on gender equality and feminism—are repackaged and repurposed by prosumers of the GB2K meme (Shifman & Lemish, 2011), and this is enabled by the most advanced information-communication technologies human civilization has yet known, the Internet and Web 2.0. In this chapter, I have divulged how a critical feminist perspective reorients our understanding of the memes, Internet memes, and, in particular, the GB2K meme as pathways or vectors for the construction and reification of domination and oppression.

"Feminist scholarship highlights the presence of multiple interests and social logics shaping technology design" (Kirkpatrick, 2008, p. 64), such as the invention and implementation of technological practices by and for male interests, capitalist profit, militaristic and imperialistic expansion, and Eurocentric cultural imperialism. For uncritical, un-reflexive minds, these social forces operate as taken-for-granted background assumptions about how and why the world operates as it does; i.e., capitalism, militarism, imperialism, and (hetero)sexism are explanatory frameworks, not ideologies in need of critical assessment and negation (Feagin & Vera, 2001). The task of a critical, emancipatory, liberation-focused sociology is to identify injustice and inequality, and to unmask and undermine the social structures that justify, legitimate, support, lead to, and/or cause them (Berger, 1963; Boltanski, 2011; Feagin & Vera, 2001; Lee, 1973; Mills, 1959/2000). It is our job as critical and public sociologists (Clawson et al., 2007) to identify the beliefs and behaviors, whether consciously chosen or unconsciously acquired, that underlie and induce oppression and domination, and then it is our task to hold them under the light of methodological and theoretical scrutiny so we may sterilize and disinfect the vectors that host these pathogenic memes.

Like people who unintentionally spread communicable diseases by, for instance, not covering their mouths and noses when coughing and sneezing, those who spread the GB2K meme do not need to be thought of as conscious agents in their capacities as a prosumers; with that said, *there are* some people who use the Internet to intentionally spread communicable and deadly diseases, like HIV (Grov, 2004). Similarly, we can use our sociological imaginations to postulate that there are some prosumers who intend for their actions to not only be sexist, but to further bolster male privilege and upend gender equality and women's empowerment (Comor, 2010). The Web 2.0-wide effort to create humorous or, at the least, "likeable" or shareable content has inevitably led to the production of thousands of sexist Internet memes that serve to undermine the push toward gender equality that has taken a great many bodies and minds generations to accomplish only the modest egalitarianism we currently enjoy (Fogel, 2000; Shifman & Lemish, 2010; Shifman & Lemish, 2011). And, like how some communicable diseases become resistant and immune to their cures over time due to mutations and natural selection, which leads to innovations (and profits) by the biomedical industry in their production of new vaccines (e.g., see ter Meulen et al., 2015), Internet memes mutate and evolve, taking on ever more extreme measures to titillate and amuse prosumers—this chapter, regretfully, will not delve into how to counteract GB2K and similar memes.

Prosuming Symbolic and Violent Sexism on Web 2.0

Constructing a *popular* Internet meme elevates the status of the prosumer within their online subcultures, and if they are successful enough, whether by intention or luck, then their Internet meme might take on a life of its own, bringing not only fame but possibly fortune as well. One-upping the competition by modifying, mocking, and parodying to new extremes any given existing Internet meme is one way to construct a popular Internet meme as well as to shore up one's self-esteem and sense of mastery. Whatever the driving force is behind the production of Internet memes, whether it is (perceived) power prestige, prosperity, or simple psychological satisfaction, if Internet memes that tap into dominant social structures are more likely to become popular than those that focus on less well-known phenomena, and if hegemonic masculinity, militarism, and the patriarchal order are as pervasive as feminists proclaim (Bennet, 2006; Connell, 2005; Hearn, 2004; Rupp, 2008), then we might suspect that the GB2K meme would transform and morph in terms of the logics of these particular social structural forces as well as in terms of the GB2K meme's own logics and those of the other Internet memes with which it is recombined. Since aggression and violence are features and outcomes of hegemonic masculinities, militarism,

FIGURE 13.5

and patriarchy (Bryson, 1999; Higate & Hopton, 2005; Hunnicutt, 2009; Kaplan, 1996; Reardon, 1994), we should expect further that violence would arise as a catalyst for the mutation of GB2K. This is most acutely observed in variants of GB2K that portray male violence against women.

The particular Internet meme displayed in Figure 13.5 brings us close to a specific representation of male violence against women, but this image is most accurately interpreted in terms of militaristic statism. Defined as the institution that has a monopoly on the legitimate initiation and use of force, meaning any *body* (male, female, etc.) can be its target, the state has been identified by feminist scholars as an institution controlled by, for, and of the patriarchal (male) establishment in society (MacKinnon, 1989). The status of these males as (militarized) law enforcement officers positions them as actors who are able to legitimately use aggression and violence on any human (or animal), not women solely (Westley, 1970). U.S. police forces, historically, have been used by ruling elites to subdue and repress sit-ins, strikes, protests, and other mass demonstrations, with an increasing prevalence of state-initiated violence taking rise during the 1960s to repress the anti-war and civil rights movements, out of which the women's liberation movement arose (Evans, 1979; Platt & Cooper, 1974). State-initiated force against women *has* taken place throughout U.S. history, most notably in the form of the forced sterilizations of females that have taken place in government-run institutions and via court mandates, particularly with women of color (Bruinius, 2006).

Whereas we can interpret the above image (Figure 13.5) as a depiction of males' violence on a woman, it is not a representation of male violence against women per se. Rather, it is an image of state repression of public collective action, for why else would these agents of social control be dressed in full riot gear? Continuing into the 21st century, during the age of Web 2.0, we have witnessed the continuation of the militarization of police forces, and almost by default they, the militarized police forces, tend to respond to incidents of public unrest and peaceful protest alike with armored vehicles, full body armor, gas masks, the use of non-lethal weapons, and the threat and initiation of mass arrests. "In the most infamous incident, now forever captured in countless Internet memes and mashups," says Radley Balko (2013, p. 296) in reference to the "overkill" responses to protests by militarized police departments, "Lt. John Pike of the University of California-Davis campus police casually hosed down a peaceful group of protesters with a pepper-spray canister." This incident manifested itself in the Casually Pepper Spray Everything Cop meme[9], which features the image of Lt. Pike spraying the infamous orange mist cut and pasted into scenes like John Trumbull's painting of the "Signing of the Declaration of Independence"[10] to an image of the actual scene of Lt. Pike dousing seated demonstrators with military-grade MK-9 pepper spray and a caption that reads, "Don't mind me, just watering my hippies."[11]

The particular prosumer who produced the particular version of GB2K displayed in Figure 6—whether or not they modeled it after the dozens of similarly structured GB2K memes that focus *only* or *primarily* on male violence against women with *no* reference to domestic objects, actions, or situations—interpreted these images as opportunities to draw upon his (or her) affinities

FIGURE 13.6 ▷

with the subculture that prosumes the GB2K meme *as well as* patriarchal militarism, which is predicated on the enactment of violence, particularly male violence against women. As opposed to a real-life or live-action photo of humans engaging in aggressive or hostile behaviors, the image in Figure 13.6 is a total fiction, a cartoon that only signifies actual human interactions. One might contest whether or not Figure 13.6 is showing the weaponized appendage of a male's or a female's body—though it seems to me to be male in origin, but one might also contest whether or not the aggression depicted in Figure 13.5 is actually male violence against women legitimated by the patriarchal state's monopoly on force. Regardless, the importance of the version of the GB2K meme in Figure 13.6 is the image's absence of *any domestic symbol* and the omnipresence of male violence against women, thus it is a new breed of the Get Back to the Kitchen Meme, i.e., the GB2Kv$_{(violence)}$ meme.

The existence of the GB2Kv meme, as represented in Figure 6, and its myriad imitations, replications, and predecessors indicates that some Web 2.0 prosumers have so thoroughly adopted the logics of the GB2K meme and patriarchal militarism that they began to use the *underlying* logics of a variety of social structures via the vector of prosumerism. GB2Kv's existence tells us that not only do the logics of particular Internet memes guide the prosumption and transformation of those memes, but it also shows us that Internet memes do not transform solely due to the application of the logics of other Internet memes (see Figures 3 and 4) or the guiding social structure (i.e., patriarchy for GB2K) behind their central logics. Not only does the GB2K meme ridicule, stigmatize, and silence women much in the same ways that women's movements have experienced in the offline world (Ferree, 2005), but it relies upon the logics of and enacts the most dangerous of the "five faces of oppression," which are exploitation, marginalization, powerlessness, cultural imperialism, and, most clearly, *violence* (Young, 1990). Male violence against women is the guiding logic of GB2Kv. Its mutation is the result of the internalization of hegemonic masculinities and patriarchal militarism as expressed through the vector of prosumerism on Web 2.0.

DISCUSSION AND CONCLUSION

The forces of modernization—democracy, science, capitalist production, literacy, liberty, and equality—have produced both wonderful and terrible developments in our contemporary age

(Giddens, 1990), and one of the mechanisms behind the process(es) of bringing modernity to societies around the world has been cultural imperialism, which has typically been expressed in terms of Eurocentrism and Americanism (Tomlinson, 1991). One of the many consequences of cultural imperialism is that

> the dominant cultural products of the society, that is, those most widely disseminated, express the experience, values, goals, and achievements of these groups. Often without noticing they do so, the dominant groups project their own experience as representative of humanity as such. Cultural products also express the dominant group's perspective on and interpretation of events and elements in the society, including other groups in the society, insofar as they attain cultural status at all. (Young, 1990, p. 59)

Patriarchal stereotypes that guide the GB2K meme rely on ideologies from an outdated, unrealistically appraised, and contested era of U.S. history (Coontz, 1992). The central logics of the GB2K meme, guided primarily by patriarchy, are that women's bodies should be relegated to one physical space (either the kitchen or the house) and women's identities should express nothing other than the role of the caretaker housewife. Thus, females (not to mention the never-present trans-person) are stripped of their dignity as sovereign individuals and forced into the standardized uniform of a domestic(ated) servant. To a great extent, prosumers must be conscious of their spreading the GB2K meme, because they must actively generate, post, share, and evaluate such digital content in order to engage in the prosumption process on Web 2.0, but their gendered cultural imperialism can be, to some extent, viewed (however willfully) as a product of ignorance or unconscious motivations. However, the existence of the GB2Kv challenges this assumption.

The violent acts portrayed in the GB2Kv meme are disturbing, at least to those of us who abhor the initiation of violence, but it is not the display of the violent acts themselves that is the most concerning feature of this particular (Internet) meme's expression. "What makes violence a face of oppression is less the particular acts themselves, though these are often utterly horrible, than the social context surrounding them, which makes them possible and even acceptable" (Young, 1990, p. 61). Violence, or the enactment of aggression upon another person or group to the extent that bodily injury ensues, is one facet of oppression where conscious intent is necessary. Regardless of the extent to which the mechanical or muscular actions must be consciously initiated, the immediate motivations or intentions to aggress upon another person can be guided by taken-for-granted assumptions about one's relationship with that person—and this is where cultural imperialism plays itself out through violence. However, in the digital realm of Web 2.0, symbolic violence against females, women, and femininities through GB2Kv calls into question where in the realm of consciousnesses of male violence again women it is originated, promulgated, manifested, and perpetuated.

If a male views women as an inferior social category, then he is likely to mistreat people he views as belonging to that category. This includes viewing non-men, non-masculine, and/or non-males as unworthy of the respect and dignity that all humans deserve by the sheer virtue of our shared humanity (Feagin & Vera, 2001), and if this same male has violent tendencies, then the patriarchal militarism of his society (wherein that is a predefining context) can facilitate, encourage, and legitimate his internalized, taken-for-granted, and/or unconscious fears and hatred of females, women, and, femininities, which can potentially result in violence, symbolic or physical, against individuals simply because they are females, women, or exhibit perceived characteristics of femininities. Because patriarchy works in concert with other systems of domination and oppression, such as (hetero)sexism, racism, classism, ageism, militarism, imperialism, and nationalism (hooks, 2000), when an individual's values and beliefs are socialized, contextualized, and sometimes even justified or legitimated by reinforcing social systems that promote or facilitate domination and oppression, especially those that encourage violence, they are more likely to, for example, construct virulent Internet memes like $GB2K_V$ than those who are not guided by or who critically assess those same ideological systems (Hunnicutt, 2009).

While there is not necessarily a direct relationship between patriarchy, or male power and privilege as a dominant form of social organization, and violence toward women (e.g., see Dutton, 1994), this social structure provides the background, context, and taken-for-granted assumptions that can and do sometimes make possible male violence against women (Brown, Chesney-Lind, & Stein, 2007; Jasinski, 2001; Smith, 1990). As a social structural force that has collided and colluded with patriarchy, prosumerism on Web 2.0 produced GB2K, but the (re)combination of GB2K with patriarchal militarism enabled it to transmutate into its more pathogenic variant, GB2Kv. The Internet, Web 2.0, and prosumerism act as vectors for many offline and online memes alike, and they sometimes go viral via the many dimensions of modernization that have heightened thought contagion to its advanced state. Regarding our concerns here, patriarchal prosumerism has acted as the vessel throughout which sexist oppression has worked its way out in the prosumption of digitized graphic information in the form of GB2K and its more pathogenic mutation, GB2Kv.

REFERENCES

Adelman, M. (2003). The military, militarism, and the militarization of domestic violence. *Violence Against Women*, *9*(9), 1118–1152.

amanda b. (2015). What color is this dress? Retrieved from http://knowyourmeme.com/memes/what-color-is-this-dress.

Aunger, R. (2002). *The electric meme: A new theory of how we think*. New York: The Free Press.

Balko, R. (2013). *Rise of the warrior cop: The militarization of America's police forces*. New York: PublicAffairs.

Beer, D., & Burrows, R. (2007). Sociology and, of and in Web 2.0: Some initial considerations. *Sociological Research Online, 12*(5). Retrieved from www.socresonline.org.uk/12/5/17.html.

------. (2010). Consumption, prosumption and participatory web cultures: An introduction. *Journal of Consumer Culture, 10*(1), 3–12.

Bennett, J. M. (2006). *History matters: Patriarchy and the challenge of feminism*. Philadelphia: University of Pennsylvania Press.

Berger, P. L. (1963). *Invitation to sociology: A humanistic perspective*. New York: Doubleday.

Berger, P. L., & Luckmann, T. (1966). *The social construction of reality: A treatise in the sociology of knowledge*. New York: Anchor Books.

Bernardi, F., J. J. Gonzalez, & M. Requena. (2007). The sociology of social structure. In C. D. Bryant and D. L. Peck (Eds.), *21st century sociology: A reference handbook*. Thousand Oaks, CA: SAGE Publications, Inc.

Blute, M. (2005). Memetics and evolutionary social science. *Journal of Memetics*, 6, http://jom-emit.cfpm.org/2005/vol9/blute_m.html.

Boltanski, L. (2011). *On critique: A sociology of emancipation*. Malden, MA: Polity Press.

Bossarte, R. M. (Ed.). (2013). *Veteran suicide: A public health imperative*. Washington, DC: American Public Health Association.

Brown, L. M., Chesney-Lind, M., & Stein, N. (2007). Patriarchy matters toward a gendered theory of teen violence and victimization. *Violence Against Women, 13*(12), 1249–1273.

Bruinius, H. (2006). *Better for all the world: The secret history of forced sterilization and America's quest for racial purity*. New York: Vintage Books.

Bryson, V. (1999). "Patriarchy": A concept too useful to lose. *Contemporary Politics, 5*(4), 311–324.

Chen, C. (2012). The creation and meaning of internet memes in 4chan: Popular internet culture in the age of online digital reproduction. *HABITUS: Institutions*, Volume III. Yale College.

Cohen, P. (2014). Family diversity is the new normal for America's children. *Briefing paper prepared for the Council on Contemporary Families*. Retrieved from https://familyinequality.files.word-press.com/2014/09/family-diversity-new-normal.pdf.

Clawson, D., Zussman, R., Misra, J., Gerstel, N., Stokes, R., Anderton, D. L., & Burawoy, M. (2007). *Public sociology: Fifteen eminent sociologists debate politics & the profession in the twenty-first century*. Berkeley: University of California Press.

Collins, S. (2010). Digital fair: Prosumption and the fair use defence. *Journal of Consumer Culture*, *10*(1), 37–55.

Comor, E. (2010). Contextualizing and critiquing the fantastic prosumer: Power, alienation and hegemony. *Critical Sociology*, *37*(3), 309–327.

Connell, R. W. (2005). *Masculinities: Second edition*. Berkeley: University of California Press.

Coontz, S. (1992). *The way we never were: American families and the nostalgia trap*. New York: Basic Books.

Cormode, G., & B. Krishnamurthy. (2008). Key differences between web 1.0 and web 2.0. *First Monday*, *13*(6-2), doi: http://dx.doi.org/10.5210/fm.v13i6.2125.

Dahlen, J. (2011). Get back to the kitchen. Retrieved from http://knowyourmeme.com/memes/get-back-to-the-kitchen.

Dawkins, R. (1989). *The selfish gene*. New York: Oxford University Press.

Della Porta, D., & Diani, M. (2009). *Social movements: An introduction*. Malden, MA: Blackwell Publishing.

Despair, Inc. (2015). *Demotivators*. Retrieved from http://www.despair.com/demotivators.html

DiMaggio, P., Hargittai, E., Neuman, W. R., & Robinson, J. P. (2001). Social implications of the internet. *Annual Review of Sociology*, 27, 307–336.

Do Rozario, R. A. C. (2004). The princess and the Magic Kingdom: Beyond nostalgia, the function of the Disney princess. *Women's Studies in Communication*, *27*(1), 34–59.

Dutton, Donald G. (1994). Patriarchy and wife assault: The ecological fallacy. *Violence and Victims*, *9*(2), 167–182.

Dyer-Witheford, N., & de Peuter, G. (2009). *Games of empire: Global capitalism and video games*. Minneapolis: University of Minnesota Press.

eBizMBA Guide. (2015, February). Top 15 most popular web 2.0 websites. Retrieved from http://www.ebizmba.com/articles/web-2.0-websites.

Evan, S. M. (1979). *Personal politics: The roots of women's liberation in the civil rights movement & the new left*. New York: Random House.

Feagin, J. R., & Vera, H. (2001). *Liberation sociology*. Cambridge, MA: Westview Press.

Ferree, M. M. (2005). Soft repression: Ridicule, stigma, and silencing in gender-based movements. In C. Davenport, H. Johnston, & C. Mueller (Eds.), *Repression and mobilization* (pp. 138–155). Minneapolis: University of Minnesota Press.

Fogel, R. W. (2000). *The fourth great awakening and the future of egalitarianism*. Chicago: University of Chicago Press.

Giddens, A. (1979). *Central problems in social theory: Action, structure, and contradictions in social analysis*. Berkeley: University of California Press.

------. (1990). *The consequences of modernity*. Stanford, CA: Stanford University Press.

------. (1991). *Modernity and self-identity: Self and society in the late modern age*. Stanford, CA: Stanford University Press.

Grov, C. (2004). "Make me your death slave": Men who have sex with men and use the internet to intentionally spread HIV. *Deviant Behavior*, 25(4), 329–349.

Grumpy Cat®. (2015a). *About Grumpy Cat*. Retrieved from http://www.grumpycats.com/about-grumpy-cat.

------. (2015b). *Grumpuccino TM Coffee*. Retrieved from http://www.grumpycats.com/grumpy-cat-merchandise/grumppuccino.

Guadagno, R. E., Rempala, D. M., Murphy, S., & Okdie, B. M. (2013). What makes a video go viral? An analysis of emotional contagion and internet memes. *Computers in Human Behavior*, 29(6), 2312–2319.

Habermas, J. (2008). Notes on post-secular society. *New Perspectives Quarterly, 25*(4), 17.

Hearn, J. (2004). From hegemonic masculinity to the hegemony of men. *Feminist Theory*, 5(1), 49–72.

Higate, P., & Hopton, J. (2005). War, militarism, and masculinities. In M. S. Kimmel, J. Hearn, & R. W. Connell (Eds.), *Handbook of studies on men and masculinities* (pp. 432–445). Thousand Oaks, CA: SAGE Publications, Inc.

hooks, b. (2000). *Feminist theory: From margin to center* (2nd ed.). London: Pluto Press.

Hunnicutt, G. (2009). Varieties of patriarchy and violence against women: Resurrecting "patriarchy" as a theoretical tool. *Violence Against Women*, 15(5), 553–573.

Huntemann, N. B., & Payne, M. T. (Eds.). (2010). *Joystick soldiers: The politics of play in military video games*. New York: Routledge.

Hunter, J. D. (1992). *Culture wars: The struggle to control the family, art, education, law, and politics in America*. New York: Basic Books.

Jasinski, J. L. (2001). Theoretical explanations for violence against women. In C. M. Renzetti, J. L. Edleson, & R. K. Bergen (Eds.), *Sourcebook on violence against women* (pp. 5–22). Thousand Oaks, CA: SAGE Publications, Inc.

Johnson, M. P. (1995). Patriarchal terrorism and common couple violence: Two forms of violence against women. *Journal of Marriage and the Family, 57*(2), 283–294.

Kaplan, L. D. (1994). Woman as caretaker: An archetype that supports patriarchal militarism. *Hypatia, 9*(2), 123–133.

Kelemen, M., & Smith, W. (2001). Community and its "virtual" promises: A critique of cyberlibertarian rhetoric. *Information, Communication & Society, 4*(3), 370–387.

Kelly, K. (2009, May 22). The new socialism: Global collectivist society is coming online. *Wired.* Retrieved from http://www.wired.com/culture/culturereviews/magazine/17-06/nep_newsocialism.

Kelner, J., & Munves, J. (1980). *The Kent State coverup.* New York: Harper and Row.

kikinak. (2010). Philosoraptor. Retrieved from http://knowyourmeme.com/memes/philosoraptor.

Killian, L. M. (1971). Optimism and pessimism in sociological analysis. *The American Sociologist, 6*(4), 281–286.

Kimball, Will. (2010). Demotivational posters. Retrieved from http://knowyourmeme.com/memes/demotivational-posters.

Kirkpatrick, G. (2008). *Technology & social power.* New York: Palgrave Macmillan.

Knobel, M., & Lankshear, C. (2007). Online memes, affinities, and cultural production. In M. Knobel and C. Lankshear (Eds.), *A new literacies sampler* (pp. 199–227). New York: Peter Lang.

Knottnerus, J. D. (1996). Social structure: An introductory essay. *Humboldt Journal of Social Relations, 22*(2), 7–13.

------. (2011). *Ritual as a missing link: Sociology, structural ritualization theory and research.* Boulder, CO: Paradigm Publishers.

Koss, M. P., Goodman, L. A., Browne, A., Fitzgerald, L. F., Keita, G. P., & Russo, N. F. (1994). No safe haven: Male violence against women at home, at work, and in the community. *American Psychological Association.*

Lankshear, C., & Knobel, M. (2007). Digital remix: The art and craft of endless hybridization. Keynote address: *The International Reading Association Pre-Conference Institute.* Toronto.

Lee, A. M. (1973). *Toward a humanist sociology.* Englewood Cliffs, NJ: Prentice-Hall, Inc.

Lewis, C. (2007). New literacies. In M. Knobel and C. Lankshear (Eds.), *A new literacies sampler* (pp. 229–237). New York: Peter Lang.

Lynch, A. (1996). *Thought contagion: How belief spreads through society.* New York: Basic Books.

MacKinnon, C. A. (1989). *Toward a feminist theory of the state.* Cambridge, MA: Harvard University Press.

Marx, K., & Engels, F. (1845/2011). *The German ideology.* Malden, MA: Wiley-Blackwell.

Mills, C. W. (1959/2000). *The sociological imagination.* New York: Oxford University Press.

Misa, T. J., Brey, P., & Feenberg, A. (Eds.). (2003). *Modernity and technology*. Cambridge, MA: MIT Press.

Orr, J. (2004). The militarization of inner space. *Critical Sociology, 30*(2), 451–481.

Parsons, T., & Bales, J. (1955). *Family, socialization and interaction process*. New York: The Free Press.

Perl, L. (2012). *Veterans and homelessness*. (CRS Report, RL34024). Washington, DC: U.S. Government Printing Office.

Peters, M. A. (2010). Creativity, openness, and the global knowledge economy: The advent of user-generated cultures. *Economics, Management, and Financial Markets, 3*, 15–36.

Platt, A., & Cooper, L. (1974). *Policing America*. Englewood Cliffs, NJ: Prentice-Hall, Inc.

Powell, W. W., & Snellman, K. (2004). The knowledge economy. *Annual Review of Sociology, 30*, 199–220.

Reardon, B. (1996). Militarism and sexism: Influences on education for war. In R. J. Burns, & R. Aspeslagh (Eds.), *Three decades of peace education around the world: An anthology* (pp. 143–160). New York: Routledge.

Reicher, S., Haslam, S. A., & Hopkins, N. (2005). Social identity and the dynamics of leadership: Leaders and followers as collaborative agents in the transformation of social reality. *The Leadership Quarterly, 16*(4), 547–568.

Ritzer, G. (2013). *The McDonaldization of society, 20th anniversary edition*. Thousand Oaks, CA: SAGE Publications, Inc.

Ritzer, G., Dean, P., & Jurgenson, N. (2012). The coming of age of the prosumer. *American Behavioral Scientist, 56*(4), 379–398.

Ritzer, George, & Nathan Jurgenson. (2010). Production, consumption, prosumption: The nature of capitalism in the age of the digital "prosumer." *Journal of Consumer Culture, 10*(1), 13–36.

Rupp, L. J. (2008). Revisiting patriarchy. *Journal of Women's History, 20*(2), 136–140.

Scott, M. C. (2012). *Casually pepper spray everything cop*. Retrieved http://knowyourmeme.com/memes/casually-pepper-spray-everything-cop.

Shifman, L. (2014). *Memes in digital culture*. Cambridge, MA: The MIT Press.

Shifman, L., & Lemish, D. (2010). Between feminism and fun(ny)mism. *Information, Communication & Society, 13*(6), 870–891.

------. (2011). "Mars and Venus" in virtual space: Post-feminist humor and the internet. *Critical Studies in Media Communication, 28*(3), 253–273.

Situngkir, H. (2004). On selfish memes: Culture as complex adaptive system. *Journal of Social Complexity, 2*(1), 20–32.

Smicker, J. (2010). Future combat, combating futures: Temporalities of war video games and the performance of proleptic histories. In N. B. Huntemann & M. T. Payne (Eds.), *Joystick soldiers: The politics of play in military video games* (pp. 106–121). New York: Routledge.

Smith, M. D. (1990). Patriarchal ideology and wife beating: A test of a feminist hypothesis. *Violence and Victims, 5*(4), 257–273.

Snow, E. (1989). Theorizing the male gaze: Some problems. *Representations, 25,* 30–41.

StumbleUpon.com. (2015). *About.* Retrieved from http://www.stumbleupon.com/about.

Tanielian, T., & Jaycox, L. H. (Eds.). (2008). *Invisible wounds of war: Psychological and cognitive injuries, their consequences, and services to assist recovery.* Arlington, VA: Rand Corporation.

Tarrow, S. (1994). *Power in movement: Social movements, collective action and politics.* New York: Cambridge University Press.

ter Meulen, J., Casimiro, D., Coller, B. A., Heinrichs, J., & Bhambhani, A. (2015). Winning a race against evolving pathogens with novel platforms and universal vaccines. In M. Singh & M. Salnikova (Eds.), *Novel approaches and strategies for biologics, vaccines and cancer therapies* (pp. 251–288). Waltham, MA: Academic Press.

Thornton, P. H., Ocasio, W., & Lounsbury, M. (2012). *The institutional logics perspective: A new approach to culture, structure, and process.* New York: Oxford University Press, Inc.

Tomlinson, J. (1991). *Cultural imperialism: A critical introduction.* Baltimore: Johns Hopkins University Press.

Varny, W. (2000). Playing with "war fare." *Peace Review, 12*(3), 385–391.

Walby, S. (1989). Theorising patriarchy. *Sociology, 23*(2), 213–234.

Westley, W. A. (1970). *Violence and the police: A sociological study of law, custom, and morality.* Cambridge, MA: MIT Press.

White, J. W. & Kowalski, R. M. (1998). Male violence toward women: An integrated perspective. In R. G. Geen & E. Donnerstein (Eds.), *The Social Psychology of Aggression* (pp. 203–228). San Diego: Academic Press.

ENDNOTES

1. This project developed from a lecture given during the spring 2013 semester for my Social Stratification course, and it might have fallen by the wayside had two of my students not taken an interest in it. I would like to thank Oklahoma State University and its sociology department for the years of dedicated training, as well as all the helpful comments and feedback from audiences, reviewers, and editors, but I would like to especially thank Kevin Gonzales and Rachelynn Coffman for going the extra mile for SOC 4383. It was already difficult, but they wanted more!

2. This is the URL for the image in Figure 1: http://www.memecenter.com/fun/161791/women-know-your-place

3. This is the URL for the StumbleUpon.com webpage: http://www.stumbleupon.com/su/1s0Etk/knowyour-meme.com/photos/47958-get-back-to-the-kitchen/, and here is the URL to the particular website: http://knowyourmeme.com/photos/47958-get-back-to-the-kitchen/

4. This is the URL for the image in Figure 2: http://knowyourmeme.com/photos/423106-get-back-to-the-kitchen?ref=next-arrow#media-title

5. This is the URL for the image in Figure 3: http://cheezburger.com/5697279488

6. "**Philosoraptor** is an image macro series featuring a clip art of Velociraptor deeply immersed in metaphysical inquiries or unraveling quirky paradoxes. One of the more thoughtful (and successful) Advice Dog variations, Philosoraptor challenges the reader with his deep, existential, Paleolithic questions" (kikinak, 2010).

7. This is the URL for the image in Figure 4: http://knowyourmeme.com/photos/145128-get-back-to-the-kitchen?ref=prev-arrow#media-title

8. This is the URL for the image in Figure 5: http://www.memecenter.com/fun/337505/nice-try

9. "Pepper Spray Cop (also known as "Casually Pepper Spray Everything Cop") is a photoshop meme based on a photograph of a police officer offhandedly pepper spraying a group of Occupy protesters at the University of California Davis in November 2011" (scott, 2012).

10. This is the URL for the image of the Casually Pepper Spray Everything meme spraying The Declaration of Independence: http://i3.kym-cdn.com/entries/icons/original/000/007/647/320665_309085722453433_1000 00560234460_1161317_489395404_n.jpg.

11. This is the URL for the Casually Pepper Spray Everything meme: http://knowyourmeme.com/photos/203669-casually-pepper-spray-everything-cop

12. This is the URL for the image in Figure 6: http://knowyourmeme.com/photos/42469-get-back-to-the-kitchen

Compulsive Heterosexuality

MASCULINITY AND DOMINANCE

by C.J. Pascoe

The weight room, a freestanding module by the football field, stank with a familiar musty smell of old sweat, metal, and rubber. Colorful diagrams of deltoids, biceps, quads, and other muscle groups adorned the walls. Each day Coach Ramirez, a gentle, soft-spoken man, called roll and told the (mostly male) students to run a lap or two as he entered the module to place his folders in his office and turn on the stereo. After running their laps, the sweaty boys filed in as loud hip-hop music blared from the stereo. Dressed in regulation black gym shorts and T-shirts, boys milled about, picking up weights, completing a few sets, and then moving on to other machines. Some of the African American boys danced to the music, while, inevitably, Josh and his white friends asked for country music.

One fall morning, as some of the boys grew tired of lifting, they gathered around a set of benches in the front of the weight room. Reggie, a white rugby-playing junior, asked the gathering group, "Did you hear about the three 'B's?' " Before anyone had a chance to respond, Reggie announced triumphantly, "Blow job, back massage, and breakfast in bed!" Rich asked skeptically, "Shouldn't the back massage come first?" The conversation soon turned to the upcoming Winter Ball and their prospects for sex with their dates. Jerome complained that he was not "gonna get laid at Winter Ball." Josh admonished, "That's why you gotta go for the younger ones, fool!

Like twelve years old!" Reggie, Rich, and Pedro laughed at Josh's advice. Pedro, never quiet for long, told the rest, "If you can put their legs behind their head and eat them out they'll have the fattest orgasm." The conversation quickly evolved into a game of sexual one-upmanship as Reggie, Rich, Jerome, and Josh began talking over each other, each with a more fantastic story. Josh claimed he was "so good" that he couldn't "control the girl from thrashing around on the bed and hurting herself on the headboard." In response Jerome advised, "That's why you gotta start out at the headboard!" Reggie shouted, "My girlfriend's bed broke!" Rich jumped in with "One time my girlfriend's dad came home while we were doing it and I had to hide in the closet." Josh, not to be outdone, replied, "Hey man, try getting a b.j. [blow job] while you are driving home!" This challenge was answered by a chorus of groans and "I've done that!"

This sort of locker-room talk is what one expects to find when researching teenage boys and masculinity. Indeed, the public face of male adolescence is filled with representations of masculinity in which boys brag about sexual exploits by showing off a girl's underwear (as in the 1980s film *Pretty in Pink*), spend the end of their senior year talking about how they plan to lose their virginity (*American Pie*), or make cruel bets about who can bed the ugliest girl in the school (*She's All That*). In many ways, the boys at River High seemed much like their celluloid representatives. As this scene in the weight room indicates, heterosexual innuendoes, sexual bravado, and sexual one-upmanship permeated these primarily male spaces. This chapter looks at these gender practices and, instead of taking them at face value as testosterone-fueled verbal jockeying, pays attention to the meanings of masculinity embedded in them. In these sorts of interactions and gendered spaces, masculinity, in spite of boys' talk about the gay boys' ability to be masculine as discussed in the previous chapter, is assumed to be synonymous with heterosexuality. But, as they do when invoking the fag discourse, boys talking about heterosexuality are and are not talking about sex. Their talk about heterosexuality reveals less about sexual orientation and desire than it does about the centrality of the ability to exercise mastery and dominance literally or figuratively over girls' bodies (Wood 1984). These heterosexually based gender practices serve to defend boys against emasculating insults like those in the fag discourse (Hird and Jackson 2001). Engaging in very public practices of heterosexuality, boys affirm much more than just masculinity; they affirm subjecthood and personhood through sexualized interactions in which they indicate to themselves and others that they have the ability to work their will upon the world around them. Imposing one's will and demonstrating dominance in this way aligns boys with personhood and subjectivity, historically coded as masculine (Jaggar 1983; Mackinnon 1982). Demonstrating dominance in a variety of ways is a central part of contemporary American masculinity (Peirce 1995).

Compulsive heterosexuality[1] is the name I give to this constellation of sexualized practices, discourses, and interactions. This term builds on Adrienne Rich's (1986) influential concept of "compulsory heterosexuality."[2] Rich argues that heterosexuality not only describes sexual desires, practices and orientations but is a "political institution" (23). The "enforcement of heterosexuality for women as a means of assuring male right of physical, economic and emotional access" (50) is a central component of gender inequality. The microprocesses of heterosexuality as an institution are so embedded in daily life that, while heterosexuality may be personally meaningful, it can simultaneously function as an oppressive social institution. While compulsory heterosexuality may regulate both men and women, "their experiences of it and the power and privilege that accompany it are different" (V. Robinson 1996, 120).

Practices of "compulsive heterosexuality" exemplify what Butler (1995) calls "gender performativity," in which gender "is produced as a ritualized repetition of conventions, and . . . this ritual is socially compelled in part by the force of a compulsory heterosexuality" (31). Compulsive heterosexuality is not about desire for sexual pleasure per se, or just about desire to be "one of the guys"; rather, it is "an excitement felt as sexuality in a male supremacist culture which eroticizes male dominance and female submission" (Jeffreys 1998, 75). Indeed, ensuring positions of power entails boys' constant "recreation of masculinity and femininity" through rituals of eroticized dominance (Jeffreys 1998, 77). Looking at boys' ritualistic sex talk, patterns of touch, and games of "getting girls" indicates how this gender inequality is reinforced through everyday interactions. Taken together, these ritualized interactions continually affirm masculinity as mastery and dominance. By symbolically or physically mastering girls' bodies and sexuality, boys at River High claim masculine identities.

A STUD WITH THE LADIES

Not surprisingly, the most popular boys at River High are heterosexual. Expressing heterosexual desire establishes a sort of baseline masculinity. Bradley, a charming blond, blue-eyed sophomore who could hardly contain his excitement about being interviewed, explained, "To be the coolest guy? If you're just like a stud at sports and you're a stud with the ladies." If anyone at River High was a "stud at sports" and a "stud with the ladies," it was Chad, a tall, well-muscled, strikingly good-looking senior football player of mixed white and Latino heritage. Chad spent much of his interview describing how he was "*that guy*" on campus: "I'm Chad Rodgers. I play football. I'm going to college. All that kind of shit. Bad-ass, you know?" He said that because of this, other guys were envious of him. When I asked him why this was the case, he answered confidently, with a bit of a sneer, "Probably 'cause they can't get girls. I work out. I got muscles and a nice body." In her interview, Cathy confirmed Chad's view of himself, saying, with admiration, "Chad? He's a big, cocky man. But he deserves the right to be cocky. He is *really* hot. But he knows it. That's just Chad. He just thinks the world revolves around him." Indeed, after interviewing him, I received the same impression of Chad.

Chad told me that he, along with some of his football teammates, frequently teased another teammate: "This dude, Dax Reynolds, he gets made fun of a lot 'cause he's always holding his girlfriend's hand. To the other guys it's funny. We just make fun of him." According to Chad, a successful sex life was more important than public displays of affection. If a guy wasn't having sex, "he's no one. He's nobody." Chad explained that some guys tried to look cool by lying about sex, but they "look like a clown, [they get] made fun of." He assured me, however, that he was not one of those "clowns" forced to lie about sex, bragging, "When I was growin' up *I* started having sex in the eighth grade." However, his description of these sexual adventures sounded scarily close to date rape. He told me, "The majority of the girls in eighth and ninth grade were just stupid. We already knew what we were doing. They didn't know what they were doing, you know?" When I asked him to explain this, he continued, "Like say, comin' over to our house like past 12:00. What else do you do past 12:00? Say we had a bottle of alcohol or something. I'm not saying we forced it upon them. I'm sayin' . . . " He trailed off here as he tried to explain that he didn't need to actually rape girls, though his friends did: "Kevin Goldsmith and uh, Calvin Johnson, they got charged with rape." Chad assured me that in spite of his statement that he had used alcohol with underage girls he had never had to force a girl to have sex: "I'll never [be in] that predicament, you know. I've never had a hard time, or had to, you know, alter their thinking."

Other boys echoed Chad's assertions about the importance of sex, saying that they felt the pressure to have sex, or at least act like they were having sex. Connor, a white junior who frequently wore Harley David-son insignia T-shirts and a black leather jacket, suggested that sex was important to maintain one's image:

> If his friends are talking about it [sex] and they got some and this guy is like "oh man, they're cool and I wanna be cool." So they go and do whatever as far as prostitution or actually drugging a girl or whatever. As far as image goes—yeah, they think it's [sex] important.

Angela told me that one of her male friends was so desperate to be seen as sexually experienced that he lied about it:

> They brag about it. They lie about it. I noticed a lot of guys lie about it. Like that guy I like. He's my best friend now, one of them. And he messed around with one of my friends before me and him started talking. He told people at football camp that they had sex. But he told me he was still a virgin. He was like, bragging about it. I asked him, "Are you still a virgin?" All of his other close friends were like, "Yeah. He's still a virgin." I said, "Why did you lie about it?" He was like, "I just wanted people to think I was cool."

Ben concurred with this analysis: "Of course they lie about it . . . It's like, tell your friends, 'Last night it was good.' And then the girl walks up and they talk about something else. You know how it is."

The way boys talked about heterosexual practices and orientations in their interviews reveals that their public sexuality was as much about securing a masculine social position as it was about expressions of desire or emotion. David explicitly talked about this "image" problem as one of "peer pressure," saying, "If you haven't scored with someone, then you are not adequate to anyone else, you know?"

In this sense, Chad was both an exemplar and an arbiter of heterosexuality. Like other boys, he recognized only specific expressions of heterosexuality as masculine. In groups boys act as a sort of "sexual police" (Hird and Jackson 2001), deriding each other's expressions of love, romance, or emotional desire, such as Dax's holding of his girlfriend's hand. Chad also had the ability to discern whether other guys were lying about their sexual activities. It seems that lying about it might actually make one less masculine than simply not engaging in it! Finally, as noted by Cathy and Chad himself, Chad was the paragon of masculinity at River High. He was "really hot" and "muscular" and could "get girls" when other guys couldn't.

If boys couldn't actually bed a girl, they had to at least act as if they were sexually attracted to girls. Jace told me that guys who weren't interested in girls were "all gay guys." Indeed, Gary confirmed that having a girlfriend served as proof of heterosexuality. I asked Gary, a white senior with spiky burgundy hair and a smartly assembled Abercrombie and Fitch outfit who was involved in drama and choir, "Is it important that guys have girlfriends?" He explained,

> Probably. Yeah. It shows you're a man. I think it's important. Let's say the top actor guy who everybody thought was gay had a really nice girlfriend. That might happen just for a cover-up so that guy can be left alone from the stereotypes and the teasing. I think it may be important to some people just so they can go through high school without worrying about anybody talking about them.

Girlfriends both protected boys from the specter of the fag and bolstered their masculinity. In fact, in the "Revenge of the Nerds" skit discussed in the introduction, the deciding factor in the nerds' ascendance to masculinity was their ability to reclaim "their" girlfriends.

Not surprisingly, given Chad's comment that if a guy hadn't had sex he was no one, boys felt pressured to make sure others knew that they thought about sex. In fact, thinking about sex was so important that boys often named it (much like homophobia) as a defining facet of adolescent masculinity. Connor explained this in response to my question "How would you describe teenage guys?"

> I *do* think it's true for 99.9 percent of the guys that they think about girls every 5.2 seconds . . . Every time they think of a girl they think of something sexually. Like every time they see a girl they look at her ass or whatever. Guys are into girls.

Connor's comments reflected what many boys at River told me, that teenage guys think about sex all of the time. What Connor left out was that boys not only thought about girls "every 5.2 seconds" but constantly, compulsively expressed this thought process. Like Connor, Tal, a slim white underclassman, also positioned thinking about sex as a defining aspect of teen masculinity. As we walked out of the weight room one day, I asked if there was anything he'd like me to include in my notes. He replied, "I got something for you! All guys think about is eating pussy twenty-four-seven!"

At River High, sex, thinking about sex, and talking about sex were framed repeatedly as specifically masculine concerns, even in the classroom. In drama class Mr. McNally was walking the class through the different components of a story—the introduction, the buildup, and then the climax. A boy in the back of the class yelled out, "Climax! Every guy knows what that is!" The class laughed. While girls might have thought about it, enjoyed it, and even desired it, sex tended to be marked as a male domain.

Heath, a tall, white attractive junior involved in the drama program who was known for his unique clothing style, told me that this sort of behavior was expected of boys; teenage guys were supposed to be "more outspoken about sexual stuff and hollering at girls and all that stuff." Darren identified auto shop as a particularly masculine arena rife with sexual discussions, explaining, "Auto shop class is a stereotype. Very typical teenage guys. All they ever talk about is sex and cars . . . it seems like sex always comes up." Jose told me something similar: "Most guys want a girl for a night and that's it. That's all it is over here. They're just looking for a girl and then they'll just forget about it the next day and then go onto something else." He told me that his friend was one of those guys:

Some guys kind of put it in their [girls'] minds that they're going to be with them and then the next day they won't call them. Like I know a guy [who is] especially good at that. He's one of my best friends. He can pull out a phone book and be like, "Who do I want to talk to tonight?" Then he'll be with them for the night. He's just a guy and he just wants as many girls as he can. Just wants girls, I guess.

For the most part boys seemed to be proud of this stereotypical "love 'em and leave 'em" behavior. While seemingly promiscuous girls were quickly and shamefully labeled *slut,* boys proudly donned the moniker of *male whore.* One of my interviewees, John, laughingly described his friend as "a male whore. Guys just don't care! Like my friend, Jeff—a male whore. I swear to God, that guy!" I asked, surprised, "He's proud?" John answered, "Oh yeah! He's proud!" Similarly Heath told me that "double standards" applied to girl and boy sexual behaviors: if a "guy sleeps around, he's the man. Girl sleeps around, oh, she's a slut. It's weird. I don't know why."

Sadly, it seems that for all the feminist activism of the past several decades little has changed in the day-to-day public sexual practices and discourses of adolescent boys. Boys still look to "score," and girls' bodies still serve as proof of masculinity. Girls who have sex are still labeled sluts, and boys who have sex are still vaulted to popularity.

GETTING GIRLS

Chad sneered at boys who, unlike him, couldn't "get girls." Getting girls, like the "girl watching" documented by Beth Quinn (2002), "functions as a game men play to build shared masculine identities and social relations" (387). Boys who couldn't engage in this game of "getting girls" lost masculine capital. School rituals such as the homecoming assembly mirrored Chad's derision of boys who failed to play at "getting girls." At the Homecoming Assembly two boys, Lamar and Tonio, stood in front of the cheering student body, lip-synching a comedy routine between Chris Rock and Michael Jackson.[3] Leering and pointing at two attractive girls clad in hip-high leather boots, black miniskirts, and white tank tops walking across the stage, the two boys pulled each other aside. Lamar, as Chris Rock, dared Tonio, as Jackson, to "get a girl." They paced back and forth in front of the girls, "Chris Rock" saying, "That girl! Oh man!" "Michael Jackson" responded in a high-pitched voice, "Goodness gracious! She is too fine!" "Rock" agreed, "She sho' is fine!" "Rock" turned to "Jackson," challenging him, "You can't get that girl!" "Jackson" responded defensively, in a high voice, "I *can* get her!" Again "Rock" challenged him, "I *bet* you can't get that girl! Michael, you are going to Neverland again!" The students roared in laughter as the two boys strutted back to "get" the girls.

The ritual of "getting girls" played out in this homecoming skit illustrates one of the ways compulsive heterosexuality becomes a part of boys' friendships and interactional styles. "Rock" and "Jackson," like boys at River High, jokingly challenged each other to dominate—or, in their words, to "get"—a girl. In these rituals girls' bodies functioned as a symbol of male heterosexuality and tangible evidence of repudiation of same sex-desire (Butler 1999). That is, if boys desired girls, then they couldn't possibly desire each other.

Both of the Mr. Cougar sketches I have outlined thus far involved stories of getting girls. In each one the victorious pair of boys was rewarded with girls as confirmation of their dominance. When Brent and Greg defeated the "gangstas," they were rewarded with "their girls," and when Freddy and Randy, as River High wrestlers, defeated their wrestling foes, the "dancing girls" ripped off their shirts to reveal a color pattern that symbolically linked them to Freddy and Randy. Rituals of getting girls allowed boys to find common ground in affirming each other's masculinity and positioned them as subjects who had a right to control what girls did with their bodies. A close examination indicates that rituals of "getting girls" relied on a threat of sexualized violence that reaffirmed a sexualized inequality central to the gender order at River High.

On Halloween, Heath arrived at school dressed as an elf carrying a sprig of mistletoe and engaged in a fairly typical ritual of getting girls. He told anyone who would listen that an elf costume was a brilliant idea for Halloween because "it's the wrong holiday!" We stood by his friends at the "water polo" table who tried to sell greeting cards as a fundraiser for the team. Heath attempted to "help" by yelling at girls who passed by, "Ten dollars for a card and a kiss from the elf! Girls only!" Girls made faces and rolled their eyes as they walked past. Graham walked up and Heath yelled to him, arms outstretched, "Come here, baby!" Graham walked toward him with his hips thrust forward and his arms open, saying, "I'm coming!" and quickly both of them backed away laughing. Graham challenged Heath's kissing strategy, saying that the mistletoe sticking out of his green shorts wouldn't work because it wasn't Christmas. Heath, to prove his point that mistletoe worked at any time of the year, lifted the mistletoe above his head and, moving from behind the table, walked up to a group of girls. They looked at him with a bit of trepidation and tried to ignore his presence. Finally one acquiesced, giving him a peck on the cheek. Her friend followed suit. Heath strutted back to the table and victoriously shook hands with all the boys.

Heath, in this instance, became successfully masculine both through renouncing the fag—he emphasized he was kissing "girls only," he imitated a fag by coming on to Graham—and through "getting girls" to kiss him.[4] Graham then congratulated Heath on his ability to overcome the girls' resistance to his overtures. This sort of coercion, even when seemingly harmless, embeds a sense of masculinity predicated upon an overcoming of girls' resistance to boys' desire (Hird and Jackson 2001). Indeed, if one of the important parts of being masculine, as stated by the boys earlier, was not just to desire girls, which Heath indicated through his "girls only" admonition, but also to be desired by girls, Heath demonstrated this in a quite public way, thus ensuring a claim, at least for a moment, on heterosexuality.

While the boys laughed and celebrated Heath's triumph of will, the girls may not have had the same reaction to his forced kisses. In a study of teenagers and sexual harassment, Jean Hand and Laura Sanchez (2000) found, not surprisingly, that in high school girls experienced higher levels of sexual harassment than boys did and were affected more seriously by it. The girls in their study described a hierarchy of sexually harassing behaviors in which some behaviors were described as more problematic than others. The girls overwhelmingly indicated that being kissed against their will was the worst form of sexual harassment, rated more seriously than hearing boys' comments about their bodies or receiving other types of unwanted sexual attention.

Of course, it is unlikely that boys, or girls, would recognize these sorts of daily rituals as sexual harassment; they are more likely seen as normal, if perhaps a bit aggressive, instances of heterosexual flirtation and as part of a normal adolescence (N. Stein 2005).[5] In fact, I never saw a teacher at River recognize these seemingly flirtatious interchanges as harassment. In auto shop, Tammy, the only girl, often faced this sort of harassment, often at the hands of Jay, a stringy-haired white junior with a pimpled face. One afternoon he walked up to Tammy and stood behind her deeply inhaling, his nose not even an inch away from her hair. Clearly uncomfortable with this, she moved to the side. He asked her if she was planning to attend WyoTech (Wyoming Technical College, a mechanic school), and she responded, "Yes." He said, "I'm going too! You and me. We're gonna be in a room together." He closed his eyes and started thrusting his hips back and forth and softly moaning as if to indicate that he was having sex. Tammy said, "Shut up" and walked away. Used to this sort of harassment, she had developed a way of dealing with such behavior. But no matter how many times she dismissed him, Jay continued to pepper her with sexual innuendoes and suggestive practices.

Both Jay's and Heath's behaviors show how heterosexuality is normalized as a sort of "predatory" social relation in which boys try and try and try to "get" a girl until one finally gives in. Boys, like Jay, who can't "get" a girl often respond with anger or frustration because of their presumed right to girls' bodies. Marc reacted this way when a girl didn't acknowledge his advances. As usual, he sat in the rear of the drama classroom with his pal Jason. A tall, attractive blonde girl walked into the room to speak to Mr. McNally, the drama teacher. As she turned to leave the class, Marc, leaning back with his legs up on the chair in front of him and his arm draped casually over the seat next to him, yelled across the room, "See you later, hot mama!" Jason, quickly echoed him, yelling "See you later, sweet thing." She didn't acknowledge them and looked straight ahead at the door as she left. Marc, frustrated at her lack of response, loudly stated, "She didn't hear me. Whore." Instead of acknowledging that not getting her reflected something about his gender status, he deflected the blame onto her. In fact, he transformed her into the female version of the fag: the whore.[6]

Getting, or not getting, girls also reflects and reinforces racialized meanings of sexuality and masculinity. Darnell, the African American and white football player who, in chapter 3, talked about how boys were told from a young age to avoid becoming a fag, made it clear that this sort of rejection was embedded with racialized meanings: pacing up and down the stairs that line the drama classroom, he yelled across the room to me. "There's just one thing I hate! Just one thing I hate!" Shawna, an energetic, bisexual African American sophomore, and I simultaneously asked, "What's that?" Darnell responded, frustrated, "When mixed girls date white guys! Mixed girls are for me!" Shawna attempted to interrupt his rant, saying, "What if the girl doesn't want to date you? Girls have a say too." Darnell responded, not in as much jest as one might hope, "No they don't. White boys can date white girls. There's plenty of 'em. They can even date black girls. But mixed girls are for me." Darnell's frustration reflects a way in which racialized, gendered, and sexual identities intersect. While he felt that he had a claim on "getting girls," as a "mixed" guy he saw his options as somewhat limited. Girls and girls' bodies were constructed as a limited resource for which he had to compete with other (white) guys.

TOUCHING

Just as same-sex touching puts boys at risk for becoming a fag, cross-sex touching affirms heterosexuality and masculinity. "The use of touch (especially between the sexes)" maintains a "social hierarchy" (Henley 1977, 5). In general, superiors touch subordinates, invade their space, and interrupt them in a way that subordinates do not do to superiors. At River High masculinity was established through gendered rituals of touch involving boys' physical dominance and girls' submission.

Girls and boys regularly touched each other in a way that boys did not touch other boys. While girls touched other girls across social environments, boys usually touched each other in rule-bound environments (such as sports) or as a joke to imitate fags. While boys and girls both participated in cross-sex touching, it had different gender meanings. For girls, touching boys was part of a continuum of cross-sex and same-sex touching. That is, girls touched, hugged, and linked arms with other girls on a regular basis in a way that boys did not. For boys, cross-sex touching often took the form of a ritualistic power play that embedded gender meanings of boys as powerful and girls as submissive, or at least weak in their attempts to resist the touching. Touching, in this sense, becomes a "kinesic gender marker" producing masculinity as dominance and femininity as submission (Henley 1977, 138).

At River High boys and girls constantly touched each other as part of daily interaction, communication, and flirtation. In many instances cross-sex touching was lightly flirtatious and reciprocal. In auto shop Brian, a tall white senior, wrapped his arms around Cara, a skinny, white sophomore, who had wandered in to watch the boys work on a car. She said to him, "Let me feel your muscles."[7] Brian responded proudly, "Check out these guns!" As he flexed his arms Cara wrapped her hand around his biceps, laughing and teasing: "Those aren't muscles! I can still squeeze it!" Brian, indignant, responded, "Let me feel yours." The thin girl made her best attempt at flexing her muscles. Grabbing her arms, Brian laughed at her nonexistent biceps, as did Cara. In this instance the touching was reciprocal and lighthearted, though still infused with normative notions of boys as muscular and girls as weak. Brian and Cara touched each other equally, they didn't struggle for control of the situation, and the interaction was not overtly competitive (though a hint of violence hid under the surface of the interaction, as Brian's strength and Cara's weakness were affirmed).

Like rituals of getting girls, touching rituals ranged from playfully flirtatious to assaultlike interactions. Teachers at River never intervened, at least as far as I saw, when these touching interactions turned slightly violent. In her study of sex education practices in high school, Bonnie Trudell (1993) noted that teachers don't or won't differentiate between sexualized horseplay and assault among students. I also never saw administrators intervene to stop what were seemingly clear violations of girls' bodies. While these sorts of touching interactions often began as flirtatious teasing, they usually evolved into a competition that ended with the boy triumphant and the girl yelling out some sort of metaphorical "uncle."

Darnell and Christina, for instance, engaged in a typical touching ritual during a morning drama class. The students had moved into the auditorium, where they were supposed to be rehearsing their scenes. Christina, a strikingly good-looking white junior with long blonde hair, donned Tim's wrestling letterman's jacket. Darnell asked her if she was a wrestler. In response she pretended to be a wrestler and challenged him to a wrestling match. They circled each other in mock-wrestling positions as Darnell, dressed in baggy jeans and a T-shirt, yelled, "I don't need a singlet to beat you, lady!" She advanced toward Darnell, performing karate kicks with her legs and chops with her arms. Darnell yelled, "That's not wrestling!" and grabbed her torso, flipping her flat on her back. She pulled him down and managed to use her legs to flip him over so that he ended up underneath her on his back while she straddled him, sitting on his waist. Graham yelled out, watching in fascination, "What is going on?!" Many of the students had gathered around to watch and laugh at the faux wrestling match. Finally Darnell won the match by picking Christina up and throwing her over his shoulders. He spun her around as she squealed to be put down.

The general pace and sequence of this interaction were mirrored in many boy-girl touching rituals. Boys and girls antagonized each other in a flirtatious way. The flirtatious physical interaction escalated, becoming increasingly violent, until a girl squealed, cried, or just gave up. This sort of daily drama physically engendered meanings of power in which boys were confirmed as powerful and girls as weak.

While the "wrestling incident" between Darnell and Christina expressed seemingly harmless notions of dominance and submission, other "touching" episodes had a more explicitly violent tone. In this type of touching the boy and the girl "hurt" each other by punching or slapping or pulling each other's hair until in the end the girl lost with a squeal or scream. Shane and Cathy spent a large part of each morning in government class beating up on each other in this sequence of domination. While it was certainly not unidirectional, the interactions always ended with Cathy giving up. One of the many instances in which Cathy ended up submitting to Shane's touch began when Shane "punched" Cathy's chin. Cathy, trying to ignore the punch, batted her eyelashes and in a whiny voice pleaded, "Take me to In and Out for lunch." In response Shane grabbed her neck with one hand and forehead with the other, shoving her head backward and forward. Cathy squealed, "You're messing up my hair!" As he continued to yank her head around, Cathy tried to do her work, her pen jerking across the page. While this sort of interaction regularly disrupted Cathy's work and actually looked exceedingly painful, she never seriously tried to stop it. When I asked Cathy why they interacted like that, she answered, "He has always been like that with me. We used to have a class right on the other side of that wall together, and he always beat me in there, too. I don't know. He just beats on me." Her response echoed Karin Martin's (1996) finding that adolescent girls, especially working-class girls, don't have a strong sense that they control their own bodies. While some girls, such as Shawna, were able to assert subjectivity and deny the primacy of boys' desire—as when she confronted Darnell's "Mixed girls are for me!" comment—not all girls felt entitled to or expressed alternative definitions of gender. It may be that Shawna, with her baggy pants, hip-hop style, and "tough girl" demeanor, found it easier to confront Darnell than did a normatively feminine girl like Cathy, whose status depended on her electability to the homecoming court. Cathy's affectively flat response to my question revealed that she simply didn't have access to or couldn't express her own bodily needs, desires, and rights.

Interactions such as the one between Cathy and Shane rarely drew the notice of teachers (except to the extent that the two were disrupting class time), most likely because these encounters were read as harmless flirting. But in the larger context of the school's gender and sexual order they reflected a more serious pattern in which both heterosexuality and masculinity presumed female passivity and male control. River boys often physically constrained girls in a sexual manner under the guise of flirtation. For instance, in the hallway a boy put his arms around a girl as she was walking to lunch and started "freaking" her, rubbing his pelvis against her behind as she walked. She rolled her eyes, broke away, and continued walking. What really undergirded all of these interactions is what some feminists call a "rape paradigm," in which masculinity is predicated on overcoming women's bodily desire and control. A dramatic example of this "rape paradigm" happened between classes during passing period.[8] Walking between government and drama classes, Keith yelled, "GET RAPED! GET RAPED!" as he rhythmically jabbed a girl in the crotch with his drumstick. She yelled at him to stop and tried to kick him in the crotch with her foot. He dodged and started yelling, "CROTCH! CROTCH!" Indeed, the threat of rape was what seemed to underlie many of these interactions where boys repeatedly showed in cross-gender touching that they were more physically powerful than girls.

In all-male spaces some boys talked angrily and openly about accusations of rape. In auto shop Jay told a story about how a girl had accused him of holding a gun to her head and forcing her to have sex with him. For this offense he was put under house arrest for the better part of a year. He angrily reported the injustice of this accusation but followed this with one of his relatively frequent threats about rape. He talked about a girl he thought was "hella ugly" but had "titties": "She's a bitch. I might take her out to the street races and leave her there so she can get raped." All the other boys in auto shop, as usual, responded in laughter.

This sort of thing happened more frequently in predominately male spaces. In the weight room, an extremely physical space, girls were routinely physically restrained or manipulated. Often boys teamed up to control a girl. One day Monte wrapped his arms around a girl's neck as if to put her in a headlock and held her there while Reggie punched her in the stomach, albeit lightly. She squealed and laughed in response. Another day Malcolm and Cameron held a girl down on the quadriceps press machine while she screamed a high-pitched wail. They let her up, but moments later Malcolm snuck up behind her and poked her in the behind. She screamed and laughed in response. These examples show how the constraint of female bodies gets translated as masculinity and femininity, embedding sexualized meanings in which heterosexual flirting is coded as female helplessness and male bodily dominance.

SEX TALK

As Chad noted in his interview, boys needed to ensure their masculinity by talking about sex in a way that was perceived by other boys as authentic so that they wouldn't look like "clowns." Boys' sex talk involves talking about bodies, dating, and girls in general. Often it takes the form of "mythic-story telling" in which boys tell larger-than-life tales about their sexual adventures, their bodies, and girls' bodies (Kehily and Nayak 1997). At River High, these sorts of "sex talk" competitions often erupted in predominately male environments but also occurred in mixed-gender groups.

Sometimes, in their desperate attempts to show they knew about sex, some boys misspoke, revealing themselves, in Chad's words, as "clowns." Standing outside the weight room one day, Jeff desperately tried to maintain a convincing, sexually knowledgeable stance. Pedro and Jeff were discussing the merits of various hair replacement therapies such as Rogaine. Pedro mused about alternative hair replacement strategies, saying, "You could take hair from your butt!" Laughing, Craig suggested "pube," or pubic, hair. This began a debate about the sexual efficacy of shaving "down there." Jeff, looking wary, said, "I don't like sharp objects down there." Josh, having long since established himself as sexually experienced, looked at Jeff incredulously, crying, "You don't like blow jobs?!" Jeff, realizing he had said something wrong but still looking confused, quickly stammered, "Sure I do!" Josh, looking at Jeff disdainfully said, as if speaking to a child, "Teeth." Jeff, quickly trying to recover from his mistake, alleged with hollow bravado, "Oh, if they don't know what they're doing." Josh, with the assurance of experience, argued, "Even if they do!" In this instance, Josh treated Jeff's comment as an inadvertent revelation of sexual inexperience. Of course, whether it actually revealed anything about his past history with blow jobs was not really the point. The point was that he sounded, for a moment, sexually incompetent. Even his attempts at recovery sounded shallow as Josh discursively trumped Jeff's knowledge of blow jobs.

Asserting sexual dominance was, somewhat paradoxically, fraught with danger. On the one hand, overpowering a girl sexually was masculine (as indicated earlier in the rituals of cross-sex touching). On the other hand (as indicated through interviews with boys about the importance of girlfriends), girls' sexual desire undergirded a boy's masculinity. The following example indicates that many boys must tread lightly when talking about how much persuasion they need to deploy in order to convince a girl to have sex with them. In talking about their plans for Winter Ball, Josh told Reggie, "I'll be fucking pissed if I don't get some." Reggie advised him, "That's why you take a girl who's gonna do something." "I got JD!"[9] Josh countered, "I got a big bag of marijuana. The sooner I get her drunk, the sooner I get laid." Reggie laughed. "You have to get her drunk to get laid?" The other boys turned to laugh at Josh. Sean admonished Josh, "You have to change your confidence level." Reggie triumphantly bragged, "I can get laid any time, anywhere." Thus, while overpowering girls' control over their own bodies certainly confirmed masculinity, it was apparently much more masculine simply to overpower them by sheer virility, so that the girls couldn't help desiring a given boy. The sort of "date rape" talk that Josh exemplified simultaneously confirmed and cast doubt upon a given boy's masculinity. As in other practices of compulsive heterosexuality, boys showed that they could overpower girls' desire, will, and bodily control by convincing them (in this case through the use of drugs) to have sex. But if a part of being successfully masculine was, as Chad indicated, being desired by girls, then in this case Reggie and Josh indicated that they were not fully successful at being masculine, since the girls didn't necessarily desire them.

A popular topic of conversation in these male spaces was how and when a given boy was going to have or had had sex. In weight-lifting class, Pedro especially loved to share his exploits. Josh frequently joined in. Often by the end of class a group of boys had gathered around them either staring in amazement or desperately trying to keep up with the tall tales flowing from Josh and Pedro. One afternoon, egged on by the other boys' excited responses to his story about how badly Brittany "wanted" him, Pedro proceeded to act out his previous night's sexual adventures: "Dude, I had sex with my girlfriend last night. She tied me to the bed! I was like, damn!" Josh chimed in, shaking his head knowingly: "Never let a girl tie you up." Pedro laughed and added proudly: "I did her so hard when I was done she was bleeding. I tore her walls!" He acted out the story as he told it, leaning back up against the wall, legs and arms spread above him, thrusting his hips back and forth as he turned his head side to side. In this sort of fantastical storytelling boys assert their heterosexuality by sharing often incoherent sexual fantasies (Wood 1984). Curry (2004) calls these "women-as-objects-stories" in which female bodies serve as the crux of a heterosexual performance designed to bolster a boy's claim on heterosexuality.

Telling stories about sex confirmed boys' knowledge of sex. Sometimes these mythic stories became a contest in which one boy tried to beat out the previous story with an outlandish tale of his own. One day in the weight room, for example, Rich sat down on a weight bench and five boys gathered around him as he told a story, after much urging, about sex with his now ex-girlfriend. He explained that they were having sex and "she said it started to hurt. I said we can stop, and she said no. Then she said it again and she started crying. I told her to get off! Told her to get off! Finally I took her off," making a motion like he was lifting her off him. Then he said there was "blood all over me! Blood all over her! Popped her wall! She had to have stitches." Boys start cracking up and moaning. Not to be outdone, other boys in the circle begin to chime in about their sexual exploits. Even those who didn't have stories about themselves asserted their knowledge of sex through vicarious experiences. Troy joined the discussion with a story about his brother, a professional basketball player for a nearby city. He "brought home a twenty-four-year-old drunk chick! She *farted* the whole time they were doing it in the other room! It was *hella* gross!" All the boys cracked up again. Adam, not to be outdone, claimed, "My friend had sex with a drunk chick. He did her in the butt! She shit all over the place!" The boys all laughed raucously and yelled out things like "Hella gross!" or "That's disgusting!" Finally, Travis seemed to top all of their stories with his. "I had sex with this one girl and then the next week she had sex with her cousin!" The boys fell backwards in laughter, yelling "Eeew! Gross!" Eventually they moved back to lifting weights. These stories expressed boys' heterosexuality by demonstrating that they were fluent in sex talk, knew about sex acts, and desired heterosexual sex. Girls' bodies, in this sense, became the conduit through which boys established themselves as masculine.

None of these stories were about sexual desire or how attractive the girls were; rather, they were quite gross, about farts, feces, and blood. These stories were about what boys could make girls' bodies do. That is, the sexual tall tales these boys told when they were together were not so much about indicating sexual desire as about proving their capacity to exercise control on the world around them, primarily through women's bodies by making them bleed, pass gas, or defecate. These stories also highlighted femininity (much like the fag) as an abject identity. Girls had out-of-control bodies, whereas boys exhibited mastery not only over their own bodies but over girls' bodies as well.

These sorts of girl-getting rituals and storytelling practices constitute "compulsive heterosexuality." While on the surface they appear to be boys-will-be-boys locker-room talk in which boys objectify girls through bragging about sexual exploits or procuring a kiss, a closer look indicates that they are also about demonstrating the ability to impose a sexualized dominance.

GIRLS RESPOND

Girls frequently colluded in boys' discourses and practices of compulsory heterosexuality. When interacting with boys, many girls emphasized their own sexual availability or physical weakness to gain and maintain boys' attention. Because a girl's status in high school is frequently tied to the status of the boys she dates, this male erotic attention is critical. Of course, gender practices like this are not limited to teenagers. Grown women "bargain with patriarchy" by submitting to sexist social institutions and practices to gain other forms of social power (Kandiyoti 1988).

The day before winter break, I handed out lollipops shaped like Christmas trees and candy canes to thank students for their help with my research. In government class Cathy took a Christmas tree lollipop, tipped her head back, and stuck the long candy down her throat, moaning as if in ecstasy. Jeremy and Shane laughed as Cathy presumably showed off her roomy mouth or throat and her lack of a gag reflex, both highly prized traits by boys when receiving "blow jobs." Cathy responded with a smirk, "I don't think I'm *that* good." The group laughed at her conclusion. It seems that the social power girls gained from going along with this behavior was more than they gained by refusing. A way to gain male attention and thus in-school status was to engage in these boys' discourses and practices about sexuality.

This approach, illustrating sexual prowess, was danger laden for girls at River and is dangerous for teenage girls in general as they tread the shifting and blurry boundary between sexy and slutty (Tanenbaum 1999). To negotiate this boundary, girls invoked a variety of gender strategies. Some, like Cathy, promoted their own sexual prowess or acted as if the boys' comments were compliments; others suffered quietly; and some actually responded angrily, contradicting boys' claims on girls' sexuality. Teresa, like most girls, quietly put up with boys' daily practices of compulsive heterosexuality. She was one of the few girls who had enrolled in the weight-lifting class. While she told me that she signed up for weight lifting because "I like to lift weights," she continued by saying she didn't like exercising in a class with all boys. "It's really annoying because they just stare at you while you lift. They just stare at you." Like many girls, she quietly put up with this treatment. I didn't see her confronting any of the boys who stared at her.

Other girls developed a more defensive response, though not one couched in feminism or in opposition to sexism. In auto shop Jay expressed frustration about his upcoming eighteenth birthday, saying that soon he couldn't "have sex with girls younger than eighteen. Statutory rape." He continued angrily (presumably referring to his rape charge), "Younger girls, they lie, stupid little bitches." He laughed, "God, I hate girls." He saw Jenny, the female student aide in the class, look at him as he said this. So he looked directly at her and said loudly, "They're only good for making sandwiches and cleaning house. They don't even do that up to speed!" She just looked at him and shook her head. Brook, another auto shop student, said to me, "Write that down!" Jay continued to harass Jenny by throwing licorice at her and yelling, "I agree, her sister is a lot hotter!" Jenny looked at him and shook her head again. Jay commanded, sitting back and folding his arms, "Make me a sandwich!" At first she ignored him with a "whatever." Then Jenny carried back the licorice he threw at her and dumped it on him. Jay responded dismissively, shaking his head and muttering, "Fucking crybaby." In this instance Jenny both acquiesced to and resisted Jay's sexist treatment. She sort of ignored him while he made blatantly sexist remarks and tried to get even with him by dumping licorice on him. Like the girl who tried to fight back as she was being jabbed in the crotch with a drumstick, Jenny developed an off-the-cuff response to let the boys know she didn't appreciate their sexism.

Other girls, like Cathy, seemed flattered by boys' behavior, responding with giggles and smiles. In the drama class Emir, who had imitated a fag by "lusting" after the boys on the basketball court, "flirted" regularly with two girls, Simone and Valerie, throughout the class period. He made kissing motions with his lips, ran his tongue slowly over his teeth, and lustfully whispered or mouthed comments such as "Come on, baby. Oooh baby. Yeah, I love you." The girls responded with laughs and giggles, occasionally rolling their eyes in mock frustration. Other girls frequently adopted the smile and giggle strategy. While I interviewed Darnell, he yelled at a passing girl that he liked her "astronaut skirt." She laughed and waved. I asked him what "astronaut skirt" meant, and he explained, "Oh, it's just a little joke. That's an astronaut skirt 'cause your butt is outta this world." As Nancy Henley (1977) points out, this giggle and smile response signifies submission and appeasement, usually directed from a lower- to a higher-status person.[10]

Though most girls submitted to this sort of behavior, not all of them did. As recounted earlier, Shawna told Darnell, when he was declaring, "Mixed girls are for me!" that girls had a say in the matter too. Darnell didn't listen to her, but she didn't accept this definition of the situation. The most apparent resisters were the girls in the Gay/Straight Alliance, whom I discuss at length in the next chapter. But even girls without an espoused political orientation sometimes rejected boys' control of girls' bodies. In the hallway, for instance, Jessica stood behind Reggie as he backed up and rubbed his behind into her crotch. In response, she smacked him hard and he stopped his grinding. Similarly, in the weight room, Teresa sometimes resisted in her own way. Reggie once said to her, "When we gonna go and have sex? When we gonna hit that?" Teresa responded with scorn, "Never!" and walked away. This, unfortunately, happened more rarely than one would hope.

I'M DIFFERENT FROM OTHER GUYS

Thus far this chapter has focused on boys who treated girls as resources to be mobilized for their own masculinity projects, but not all boys engaged in practices of compulsive heterosexuality at all times. Most boys engaged in these sorts of practices only when in groups, and some boys avoided them in general.

When not in groups—when in one-on-one interactions with boys or girls—boys were much less likely to engage in gendered and sexed dominance practices. In this sense boys became masculine in groups (Connell 1996; Woody 2002). With the exception of Chad, none of the boys spoke with me the way they spoke with other boys about girls, girls' bodies, and their own sexual adventures. When with other boys, they postured and bragged. In one-on-one situations with me (and possibly with each other) they often spoke touchingly about their feelings about and insecurities with girls. While the boys I interviewed, for the most part, asserted the centrality of sexual competence to a masculine self, several of them rejected this definition or at least talked differently about girls and sexuality in their interviews.

When alone some boys were more likely to talk about romance and emotions, as opposed to girls' bodies and sexual availability. Darnell, for instance, the boy who had announced, "Mixed girls are for me!" and who had "wrestled" Christina, talked to me in private and with great emotion about a girl with whom he had recently broken up:

> I never wanted a girlfriend, but I got a girlfriend and I never wanted to lose her. Now I don't go out with that girl any more, but I still see her. We actually live in the same apartment complex. She goes to Chicago High School. She's not supposed to go to Chicago and I'm not supposed to go to River, so we kind of stay apart. It's a little hard. It's kind of easy if you were that kind of guy you could just have a girlfriend over there and a girlfriend over here.

While in groups with other boys Darnell behaved much like "the kind of guy who could just have a girlfriend over there and a girlfriend over here," claiming things like "Mixed girls are for me!" But in the interview with me he spoke tenderly about his former girlfriend. When I asked him why he thought he was different, he said, "I had a whole bunch of girls when I was little. I know how certain things can hurt their feelings. I don't like hurting people's feelings." Darnell's discussion of girls and his ability to hurt their feelings provided a very different picture of his approach to women than did his proclamations about which women belonged to him.

In interviews boys often posited themselves as "different from other guys," while in public they acted just like the guys they derided. Heath, for instance, told me he was "probably less" like an average guy because "I don't try and get with every girl I see." Like others, Heath became a "guy" in public, not in private interactions. Heath was the boy who had dressed like an elf for Halloween and accosted the passing girls in order to procure a kiss. Outside this sort of group setting, Heath dismissed lecherous behavior as something "other guys" did, but when in public he acted just like these "other guys." As Jace told me, when talking about a generic teenage boy, "By himself, he'd probably be cool. He wouldn't do stupid stuff. But in a group he'd do stupid stuff." When I asked him for an example of stupid stuff, he said, "Well, guys check out girls anyway, yell at 'em, 'Oh, yeah, you look good today, what's up?' " Indeed, looking at the differences between both Darnell's and Heath's behavior in groups and individually indicates that Jace highlights an important component of adolescent masculinity—that it happens in groups.

That said, boys not widely considered masculine did, on occasion, speak about girls and their relationships with girls in kind and nonobjectifying ways, even in groups of boys. In the following example a group of boys shared some tender observations about their relationships in a highly masculinized space, auto shop. Ryan looked at a note written to him by his girlfriend before he handed it to me. His girlfriend, who was moving away, wrote that she cared about and would "never forget" him, even though she thought he would forget her. She wrote, among other things, "I feel safe in your arms." I asked Ryan if he wrote notes back. He and his friend Chet both said that they wrote notes to their girlfriends. Both of them also told me they kept their girlfriends' notes in special boxes. They did, however, debate what sort of notes they kept. Chet said he kept all the notes: "It doesn't even matter if it's important." Ryan said he only kept the note if it was important. Another friend, John, chimed in, announcing he kept them because "it's hella long, they spent all that time writing it." While this might initially sound silly, John's comment actually signaled a sweet acknowledgment of a girl's perspective and experience. K. J., the popular dancer we met at the end of the last chapter, spoke up at this point and rerouted the discussion back to the familiar territory of compulsive heterosexuality. He received multiple notes each day from his legions of female fans. His comments about these notes sounded quite different from the sweet comments of Chet and Ryan. K. J. laughed about a note he had received that read, "Every time you dance I have an orgasm." As a sexual actor, K. J. was so virile he could cause a girl to have an orgasm without even touching her. Ryan, Chet, and John laughed, and the conversation soon dissipated. K. J., a high-status, masculine boy, redirected a conversation about girls' perspectives and boys' emotions back to the familiar terrain of boys as sexual actors.

Though discussions among boys like the one between Ryan and Chet were rare, on another occasion I heard a boy, in a group of other boys, refuse to engage in practices of compulsive heterosexuality by claiming that he couldn't talk about his girlfriend like that. Pedro, as usual, was talking to the other boys in the weight room about a variety of sexual practices. He lectured, "You are getting your girl from behind. You spit on her ass cheeks . . . " As he continued he was drowned out by the other boys yelling, "You watched that on a porno!" Undaunted, Pedro said, "Next time you get buttered, hit her on the back of her head after you cum and it will come out her nose!" The other boys howled in laughter as they pictured this highly unlikely sexual scenario. As Pedro goaded the other boys into promising that they would try this particular sexual practice the next time they had the opportunity, a good-looking African American boy spoke up, saying quietly that he wouldn't: "I got a girlfriend, man." As the other boys scoffed he said, "I wouldn't do that to her." The only safe terrain from which to challenge these sexually oriented definitions of masculinity was a relationship. A boy probably could not have argued that talking this way about girls was derogatory on principle without claiming he was speaking about a girlfriend.

Other boys who refrained from participating in these sorts of conversations frequently identified as Christian. Though they professed the same religion, they did not constitute a distinct peer group in the school but were scattered throughout the social scene at River High. Sean, a recent convert to evangelical Christianity, talked through much of his interview about struggling to maintain secular friendships while simultaneously practicing Christianity because of his different views on both sexuality and drug use:

> I know if I wasn't with God, I'd be doing everything that they are doing. I don't feel like saying that, but it's the truth. I am like them. But I choose not to do as they do.

Before he converted, Sean, a muscular, handsome white senior who identified with hip-hop culture, had been sexually active with several girls. He found it challenging to refrain from having sex after he converted, saying, "That was a hard one. That was really tough." He looked down on boys who tried to "get girls":

> There will be some guys that they'll go up to a girl, you know? "Hey, girl, come here." And they will keep on bugging them. They'll try to grab and touch them and stuff like this. They're just letting all their, they're acting on emotions pretty much.

Sean saw these boys as out of control. He used a feminized insult, implying that the boys engaged in practices of "getting girls" because they were ruled by their emotions and thus not able to refrain from sexist practices.

Connor, who also identified as a Christian, similarly distanced himself from other boys and their views of sexuality. "I don't care if I have sex or not because I want to save myself until I'm married, because that's something special. I'm really less than most average guys, that's what I think." Connor saw himself as less interested in sex than other teenage boys because he saw it as inappropriate behavior outside a marriage. Ben also refused to engage in sexualizing discourses of girls. He explained:

> I remember the first day we were disassembling a lawn mower and she [Teresa, the only girl in auto shop] was like, right over by me. And there's these two other guys

by me. She walks away and then he's like, "Hey dude, can you beat those?" And I'm like . . . "I'm just not into that kind of stuff." He goes, "Oh, okay, good stuff."

Like the boy who refused to engage in compulsive heterosexuality by claiming a girlfriend, some boys claimed a religious affiliation.

Christian boys, like Sean, frequently cast themselves as more mature than other boys because of their sexual restraint, drawing on masculinizing discourses of self-control and maturity. Like practices of compulsive heterosexuality, these sorts of gender practices indicated control and mastery, not over others (girls), but over themselves. Talking with Darren and Brook, who both identified as Christian, during auto shop, I asked them if they ever felt left out of conversations with other guys. Brook responded, "Yeah, sometimes. But I'm not, like, ashamed of what I think, you know?" I asked in response, "Do you ever feel less masculine because of it?" Brook said, "No. If anything, more. Because you can resist. You don't have to give in to it." Darren chimed in, "That was profound, dude!" I then asked, "Do you think other guys ever think, 'Oh, those guys are such pussies. They just can't get laid and it's an excuse'?" Brook replied, "Probably, yeah. There are going to be those stereotypical teenage guys again that think that." Unlike other boys, who, for the most part, talked about sex as if it were a recreational activity, both Brook and Darren wanted sex to be "special." Brook said that while "sex is all over the place, I haven't had sex." Like other boys, he hurried to assure me that "I'm a teenage guy, don't think I don't think about it." But unlike other boys, he exercised will and mastery, not over girls' bodies, but over his own by waiting to have sex. Like these boys, Cid explicitly invoked a discourse of control as he spoke about how "most guys are gawking at the girls. I notice that and I just don't want to be like that. I don't know if I'm controlling myself or if it just happens. Either way I don't want to be like that . . . It makes me feel better about myself, like I don't have to be like them."

Religion played a key role in how or if boys deployed practices of compulsive heterosexuality to shore up a masculine appearance and sense of self. In fact the table at which the Latter Day Saints students convened during lunch was (apart from Gay/Straight Alliance meetings and the drama classroom) the least homophobic and sexist location on campus! At first this seems to be a strange finding because many Christian sects or denominations are regarded as conservative and sexist. These boys weren't necessarily any less invested in a masculine identity predicated on gender inequality. However, Christian boys at River High had institutional claims on masculinity such that they didn't need to engage in the sort of intense interactional work that Kimmel (1987) claims is characteristic of contemporary "compulsive masculinity." As a result, unlike nonreligious boys, they did not need to engage in the continual interactional repudiation of equality with girls. Their respective religions buttressed male power through their teachings such that the interactional accomplishment of masculinity was less central to their identity projects. Thus the Christian boys at River may have been less interactionally sexist, but their investment in gender difference and gender inequality was little different from that of the other boys at River. In a society in which the gendered order has undergone a rapid change due to challenges to male power, and men and women are relatively equal under the law, one of the ways to maintain power is through interactional styles. But because the Christian institutions of which these boys were a part have remained relatively stable regarding issues of gender difference and equality, these boys had less need for interactional practices of gendered power.

FEMALES ARE THE PUPPETS

At a country square dance a few years ago I saw an offensive game between two men on opposite sides of a square, to see who could swing the women hardest and highest off the ground. What started out pleasantly enough soon degenerated into a brutal competition that left the women of the square staggering dizzily from place to place, completely unable to keep up with what was going on in the dance, and certainly getting no pleasure from it. The message that comes through to women in such physical displays is: you are so physically inferior that you can be played with like a toy. Males are the movers and the powerful in life, females the puppets.

It is heartbreaking, thirty years after Nancy Henley (1977, 150) wrote this passage, to document the continuing centrality of what she called "female puppetry" to adolescent masculinity. Like these square-dancing men, boys at River High repeatedly enforced definitions of masculinity that included male control of female bodies through symbolic or physical violence.

As a feminist researcher I was saddened and quite frankly surprised to discover the extent to which this type of sexual harassment constituted an average school day for youth at River High. Though much of the media and many cultural critics repeatedly claim that we have entered a postfeminist age, these scenes at River High indicate that this age has not yet arrived. In fact gender practices at the school—boys' control of girls' bodies, almost constant sexual harassment, and continual derogatory remarks about girls—show a desperate need for some sort of sexual harassment education and policy enforcement in schools.

Just as in the square dance that Henley described, girls' bodies at River High provided boys the opportunity to demonstrate mastery and dominance. These practices of compulsive heterosexuality indicate that control over women's bodies and their sexuality is, sadly, still central to definitions of masculinity, or at least adolescent masculinity. By dominating girls' bodies boys defended against the fag position, increased their social status, and forged bonds of solidarity with other boys. However, none of this is to say that these boys were unrepentant sexists. Rather, for the most part, these behaviors were social behaviors. Individually boys were much more likely to talk empathetically and respectfully of girls. Even when they behaved this way in groups, boys probably saw their behavior as joking and in fun (Owens, Shute, and Slee 2005). Maintaining masculinity, though, demands the interactional repudiation of this sort of empathy in order to stave off the abject fag position. It is precisely the joking and sexual quality of these interactions that makes them so hard to see as rituals of dominance. These interactional rituals maintain the "cruel power of men over women by turning it into just sex" (Jeffreys 1998, 75). The data presented in this chapter make gender equality seem a long way off. The next chapter shows how several groups of girls, much like the boys in the drama performances, provide alternative models of gender practices in adolescence, emphasizing play, irony, and equality rather than dominance and submission.

ENDNOTES

1. This is not to say that similar enactments of dominance and control don't occur among gay men. But such behavior is out of the scope of this study, since there were not enough self-identified gay boys at this school from which to draw conclusions about the way sexual discussions and practices interacted with masculinity for gay boys.

2. I am also indebted to Michael Kimmel's (1987) argument that masculinity itself must be compulsively expressed and constantly proven, something he calls "compulsive masculinity."

3. Chris Rock is a popular comedian. This routine is a fictionalized account in which he both plays himself and imitates Michael Jackson. The "Neverland" Chris Rock refers to is Michael Jackson's whimsical ranch in California.

4. Heath's behavior is a good illustration of how a boy's engagement with the "fag discourse" might vary by context. While in drama performances neither he nor Graham engaged in the fag discourse, outside that context both of them did.

5. That said, if anyone called this sort of behavior sexual harassment, it would more likely be girls than boys, since women are more likely than men to label so-called flirtatious behaviors as harassment (Quinn 2002).

6. Whore, however, is equivalent to fag only in that both boys and girls agree it is the worst insult one can direct toward a girl, much as fag is for a boy. That said, girls do not frantically lob the insult whore at one another in order to shore up a feminine identity the way boys do with fag regarding a masculine identity. Both fag and whore, however, do invoke someone who has been penetrated, which is a powerless position.

7. Muscles, in many boys' interviews, were central to understandings of oneself and others as masculine. Later in the chapter we see that boys are obsessed with size; in just about every realm, bigger is better.

8. Transitional periods are the time when students are most at risk for harassment and bullying (N. Stein 2002).

9. Jack Daniels, a relatively inexpensive whiskey.

10. The research on smiling and giggling as practices of submission is mixed. Most of the research indicates that the meanings invoked by a smile depend on the context in which it is given, by whom and to whom (LaFrance 2002; Mast and Hall 2004).

Representations of Whiteness in the Black Imagination

by bell hooks

Although there has never been any official body of black people in the United States who have gathered as anthropologists and/or ethnographers to study whiteness, black folks have, from slavery on, shared in conversations with one another "special" knowledge of whiteness gleaned from close scrutiny of white people. Deemed special because it was not a way of knowing that has been recorded fully in written material, its purpose was to help black folks cope and survive in a white supremacist society. For years, black domestic servants working in white homes, acting as informants, brought knowledge back to segregated communities—details, facts, observations, and psychoanalytic readings of the white Other.

Sharing the fascination with difference that white people have collectively expressed openly (and at times vulgarly) as they have traveled around the world in pursuit of the Other and Otherness, black people, especially those living during the historical period of racial apartheid and legal segregation, have similarly maintained steadfast and ongoing curiosity about the "ghosts," "the barbarians," these strange apparitions they were forced to serve. In the chapter on "Wildness" in *Shamanism, Colonialism, and the Wild Man*, Michael Taussig urges a stretching of our imagination and understanding of the Other to include inscriptions "on the edge of official history." Naming his critical project, identifying the passion he brings to the quest to know more deeply *you who are not ourselves*, Taussig explains:

> I am trying to reproduce a mode of perception—a way of seeing through a way of talking—figuring the world through dialogue that comes alive with sudden transformative force in the crannies of everyday life's pauses and juxtapositions, as in the kitchens of the Putumayo or in the streets around the church in the Niña Maria. It is always a way of representing the world in the round-about "speech" of the college of things.. . . It is a mode of perception that catches on the debris of history. . ..

I, too, am in search of the debris of history. I am wiping the dust off past conversations to remember some of what was shared in the old days when black folks had little intimate contact with whites, when we were much more open about the way we connected whiteness with the mysterious, the strange, and the terrible. Of course, everything has changed. Now many black people live in the "bush of ghosts" and do not know themselves separate from whiteness. They do not know this thing we call "difference." Systems of domination, imperialism, colonialism, and racism actively coerce black folks to internalize negative perceptions of blackness, to be self-hating. Many of us succumb to this. Yet blacks who imitate whites (adopting their values, speech, habits of being, etc.) continue to regard whiteness with suspicion, fear, and even hatred. This contradictory longing to possess the reality of the Other, even though that reality is one that wounds and negates, is expressive of the desire to understand the mystery, to know intimately through imitation, as though such knowing worn like an amulet, a mask, will ward away the evil, the terror.

Searching the critical work of post-colonial critics, I found much writing that bespeaks the continued fascination with the way white minds, particularly the colonial imperialist traveler, perceive blackness, and very little expressed interest in representations of whiteness in the black imagination. Black cultural and social critics allude to such representations in their writing, yet only a few have dared to make explicit those perceptions of whiteness that they think will discomfort or antagonize readers. James Baldwin's collection of essays *Notes of a Native Son* explores these issues with a clarity and frankness that is no longer fashionable in a world where evocations of pluralism and diversity act to obscure differences arbitrarily imposed and maintained by white racist domination. Addressing the way in which whiteness exists without knowledge of blackness even as it collectively asserts control, Baldwin links issues of recognition to the practice of imperialist racial domination. Writing about being the first black person to visit a Swiss village with only white inhabitants in his essay "Stranger in the Village," Baldwin notes his response to the village's yearly ritual of painting individuals black who were then positioned as slaves and bought so that the villagers could celebrate their concern with converting the souls of the "natives":

> I thought of white men arriving for the first time in an African village, strangers there, as I am a stranger here, and tried to imagine the astounded populace touching their hair and marveling at the color of their skin. But there is a great difference between being the first white man to be seen by Africans and being the first black man to be seen by whites. The white man takes the astonishment as tribute, for he arrives to conquer and to convert the natives, whose inferiority in relation to himself is not even to be questioned, whereas I, without a thought of conquest, find myself among a people whose culture controls me, has even, in a sense, created me, people who have cost me more in anguish and rage than they will ever know, who yet do not even know of my existence. The astonishment with which I might have greeted them, should they have stumbled into my African village a few hundred years ago, might have rejoiced their hearts. But the astonishment with which they greet me today can only poison mine.

My thinking about representations of whiteness in the black imagination has been stimulated by classroom discussions about the way in which the absence of recognition is a strategy that facilitates making a group the Other. In these classrooms there have been heated debates among students when white students respond with disbelief, shock, and rage as they listen to black students talk about whiteness, when they are compelled to hear observations, stereotypes, etc., that are offered as "data" gleaned from close scrutiny and study. Usually, white students respond with naive amazement that black people critically assess white people from a standpoint where "whiteness" is the privileged signifier. Their amazement that black people watch white people with a critical "ethnographic" gaze is itself an expression of racism. Often their rage erupts because they believe that all ways of looking that highlight difference subvert the liberal belief in a universal subjectivity (we are all just people) that they think will make racism disappear. They have a deep emotional investment in the myth of "sameness," even as their actions reflect the primacy of whiteness as a sign informing who they are and how they think. Many of them are shocked that black people think critically about whiteness because racist thinking perpetuates the fantasy that the Other who is subjugated, who is subhuman, lacks the ability to comprehend, to understand, to see the working of the powerful. Even though the majority of these students politically consider themselves liberals and anti-racist, they too unwittingly invest in the sense of whiteness as mystery.

In white supremacist society, white people can "safely" imagine that they are invisible to black people since the power they have historically asserted, and even now collectively assert over black people, accorded them the right to control the black gaze. As fantastic as it may seem, racist white people find it easy to imagine that black people cannot see them if within their desire they do not want to be seen by the dark Other. One mark of oppression was that black folks were compelled to assume the mantle of invisibility, to erase all traces of their subjectivity during slavery and the long years of racial apartheid, so that they could be better, less threatening servants. An effective strategy of white supremacist terror and dehumanization during slavery centered around white control of the black gaze. Black slaves, and later manumitted servants, could be brutally punished for looking, for appearing to observe the whites they were serving, as only a subject can observe, or see. To be fully an object then was to lack the capacity to see or recognize reality. These looking relations were reinforced as whites cultivated the practice of denying the subjectivity of blacks (the better to dehumanize and oppress), of relegating them to the realm of the invisible. Growing up in a Kentucky household where black servants lived in the same dwelling with the white family who employed them, newspaper heiress Sallie Bingham recalls, in her autobiography *Passion and Prejudice*, "Blacks, I realized, were simply invisible to most white people, except as a pair of hands offering a drink on a silver tray." Reduced to the machinery of bodily physical labor, black people learned to appear before whites as though they were zombies, cultivating the habit of casting the gaze downward so as not to appear uppity. To look directly was an assertion of subjectivity, equality. Safety resided in the pretense of invisibility.

Even though legal racial apartheid no longer is a norm in the United States, the habits that uphold and maintain institutionalized white supremacy linger. Since most white people do not have to "see" black people (constantly appearing on billboards, television, movies, in magazines, etc.) and they do not need to be ever on guard nor to observe black people to be safe, they can live as though black people are invisible, and they can imagine that they are also invisible to blacks. Some white people may even imagine there is no representation of whiteness in the black imagination, especially one that is based on concrete observation or mythic conjecture. They think they are seen by black folks only as they want to appear. Ideologically, the rhetoric of white supremacy supplies a fantasy of whiteness. Described in Richard Dyer's essay "White," this fantasy makes whiteness synonymous with goodness:

> Power in contemporary society habitually passes itself off as embodied in the normal as opposed to the superior. This is common to all forms of power, but it works in a peculiarly seductive way with whiteness, because of the way it seems rooted, in common-sense thought, in things other than ethnic difference. . . . Thus it is said (even in liberal textbooks) that there are inevitable associations of white with light

and therefore safety, and black with dark and therefore danger, and that this explains racism (whereas one might well argue about the safety of the cover of darkness, and the danger of exposure to the light); again, and with more justice, people point to the Jewish and Christian use of white and black to symbolize good and evil, as carried still in such expressions as "a black mark," "white magic," "to blacken the character" and so on. Socialized to believe the fantasy, that whiteness represents goodness and all that is benign and non-threatening, many white people assume this is the way black people conceptualize whiteness. They do not imagine that the way whiteness makes its presence felt in black life, most often as terrorizing imposition, a power that wounds, hurts, tortures, is a reality that disrupts the fantasy of whiteness as representing goodness.

Collectively black people remain rather silent about representations of whiteness in the black imagination. As in the old days of racial segregation where black folks learned to "wear the mask," many of us pretend to be comfortable in the face of whiteness only to turn our backs and give expression to intense levels of discomfort. Especially talked about is the representation of whiteness as terrorizing. Without evoking a simplistic essentialist "us and them" dichotomy that suggests black folks merely invert stereotypical racist interpretations so that black becomes synonymous with goodness and white with evil, I want to focus on that representation of whiteness that is not formed in reaction to stereotypes but emerges as a response to the traumatic pain and anguish that remains a consequence of white racist domination, a psychic state that informs and shapes the way black folks "see" whiteness. Stereotypes black folks maintain about white folks are not the only representations of whiteness in the black imagination. They emerge primarily as responses to white stereotypes of blackness. Lorraine Hansberry argues that black stereotypes of whites emerge as a trickle-down process of white stereotypes of blackness, where there is the projection onto an Other all that we deny about ourselves. In *Young, Gifted, and Black*, she identifies particular stereotypes about white people that are commonly cited in black communities and urges us not to "celebrate this madness in any direction":

> Is it not "known" in the ghetto that white people, as an entity, are "dirty" (especially white women—who never seem to do their own cleaning); inherently "cruel" (the cold, fierce roots of Europe; who else could put all those people into ovens *scientifically*); "smart" (you really have to hand it to the m.f.'s), and anything *but* cold and passionless (because look who has had to live with little else than their passions in the guise of love and hatred all these centuries)? And so on.

Stereotypes, however inaccurate, are one form of representation. Like fictions, they are created to serve as substitutions, standing in for what is real. They are there not to tell it like it is but to invite and encourage pretense. They are a fantasy, a projection onto the Other that makes them less threatening. Stereotypes abound when there is distance. They are an invention, a pretense that one knows when the steps that would make real knowing possible cannot be taken or are not allowed.

Looking past stereotypes to consider various representations of whiteness in the black imagination, I appeal to memory, to my earliest recollections of ways these issues were raised in black life. Returning to memories of growing up in the social circumstances created by racial apartheid, to all black spaces on the edges of town, I reinhabit a location where black folks associated whiteness with the terrible, the terrifying, the terrorizing. White people were regarded as terrorists, especially those who dared to enter that segregated space of blackness. As a child, I did not know any white people. They were strangers, rarely seen in our neighborhoods. The "official" white men who came across the tracks were there to sell products, Bibles, and insurance. They terrorized by economic exploitation. What did I see in the gazes of those white men who crossed our thresholds that made me afraid, that made black children unable to speak? Did they understand at all how strange their whiteness appeared in our living rooms, how threatening? Did they journey across the tracks with the same "adventurous" spirit that other white men carried to Africa, Asia, to those mysterious places they would one day call the "third world"? Did they come to our houses to meet the Other face-to-face and enact the colonizer role, dominating us on our own turf?

Their presence terrified me. Whatever their mission, they looked too much like the unofficial white men who came to enact rituals of terror and torture. As a child, I did not know how to tell them apart, how to ask the "real white people to please stand up." The terror that I felt is one black people have shared. Whites learn about it secondhand. Confessing in *Soul Sister* that she too began to feel this terror after changing her skin to appear "black" and going to live in the South, Grace Halsell described her altered sense of whiteness:

> Caught in this climate of hate, I am totally terrorstricken, and I search my mind to know why I am fearful of my own people. Yet they no longer seem my people, but rather the "enemy" arrayed in large numbers against me in some hostile territory. . . . My wild heartbeat is a secondhand kind of terror. I know that I cannot possibly experience what *they*, the black people, experience. . . .

Black folks raised in the north do not escape this sense of terror. In her autobiography, *Every Good-bye Ain't Gone*, Itabari Njeri begins the narrative of her northern childhood with a memory of southern roots. Traveling south as an adult to investigate the murder of her grandfather by white youth who were drag racing and ran him down in the streets, Njeri recalls that for many years "the distant and accidental violence that took my grandfather's life could not compete with the psychological terror that had begun to engulf my own." Ultimately, she begins to link that terror with the history of black people in the United States, seeing it as an imprint carried from the past to the present:

> As I grew older, my grandfather assumed mythic proportions in my imagination. Even in absence, he filled my room like music and watched over me when I was fearful. His fantasized presence diverted thoughts of my father's drunken rages. With age, my fantasizing ceased, the image of my grandfather faded. What lingered was the memory of his caress, the pain of something missing in my life, wrenched away by reckless white youths. I had a growing sense—the beginning of an inevitable comprehension—that this society deals blacks a disproportionate share of pain and denial.

Njeri's journey takes her through the pain and terror of the past, only the memories do not fade. They linger as does the pain and bitterness: "Against a backdrop of personal loss, against the evidence of history that fills me with a knowledge of the hateful behavior of whites toward blacks, I see the people of Bainbridge. And I cannot trust them. I cannot absolve them." If it is possible to conquer terror through ritual reenactment, that is what Njeri does. She goes back to the scene of the crime, dares to face the enemy. It is this confrontation that forces the terror of history to loosen its grip.

To name that whiteness in the black imagination is often a representation of terror. One must face written histories that erase and deny, that reinvent the past to make the present vision of racial harmony and pluralism more plausible. To bear the burden of memory one must willingly journey to places long uninhabited, searching the debris of history for traces of the unforgettable, all knowledge of which has been suppressed. Njeri laments that "nobody really knows us." She writes, "So institutionalized is the ignorance of our history, our culture, our everyday existence that, often, we do not even know ourselves." Theorizing black experience, we seek to uncover, restore, as well as to deconstruct, so that new paths, different journeys, are possible. Indeed, Edward Said, in his essay "Traveling Theory," argues that theory can "threaten reification, as well as the entire bourgeois system on which reification depends, with destruction." The call to theorize black experience is constantly challenged and subverted by conservative voices reluctant to move from fixed locations. Said reminds us:

> Theory . . . is won as the result of a process that begins when consciousness first experiences its own terrible ossification in the general reification of all things under capitalism; then when consciousness generalizes (or classes) itself as something opposed to other objects, and feels itself as contradiction to (or crisis within) objectification, there emerges a consciousness of change in the *status quo*; finally, moving toward freedom

and fulfillment, consciousness looks ahead to complete self-realization, which is of course the revolutionary process stretching forward in time, perceivable now only as theory or projection.

Traveling, moving into the past, Njeri pieces together fragments. Who does she see staring into the face of a southern white man who was said to be the murderer? Does the terror in his face mirror the look of the unsuspecting black man whose death history does not name or record? Baldwin wrote that "people are trapped in history and history is trapped in them." There is then only the fantasy of escape, or the promise that what is lost will be found, rediscovered, and returned. For black folks, reconstructing an archaeology of memory makes return possible, the journey to a place we can never call home even as we re-inhabit it to make sense of present locations. Such journeying cannot be fully encompassed by conventional notions of travel.

Spinning off from Said's essay, James Clifford, in "Notes on Travel and Theory," celebrates the idea of journeying, asserting:

> This sense of worldly, "mapped" movement is also why it may be worth holding on to the term "travel," despite its connotations of middle class "literary" or recreational journeying, spatial practices long associated with male experiences and virtues. "Travel" suggests, at least, profane activity, following public routes and beaten tracks. How do different populations, classes and genders travel? What kinds of knowledges, stories, and theories do they produce? A crucial research agenda opens up.

Reading this piece and listening to Clifford talk about theory and travel, I appreciated his efforts to expand the travel/theoretical frontier so that it might be more inclusive, even as I considered that to answer the questions he poses is to propose a deconstruction of the conventional sense of travel, and put alongside it, or in its place, a theory of the journey that would expose the extent to which holding on to the concept of "travel" as we know it is also a way to hold on to imperialism.

For some individuals, clinging to the conventional sense of travel allows them to remain fascinated with imperialism, to write about it, seductively evoking what Renato Rosaldo aptly calls, in *Culture and Truth*, "imperialist nostalgia." Significantly, he reminds readers that "even politically progressive North American audiences have enjoyed the elegance of manners governing relations of dominance and subordination between the 'races.'" Theories of travel produced outside conventional borders might want the Journey to become the rubric within which travel, as a starting point for discourse, is associated with different headings—rites of passage, immigration, enforced migration, relocation, enslavement, and homelessness. "Travel" is not a word that can be easily evoked to talk about the Middle Passage, the Trail of Tears, the landing of

Chinese immigrants, the forced relocation of Japanese Americans, or the plight of the homeless. Theorizing diverse journeying is crucial to our understanding of any politics of location. As Clifford asserts at the end of his essay:

> Theory is always written from some "where," and that "where" is less a place than itineraries: different, concrete histories of dwelling, immigration, exile, migration. These include the migration of third world intellectuals into the metropolitan universities, to pass through or to remain, changed by their travel but marked by places of origin, by peculiar allegiances and alienations.

Listening to Clifford "playfully" evoke a sense of travel, I felt such an evocation would always make it difficult for there to be recognition of an experience of travel that is not about play but is an encounter with terrorism. And it is crucial that we recognize that the hegemony of one experience of travel can make it impossible to articulate another experience or for it to be heard. From certain standpoints, to travel is to encounter the terrorizing force of white supremacy. To tell my "travel" stories, I must name the movement from racially segregated southern community, from rural black Baptist origin, to prestigious white university settings. I must be able to speak about what it is like to be leaving Italy after I have given a talk on racism and feminism, hosted by the parliament, only to stand for hours while I am interrogated by white officials who do not have to respond when I inquire as to why the questions they ask me are different from those asked the white people in line before me. Thinking only that I must endure this public questioning, the stares of those around me, because my skin is black, I am startled when I am asked if I speak Arabic, when I am told that women like me receive presents from men without knowing what those presents are. Reminded of another time when I was strip-searched by French officials, who were stopping black people to make sure we were not illegal immigrants and/or terrorists, I think that one fantasy of whiteness is that the threatening Other is always a terrorist. This projection enables many white people to imagine there is no representation of whiteness as terror, as terrorizing. Yet it is this representation of whiteness in the black imagination, first learned in the narrow confines of poor black rural community, that is sustained by my travels to many different locations.

To travel, I must always move through fear, confront terror. It helps to be able to link this individual experience to the collective journeying of black people, to the Middle Passage, to the mass migration of southern black folks to northern cities in the early part of the twentieth century. Michel Foucault posits memory as a site of resistance. As Jonathan Arac puts it in his introduction to *Postmodernism and Politics*, the process of remembering can be a practice which "transforms history from a judgement on the past in the name of a present truth to a 'counter-memory' that combats our current modes of truth and justice, helping us to understand and change the present by placing it in a new relation to the past." It is useful, when theorizing black experience, to examine the way the concept of "terror" is linked to representations of whiteness.

In the absence of the reality of whiteness, I learned as a child that to be "safe" it was important to recognize the power of whiteness, even to fear it, and to avoid encounter. There was nothing terrifying about the sharing of this knowledge as survival strategy; the terror was made real only when I journeyed from the black side of town to a predominantly white area near my grand-mother's house. I had to pass through this area to reach her place. Describing these journeys "across town" in the essay "Homeplace: A Site of Resistance," I remembered:

> It was a movement away from the segregated blackness of our community into a poor white neighborhood. I remember the fear, being scared to walk to Baba's, our grandmother's house, because we would have to pass that terrifying whiteness—those white faces on the porches staring us down with hate. Even when empty or vacant those porches seemed to say *danger*, you do not belong here, you are not safe.

Oh! that feeling of safety, of arrival, of homecoming when we finally reached the edges of her yard, when we could see the soot black face of our grandfather, Daddy Gus, sitting in his chair on the porch, smell his cigar, and rest on his lap. Such a contrast, that feeling of arrival, of homecoming—this sweetness and the bitterness of that journey, that constant reminder of white power and control. Even though it was a long time ago that I made this journey, associations of whiteness with terror and the terrorizing remain. Even though I live and move in spaces where I am surrounded by whiteness, there is no comfort that makes the terrorism disappear. All black people in the United States, irrespective of their class status or politics, live with the possibility that they will be terrorized by whiteness.

This terror is most vividly described by black authors in fiction writing, particularly Toni Morrison's novel *Beloved*. Baby Suggs, the black prophet, who is most vocal about representations of whiteness, dies because she suffers an absence of color. Surrounded by a lack, an empty space, taken over by whiteness, she remembers: "Those white things have taken all I had or dreamed and broke my heartstrings too. There is no bad luck in the world but white folks." If the mask of whiteness, the pretense, represents it as always benign, benevolent, then what this representation obscures is the representation of danger, the sense of threat. During the period of racial apartheid, still known by many folks as Jim Crow, it was more difficult for black people to internalize this pretense, hard for us not to know that the shapes under white sheets had a mission to threaten, to terrorize. That representation of whiteness, and its association with innocence, which engulfed and murdered Emmett Till, was a sign; it was meant to torture with the reminder of possible future terror. In Morrison's *Beloved*, the memory of terror is so deeply inscribed on the body of Sethe and in her consciousness, and the association of terror with whiteness is so intense, that she kills her young so that they will never know the terror. Explaining her actions to Paul D., she tells him that it is her job "to keep them away from what I know is terrible." Of course Sethe's attempt to end the historical anguish of black people only reproduces it in a different form. She conquers the terror through perverse reenactment, through resistance, using violence as a means of fleeing from a history that is a burden too great to bear.

It is the telling of our history that enables political self-recovery. In contemporary society, white and black people alike believe that racism no longer exists. This erasure, however mythic, diffuses the representation of whiteness as terror in the black imagination. It allows for assimilation and forgetfulness. The eagerness with which contemporary society does away with racism, replacing this recognition with evocations of pluralism and diversity that further mask reality, is a response to the terror. It has also become a way to perpetuate the terror by providing a cover, a hiding place. Black people still feel the terror, still associate it with whiteness, but are rarely able to articulate the varied ways we are terrorized because it is easy to silence by accusations of reverse racism or by suggesting that black folks who talk about the ways we are terrorized by whites are merely evoking victimization to demand special treatment.

When I attended a recent conference on cultural studies, I was reminded of the way in which the discourse of race is increasingly divorced from any recognition of the politics of racism. Attending the conference because I was confident that I would be in the company of like-minded, "aware," progressive intellectuals, I was disturbed when the usual arrangements of white supremacist hierarchy were mirrored both in terms of who was speaking, of how bodies were arranged on the stage, of who was in the audience. All of this revealed the underlying assumptions of what voices were deemed worthy to speak and be heard. As the conference progressed, I began to feel afraid. If these progressive people, most of whom were white, could so blindly reproduce a version of the status quo and not "see" it, the thought of how racial politics would be played out "outside" this arena was horrifying. That feeling of terror that I had known so intimately in my childhood surfaced. Without even considering whether the audience was able to shift from the prevailing standpoint and hear another perspective, I talked openly about that sense of terror. Later, I heard stories of white women joking about how ludicrous it was for me (in their eyes I suppose I represent the "bad" tough black woman) to say I felt terrorized. Their inability to conceive that my terror, like that of Sethe's, is a response to the legacy of white domination and the contemporary expressions of white supremacy is an indication of how little this culture really understands the profound psychological impact of white racist domination.

At this same conference, I bonded with a progressive black woman and her companion, a white man. Like me, they were troubled by the extent to which folks chose to ignore the way white supremacy was informing the structure of the conference. Talking with the black woman, I asked her: "What do you do, when you are tired of confronting white racism, tired of the day-to-day incidental acts of racial terrorism? I mean, how do you deal with coming home to a white person?" Laughing she said, "Oh, you mean when I am suffering from White People Fatigue Syndrome? He gets that more than I do." After we finish our laughter, we talk about the way white people who shift locations, as her companion has done, begin to see the world differently. Understanding how racism works, he can see the way in which whiteness acts to terrorize without seeing himself as bad, or all white people as bad, and all black people as good. Repudiating us-and-them dichotomies does not mean that we should never speak of the ways observing the world from the standpoint of "whiteness" may indeed distort perception, impede understanding of the way racism works both in the larger world as well as in the world of our intimate interactions.

In *The Post-Colonial Critic*, Gayatri Spivak calls for a shift in locations, clarifying the radical possibilities that surface when positionality is problematized. She explains that "what we are asking for is that the hegemonic discourses, and the holders of hegemonic discourse, should dehegemonize their position and themselves learn how to occupy the subject position of the other." Generally, this process of repositioning has the power to deconstruct practices of racism and make possible the disassociation of whiteness with terror in the black imagination. As critical intervention it allows for the recognition that progressive white people who are anti-racist might be able to understand the way in which their cultural practice reinscribes white supremacy without promoting paralyzing guilt or denial. Without the capacity to inspire terror, whiteness no longer signifies the right to dominate. It truly becomes a benevolent absence. Baldwin ends his essay "Stranger in the Village" with the declaration: "This world is white no longer, and it will never be white again." Critically examining the association of whiteness as terror in the black imagination, deconstructing it, we both name racism's impact and help to break its hold. We decolonize our minds and our imaginations.

SECTION 4

POWER AND PRIVILEGE

Copyright © by Depositphotos / Yaruta.

On Diversity in the United States

by David G. Embrick

Illusion is the most tenacious weed in the collective consciousness.

—Antonio Gramsci[1]

Diversity. What exactly is diversity? A cursory Google search reveals 230 million results.[2] It certainly has become one of the most commonly used words in our society these days. University of Illinois at Chicago professor Walter B. Michaels noted that diversity "has become virtually a sacred concept in American life today" (2006, p. 12). In that same sentence Michaels goes on to say that although most people are not against diversity, they tend to have different degrees of enthusiasm toward the concept. Scholars such as Joyce Bell and Douglas Hartmann (2007) found in their research on diversity that the idea of diversity is one that is ambiguous and often confusing. They argue that although folks are usually confused with the term "diversity," most think of the term in a "happy" way. In fact, few other words generate the uplifting feeling of what it means to live in a democratic and free society. But what exactly does it mean to be diverse? Does it mean that we should accept the racial and ethnic differences of others? Or, perhaps diversity refers to class tolerance? What about gender, sexual orientation, age, culture, religion, or any multitude of other differences between people who live in our society?

Increasingly, diversity has come to refer to all of the aforementioned identities. Moreover, the use of the term diversity has seemingly expanded in the last two decades so that more differences are embraced under its umbrella every day: personality, politics, education, perspectives, ideas, and grooming styles, to name just a few examples. Such broad defining of diversity has even led to the decision of many businesses and numerous other organizations to create support groups that celebrate peoples' differences in marital status, animal ownership, clothing styles, and, to invoke an old cliché, just about everything but the kitchen sink.[3] In addition to the celebration of difference that is attached to the word diversity is the underlying perception of equality that is often also associated with the term. That is, the term diversity elicits the assumption that not only are many institutions interested in the differences between people, but, somehow, institutions that are interested in promoting diversity are also interested in issues of justice and equality. However, in reality, rarely do we find variety or equality in our U.S. institutions, both at the lower and middle strata, but especially at the upper administrative levels.

The notion of diversity, especially as it relates to equality and equal opportunity, is not problematic. What is problematic, however, is how gender and racial inequalities continue to be overlooked in many institutions, partly as a result of the broadening of the term "diversity." And, while diversity is not necessarily about race or gender, specifically, the broad defining of diversity by mainstream America has helped to downplay the racial and gender inequalities that continue to plague institutions in the U.S. As diversity comes to represent more of the differences between people in society, less attention is paid to historical and persistent racial, ethnic, and gender discrimination in organizations. For women and minorities, progressive steps to ensure racial and gender justice has seemingly plummeted since the civil rights triumphs of the sixties. Thus, although there has been an increase in the rise of organizational philosophy espousing diversity, there is also overwhelming data that suggest minorities and women are still unable to obtain opportunities or to achieve success at the same rates as their white male counterparts. In fact, while the amount of money spent on diversity by companies has increased (with estimates as high as $8 billion annually on diversity training alone) since the late nineties, so too have risen the number of racial and gender discrimination lawsuits filed against these companies (see also Rice & Arekere, 2005). More frequent than ever are examples of major companies such as Xerox that have been successfully sued for having African American dolls with hangman's nooses around their necks prominently displayed in several of their workplaces, yet still manage to win numerous awards for their "sincerity" and "efforts" toward diversity (for more information on the lawsuit against Xerox, see Hansen, 2003).

Accordingly, women and racial minorities continue to be overlooked in corporate positions that hold any serious decision-making power (Burk, 2005; see also Acker, 2006). They also continue to be underrepresented in higher education, both as students and as faculty members (Feagin et al., 1996; see also Renzulli et al., 2006). And, contrary to the few token representatives who are frequently paraded by the media (e.g., Condoleezza Rice, Colin Powell, and more recently Barack Obama), women and racial minorities get very little representation in U.S. politics. According to a June 2006 report by *DiversityInc*,[4] although racial minorities comprise over 30% of the U.S. population and over 34% of the labor force, they represent only 6% of the 4,100 U.S. senate employees across America. The article further states, "The top Washington, D.C.-based positions in almost every Senate office—chief of staff, legislative director and communications director—are practically reserved for white men and women" (p. 171). Not only do blacks and other racial minorities have little say in the political decision-making that goes on in the U.S. senate, they have little power in influencing those who do hold power. Hence, recommendations to U.S. senators from their staff, ranging from hiring personnel to policy making, are made without the benefit of having minorities' views represented. These numbers continue to hold true in 2015 and there is little indication that change is likely to occur in the near future.

The purpose of this chapter is to provide an overview of the concept of diversity, currently and historically, and to examine diversity's parallel over the years with progressive policies such as affirmative action and multiculturalism. In addition, I argue that, in an age of color-blind racism (see Bonilla-Silva, 1997, 2001, 2014), the language of diversity is increasingly being evoked by many institutions in order to curtail deeper public investigations into the gender and racial inequalities that continue to persist in the workplace. That is, many institutions argue that they value diversity, yet make no attempts to ensure that minorities and women get fair and equal treatment in comparison to their white male counterparts.

Diversity Prior to the 1960s

The notion that all people are equal, imbued with certain inalienable rights, and should be treated fairly and justly is relatively new in America. According to Feagin[5] (2006), the U.S. Constitution was instrumental in helping to set the stage for the development of a racist and sexist society. Women had few rights compared to men in the early history of the U.S. and the intentions of the founding fathers had always been one of white male supremacy. The racial and gender practices of our nation are so deeply embedded in our institutions and have such a long and intentional history that according to Bonilla-Silva[6] (2006), it will take much more than superficial changes in our institutions (in our educational system, social structure, etc.) to create total racial and gender harmony.

Abraham Lincoln's Emancipation Proclamation on January 1, 1863, paved the way for the dismantling of slavery in the U.S. However, whites continued to maintain social, economic, and political control through the use of Jim Crow legislation, highly racialized scare tactics, and a court system that was openly hostile to minorities. And white males were systematically able to thwart an increasing women's suffrage movement that would not gain momentum until the early twentieth century. Indeed, it was not until the 19th Amendment to the Constitution was ratified on August 26, 1920 that women could finally vote. Similarly, it was not until the early 1930s that federal court decisions were finally made to stop overt racial segregation at all white universities, the culmination of which many would claim to be the 1954 landmark *Brown v. Topeka Board of Education* case that declared that denying education to anyone, regardless of race, was unconstitutional.

A major win for women and minorities came in the form of President Franklin D. Roosevelt's Executive Order 8802, better known as the Fair Employment Act. Under pressure from a massive protest organized by the Brotherhood of Sleeping Car Porters (led by Bayard Rustin, A. Philip Randolph, & A. J. Muste), Roosevelt signed the Executive Order on the eve of WWII, June 25, 1941, prohibiting racial discrimination in the national defense and other government-related industries. The Fair Employment Act was the first federal law prohibiting discrimination in the U.S. It established the Committee on Fair Employment Practices, headed by the Office of Production Management, whose job was to investigate discrimination violations and take appropriate action. Although the Fair Employment Act served as acknowledgment from the government to address racial issues, Executive Order 8802 carried no punitive measures for companies that did not comply. President Roosevelt's intent in creating the executive order was to curtail protests and strikes to ensure the production of military weapons and supplies as the U.S. prepared for war (Burstein, 1985). Nonetheless, the executive order served as precedent for future presidential orders dealing with discrimination in the workplace.

As World War II became an inevitable situation for the U.S., the idea of America as a great big "melting pot"[7] became a central theme for a government trying to unite its people to a common cause. World War II also created a new dilemma for businesses that had lost the majority of their workforce to war. As men were being shipped off to fight overseas, increasing numbers of companies had to resort to women laborers as well as minority and immigrant male workers who were unable or ineligible to serve in the Armed Forces. As a result, record numbers of women and minorities were given the opportunity to enter into the U.S. labor force and into jobs that were previously dominated by white men. Although World War II provided unprecedented opportunities for women and minorities to obtain better-paying jobs than they previously had, racial and gender barriers were not erased and discrimination continued, albeit on a somewhat lesser scale when compared to before the war. The end of World War II signaled a return to white male supremacy ideals that had plagued America since long before the revolution. With increased blatant and overt sex discrimination came racial hostility, not only from mainstream white males, but also from the educational, political, and U.S. court systems, all of which were composed mostly of white males. America's melting pot was an exclusive club, and excluded from this club were blacks, Asians, Latinos, and some dark-skinned European groups. Around the same time, the U.S. government was busy supporting a large political campaign designed to get women out of the workforce and back into the homes where they were before the war started.

Favorable changes came once again for minorities when the courts declared school segregation to be illegal. The *Brown v. Topeka Board of Education* case marked more than just a win for minorities wanting a better education: It marked a significant time of change in U.S. history. Along with changes in the law favoring women and minorities, laws were also being changed to allow at least token numbers of immigrants into the U.S., some from countries whose people were previously barred or limited from the United States. The late 1940s and early 1950s were also times of strife. Increased racial riots and frequent protests created uncomfortable situations for many white men. As Omi & Winant[8] (1994) have noted, the social and political movements of many minority groups posed a real challenge to the political, cultural, and social structures in America. But while riots and protests against racial and gender discrimination were effective tools for creating social change, real progress came about as a result of changes in the legality of racial and sex discrimination. It was these legal changes that forced businesses and other organizations to change their tactics when it came to dealing with minorities and women, both as customers and as employees. The biggest change for many businesses and government agencies came about with the ratification of Civil Rights Act of 1964, which read:

> An Act. To enforce the constitutional right to vote, to confer jurisdiction upon the district courts of the United States to provide injunctive relief against discrimination in public accommodations, to authorize the Attorney General to institute suits to protect constitutional rights in public facilities and public education, to extend the Commission on Civil Rights, to prevent discrimination in federally assisted programs, to establish a Commission on Equal Employment Opportunity, and for other purposes. Be it enacted by the Senate and House of Representatives of the United States of America in Congress assembled, that this Act may be cited as the "Civil Rights Act of 1964."[9]

Of particular interest to businesses was Title VII (Section 2000e-2, 703) of the 1964 Civil Rights Act that provided equal protection under the law for women and minorities as well as enforcement of that law. Title VII was written as an equal employment opportunity clause that prohibited employers, labor organizations, and employment agencies from discriminating based on an individual's race, color, religion, sex, or national origin. For many companies, Title VII (along with other laws such as the Equal Pay Act of 1963[10], the Voting Rights Act of 1965, and the Immigration Act of 1965) posed serious threats to the white male power structure present in organizations across America. After all, it was not until after changes in the law to protect women and minorities were enacted that many businesses and organizations faced legal ramifications for racial and sex discrimination. Indeed, before this, most organizations freely and openly discriminated against women and minorities and although record numbers of women and minorities were being employed by many businesses compared to pre–World War II times, most of the jobs tended to be menial and low paid, and opportunities for advancement in the company were few and far between (Burstein, 1985; Collins, 1997; DiTomaso & Smith, 1996; Farley, 1984; Farley & Allen, 1987; Wilson, 1978). In fact, according to Burstein (1985, p. 1), it was not uncommon for "employers seeking white-collar workers to specify that they were interested only in Protestant or 'Nordic' applicants." Minorities and women were denied access to many jobs. And skilled labor unions (such as American Federation of Labor—AFL), which presented better opportunities compared to other non-skilled unions for managerial promotions (such as Congress of Industrial Organizations (CIO)), often excluded women and minorities from their organizations (Green, 1978, 1980). Reserved for white men were the managerial and executive positions of an organization, a social incubator that helped them to maintain their social status, their white privilege, and their exclusive power.

Multiculturalism in the 1960s and 1970s

The Civil Rights Act of 1964 alone was not responsible for the internal changes that were taking place in many businesses and organizations in the late 1960s and early 1970s. As a result of a number of social movements, to include the civil rights movement, new policies and programs were needed to quell the growing public image of America as a racist and sexist society, as well as the growing public dissent. Thus, the notion of "multiculturalism" was introduced to the U.S. First used in 1957 to describe Switzerland (Parrillo, 2005), multiculturalism is a theory centered on the idea that countries should embrace the rich ethnic and cultural variety that makes up their population. The idea of multiculturalism spread in the 1970s through the political agendas of several countries, varying from country to country. For example, the idea of multiculturalism was adopted into Canadian law in 1971 (known as the Official Multiculturalism Act of 1971) as a political response to the grievances filed by Canada's French-speaking minority. Initially, the Canadian government wanted to implement a series of programs guided by the notions of biculturalism. However, that idea was overwhelmingly attacked on a number of fronts, the major argument being that biculturalism did not respect or recognize Canadians who were not of French or English descent. Subsequently, the Official Multiculturalism Act of 1971 was added to Canada's 1982 constitution.

Multiculturalism took on a different agenda, however, in the U.S. as more effort was placed on promoting multiculturalism in order to curb the growing global view of Americans as bigots and hypocrites rather than embracing the idea of racial and ethnic pluralism (Layton, 2000[11]). In an attempt to improve the economic and social status of minorities, the federal government not only implemented a series of legislative acts to help protect minorities' rights, but multicultural policies became the standard in various federal departments and in the everyday business conducted between the U.S. government and companies that wanted to do business with it. Although the notion of multiculturalism was never ratified into law, the Equal Employment Opportunity Commission (EEOC)—put into place by the Civil Rights Act of 1964, as well the Office of Federal Contract Compliance Programs (OFCCP), established in 1965 and governed by the Department of Labor—created pressure for many businesses through the implementation of new federal purchase and federal compliance programs designed around the ideas of equal opportunity and cultural pluralism (Collins, 1997). Not all businesses agreed with these new federal guidelines, but many companies that were interested in doing business with the U.S. government complied by creating new offices of multiculturalism and affirmative action in an effort to meet the new workplace standards (Heckman & Wolpin, 1976).

Though the pressure from the EEOC on businesses to open up their workplaces to women and minorities was high, a number of corporations embraced multiculturalism early on in an effort to move ahead of what was already a growing trend in the federal government. Following the lead of many government agencies and corporate businesses, growing numbers of colleges and universities also began to create offices of multicultural services. This was a rational act, given the likelihood that EEOC would make multicultural policies a staple in their new agenda, but it was also seen as good politics, given the changing demographic context. Many organizations that implemented multicultural policies in the workplace early on were seen as progressive leaders at a time when mainstream conservatives in the United States were facing the onslaught of a number of large progressive movements. According to Zweigenhaft & Domhoff (2003, 2006), the early 1970s represented an unprecedented time in history for educated women and blacks who were previously denied access to higher education, government jobs, and jobs in the business industry (see also Collins, 1997; Wright, 1996). And while the numbers of women and blacks entering these positions were relatively small, they represented a breakthrough in an area that previously was dominated by white males.

Affirmative Action

If multiculturalism was the mantra during the middle to late 1960s through early 1980s, affirmative action[12] policies and programs ensured that women and minorities would gain entry into jobs previously denied them (Collins, 1997; DiTomaso & Smith, 1996; Heckman & Payner, 1989; Herring & Collins, 1995). Affirmative action programs were widely implemented in many educational, government, and business organizations early on and created a unique opportunity for women and minorities who wanted a piece of the American Dream. According to West (1996, p. 32), the fundamental purpose of affirmative action was to "put a significant dent in the tightly controlled networks of privileged white male citizens who monopolized the good jobs and influential positions in American society." Thus, affirmative action was not simply a means by which women and minorities could gain access to better-paid jobs and higher-level positions. It was a counter to the continuing legacy of white male supremacy.[13]

Used as a counterargument to the prevailing notion of meritocracy, President Lyndon B. Johnson justified the use of affirmative action programs in his 1965 talk at Howard University.[14] In his famous speech, President Johnson remarked, "You do not take a person who, for years, has been hobbled by chains and liberate him, bring him up to the starting line in a race and then say, 'you are free to compete with all the others', and still justly believe that you have been completely fair." Affirmative action received widespread attention in the late 1960s to early 1970s through Executive Order 10925[15], implemented by President John F. Kennedy, and Executive Order 11246[16] which was implemented by President Lyndon B. Johnson. Both executive orders were administered and enforced by OFCCP and served as mechanisms to reduce barriers to women and minorities in private as well as public employment. New programs were added and old ones renewed throughout the 1970s, as the Nixon and Ford administrations were active supporters of affirmative action and other policies that promoted equal opportunity, a strategy that, according to Marable (1996), allowed the Republican Party to better connect with an expanding black middle class. According to Williams (1996, p. 244), it was President Nixon's administration that created a new set of policies that required all affirmative action programs to include "minority and female hiring goals and timetables to which the contractor must commit its 'good-faith' efforts," a requirement that Laurence Silberman as under-secretary of labor claimed would ensure opportunities for women and minorities.

In addition to the federal government, affirmative action became popular on college campuses as a number of student movements called for their schools to actively recruit minority students. Although in many instances the affirmative action agenda was led by minority groups [e.g., Black Student Movement (BSM), El Movimienta Estudiantil Chicano de Aztlan (MEChA), Mexican American Student Association (MASA)], the spurring of students on campus came from other fronts as well [e.g., Students for a Democratic Society (SDS), Southern Student Organizing Committee (SSOC)]. In the business world, companies faced heated pressure from the EEOC and OFCCP to conform to multicultural and nondiscriminatory practices (Collins, 1997). Many companies found themselves on the losing end of discrimination lawsuits filed by the EEOC and many settlements were arranged to not only pay monetary compensation to women and minorities for violating their rights, but to also establish company programs and policies that would help fuel the success of women and minority in the workplace.[17]

Regardless, mixed in with the growing social, policial, and economic pressures to become multicultural, there was also little social or political backlash during the late 1960s and early to middle 1970s to affirmative action programs and policies (at least the complaints of whites were less vocal compared to the backlash multiculturalism and affirmative action faced in 1980s). Consequently, a number of corporations took advantage of the situation and voluntarily implemented affirmative action programs on their own. Indeed, organizations such as Plans for Progress, a collaboration of over 165 Fortune 500 companies, freely engaged in affirmative action efforts to recruit women and minorities into their workplaces.[18]

The Reagan Years and the Affirmation Action Backlash

Starting in the late 1970s, and further fueled by the Reagan Administration in the 1980s that slashed and burned many social welfare and EEOC programs, affirmative action became a national controversy (DiTomaso & Smith, 1996). In her article "The Politics of Affirmative Action," Williams (1996) provides three reasons to explain the growth of hostility toward affirmative action during this time. First, the post–World War II boom had severely waned and with an increasing economic globalization also came job loss for many U.S. citizens, especially in the manufacturing sector. Competition and cheap labor markets overseas also helped to increase hostility toward immigrants, a situation that did not help minorities who were citizens of the U.S., as they became "otherized" along with anyone who did not fit the skin tone and phenotype of white Europeans. Second, increases in technology fueled a growing anxiety of job security. Automation in the factories led to a phenomenal level of clerical and technical job loss. And third, a factor agreed upon by most liberal scholars studying the issue of affirmative action, the economic policies of the Reagan and Bush administrations intentionally devised a series of plans to generate public discontent with affirmative action. These plans included not only severe cuts to many welfare and social programs, but also racially coded language designed to appeal to white voters and public discourse that argued that since racism was no longer an issue in the U.S., programs designed to create opportunities for minorities were no longer needed. The idea that everyone was on a level playing field generated new hope for whites (white males, in particular) in the form of "reverse discrimination," a notion suggesting that whites were being racially discriminated against. In addition to the changes made by the Reagan and Bush administrations, Executive Orders 10925 and 11246 were amended and made ineffective and the EEOC and OFCCP found themselves targets of the Department of Justice as well as the White House. Amazingly, though affirmative action rapidly lost ground in the political and social arenas of the U.S. starting in the late seventies, most businesses in corporate America retained their affirmative action programs throughout the eighties until it became replaced with a phenomenon of a new kind: diversity.

Birth of Diversity

Diversity is the latest oft-used term following its predecessor multiculturalism to counter the growing controversies multiculturalism and affirmative action programs were generating in the late 1970s and early 1980s. Made famous in the 1978 Supreme Court Case, *Bakke v. Board of Regents*[19], the word diversity became co-opted by major corporations and other organizations shortly after. The word "diversity" served many organizations well, especially corporate and later educational interests, because it was not as limiting as "multiculturalism," nor was it tied to the growing perception that policies such as affirmative action were discriminatory in themselves. This did not mean that government agencies, major corporations, and educational institutions necessarily abandoned affirmative action programs. For some organizations, affirmative action policies were taken apart, rearranged, and placed under the new title of "diversity programs" (see

Kelly & Dobbin, 1998; also Thomas, 1990). In other organizations, affirmative action continued to serve as the centerpiece in their diversity policies (a recent example of this is illustrated by the large number of corporations—65 leading Fortune 500 companies to include General Motors, the world's largest car manufacturing company—that sided with Michigan in the Michigan law school case, *Grutter v. Bollinger*[20]; see Green, 2004).

Organizations adopting diversity policies were seen as the front runners of progressiveness, especially at a time when various social movements, this time on a more global scale, were questioning whether or not America was truly an egalitarian nation. Multiculturalism became the central theme after World War II, when thousands of black and minority soldiers were returning to the United States in search of career opportunities. With the Civil Rights Act of 1964 came the expectation of fair and equal opportunites for workers of all colors. Between 1950 and 1976, the number of women in the U.S. workforce increased from 18.4 million to over 38.4 million (Green, 1980). During this time, unprecedented numbers of women were also pursuing higher education to increase their chances of competing effectively in the job market. With the 1980s and 1990s came political assaults on multicultural policies and practices. However, also prominent, and mostly as a result of conservative Reaganomic politics and new legislation, were the increased numbers of racial riots and social unrest from minorities and other supporters of their cause of racial equality. Diversity was seen as the new solution for many organizations trying to get away from the unpopularity of multiculturalism and affirmative action policies and practices (DiTomaso & Smith, 1996; Thomas, 1990). Unfortunately, diversity has also served as the new rallying cry for many organizations to hide the racial and gender inequalities that continued to persist in their workplaces.

The idea that corporations, government agencies, and educational institutions are interested in developing and maintaining a diverse and inclusive work environment is rather new, one that was around in the 1950s through 1970s with multiculturalism and affirmative action and continues on today with notions of diversity. Before the 1960s, it was uncommon for women and minorities to occupy top managerial and executive positions in businesses (Collins, 1997; DiTomaso & Smith, 1996). This is not to say that minorities and women were not allowed to work for many companies, rather they were mostly excluded from positions of power and authority. A close examination of U.S. corporate history illustrates a long pattern of resentment and hostility toward women and minorities that did not change, publicly in any event, until recently (Burstein, 1985; Farley, 1984; Farley & Allen, 1987; Wilson, 1978). However, workforce data continue to indicate that minorities and women are not even close to achieving parity with their white male counterparts (Fernandez, 1999; Stith, 1998). Furthermore, many organizations continue to implement various tactics to prevent women and minorities from achieving any sense of real power or authority in the workplace (e.g., sex segregation and glass ceilings; see Cohn, 2000; also Fernandez, 1981). Given the history of racism and sexism in America and the fact that racial and gender discrimination continue to pose major problems for achieving racial and gender equality, should we be somewhat skeptical about diversity policies and practices that are advertised by many U.S. institutions?

Diversity Today

In his 1997 *American Sociological Review* article titled "Rethinking Racism: Toward a Structural Interpretation," Bonilla-Silva argued that since the civil rights movement in the late 1950s and early 1960s, new covert and subtle racial practices have replaced the old overt and in-your-face Jim Crow techniques that were previously used by whites to keep minorities in their place. Bonilla-Silva coins this shift in America's racial practices as new racism. As a result of new racism practices, an ideology of colorblindness has emerged to justify and rationalize continued racial oppression[21] (for other studies on how racism works in the post–civil rights era, see also Kinder & Sears, 1981; McConahay & Hough, 1976; Smith, 1995). Thus, whites (and to some extent, non-whites) claim that racism does not exist, that racial segregation is a natural occurrence, or that culture explains why minorities do not do as well as their white counterparts.

Similarly, I have argued in previous articles (Embrick, 2008, 2011) that a diversity ideology has also emerged as a byproduct of the changes that occurred as a result of the civil rights triumphs of the sixties. It works hegemonically by accepting the language and even the moral order of diversity, without dealing with the practical and political elements involved in creating a truly diverse workplace. The diversity ideology is steeped in lore that suggests our society has come to a point in time where everyone, to include women and all racial and ethnic groups, in particular, is treated fairly and equally. It is comparable to the age-old notion of the American dream in that there is an idea that opportunity exists for anyone who will work hard enough for it. Similar to the mainstream logic surrounding the American dream, the diversity ideology suggests there is a level playing field when it comes to opportunities in such avenues as education, politics, public administration, and corporate America. Thus, the diversity ideology advocates not just opportunity, but equal opportunity. As a result of the widespread influence of the diversity ideology, when institutions such as major corporations, universities, and government agencies publicly advertise that they are interested in promoting diversity, the public perception is often that these organizations have a vested interest in promoting equality for morale, economic, or some other organizational benefit.[22]

Increasingly, research on diversity in corporate settings, higher education, and other institutions have found that while diversity was touted as an extremely important and valued concept, rarely was there any genuine interest in promoting racial and gender equality; indeed, rarely did conversations or discussions regarding diversity include issues of race and gender (Bell & Hartmann, 2007; Berrey, 2011; Embrick, 2008, 2011; Jackson et al., 2015; Moore & Bell, 2011). Findings such as these suggest that the concern of many organizations over diversity may not be as straightforward as they appear. It also suggests that the issue of diversity is a much more complex issue than many scholars have previously noted. With the recent attacks on affirmative action, diversity may not represent so much equal opportunity in the workplace for women and minorities in many U.S. organizations as it does a colorblind tactic that creates the illusion of egalitarianism.

Conclusion

To quote a line from Rice (2003, p. 14), in order for corporations, organizations and other institutions to make serious their commitments on diversity, they have to first "get their own houses in order." Diversity policies and practices must be enforced and serious efforts must be placed on placing women and minorities into higher-level positions where they will be able to have effective control over how their workplaces will be managed. However, the data suggests that women and minorities have a long way to go before achieving parity with white men in higher education, in the corporate world, and in public administration (Feagin et al., 1996; Fernandez, 1999, 1981). As it stands, it is questionable whether organizations are truly interested in creating a racially and gender diverse workforce, or simply interested in maintaining the status quo.

Diversity, when managed and implemented properly, can be a very effective tool in creating a successful, prosperous, and egalitarian environment (see Rice & White, 2005). However, as it stands, the diversity ideology has effectively allowed many major institutions to shield the racial and gender inequality that continue to persist in their various environments. We should question not only the policies and practices of organizations that claim they are interested in creating a more diverse workforce, but also the sincerity of such claims. Further, while diversity is not simply limited to racial and gender equality, neither should it exclude them.

References

Acker, Joan. (2006). Inequality regimes: Gender, class, and race in organizations. *Gender & Society, 20*(4), 441–464.

Bell, Joyce, & Douglas Hartmann. (2007). Diversity in everyday discourse: The cultural ambiguities and consequences of "happy talk." *American Sociological Review, 72,* 895–914.

Berrey, Ellen. (2011). Why diversity became orthodox in higher education, and how it changed the meaning of race on campus. *Critical Sociology, 37*(5), 573–596.

Bonilla-Silva, Eduardo. 1997. Rethinking racism: Toward a structural interpretation. *American Sociological Review, 62*(3), 465–480.

_____. (2001). *White supremacy & racism in the post-civil rights era.* Boulder, CO: Lynne Rienner Publishers.

_____. (2014/2003). *Racism without racists: Color-blind racism and the persistence of racial inequality in the USA.* Boulder, CO: Rowman and Littlefield Publishers, Inc.

Burk, Martha. (2005). *Cult of power: Sex discrimination in corporate America and what can be done about it.* New York: Scribner.

Burstein, Paul. (1985). *Discrimination, jobs, and politics: The struggle for equal employment opportunity in the United States since the New Deal.* Chicago: University of Chicago Press.

Cohn, Samuel. (2000). *Race, gender, and discrimination at work.* Boulder, CO: Westview Press.

Collins, Sharon M. (1997). *Black corporate executives: The making and breaking of a black middle class.* Philadelphia: Temple University Press.

DiTomaso, Nancy, & Steven A. Smith. (1996). Race and ethnic minorities and white women in management: Changes and challenges. In Joyce Tang & Earl Smith (Eds.), *Women and minorities in American professions* (pp. 87–110). New York: State University of New York Press.

Embrick, David G. (2008). The diversity ideology: Keeping major transnational corporations white and male in an era of globalization. In Angela Hattery, David G. Embrick, & Earl Smith (Eds.), *Globalization and America: Race, human rights & inequality.* Lanham, MD: Rowman and Littlefield.

_____. (2011). Diversity ideology in the business world: A new oppression for a new age. *Critical Sociology, 37*(5), 541–556.

Farley, Reynolds. (1984). *Blacks and whites: Narrowing the gap?* Cambridge, MA: Harvard University Press.

Farley, Reynolds, & Walter A. Allen. (1987). *The color line and the quality of life in America.* New York: Russell Sage.

Feagin, Joe R. (2006). *Systemic racism: A theory of oppression.* New York: Routledge.

Feagin, Joe R., Hernan Vera, & Nikitah Imani. (1996). *The agony of education: Black students at white colleges and universities.* New York: Routledge.

Fernandez, John P. (1999). *Race, gender & rhetoric: The true state of race and gender relations in corporate America.* New York: McGraw-Hill.

_____. (1981). *Racism and sexism in corporate life.* Lexington, MA: Lexington Books, D.C. Heath and Company.

Green, Denise O'Neil. (2004). Justice and diversity: Michigan's response to *Gratz, Grutter,* and the affirmative action debate. *Urban Education, 39*(4), 374–393.

Green, James R. (1980). *The world of the worker: Labor in twentieth-century America.* Champaign: University of Illinois Press.

_____. (1978). *Grass roots socialism: Radical movements in the Southwest: 1895–1943.* La Vergne, TN: Lightning Source, Inc.

Hansen, Fay. (2003, April). Diversity's business case doesn't add up. *Workforce Management,* 28–32.

Heckman, James J., & Brook S. Payner. (1989). Determining the impact of federal antidiscrimination policy on the economic status of blacks: A study of South Carolina. *American Economic Review, 79,* 138–177.

Heckman, James J., & Kenneth Wolpin. (1976). Does the Contract Compliance Program work? An analysis of Chicago data. *Industrial and Labor Relations Review, 29*(4), 544–564.

Herring, Cedric, & Sharon Collins. (1995). Retreat from equal opportunity? The case of affirmative action. In Michael Peter Smith & Joe R. Feagin (Eds.), *The bubbling cauldron: Race, ethnicity and the urban crisis* (pp. 143–162). Minneapolis: University of Minnesota Press.

Jackson, Crystal, David G. Embrick, & Carol S. Walther. (2015). The white pages: Diversity and the mediation of race in public business media. *Critical Sociology, 41*(3), 537–551.

Kelly, Erin, & Frank Dobbin. (1998). How affirmative action became diversity management: Employer response to anti-discrimination law, 1961–1996. *American Behavioral Scientist, 41,* 960–984.

Kinder, Donald R., & David O. Sears. (1981). Prejudice and politics: Symbolic racism versus racial threats to the good life. *Journal of Personality and Social Psychology, 40*(1), 414–31.

Layton, Azza Salama. (2000). *International politics and civil rights policies in the United States, 1941–1960.* Cambridge, UK: Cambridge University Press.

Marable, Manning. (1996). Staying on the path to racial equality. In George E. Curry (Ed.), *The affirmative action debate* (pp. 3–15). Reading, MA: Addison-Wesley Publishing Company, Inc.

McConahay, John B., & J. C. Hough. (1976). Symbolic racism. *Journal of Social Issues, 32*(2), 23–46.

Michaels, Walter B. (2006). *The trouble with diversity: How we learned to love identity and ignore inequality.* New York: Henry Holt and Company, L.L.C.

Moore, Wendy Leo, & Joyce M. Bell. (2011). Maneuvers of whiteness: "Diversity" as a mechanism of retrenchment in the affirmative action discourse. *Critical Sociology, 37*(5), 597–613.

Omi, Michael, & Howard Winant. (1994). *Racial formation in the United States: From the 1960s to the 1980s.* New York: Routledge.

Parrillo, Vincent N. (2005). *Diversity in America,* (2nd ed.). Thousand Oaks, CA: Pine Forge Press.

Renzulli, Linda A., Linda Grant, & Sheetija Kathuria. (2006). Race, gender, and the wage gap: Comparing faculty salaries in predominantly white and historically black colleges and universities. *Gender & Society, 20*(4), 491–510.

Rice, M. R. (2004). Organizational culture, social equity, and diversity: Teaching public administration education in the postmodern era. *Journal of Public Affairs Education, 2,* 143–154.

_____. (2003). Organizational culture, social equity and diversity: Teaching public administration education in the postmodern era. *Bush School of Government and Public Service Working Paper # 314.*

Rice, Mitchell F., & Harvey L. White. (2005). Embracing workplace diversity in public organizations: Some further considerations. In Mitchell F. Rice (Ed.), *Diversity and public administration: Theory, issues, and perspectives* (pp. 230–236). New York: M. E. Sharpe.

Smith, Robert Charles. (1995). *Racism in the post-civil rights era.* Albany: State University of New York Press.

Stith, Anthony. (1998). *Breaking the glass ceiling: Sexism & racism in corporate America: The myths, the realities & the solutions.* Los Angeles: Warwick Publishing.

Thomas, R. Roosevelt, Jr. (1990 March–April). From affirmative action to affirming diversity. *Harvard Business Review,* 107–117.

West, Cornell. (1996). Affirmative action in context. In George E. Curry (Ed.), *The affirmative action debate* (pp. 31–35). Reading, MA: Addison-Wesley Publishing Company, Inc.

Williams, Linda Faye. (1996). The politics of affirmative action. In George E. Curry (Ed.), *The affirmative action debate* (pp. 241–257). Reading, MA: Addison-Wesley Publishing Company, Inc.

Wilson, William Julius. (1978). *The declining significance of race: Blacks and changing American institutions.* Chicago: University of Chicago Press.

Wood, Peter. (2003). *Diversity: The invention of a concept.* San Francisco: Encounter Books.

Wright, Rosemary. (1996). Women in computer work: Controlled progress in a technical occupation. In Joyce Tang & Earl Smith (Eds.), *Women and minorities in American professions* (pp. 43–64). New York: State University of New York Press.

Zweigenhaft, Richard L., & G. William Domhoff. (2006/1998). *Diversity in the power elite: Have women and minorities reached the top?* New Haven, CT: Yale University Press.

_____. (2003). *Blacks in the white elite: Will the progress continue?* Boulder, CO: Rowman and Littlefield Publishers, Inc.

ENDNOTES

1. Gramsci, Antonio. (1978). *Selections from political writings, 1921–1926.* Museum Street, London: Lawrence & Wishad Ltd.

2. Google search for the word "diversity" revealed 230,000,000 results on March 19, 2015.

3. According to a 2003 article in *Workforce Management,* the increasing numbers of groups that are covered by diversity initiatives have helped to trivialize racial discrimination in many companies. Some examples of more recently created groups in various organizations such as Microsoft are groups for single parents, people with attention deficit disorder, dog ownership, any number of ethnic, cultural, or national identities, and birth order, among others.

4. Brown, C. Stone, & Mark Lowery. (2006). Who is worst for diversity? The United States senate. *DiversityInc Top 50 Companies for Diversity, 5*(5), 170–180.

5. Feagin, Joe R. (2006). *Systemic racism: A theory of oppression.* New York: Routledge.

6. For more details on combating the racialized social system, see chapter 9 of Eduardo Bonilla-Silva's book, *Racism without Racists: Color-Blind Racism and the Persistence of Racial Inequality in the United States* (2nd ed.). Boulder, CO: Rowman & Littlefield Publishers, Inc.

7. The "Melting Pot" theory suggested that as immigrants began to take on more identifiable characteristics (e.g., speak English, lose their accents, become middle class), they would eventually shed their ethnic identities and become accepted as "Americans."

8. See pg. 95 in Michael Omi and Howard Winant's 1994 book, *Racial Formation in the United States: From the 1960's to the 1990's.* New York: Routledge.

9. See the U.S. Equal Employment Opportunity Commission's website for a complete description of the Civil Rights Act of 1964.

10. The Equal Pay Act of 1963 outlawed sex-based discrimination in wages where work was essentially the same.

11. A full text version of this reference can be found on the Internet: http://books.google.com/books?id=t7q3_uNi570C&dq=Civil+Rights+Movement+%2B+Internations+Opinion+of+the+U.S.

12. The term "affirmative action" was first used by President Kennedy in his Executive Order 10925 to refer to measures designed to achieve non-discrimination.

13. Although West notes that affirmative action was a weak and imperfect response to the lasting legacy of white supremacy. For more information, see West, Cornell. (1996). Affirmative action in context. In George E. Curry (Ed.), *The Affirmative Action Debate* (pp. 31–35). Reading, MA: Addison-Wesley Publishing Company, Inc.

14. The title of the speech was "To Fulfill These Rights" and was given by President Lyndon B. Johnson on June 4, 1965.

15. Signed March 6, 1961 by President John F. Kennedy, Executive Order 10925 established a President's Committee on Equal Employment Opportunity that was charged with ensuring discrimination did not occur in government jobs based on race, creed, color, or national origin.

16. Executive Order 11246, signed by President Lyndon B. Johnson, Sept. 24, 1965, was established to set EEO and Affirmative Action Guidelines for Federal Contractors Regarding Race, Color, Gender, Religion, and National Origin. The charges of Executive Order 11246 were placed in the care of OFCCP.

17. An example of such a case is the January 1973 settlement between the Equal Employment Opportunity Commission and AT&T, a prominent communications company. Although AT&T did not enter a plea of guilty to the charge of racial and sex discrimination against its employees, it did sign a settlement agreement calling for millions of dollars of back pay as well as the implementation of company goals calling for increased attention to multicultural practices in the workplace.

18. See Williams, Linda Faye's 1996 article "The Politics of Affirmative Action" for more information on corporate support for affirmative action in the 1960s and 1970s. In George E. Curry (Ed.) *The Affirmative Action Debate* (pp. 241–257). Reading, MA: Addison-Wesley Publishing Company, Inc.

19. The U.S. Supreme Court ruled that the race of an applicant could be used as a criterion in admitting students to the University of California system if it served "the interest of diversity."

20. In 2003, the U.S. Supreme Court ruled in support of universities that wanted to use affirmative action to achieve diversity in the admissions process. The *Grutter v. Bollinger* case was seen as a setback to the Bush Administration, which publicly opposed affirmative action.

21. See also Bonilla-Silva's 2001 book, *White Supremacy & Racism in the Post-Civil Rights Era* (Boulder, CO: Lynne Rienner Publishers) as well as his 2006 book, *Racism Without Racists: Color-Blind Racism and the Persistence of Racial Inequality in the USA* (Boulder, CO: Rowman & Littlefield Publishers, Inc.) for more details on "new racism" since the civil rights era.

22. See Mitchell F. Rice's 2004 article, "Organizational Culture, Social Equity, and Diversity: Teaching Public Administration Education in the Postmodern Era," for a more in-depth analysis of how diversity is typically organizationally defined.

Critical Race Theory Critique of Colorblindness

by Margaret M. Zamudio, Caskey Russell, Francisco A. Rios, and Jacquelyn L. Bridgeman

One of the most profound problems that critical race theory scholars confront in addressing racial inequality is the widely held idea that, as a result of the Civil Rights Movement, the United States is now a colorblind society. This notion is further problematized with the election of Barack Obama to the presidency, an event to which political pundits point to suggest that we are not only a colorblind society, but a post-racial society. According to this view, not only do we no longer see or consider race—race no longer exists. Colorblindness suggests that today everybody enjoys equal treatment without regard to race. The notion of colorblindness is a product of liberal ideology that equates political rights with social equality without interrogating the many ways that race and racism play out in contemporary society to reproduce ongoing social inequality.

The civil rights laws elevating racial neutrality over racial discrimination addressed the most blatant forms of discrimination. Today, it is unlawful to ban students from attending schools based on race or to explicitly segregate students into particular classrooms based on race. These types of laws have served to advance the social position of people of color up to a point. Delgado and Stefancic (2001) point out the following:

> . . .critical race theorists (or "crits," as they are sometimes called) hold that color blindness will allow us to redress only extremely egregious racial harms, ones that everyone would notice and condemn.

But if racism is embedded in our thought processes and social structures as deeply as many crits believe, then the "ordinary business" of society—the routines, practices, and institutions that we rely on to effect the world's work—will keep minorities in subordinate positions. (p. 22)

The notion of colorblindness assumes that racism only operates as a consequence of political rights and the laws that govern them. It fails to consider the extent that society is racialized both interpersonally and institutionally. At the interpersonal level, it is impossible for us to not notice color and CRT legal scholar Neil Gotanda (2000) challenges the viability of colorblind laws. He states that

. . .in everyday American life, nonrecognition is self-contradictory because it is impossible not to think about a subject without having first thought about it at least a little. . . . The characteristics of race that are noticed (before being ignored) are situated within an already existing understanding of race. That is, race carries with it a complex social meaning. This pre-existing race consciousness makes it impossible for an individual to be truly nonconscious of race. (p. 36)

More directly, Brooks (2009) maintains that due to power differentials, colorblindness implicitly values whiteness and devalues all that is not white. He writes that ". . .when society proceeds in a colorblind fashion, it does not see monochrome: it sees white. Whiteness is the default cultural standard, and, thus, it is easy to view even the positive features of black culture as morally questionable" (p. xviii).

The basic CRT assumption at work here is that the laws of a liberal, democratic, capitalist society, even those granting people of color formal equality, are inadequate in remedying the legacy of over 200 years of state-sponsored racial inequality. The notions, ideas, forms of interaction developed to produce and reproduce inequality have moved beyond the legal scriptures that allowed man and woman to own man and woman, to force people off their land, to colonize them for their labor, to marginalize their children, to determine their status and place in society, and to develop ways of thinking and knowing that legitimized the inequality created in the process. Society's understandings of race, the meaning it has placed on blackness, redness, brownness, and whiteness is not undone with the stroke of a pen that brought us the Civil Rights Act of 1964. Thus, race as a socially constructed category carries with it historically derived meanings that continue to influence our present race-based ideas and interactions.

In fact, as Charles Lawrence (1987) illustrates in his groundbreaking work, *The Id, the Ego, and Equal Protection: Reckoning with Unconscious Racism*, and as numerous social and cognitive psychological experiments have shown, race is so much a part of our social and cultural heritage it is not only next to impossible to be colorblind—to not take race into account—it is also quite difficult to not act on biases, unconscious biases, which correlate with our automatic recognition of race when interacting with other human beings (see, e.g., Eberhardt and Fiske 1998; Fiske 1998; Fiske and Taylor 1991). As Lawrence explains:

> [T]he theory of cognitive psychology states that the culture—including, for example, the media and an individual's parents, peers, and authority figures—transmits certain beliefs and preferences. Because these beliefs are so much a part of the culture, they are not experienced as explicit lessons. Instead, they seem part of the individual's rational ordering of her perceptions of the world. The individual is unaware, for example, that the ubiquitous presence of a cultural stereotype has influenced her perception that blacks are lazy or unintelligent. Because racism is so deeply ingrained in our culture, it is likely to be transmitted by tacit understandings: Even if a child is not told that blacks are inferior, he learns that lesson by observing the behavior of others. These tacit understandings, because they have never been articulated, are less likely to be experienced at a conscious level. (p. 323)

As Lawrence explained in an article 20 years later, his purpose in employing psychological concepts was to illustrate the way in which the ideology of white supremacy holds a unique place in our conscious and unconscious beliefs and the way in which invidious discrimination is ubiquitous even if we do not realize it (2008). Addressing the unconscious component of racism, including how it conflates with colorblind rhetoric to keep in place the present racial hierarchy, is an avenue which CRT scholars continue to explore when seeking ways to effectively address America's perpetual race problem. (For recent work involving CRT and psychology see *California Law Review*, Volume 94, July 2006; *Connecticut Law Review*, Volume 40, May 2008.) CRT scholars also employ insights gleaned from cognitive and social psychology to call into question the mainstream assumption that our nation is in fact colorblind and to question whether implementing color-blind mandates such as those required by Propositions 209 and 2 (anti-affirmative action initiatives, to be described later) is even plausible (Carbado and Harris 2008; see also discussion in chapters 6 and 7 of this volume).

At the institutional level, colorblind policies have a profound effect on the maintenance of inequality. The post-civil rights period witnessed a number of liberal reforms directed at making social institutions more accessible and responsive to the people historically denied access. Given the blatantly racist history that shaped race relations at the individual level, social institutions needed to initiate policies intended to curb the influence of racially motivated individual decision-makers. Anti-discrimination laws developed for this purpose. Laws banning de jure discrimination (legally sanctioned) were intended to uphold the Fourteenth Amendment guarantee of equal protection under the law. The law banning segregation in public schools that developed from the ruling in *Brown vs. Board of Education* was one of the first of these. Of course, in contemporary society we celebrate the State's action in these rulings. Schools that had been zealously upholding the color line to assure racial segregation were now forced to be colorblind in determining student enrollment.

Yet today, schools are as racially segregated as in the past. Jonathan Kozol (2005), a fervent advocate for children of color in U.S. schools, writes in *Shame of a Nation: The Restoration of Apartheid Schooling in America*:

> One of the most disheartening experiences for those who grew up in the years when Martin Luther King and Thurgood Marshall were alive is to visit public schools today that bear their names, or names of other honored leaders of the integration struggles that produced the temporary progress that took place in the three decades after Brown, and to find how many of these schools are bastions of contemporary segregation. It is even more disheartening when schools like these are not in segregated neighborhoods but in racially mixed areas in which the integration of a public school would seem to be most natural and where, indeed, it takes conscious effort on the part of parents or of school officials in these districts to *avoid* the integration option that is often right at their front door. (p. 22)

What then is the role of colorblind policies in maintaining racial inequality at the institutional level? At the least offensive level these colorblind policies practice social neglect. One of the founding CRT legal scholars Alan Freeman (1995) suggests that *Brown* failed to take a victim perspective in favor of a perpetrator perspective. A victim's perspective would have demanded that the totality of inequalities caused by a history of racial subordination be addressed. By isolating the act of de jure segregation (segregation designed to maintain the subordination of blacks to whites) or intentional discrimination (the act of an isolated individual whose full intention is to discriminate to bring about a harmful condition for the victim), the ruling neglects the totality of conditions that create de facto (real and effective) segregation and discrimination. In effect, the result is that victims have a very narrow set of alternatives in remedying the wrongs committed against them. Similarly, a colorblind approach to institutional discrimination shares features with the perpetrator perspective. Freeman (1995) writes, "among these features is the emphasis on negating specific invalid practices rather than affirmatively remedying conditions. . ." (p. 32). Focusing on very narrow institutional practices allows for racism to continue unchecked while at the same time absolving the institution for ongoing de facto racial practices that are outside the realm of legally sanctioned discrimination.

Further, as recent scholarship regarding colorblindness shows, color-blind policies go beyond social neglect and work to affirmatively dismantle gains made in the post-civil rights era. By equating pre-civil rights subordination with programs such as affirmative action, which are meant to help remedy hundreds of years of subjugation, current colorblind rhetoric and the policies it has engendered has served to make suspect and call into question any and all race-based remedies regardless of whether such remedies are serving the purpose of equality and social justice (Haney Lopez 2007). Deploying colorblindness in this way has worked to dismantle programs meant to combat racism and move us closer to equality. At the same time, rhetoric asserting that requiring colorblindness is the same as having achieved it makes it harder to push for a social justice agenda that seeks to continue to work to eradicate the vestiges of racism.

Additionally, as noted CRT scholar Sumi Cho has explained, this problem is exacerbated by the recent shift from colorblindness to post-racialism. Cho defines post-racialism as "a twenty-first-century ideology that reflects a belief that due to the significant racial progress that has been made, the state need not engage in race-based decision-making or adopt race-based remedies, and that civil society should eschew race as a central organizing principle of social action" (2009, p. 1594). In her recent work, Cho asserts that the current shift from colorblindness to post-racialism was prompted in no small part by the recent election of Barack Obama as president. While there is significant overlap between colorblindness and pos-racialism as Cho explains, they are not one and the same.

> . . .[W]hile the ideology of colorblindness shares many features and objectives with the ideology of post-racialism detailed below, post-racialism is yet distinct as a descriptive matter, in that it signals a racially transcendent event that authorizes the retreat from race. Colorblindness, in comparison, offers a largely normative claim for a retreat from race that is aspirational in nature. (pp. 1597–1598)

As Cho explains further, the shift from colorblindness to post-racialism is concerning for those who continue to seek racial equality and social justice for a number of reasons. Like colorblindness, post-racialism works "to eliminate state intervention to address racial injustices through race-based remedies" (2009, p. 1644). According to Cho, post-racialism may be even more effective than colorblindness in this regard because post-racialism appeals to a broader spectrum of people and insulates white normativity from criticism in ways colorblindness does not.

The continued school segregation of students of color, as described by Kozol (2005), is a product of our failure to affirmatively remedy the totality of social conditions that have produced ongoing racial inequality. Brown v. Board removed the most visible barriers to educational discrimination. But it failed to address the less tangible forms that keep school segregation alive today: white flight from schools and neighborhoods, disinvestment in public education, semi-privatization of education, historically produced poverty in communities of color, etc.

Most importantly, not *Brown v. Board* or any other court action since then has addressed institutional white privilege and the unjust enrichment of whites at the expense of people of color. Colorblindness and the shift to post-racialism, which work to obscure and ignore the continued effects of race and to equate racial subordination with remedies meant to combat that subordination, make it increasingly less likely that the continued barriers to equal education will be torn down any time soon.

The Myth of Meritocracy, Colorblindness, and Whiteness

Now that blatant anti-discrimination policies have been in effect for over half a century, the myth of meritocracy and the concept of colorblindness suggest that continued educational inequality has more to do with individual educational choices rather than discrimination in schools, which continues to place whites at the top and people of color at the bottom of the educational hierarchy. The flip side of blaming those at the bottom for their position in society is praising those at the top for achieving their position. This is one of the most egregious falsehoods of the myth of meritocracy. If, as Freeman (1995) points out, "the Brown case was a straightforward declaration that segregation was unlawful because it was an instance of majoritarian oppression of black people, a mechanism for maintaining blacks as a perpetual underclass" (p. 33), then we have to ask who benefitted from the maintenance of blacks (in this case) as an underclass? Joe Feagin (2000) writes in *Racist America: Roots, Current Realities, and Future Reparations* of the unjust enrichment of whites. He explains:

> . . .unjustly gained wealth and privilege for whites is linked directly to undeserved immiseration for black Americans. This was true for many past generations, and it remains true for today's generations . . . The average black person lives about six years less than the average white person. An average black family earns about 60 percent of the income of an average white family—and has only 10 percent of the economic wealth of an average white family . . . Acts of oppression are not just immediately harmful; they often carry long-term effects. (p. 27)

Brooks (2009) makes a similar claim by asserting that the first two major racial "group rights" efforts, historically, were aimed at the explicit benefit of whites. These included the initial "separate and unequal" doctrine that dominated during slavery and the "separate but equal" doctrine with its Jim Crow policies which obtained thereafter (i.e., the absence of anti-discrimination laws, state rights' claims that allowed states to exercise unequal treatment, and safety and wage law exclusions for occupations dominated by people of color such as farm workers and maids).

Katznelson (2005) extends this argument to describe how the G.I. Bill of Rights served as affirmative action for whites. He shows how Mississippi used state rights' claims to allow it to provide G. I. Bill benefits to 3,229 whites and only 2 veterans of color.

But perhaps the most tangible long-term benefit that whites have accrued from a history of racial exploitation is their wealth, and subsequently their enriched position, in accessing educational resources. While income inequality has decreased since the 1960s, wealth not income provides the best indicator for one's life chances. Melvin Oliver and Thomas Shapiro (1997) in *Black Wealth White Wealth: A New Perspective on Racial Inequality* differentiate wealth and income.

> Wealth is what people own, while income is what people receive for work, retirement, or social welfare. Wealth signifies the command over financial resources that a family has accumulated over its lifetime along with those resources that have been inherited across generations. Such resources, when combined with income, can create the opportunity to secure the 'good life' in whatever form is needed—education, business, training, justice, health comfort, and so on. (p. 2)

> Today, whites enjoy considerable more wealth than people of color and, as a result, have greater access to educational resources. In fact, Shapiro (2009) points out that "the accumulative advantage or the legacy of whiteness for the typical white family is $136,174" (p. 59). Shapiro also points out that "in 2002, a typical Hispanic family owned 11 cents of wealth for every dollar owned by a typical white family, and African-American families owned only 7 cents" (p. 60).

Wealth is directly tied to a history of racial exploitation. White communities have directly enjoyed, and accumulated across generations, the benefits of a color line used to determine the allocation of public and private goods such as education, jobs, and housing: the basic foundations for the accumulation of wealth. Housing, in particular, provides the most common route for generating wealth. For working people, buying a house represents an element of achieving the American dream. However, the policies and practices surrounding housing—from the development of white suburbs in the 1940s and 1950s (which continue to serve mostly white residents) and the intentional ghettoization of black/brown people in inner cities and barrios, to the discriminatory mortgage lending, to the direct role of the Federal government in facilitating this inequality—have worked to create the contemporary racial wealth gap (Lipsitz 2009). Lipsitz explains that

. . .each of these policies widened the gap between the resources available to whites and those available to aggrieved racial communities, but the most damaging long-term effects may well have come from the impact of the racial discrimination codified by the policies of the FHA [Federal Housing Administration]. By channeling loans away from older inner-city neighborhoods and toward white home buyers moving into segregated suburbs, the FHA and private lenders after World War II aided and abetted the growth and development of increased segregation in U.S. residential neighbor-hoods. (p. 148)

When housing prices doubled in the 1970s, home owners saw their equity increase exponentially. At the same time, people of color where largely locked out of the suburban market by ongoing racial practices in the industry. Those who were fortunate enough to secure financing bought at much higher prices and were not offered the same opportunity to bank a slice of the great wealth generated in the housing boom of the 1970s. As a result of these policies, Lipsitz (2009) adds "by 1993, 86 percent of suburban whites still lived in places with a black population below 1 percent" (p. 149). While we tend to believe that economic processes are colorblind—that those who can afford to buy a house do and that they buy wherever they desire to live—decisions about who has the opportunity to buy, which neighborhoods they can buy in, and how much wealth they accumulate as a result of these activities is in reality historically and racially determined.

Closely tied to the unjust enrichment of whites and the unjust impoverishment of people of color is the unjust allocation of educational resources. Since schools often derive the bulk of their funding from their community's tax base, the issue of school funding is often considered a colorblind process. But as our discussion on wealth indicates, community formation and wealth stems from racially biased historical processes. The greater wealth in white communities provides greater funds for their local schools. White students thus have racially based advantages that appear colorblind rather than color-based; in fact, historically based racism is operating in the contemporary distribution of educational resources. However, because historical processes are not readily discernible in the absence of critical thought and questioning, the unjust enrichment of whites and the unjust impoverishment of communities of color play out as seemingly colorblind processes in determining educational advantage and disadvantage.

These seemingly colorblind processes fuel the myth of meritocracy that suggests those who achieve educationally earned their way on individual merit. In this light, individuals are taken out of their historical and contemporary context. The privileges of whiteness and disadvantages of color are completely obscured. The white student who works hard at her suburban school, earns high marks in her advanced placement classes, studies hard in her school-funded SAT courses, and makes national merit scholar to gain admission to an elite university appears to do so as an individual. This student indeed worked hard, but her accomplishments were made possible within the suburban context created distinctly to privilege whiteness. Conversely, the American Indian student who works hard at his reservation school, earns high marks, does not have access to quality SAT courses nor access to advanced placement classes, fails to achieve national merit distinction, but earns a tribal scholarship to attend a state university is often portrayed as racially advantaged in being awarded scholarship money. This latter student's achievements, despite the racial obstacles he has necessarily had to overcome, are minimized to suggest that his race rather than his hard work advantaged him in college admissions. Ultimately, the most blatant forms of racism today stem from our failure to acknowledge the unearned privilege and the unjust enrichment of whiteness. The very notion of colorblindness underlies this contemporary racism and maintains the myth of meritocracy.

Colorblind Racism

Colorblind racism can be understood as an active form of racism. Colorblind racism maintains the dominance and privilege of whiteness in the post-civil rights era. Brooks (2009) maintains, "Color blindness does nothing to change the existing racial dynamic and, for that reason, it takes sides ipso facto. . . In the end, white hegemony is the order of the day" (p. 103). This new racial project termed *colorblind racism* functions to (1) obscure the privilege of whiteness and (2) to reverse the gains of the Civil Rights Movement by attacking race-based programs designed to provide historically oppressed groups access to social resources in general, and education in particular. The latter function represents colorblind racism in its most active form.

Conservatives are at the forefront of this movement. Conservatives take liberalism to an extreme. They go beyond simply accepting liberal assumptions and instead use them to actively attack the gains of the Civil Rights Movement. Colorblindness operates as the intellectual justification for a reinvigorated racism that has turned the Civil Rights Movement on its head. Recall Martin Luther King's famous 1963 "I Have a Dream" speech. Over 40 years later, this speech still moves many. Today, conservative activists use one line in particular to oppose the programs that emerged from the Civil Rights Movement. Martin Luther King's eloquent statement, "I have a dream that my four little children will one day live in a nation where they will not be judged by the color of their skin, but by the content of their character," looked to a future when race would no longer have the stinging impact it had then and today. But conservative activists use the idea of not judging an individual based on his or her color to block race-specific policies like desegregation, affirmative action, and bilingual education. Although these progressive policies by themselves are ineffective in achieving full racial justice, they represent the few tools available in the struggle against racial oppression in the post-civil rights period.

Colorblind racism abuses the discourse of the Civil Rights Movement. An argument suggesting that racism is a thing of the past or that awarding an American Indian a scholarship, for example, constitutes reverse discrimination serves to reverse the few gains of the Civil Rights Movement, the very gains that made it possible for a black man to become president of the United States. Conservatives making these arguments in the face of entrenched racial inequality promote the interests of whiteness at the continued expense of people of color. In fact, CRT scholars see this conservative movement as an organized assault on people of color disguised under a hood of colorblindness. How might the rest of us better confront contemporary racism? Two of the authors of this book have written extensively on the problem.

> One way of demystifying the racial project of a "colorblind" racist society is simply to admit that racism exists and that all white people benefit from it. We believe that coming to an understanding of the various ways in which racism plays out and is understood, legitimated, and contested serves to demystify the racial project of a colorblind society (Zamudio and Rios 2006, p. 485).

In short, for CRT scholars, intentionality of racism is not of the greatest importance. Rather, the impact of ideologies and institutional structures that result in social inequality are racist. As Brooks (2009) quips, social subordination of people of color "is racist because it is racialized" (p. 90).

Latina/o Sociology

by Rogelio Sáenz, Karen Manges Douglas, and Maria Cristina Morales

Rogelio Sáenz, Karen Manges Douglas, and Maria Cristina Morales, "Latina/o Sociology," *Expanding the Human in Human Rights: Toward a Sociology of Human Rights*, ed. David L. Brunsma, Keri E. Lyall Smith and Brian K. Gran, pp. 54-63. Copyright © 2014 by Paradigm Publishers. Reprinted with permission.

Latina/os represent the fastest-growing racial and ethnic group in the United States. Indeed, over the period from 1980 to 2009, the Latina/o population more than tripled—from 14.6 million in 1980 to 48.4 million in 2009—while the overall US population increased by only 36 percent (Sáenz 2010a). Currently, Latina/os account for one of every two persons added to the US population. The rapid growth of the Latina/o population has been fueled by the group's youthfulness, reflected in a median age of twenty-seven compared to forty-one among the white population in 2009.

The variation in the age structures of these two groups will result in an expansion of the Latina/o representation in the United States alongside a declining presence of whites in the coming decades. It is projected that the Latina/o share of the US population is likely to increase from 16 percent in 2010 to 30 percent in 2050, while that of the white population is expected to decline from 65 percent in 2010 to 46 percent in 2050 (US Census Bureau 2008). This divergent demographic future has led to the rise of policy initiatives to halt Latina/o immigration and to apprehend and deport undocumented Latina/os.

The increasingly hostile environment against Latina/os has threatened their basic human rights for US citizens and noncitizens alike. Despite their long presence in the United States, especially in the case of Mexicans and Puerto Ricans, Latina/os continue to be viewed as an invading threat that does not belong in the United States (Chavez 2008). The antagonism against Latina/os is driven by racism and a fear that they are encroaching on the safe and comfortable space where whites have thrived and benefitted from their racial status.

Despite major encroachments on the basic human rights of Latina/os in the United States, human rights concerns continue to be a sidebar in research on Latina/os. Only in the last decade have we seen an increase in research on Latina/os directly addressing matters of human rights. For example, a search of *Sociological Abstracts* using the keywords "Hispanic," "Latino," or "Latina" and "human rights" reveals only twelve entries, all published since 1999, with two-thirds of these published since 2005. The absence of work on human rights related to Latina/os reflects the US practice of granting rights on the basis of citizenship rather than one's being a human being (Turner 2006). Nonetheless, attention to human rights issues affecting Latina/os has increased in the post-9/11 period with the heightened criminalization of immigrants and militarization of the border (Golash-Boza 2009; Sáenz and Murga 2011).

This chapter has several goals. First, we provide an overview of the theoretical perspectives and sociological tool kits that Latina/o scholars have employed in the study of Latina/os. Second, we provide the historical context in which whiteness became an asset for US citizenship along with the racialization of Latina/os. Third, we summarize the contemporary context in which Latina/os live. Finally, we conclude with a discussion of the sociology of Latina/os and its potential linkage to a human rights perspective.

SOCIOLOGICAL TOOL KITS IN THE STUDY OF LATINA/OS

Sociologists who study the Latina/o population use a variety of methodological tools to conduct their research (Rodríguez, Sáenz, and Menjívar 2008; Rodríguez 2008). As scholars try to gain a deep understanding of sociological phenomenon on Latina/os, they tend to rely on qualitative methods including ethnographies, in-depth interviews, and observations (Dunn 2009). In addition, scholars who are interested in historical and legal studies of the Latina/o population tend to make use of historical and legal archives in their research. Court cases, including Supreme Court decisions and dissenting opinions, for instance, are quite revealing of the assumptions undergirding them (López 2006). Moreover, sociologists who are interested in media studies tend to analyze textual, visual, and digital sources. Content analysis of programming content and advertisements, along with newspaper column-width coverage, are all common methodological tools used for studying the media. Furthermore, persons who examine structural forces impacting the behavior of Latina/os tend to rely on quantitative data including census information and large-scale surveys. Additionally, sociologists who examine the transnational aspects of the lives of Latina/os use a variety of methodological approaches, including ethnographies, in-depth interviews, and surveys, in the communities of origin and destination across international borders. Finally, sociologists who study the Latina/o population use a variety of theoretical approaches that capture the inequalities that continue to mark the lives of Latina/os. These approaches include the structural racism (Feagin 2006) and critical race (and LatCrit) (Trucios-Haynes 2001) perspectives.

A HISTORICAL OVERVIEW OF THE RACIALIZATION OF LATINA/OS

Ngai's (2004) concept of Latina/os as alien citizens (or Heyman's [2002] reference to "anticitizens") provides an appropriate point of departure from which to discuss human rights and the US Latina/o population. Alien citizenship ensued from the US legal racialization of people based upon their national origins. Accordingly, the use of racial categories for inclusion and exclusion from the United States dates to the nation's first immigration and naturalization laws of 1790, which limited eligibility for naturalization to free, white aliens (Ngai 2004).

Following the Civil War, naturalization laws were amended to confer citizenship on persons of African descent (former slaves) while continuing the eligibility criterion of white, thereby establishing a black-white color line for the granting of US citizenship (Daniels 2004). The 1924 National Origins Act established a racial hierarchy of the world's inhabitants (Ngai 1999, 2004) in which northern and western Europeans received large quotas, southern and eastern Europeans got small quotas, and Asians were barred from immigrating to the United States.

Western Hemisphere residents (Latin Americans and Canadians) were excluded from the act's quota restrictions, reflecting the political clout of southwestern agricultural interests desiring cheap Mexican labor. Instead the bill established visa requirements for entry into the United States, which resulted in a new category of persons in the racial taxonomy: the "illegal alien" (Bustamante 1972). Although people without proper documentation included all nationalities worldwide, over time the term became synonymous with "Mexican" (Ngai 2004).

The requirement that US citizenship be limited to those defined as either white or black meant that the courts were called upon to make racial determinations. Between 1887 and 1923, the federal courts made more than twenty-five racial determinations (López 2006; Ngai 2004). For the nation's Latina/o population, who per the US black-white citizenship requirements were legally designated white, there are numerous examples of ways the dominant white group defined Latina/os as nonwhite. In the case of *In Re: Rodriguez* (1897), Ricardo Rodriguez, a Mexican-born resident of San Antonio, Texas, was denied naturalization on the grounds that he was not white (De Genova 2005; Sáenz and Murga 2011). However, a district court judge ruled that although Rodriguez was not white, he was nevertheless eligible to become a naturalized citizen because the Texas state constitution recognized Mexicans as citizens of Texas, all citizens of Texas were granted US citizenship when Texas became a US state, and the Treaty of Guadalupe Hidalgo signed in 1848 granted US citizenship to Mexicans living on these lands (De Genova 2005; Sáenz and Murga 2011).

The discomfort of the white population over the Latina/os' default white designation is further reflected in the creation of a "Mexican" racial category for the 1930 census. Due in part to the lobbying efforts of Mexican American leaders who argued that Mexican Americans were white (Snipp 2003, 69), the issue of how to classify the Latina/o population of the United States remained a work in progress. Ironically, whites were quick to view Latina/os as white when *Brown v. Board of Education* pressured the South to desegregate. Accordingly, Texas officials sought to achieve school desegregation by placing Latina/o and black students in the same schools (San Miguel 2005).

The alien citizenship of Latina/os stems from the conquest of the two largest Latina/o groups—Mexicans and Puerto Ricans—characterized by warfare, power, and resource asymmetry between the United States and Latin America (see Bonilla-Silva 2008). US employer demand for cheap Latin American labor (particularly Mexican), supported by legislative initiatives such as the Bracero Program and more recently NAFTA, continue to pull Latina/os into the United States despite highly racialized immigration and naturalization legislation intent on limiting "undesirables." Policy initiatives in several states (notably Arizona and Alabama) are aimed squarely at the Latina/o undocumented. While individual pieces of legislation have been legally challenged, the racial nature of the efforts, the conflation of legal and illegal, citizen and noncitizen, and the Supreme Court's sanction of racial profiling of "Mexican-looking" people send an unwelcoming message. Further, these types of policy initiatives have intensified over the last few decades as the Latina/o population has grown.

THE CONTEMPORARY CONTEXT

The expanding Latina/o population and its spread to states that have historically not had a significant presence of Latina/os challenge the racial hierarchy and the power monopoly that whites have enjoyed (see Moore 2008). To stem Latina/o encroachment on the existing racial structure,

US states have employed a variety of tactics, including highly restrictive immigration laws such as Arizona's Senate Bill (SB) 1070, mobilization of local militias such as the Minutemen to patrol the border, state-mandated abolition of ethnic studies courses (e.g., Arizona's House Bill 2281), passage of English-only legislation and repealing of bilingual education in several states, and local ordinances criminalizing property rental to undocumented immigrants. These efforts have served to set Latina/os once again as a class apart.

At the federal level, revamped immigration laws such as the Illegal Immigrant Reform and Immigrant Responsibility Act of 1996 enhanced border-enforcement activities and loosened deportation criteria. Additionally, the law established a mechanism for partnerships between local law enforcement and federal immigration enforcement via the 287(g) provision. In 2006, the United States passed the Secure Fence Act of 2006 authorizing construction of a US border wall. Further, the Fourteenth Amendment to the US Constitution, which grants citizenship to all persons born in the United States, is at the epicenter of nativists' efforts to overturn the principle as a mechanism to slow the growth of the rapidly expanding US Latina/o population (Wood 1999).

As López (2006) notes, these targeted actions are far from color-blind and share the same highly racial imprimatur of earlier policies that oversaw the internment of Japanese American citizens during World War II and the deportation of Mexican Americans during Operation Wetback in the 1950s. This hostile environment against Latina/os has contributed to citizenship and human rights violations—acceptable collateral damage to maintain white supremacy.

SOCIOLOGY OF LATINA/OS

The sociological study of Latina/os is relatively new, with major developments beginning in the 1970s. However, over the past several decades, the field of the sociology of Latina/os has expanded dramatically. Major substantive areas of study include demography, crime, education, family, gender, health, immigration, inequality, and labor. While much of the research in the area has focused on Latina/os in the United States, research has also addressed the larger transnational context in which Latina/os exist.

Transnationalism describes the processes whereby immigrants maintain ties to the native/sending communities and participate in varying ways in the activities of their communities of origin and destination. In part due to the proximity to Latin American countries, Latina/o immigrants to the United States, particularly more recent arrivals, continue to be linked to their originating communities (Fink 2003; Smith 2005).

Transnationalism impacts both individuals and entire families. Transnational families are created when one or both parents emigrate from the household of origin (Menjívar and Abrego 2009; Parreñas 1998). In the context of the aftermath of 9/11, the "war on drugs," and the global economic recession, crossing borders and maintaining transnational ties has become difficult and dangerous for Latin American migrants. Human rights concerns have escalated along the US-Mexico border due to border-control measures—that is, the erection of a physical and virtual wall, increases in border agents, and the militarization of the border (use of surveillance technology and military personnel) (Dunn 2001). Consequently, what was once a circulatory migrant flow has become increasingly a one-way journey. Sending-community involvement in this migration is constricted, transnational family reunification is hindered, and undocumented immigrants are often "entrapped" along the southern border (Núñez and Heyman 2007).

Particularly alarming is the increase in migrant deaths resulting from the more dangerous and treacherous terrain migrants are forced to travel from Mexico into the United States due to enhanced urban-border enforcement (Eschbach et al. 1999; Massey, Durand, and Malone 2002). Unfortunately, these and other human rights abuses have largely been ignored in the United States. Further, because nation-states maintain power in implementing international human rights, there appears to be little legal recourse for these human rights abuses as the United States refused to sign the International Convention on the Protection of the Rights of All Migrant Workers and Their Families adopted by the UN General Assembly in 1990. This is problematic for Latina/os because many lack citizenship rights afforded by nation-states (see Turner 2006).

Border-control initiatives also create human rights abuses for US-born Latina/os. Heightened border enforcement disrupts the stability of life for all inhabiting this militarized zone. Under the pretext of the "war on drugs," the military is used for domestic policing along the US-Mexico border (Dunn 2001). The militarization that Latina/os are subjected to in the border region parallels other state-sanctioned forms of social control. Border-control operations racially profile all "brown" people regardless of citizenship status (Morales and Bejarano 2009). The Border Network for Human Rights (2003) has documented the extensive use of race as a basis for immigration-related questioning leading to constitutional violations against US citizens and documented immigrants, such as wrongful detentions, searches, confiscation of property, and physical and psychological abuse.

As Latina/os have settled in new destinations (Sáenz, Cready, and Morales 2007), border-control enforcement tactics have followed (Coleman 2007). Turner (2006) notes the increasing need for human rights enforcement in situations where everyone is vulnerable. In this case, all

US residents are vulnerable as the militarized state and border-control tactics expand across the country.

No doubt, the historical and contemporary story of the US Latina/o population is far from straightforward. Latina/os encompass a heterogeneous population with differing histories and modes of incorporation into the United States. This heterogeneity makes human rights issues more complex and not neatly encompassed in a single narrative or tradition. Although there are variations, one constant has been the inferior status of Latina/os relative to whites.

WHAT CAN THE HUMAN RIGHTS PARADIGM LEARN FROM THE SOCIOLOGY OF LATINA/OS?

The sociology of Latina/os can expand the human rights paradigm given Latina/os' status as the largest US minority group, their diversity, and their transnational lives, which create a gray area between the human and citizenship rights paradigms. To begin, despite being the nation's largest minority group, Latina/os remain marginally integrated into mainstream institutions. The sociology of Latina/os has been inspired by several societal conditions that Latina/os face, such as precarious employment situations, poverty, educational inequality, injustice in the criminal justice system, a system of rights that does not protect its immigrant community, and other human rights abuses that reflect the group's lack of integration. The human rights abuses that Latina/os confront are not merely associated with the newcomer status of a segment of the population. Indeed, despite their long historical presence in the United States, Mexican Americans continue to occupy the lowest economic positions (Sáenz, Morales, and Ayala 2004) and are largely regarded as "foreigners" (Douglas and Sáenz 2010).

The human rights implications of the extensive social control of Latina/os are reflected in public policies. For instance, SB 1070 made residing in Arizona without legal authorization a crime and conflates the policing of immigration with racial profiling (Heyman 2010; Sáenz and Murga 2011). Arguably, this state-level policy is a response to the threatening Latina/o growth (see Sáenz 2010b) and targets all Latina/os, regardless of citizenship status, who are perceived to be "foreigners" (Heyman 2010). Human rights concerns arise from the exercise of state power to disproportionately target Latina/os, leading to their subjection to extensive social controls, deportation and separation from families, harassment, and criminalization.

The sociology of Latina/os has highlighted Latina/o heterogeneity, which has important implications for the human rights paradigm. Latina/os are stratified by racial identification, skin color, citizenship status, and class (Morales 2009), which increases the complexity of applying the human rights paradigm. The diversity of the Latina/o population, particularly in terms of citizenship status, illustrates a challenge in utilizing the human rights paradigm for the equality, safety, and prosperity of the entire group. The difficult theoretical work of how to grapple with the human rights of Latina/o immigrants—many of whom are outside the umbrella of citizenship rights and simultaneously deprived of human rights given the focus of nation-states—has yet to be done.

Yet, the citizenship diversity among Latino immigrant families has a myriad of human rights implications. There are many "mixed-status families," which consist of members with a variety of statuses, including citizens, visa holders, naturalized citizens, and undocumented individuals. Indeed, Fix and Zimmermann (2001) found that one-tenth of families have mixed status, where one or both parents are noncitizens and the children are citizens. In a study of mixed-status families in the detention/deportation system, Brabeck and Xu (2010) found that parents with higher levels of legal vulnerability experienced greater problems associated with emotional well-being, ability to provide financially, and relationships with their children. In this context, children's emotional stability and academic performance are jeopardized (Brabeck and Xu 2010). Moreover, in the legal system, the onerous requirements to override deportation proceedings create a hurdle few can overcome and one that is nearly insurmountable for undocumented parents of US citizen children (Sutter 2006). Human rights perspectives must consider the cessation of individual deportations in order to maintain "intact" families, a notion that several nations recognize as important (Sutter 2006). Thus, this adds another layer of complexity to the application of human rights when considering whether the locus of protection should be the individual or the family.

INCORPORATING THE HUMAN RIGHTS PARADIGM INTO THE SOCIOLOGY OF LATINA/O RESEARCH

A review of the human rights literature concerning the Latina/o population reveals significant attention to human rights based in Latin America but not in the United States before the 9/11 period. With the rise of human rights abuses in the post-9/11 period, research addressing human rights among Latina/os has shifted toward the United States since 2000. Of the sixteen entries in *Sociological Abstracts* published since 2000, eleven were based in the United States. The research on Latina/os in the United States that has incorporated human rights dimensions includes themes such as the ambiguity of the US-Mexico border (Ortiz 2001), the militarization of the border (Dunn 2001), the US minority rights revolution associated with the civil rights era

(Skrentny 2002), abuses against immigrants (Dunn, Aragones, and Shivers 2005; Krieger et al. 2006; Redwood 2008; Vinck et al. 2009), the growth of the prison population (Modic 2008), youth activism and the struggle for human rights associated with the immigrant rights marches of 2006 (Velez et al. 2008), and antigay family policies (Cahill 2009).

Still, the relative dearth of material within the established human rights tradition represents the difficulty the perspective faces in addressing the multiple and continuing human rights violations confronting the US Latina/o population. There are several reasons for this. First, as Dunn (2009) notes, the issue of human rights remains entangled within notions of the nation-state and citizenship. Human rights are conditional on citizenship, which comes with attached rights and duties. Violations (e.g., committing felony acts) can result in the diminishment of citizenship rights (e.g., voter disenfranchisement). Indeed, it is within this tradition that human rights battles for inclusion have occurred in the United States. People of color have challenged their exclusion from the full benefits of US citizenship and sought remedies. However, these remedies are conditioned by citizenship. By definition, the extraterritorial essence of the Latina/o population is a threat to the nation-state. Just as Japanese Americans were viewed during World War II as sympathetic and inextricably linked to Japan, which provided the rationale for their imprisonment, so too, and despite multiple generations of presence in the United States, is there a conflation between Mexican Americans and Mexico. Further complicating the Latina/o human rights story is that significant numbers of the US Latina/o population remain citizens of their countries of origin. Thus, the links to their homelands are still direct and, to many in the United States, threatening.

Second, the narrow framing of human rights conditioned upon citizenship has pitted Latina/o citizen against Latina/o noncitizen. The narrow targeting of, for example, immigration laws on racial grounds has resulted not only in broken families but in an "us-versus-them" mentality that has tolerated human rights violations so long as citizens are not the target (Dunn 2009). As Ngai (2004) argues, this framing of migrants as threats, together with the prolific national discourse surrounding the need to "secure our borders," provides cover for the state to engage in a variety of racist and discriminatory acts that even the Supreme Court acknowledges "would be unacceptable if applied to citizens" (Ngai 2004, 12).

Third, as articulated in the works of LatCrit theorists, the ambiguous racial category that Latinas/os inhabit renders the application of traditional human rights perspectives problematic. Fourteenth Amendment protections are predicated on race, ancestry, or national origin. This leaves most Latina/os who lack a distinct racial category or national origin without a basis for a discrimination claim. As detailed earlier, this is problematic on several fronts, including the fact that some Latina/os are Americans with deep ties to their countries of origin. The effect of both the narrow focus of the equal protection clause and the multidimensional nature of the Latina/o population has allowed for "discrimination to remain remedied" and for "the manipulation of the Latina/o image to exploit racial fears" (Trucios-Haynes 2001, 4).

The human rights perspective offers potential redress to the nation-state/ citizenship-rights perspective. This perspective begins with the premise that all human beings have fundamental and inalienable human rights (Blau and Moncada 2005; Sjoberg, Gill, and Williams 2001). These rights are unconditional, universal, and, importantly, transnational. As Turner explains, these individual rights emerge as a result of our "shared vulnerabilities" (2006a, 47). This perspective provides a different frame (outside the citizenship/nation-state divide) from which to evaluate questionable policies despite their legality within the nation-state. Unfortunately, the platform for realizing these rights is relatively narrow. The UN offers a Declaration of Human Rights, but there are only weak enforcement capabilities at the global level. Thus, despite the recognition of inalienable and universal human rights, this perspective has gained little traction.

Further, as Bonilla-Silva (2008) argues, the human rights tradition suffers from its failure to recognize and incorporate race into its analysis. Bonilla-Silva asserts that "the HRT idealizes the autonomous individual who can be located within a universe of abstract rights, devoid of racially constraining social structures" (2008, 11). While the human rights perspective recognizes the inalienable rights of people, it "seems unwilling to temper this view with the fact that there are vast differences of power among individuals as individuals as well as members of social groups or nation-states" (Bonilla-Silva 2008, 12). In short, all people are not the same. Much of the story told, thus far, involves the successful efforts to marginalize the Latina/o population. Immigration laws, including the present-day variations, have been constructed along highly racialized lines with specific racial bogeymen as their target.

THE ROAD FORWARD

Despite the long presence of Latina/os in the United States and the fact that the majority of Latina/os are US born, Latina/os continue to be viewed as "perpetual foreigners" and "anticitizens." Hostilities toward Latina/os have risen over the last several decades as global forces and economic and political linkages between the United States and Latin America have uprooted many Latin Americans who have migrated to the United States. The youthfulness of the Latina/o population also portends a disproportionate growth of Latina/os in the coming decades in this country. Numerous policies have emerged throughout the country, but especially in states bordering Mexico, to stem the entrance of Latina/o immigrants and to roundup and deport those already here. While ostensibly undocumented Latina/ os are the target, in reality Latina/o naturalized citizens and US-born Latina/os have also been affected by such policies.

Policies such as Arizona's SB 1070, the vigilantism that has arisen along the border in the form of the Minutemen, the militarization of the border, and the rise of detention centers have made Latina/os, regardless of citizenship status, vulnerable to a wide range of human rights violations. For example, on a daily basis, Latina/o families are being split due to the deportation of family members, while others are questioned or pulled over by law enforcement for looking Latina/o. Moreover, the militarization of the border and governmental efforts to push immigrants to enter through dangerous and treacherous terrains have resulted in the deaths of countless human beings seeking better lives in the United States. Furthermore, the militarization of the border has also occasionally resulted in the killing of Latina/os and Mexican nationals (see Brice 2010). The killing of Esequiel Hernández Jr., an eighteen-year-old high school student who was herding goats in Redford, Texas, at the time of his death at the hands of a US Marine Corps antidrug patrol, best illustrates the vulnerability that Latina/os face along the border as the US government wages war against immigrants and drug traffickers (National Drug Strategy Network 1997). Reverend Mel La Follette, a retired Episcopalian priest in Redford, aptly described the situation: "We were invaded, and one of our sons was slaughtered . . . . The whole community was violated" (National Drug Strategy Network 1997). Such policies and traumatic events have undone many of the gains Latina/os achieved through civil rights legislation.

Our review of the literature reveals that only recently have we seen the incorporation of human rights concerns into the study of Latina/os. We see this as a much-needed and welcome addition to scholarship on the Latina/o population. Much of the existing literature examining the plight of the Latina/o population has merely alluded to the human rights implications without delving deeply into the human rights consequences of the conditions of the population. However, there is a need to make adjustments in the human rights perspective to better capture the racialized situation of Latina/os in the United States, along with the unequal power relations between the United States and Latin American countries (Bonilla-Silva 2008). Insights from the sociology of Latina/o literature related to the racialization of Latina/os, the heterogeneity of the Latina/o population, the agency that Latina/os possess, and the transnational aspects of the lives of Latina/os are considerations that the human rights perspective must take into account to more fully address the human rights of the Latina/o population.

The Significance of Gender Arrangements

by Juan Jose Bustamente

INTRODUCTION

Lorber (2005) defines gender as an organizing principle of institutional and individual life centered upon a set of cultural and social norms attached to feminine and masculine characteristics (Pp. 5). The underlying idea is that gender differences are part and parcel of a larger society that produces institutions and personal relationships patterned by gender inequality. While gender inequality is prevalent in many or most societies, the mechanisms, which allow it to function, are by no means universal. Given that a complex interplay of gender inequalities encircles a variety of institutions, actors, and social situations, it takes on different forms in each society (Lorber 2005: 5).

In this chapter, I focus on labor and power as large-scale bases of gender inequality. To accomplish this, I use the most thoroughly articulated account of gender as a structured system—offered by Connell (1987)—to explain my argument. In terms of labor, this approach treats the division of labor as a part of a larger initiative created to profit from the unequal gender distribution of domestic work, both paid and unpaid. To speak of free labor is to imply that housework is not work *per se;* it is women's work. Under this discursive regime, men benefit by engaging mostly in paid work. To think of paid work is to envision a gendered work force, skilled and trained to fulfill the objectives of a profit-driven society. This leads to the following point: given that gender divisions are built into social institutions, the relationship between gender and power implies a patterned organizational structure dominated by men with women as subordinates. This is not to say that power is universal and vouchsafed to all men. There are class, race, and sexuality conditions that also position many men in marginal places. Even in the family arena, where men are commonly ascribed a dominant position, there are external conditions (such as employment and immigration status) that erode male power at home (Connell 1987: 91–118). I apply this argument to understand the Mexican- and U.S.-based influence of gender, as a collective social order, on family life.

I have organized this chapter into two major sections. In the first part, I examine the gendered order on both sides of the border as larger factors affecting immigrant families. I use labor, education, and religion as major attributes to gauge gender's impact on family relations. In doing so, I examine the ways in which immigrant families engage Mexican and U.S. gender orders, and try to understand what impact this discourse has on their lives. Finally, I conclude by summarizing the effects of gender, from both sides of the border, on male and female relations.

To appreciate the extent to which the Mexican gender order permeates borders and sustains or redefines people's relationships, it is crucial to understand gender as it is lived in Mexico. The first step is to review Mexican history and determine how ideas of gender evolved there. The academic literature on women and men's relations center on patriarchy—an organizing principle of gender and sexual practices that legitimizes men's dominance and women's subordination (Lewis 1951: 52). This research situates Mexico as a latent example of a patriarchal society in which men's institutional authority shaped the gender order in terms of social, economic, political, familial, and sexual relations (see Canak and Swanson 1998: 71 for a further critique on the subject). Here, two major principles defined a patriarchal society that pressured women and men to conform to rigid codes of gender behavior: *machismo,* an overt display of physically and sexually aggressive masculine behavior, and *marianismo,* a patient, respectful, and obedient female behavior associated with the religious interpretation of the Virgin Mary. Induced by a male-dominated societal order, Stevens (1973) argues that these organizing principles of social life (machismo and marianismo) are intended to control not only relations, but also life opportunities between women and men (Pp. 59–62).

This argument reflects a negative, static and stereotypically driven view of gender in Mexico's past. Today, serious attempts to repair these deficiencies in scholarly research are in progress. Many studies using a more complex set of arguments provide exceptional insights into the current state of gender in

Mexico. Oropesa (1997), for instance, found that male dominance ". . . is neither universal nor insurmountable" (Pp. 1310). The inclusion of women in labor markets and their educational attainment has reorganized the gendered order from male domination toward more egalitarian arrangements. The basis for this argument is that employment and education "facilitate satisfaction with decision making because it fosters egalitarian relationships" (Oropesa 1997: 1311). Yet to speak of changes in the gender structure is not to argue that employment and education have somehow amplified women's working conditions. There are also other factors relating to the structure of labor market opportunities, education, and religious ideals that foster women's economic dependency on men and relegate the social and economic position of women to marginal places (Diaz Barriga Sánchez 2008: 312).

Similarly in the U.S., gender—as a social structure—compels people to conform to complementary feminine and masculine behaviors. Gender, as an organizing principle of social life, permeates social institutions and pressures both women and men to follow dissimilar gender practices that solidify men's power and control of women. Because gender inequality transpires in different dimensions, there is no monolithic theory that explains the complex interplay of inequality in its entirety; rather, feminism has evolved different ways to confront it. Although different feminist movements over time have promoted equality between genders, it is not surprising that this struggle to end inequality has spanned three centuries and remains unfinished.

During the 19th century, for example, first wave feminism—culminating in the suffragist movement—strived for equal voting and reproduction rights, as well as access to higher education, property, and the opportunity to earn money. Eventually, at least in the U.S., this social movement accomplished its goals to some degree. In time, feminism—as a social movement— underwent second and third waves. Second wave feminism questioned oppressive forces that continued to act upon women and began to offer and implement remedies. Today, the third stage of the movement confronts the gendered social order on a number of different fronts and addresses varying forms of oppression faced by people of color. It aims to end gender and race inequality as its basic premise (Lorber 2005: 1–18).

In spite of the many political and social gains feminism has achieved, today—as in the past— gender as a social force continues to differentiate men from women. Acker (1992), for instance, suggests that after years of struggle for equality, institutional structures (e.g. politics, religion) remain entrenched along gendered lines and continue to be dominated by men (Pp. 567). The shaping of what Acker (1992) calls "gendered institutions"—in terms of practices, processes, ideologies, and power distribution—maintains a system that places men in a position of dominance over women (Pp. 568). As such, it is difficult to understand a community littered with gender inequality unless we situate employment, education, and religion as key factors that affect family relations.

GENDER ON THE BORDERLANDS

While doing fieldwork on both sides of this borderlands region, I observed the operations of gender in daily lives. As mentioned in chapter three, the border area between Matamoros and Brownsville, and Miguel Alemán and Roma, is far from being a homogenous region. Rural and urban components make it quite diverse and gender arrangements vary greatly from one place to another. The two gender structures, situated in rural and urban environments, exert a range of influences upon behavior, from indisputably male-dominated configurations to more egalitarian arrangements. I observed, for instance, that rural communities tend to be more traditional concerning gender practices than urban areas. Rural dwellers observe stricter codes of gender behavior while people from urban settings are more egalitarian. Sonia, a woman who has spent most of her life living on both sides of the border, shared similar views about the gender arrangements of this region:

> Juan, when we talk about Rio Grande City, you know that we talk about (the city of) Camargo. *Camargo?* If you think about it or even if you search the Internet, this happens because most of the descendants of Rio Grande City came from Camargo. You will find a lot of Garzas, Garcías, Martinez, Lopez, and Muñozes. Here, family relations are strong. I tell you this because I used to live in that region. I spent few years with my ex-husband in Comales, two kilometers from Camargo, and all his family was in Rio Grande. Life in Camargo and Rio Grande is traditional, very similar to Miguel Aleman and Roma. Totally different to what happen in Reynosa and McAllen, and Matamoros and Brownsville. Because I have lived in this region for years, I thought many times . . . here the only thing that divides Miguel Aleman and Roma, and Rio Grande and Camargo, is the river . . . the customs and traditions are the same, not to say the way of thinking [referring to the local ideology] . . . Here, the concept of women also is very similar. When you talk with people in their 70s and older, who live in Rio Grande, their position about women is that they have to take a submissive attitude, regardless. Look Juan, we talk about the U.S.! Please!

Erica, Sonia's daughter, commented on her experience of living gender in the asymmetrical cities of Rio Grande and Brownsville:

> . . . Men in Rio Grande are jealous and they expect from you to show submissive behavior . . . Also, women don't talk back. Men decide about almost everything. *How*

come? Well, if you speak out, men will tell you, "shut the fuck up!" Where does this *(ideology) come from, for example, in your case?* From his [Erica's former partner] family customs. They were raised in Rio Grande. The grandfather is like that, the father is like that, and the son (my ex-partner) is like that [meaning that across generations, the three men have showed strong tendencies to demean women]. They are all the same: unfaithful, alcohol abusers, and verbal and physical women abusers. The grandfather, the father, and my ex are very much the same. *Is this a Río Grande City thing? Is it* *the same in Brownsville?* No! I think Río Grande is a special case. You know, I have lived in Brownsville and had some boyfriends, but they are not like that. There, life is different.

These narratives demonstrate that the Valley is neither a homogeneous rural place and nor an urbanite metropolitan area. Specifically, these narratives indicate an exchange of conventional gender arrangements between Tamaulipas' rural communities and rural areas of the Valley. It shows a region more associated with the traditional male dominant practices of rural communities than the progressive arrangements found in urban settings. Labor, education, and religion appear to be key components for understanding the variety of gender arrangements operative along both sides of the border. Given this, the subject requires further clarification or analysis.

EMPLOYMENT ON THE BORDERLANDS

In Mexico today, Ariza and de Oliveira (2002) argue, employment oftentimes undermines male dominance. Mexican women utilize income as the main tool to unsettle established patterns of gender relations. Employment also decreases women's economic dependency and enhances their position to negotiate monetary distribution in the home. It also improves women's self-esteem and empowers them to create ideal scenarios to contest gender and promote further change (Ariza and de Oliveira 2002: 61–65). In this way, Ariza and de Oliveira (2002) assert, employment income—as an economic factor—fosters egalitarian relationships and enhances the social position of women in the family milieu and the larger society. On the other hand, an opposing school of interpretation views employment not as an empowering factor but as a perpetuating aspect of gender inequality. For example, Diaz Barriga Sánchez (2008) suggests that the marginal position of women in society is largely associated with the unequal structure of the Mexican labor market in which women's work opportunities are limited to the low-wage maquiladora industry and many service sectors. Accordingly, the monetary contributions of women (38.5 percent of men) are mostly treated as a supplemental resource reflective of this group's marginal position in society (Diaz Barriga Sánchez 2008: 349). To think of limited access to higher wages not just as a loss of money, but also in terms of decreased social bargaining power, provides a clearer view of the ways in which the gendered order reproduces privileges and perpetuates inequalities.

By contrast, in the U.S. today, women's gained right entry into the labor market is now beyond any dispute. For instance, the percentage of women over 16 participating in the labor force increased from 32 percent in 1950 to 59 percent, in 2005. The most striking thing about this increase, however, is the rise in the percentage of working married women with children, from 19 percent in 1950 to 69 percent in 2005 (Cohany and Sok 2007: Chart 1). These figures imply that gender inequality has somehow diminished in America because of women's increased participation in the labor market. Nevertheless, academic scholarship shows that gender inequality remains an ambiguous issue in the occupational distribution and wage earnings. Women's Bureau figures still show a significant concentration of women and men in occupations along gendered lines. As of 2008, women in professional occupations such as engineering and computer science represented only 13.5 percent and 24.8 percent of the workforce, while in the education and healthcare fields they represented 26 percent and 23.6 percent of the professional labor force, respectively (U.S. Department of Labor 2009: Table 11). Note, however, that gender inequality is not only contextualized in terms of numbers. Women's equal treatment and access to opportunities in higher-paid male-dominated occupations are, according to Acker (2006), conditioned ". . . only if the women function like men . . . [sharing] . . . many of the same characteristics, such as strength, aggressiveness, and competiveness" (Pp. 443). Yet, as Manzano-Diaz (2010) points out, women with the same credentials and labor experience as men still earn less money ". . . despite the fact that women hold the majority of post-secondary degrees in this country" (Online Citation). For example, as of 2010, women earn only 83 cents for every dollar that men make on median weekly earnings (U.S. Department of Labor 2010: Table 2). This earnings gap, according to Eitzen and Baca Zinn (2004), appears to be associated with the concentration on women in low-wage occupations and limited labor experience (Pp. 263). Dunn (1996) additionally suggests that discriminatory practices in the labor market play a key role in producing this gap (Pp. 62).

Unlike in the *Frontera Chica*–a colloquial term used to describe the border region between Reynosa and Miguel Alemán–I found that people living in urban places such as Reynosa and Matamoros are more progressive in their attitudes about gender arrangements than in those living in rural settings. As the most industrialized and populated cities of Tamaulipas, Reynosa and Matamoros offer more employment and educational opportunities, there is a greater emphasis in these places on women's equality. I observed that, in spite of the lower wages women earned by women in the maquiladoras, their participation in the labor market provides them with job opportunities that would not otherwise be available. Sonia, a woman who has lived in both the Valley and Tamaulipas, shared her experience as an employee of a maquiladora:

> . . . One month after of being hired and working as a laborer with no experience at all, I was offered the position of supervisor. Probably they [the management] saw potential . . . I remember the owner of the maquiladora calling me into his office . . . then, I was in a conference room surrounded by industrial engineers, all men. That was an odd moment because many of those men wanted the position . . . and look[ed] at me . . . I was the chosen one, a person with no education. Then, I started to build leadership [skills] to manage between 400 and 500 employees. It was not easy, but I worked really hard to make it happen. I stayed from sunrise to sunset in the *maquiladora* showing the laborers how to work efficiently.

> *How did you manage, as a woman in a leadership position, to supervise women and men without conflict?* They, women and men, did not see me as a woman and supervisor; they saw me just as another supervisor. I remember having a trustful relation with my workers. If they [workers] had a family problem, many times, they shared with me and I listened. In fact, I was a good listener.

> *Was it the same with men?* It was the same, men and women. You know what was funny? I had problems with the educated men of the company, but I don't remember any with the laborers. I treated them in a considerate and professional way that I felt too close to them. I treated my employees as I wanted being treated.

By contrast, employment opportunities are very limited in the rural parts of the Frontera, as noted in chapter three; most workers are relegated to agricultural, ranching, small-scale retail, and low-wage service-oriented jobs. Unlike in Reynosa and Matamoros, migration from other Mexican states is almost nonexistent. By talking with people who have lived and worked in this region for generations, I discovered that women's involvement in paid work is very marginal. The majority of women stay at home doing household work and taking care of children. Men, on the other hand, seldom help with household chores, but are heavily involved in fatherhood. These social conditions appear to stifle women's financial independence and position men as the ultimate authority in the home.

In the Valley, historically, women and men have worked side-by-side in the agricultural fields as migrant workers. Today, both work in more diversified—but still low-paid—service jobs. Working opportunities remain limited to retail, fast food chains, grocery stores, and agriculture. Manufacturing is virtually nonexistent in the area. Women who also work in male-dominated occupations usually face hostility, resentment, and harassment. Aileen, a young woman with three children, commented on her experiences as the only female worker in her field:

> *Are you okay with the type of work you do?* No! This is a tiresome work, and no, I am not happy. *Tiresome because you have to wake up early and work so many hours, or just because it does not pay?* No, the thing with my work is that it pays very well, but in this field [bakery delivery] I am the only woman who distributes bakery products in the Valley for my brand. There are no women. I am the only woman for example that serves Wal-Mart. This is a kind of work for men. You have to carry a lot of things, many times very heavy. It is very tiresome because it requires a lot of your time. It drains you a lot. Also, because I work mostly around men, sometimes I feel that my self-esteem is too low. In fact, I was telling one of my friends that I feel bad because I cannot fix my hair or dress properly for a woman in this work environment . . . Because all distributers are men, I do not like that they [men] can take advantage of that, make an annoying comment, or harass me in the workplace. That's the reason why I do not use makeup or even fix my hair . . . I don't listen and talk to them, period! *How long have you been working in this field?* About a year, since last July [2009]. *So, do you plan to keep this job in the future, regardless?* No! I want get educated. I am taking college credits in South Texas College.

Although the labor market is constricted for people whose educational experience is limited to a high school diploma, others with more education compete on another level and in a different environment; this includes job opportunities at local school districts, community colleges and universities, in Maquiladora management, and with municipal, state, and federal governments. In spite of all these job opportunities, the participation of women in paid work does not enhance their social standing in a male-dominated region. Often, these women's wages are treated as marginal income. The most striking thing about this situation is that, regardless of the women's financial contributions, gender ideology still relegates them to caregiver roles–and they remain economically dependent upon their male counterparts.

EDUCATION ON THE BORDERLANDS

In Mexico today, Oropesa (1997) argues, schools—as agents of change—erode local male dominant practices by spreading progressive middle-class principles of gender relations. This, in turn, empowers women to resist their subordinated position in Mexican society (Pp. 1311). Education, Zabludovsky (2007) contends, also gives women access to better job opportunities, wages, work conditions, and the unparalleled possibility to foster egalitarian relationships and transform institutions (Pp. 38). For decades, however, girls' educational attainments have hardly passed the elementary school level (Arizpe 1993). Two issues, Post (2001) asserts, underpin this argument and rationalize the underrepresentation of girls at the middle school level: poverty and sibling order. In the first place, families living in poor communities send fewer girls to middle school than boys. In the latter case, younger siblings (mostly girls) attend middle school in higher numbers than older girls. In both scenarios, preferential systems negatively affect the fate of poor and older girls by making them the most likely candidates [over male siblings and younger girls] to drop out of school and perform domestic housework (Post 2001: 485). Despite Mexican women's advancement in educational settings (Zabludovsky 2007), the gender educational gap remains at 35 percent on the national level and at 75 percent in the southern states (Frías 2008: 228). Girls and women are enticed and influenced to conform to dominant gendered codes of behavior by the relationship between a male-oriented hierarchy and social conditions associated with education (Diaz Barriga Sánchez 2008: 365). Although this influence is declining, Zabludovsky (2007) and Frías (2008) suggest that girls and women still experience overt and covert pressure to leave school at an early age—under the assumption that an education is unnecessary to get married, raise children, and perform housework.

In America today, unlike in other developing countries—particularly Mexico where kindergarten, elementary, and middle school (K-9 level) is mandatory, but attendance is not enforced—access to elementary and secondary public education (1-12 levels) is considered a universal right. Gender inequality, in terms of access to basic public education, is beyond any dispute. Instead, as Buchmann, DiPrete, and McDaniel (2008) elaborate, debates about education generally center on ". . . the ways in which girls and women are advantaged in some aspects of education, as well as those in which they continue to trail boys and men" (Pp. 320). This means that, despite improved equity and gains in education, society continues to send a strongly gendered message. These studies refer to accounts of discriminatory practices that heighten gender differences, often embedded (either covertly or overtly) in curriculum and textbooks biases. Sadker, Sadker, and Steindam (1989), for instance, provide striking descriptions of gender inequality in school curriculums which entice more boys into mathematical and science fields and restrict more girls to literature and humanities disciplines (Pp. 47). Two similar studies produced by Evans and Davies (2000: 268) and by Zittleman and Sadker (2003: 62) found that, while textbooks portray boys and men in a very aggressive and competitive light, women's invisibility remains pervasive in much of the academic literature.

Reynosa and Matamoros offer greater educational opportunities than other borderlands communities. One can find multiple educational opportunities, from public and private to kindergarten through college and university level coursework. Children, regardless of gender, are not required to commute or relocate to access education beyond the middle school level. In these urban areas, the gender ideology is more egalitarian than in rural settings. However, limited economic and familial resources continue to restrict women's access to education. For instance, Sonia, who once wanted to be a medical doctor, remembered her frustrated educational experience in Matamoros:

> I remember that when I finished high school, I also was very disappointed because there was no money to continue the medical school. *No money?* No, because of a scholarship, I finished my high school. But, when I got accepted into the medical school, I had no economic support. It was very hard to accept it. I even questioned myself about why I finished high school if I have no future. I thought that everything I have accomplished as a student was worthless.

In the rural part of la Frontera, however, I observed the ways in which the Mexican state neglects children by failing to provide sufficient educational resources. Children of both genders living in these relatively isolated places, benefit only from elementary and middle school education opportunities. Attaining high school and college instruction require children to make a long commute or even relocate to Reynosa, Matamoros, or in some cases across the border. This has serious repercussions within the context of the particular gender discourse operative in the area. The same parents who hesitate to allow girls to move into an urbanized setting where educational opportunities flourish will encourage their boys to take this step. There are two main arguments commonly offered in support of this gendered behavioral pattern. The first sees girls as individuals who do not necessarily need an advanced education in order to raise children and maintain a household. The second perceives major cities as threatening places for girls to be alone. These social conditions again appear to benefit men over women, thereby reflecting the community's male dominance ideology.

Although it is understood that access to education in the U.S. is universal, at least at the K-12 level, the issue in the LRGV relates more to attainment than to access. For example, as of 2000, only 19 percent of the population 25 age and older held a high school diploma or its GED equivalent, and 6.8 percent of the population same population group had earned a bachelor's degree (U.S. Census Bureau 2000b: 2). These figures clearly show that the educational system in this region fails boys and girls equally. Aileen describes how being a full-time worker has heightened her desire to finish college and, thus, improve her quality of life:

> . . . this morning I was checking [the college website] to take more classes. I tell you this because since I graduated from high school I have been taking college credits . . . one class per semester . . . obviously it's taking me years and years to finish. I only take more classes when I can . . . like the summer. This past fall, I did not attend

college because of the holidays, but now since more classes are offered by internet, I want to try one more time. *You want to graduate soon?* Yes! I want to graduate. *What major you chose?* That's the problem, because I have been changing majors so many times . . . now, I am majoring in speech therapy. But, I know it will take a lot of time, I only have completed about 40 and something credit hours in so many years.

Assuming that education empowers women to question the male dominance order, these narratives show an opposite trend. The interviews reveal the continued existence of a gendered order that oppresses women and empowers men. Erica, a young 24-year-old, recalled a life-altering, bitter experience with her high school sweetheart,

> . . . to him [ex-boyfriend] my education was never a priority. I told him and his family that after graduation I wanted go back for my masters. They told me literally, when are you *fucking gonna* end? It will take you another four years to finish school, when, when . . . Erica! Then, I told him about applying to the graduate school . . . a Ph.D. program . . . he made fun of me and laugh for little time. He looked at me and said, you as a doctor! Please . . . and started making fun of me again. *Perhaps, he took that attitude because he saw your education as a threat in your relationship?* No, he does not appreciate education. He makes fun of me when we talk about what I want to do in the future . . . But, he forgets when we were in high school and I did his homework. *What did you do to correct this situation?* I had to leave him. I moved out of our place in Rio Grande and got temporary shelter in Brownsville, with friends.

RELIGION ON THE BORDERLANDS

In Mexico today, religion—as a social structure—is also patterned by gender. Emerson, Mirola, and Monahan (2010), for example, point out that religions, across all spectrums, create their own notion of *normality* about gendered behavioral codes which affect relations between women and men (Pp. 136). In Mexico today, compared with other Christian and non-Christian religions, Catholicism is very much the norm. As of 2000, almost 88 percent (87.99 percent) of the Mexican population is Catholic, 7.27 percent is Christian—protestant, evangelical, and biblical, and 4.74 percent identify as non-Christian—Jews, Atheists, and others (Aguayo Quezada 2002: 66). The Catholic Church, Diaz Barriga Sánchez (2008) argues, plays a significant role in reinforcing gender differences and maintaining a male dominant order (Pp. 357). Juárez Cerdi (2000) similarly found that protestant and evangelical churches entice women to conform to male dominant biblical codes of behavior (Pp. 87). In both cases, religion utilizes rituals, symbols, values, and norms to prescribe masculine and feminine ideals associated with male dominant gender practices. Yet, to speak of these religious constraints is not to say that women do not resist them. In fact, they do. However, power differentials associated with employment and education diminishes or enhances women's agency to contest the religious order (Juárez Cerdi 2000: 82).

In the United States today, academic research shows that religion, as an institution patterned by gender inequality, remains heavily dominated by men (Johnstone 2007: 255). As of 2007, Christians constitute 78.4 percent of all religious adherents in the U.S. This group includes Protestants (51.3 percent), Catholics (23.9 percent), and other Christian groups 3.2 percent; non-Christian groups make up the other 20.8 percent (Pew Research Center's Forum on Religion and Public Life 2008: 10). According to Johnstone (2007), Christianity—as the United States' dominant religion—perpetuates the idea that women and men have different missions in life. It presses individuals to adjust themselves to rigid gendered codes of behavior by excluding women from many organizational practices and regulating gender relations. Although the inclusion of ordained women in the organizational structure of many protestant groups is a reality, in other denominations—like Catholicism—this remains unthinkable. The ordination of women, despite its steady increase (from 2.3 percent in the 1960s to 13.8 percent in the 2000s), remains marginal (Johnstone 2007: 259–260). Similarly, McGuire (2009) argues that religion permeates everyday activities by shaping individual and collective behavior. Many Christian groups, for example, exercise significant influence over sexual behavior within and beyond the family milieu (restrictions on premarital, extramarital, and other sexual activities that deviate from the norm), to regulate reproduction (use of contraceptives), and to discourage divorce—in many cases despite the overt evidence of spousal abuse (McGuire 2009: 64–65).

During the course of my fieldwork along the border, I observed many little towns (like Camargo and Diaz Ordaz) and saw how social life evolves out of and continues to revolve mostly around religious activities. While attending church, I found Catholic priests—particularly—used religious arguments to prod couples to conform to strictly gendered codes of behavior. For example, as the main pillar of the family, a woman's life must be centered on family needs—especially in aspects related to motherhood and spiritual values. It is a moral justification often utilized by priests to keep women in a subordinate position within the family setting and at the community level. My observations also revealed a significant exchange of gendered values and practices between Mexican rural communities and the immigrant families of Rio Grande City and Roma. During our conversation, Sonia and Erica described their experience as women in a very religious setting:

Sonia: I have seen Catholic Churches in Rio Grande full of people every weekend. Because these towns are very Catholic, they don't like other *religions* like Jehovah Witness and *Cristianos*. Other Churches have no place over there. The Catholicism is very strong there. Rio Grande and Roma are something special, I would say . . . more Rio Grande. Erica: when my ex and I were together, we went to the Catholic Church. His family is very religious. Because of this, *la abuela* [the grandma] always says, if he [the ex-partner] hit you, don't say anything. Wait here until you heal . . . we support you. Just don't make him [ex-partner] angry so he does not have to hit you again. *So, were you blamed all the time for any discussions in your relationship?* All the time! When we engaged in heated arguments, *la abuela* says, why you don't keep your mouth shut so we can continue with our lives . . . look at my daughter! [ex-boyfriend's mom] she has been married for 40 years. But I said to her, yes . . . 40 years of emotional, domestic, and physical abuse. I don't want that life.

The Valley's robust religious community ensures that its social life revolves around Church activities, particularly on weekends. The region is also home to one of the most sacred Catholic shrines in the United States—the Basilica of San Juan. It is customary for Catholics from all over the community to attend a mass at least once a year in the San Juan Church. Religious services are conducted in Spanish or English, or both; the topic of most sermons remains very traditional and oriented toward patriarchal gender discourse.

In many urban areas—primarily in Reynosa and Matamoros—I observed a more egalitarian gender order in operation. The vast job opportunities for women seem to benefit their position. The maquiladora industry—operating 24 hours a day and seven days a week—requires workers to adjust their schedules to meet factory needs. This includes working weekends, day and night, demands which ultimately affect family life and church attendance.

The most striking thing I observed about gender dynamics in Reynosa and Matamoros, however, is that women and men came to these cities from other parts of Mexico to work in the maquiladora industry–mostly from Veracruz–with little to no previous international migration experience. Because these new settlers scarcely cross into the U.S. side, I found family networks between Tamaulipas and the Valley to be virtually nonexistent. It appears that the progressive gender arrangements that characterize this urban population hardly reach into the U.S. borderlands area. When these egalitarian practices do arise, women not only question the privileged position of men, but also present an alternative idea of gender relations. For instance, Maria, who was born in Mexico City and later migrated to Reynosa before moving to the Valley, shared her experience about family life and religion. Despite being a devoted Christian, Maria rejected the stereotypical religious image of a submissive woman:

Maria, to what degree religion affects your marriage? Well, if we talk about religion, we [Mario and Maria] have not followed ours the way we should. Because my marriage did not work the way I wanted, I got so close to my church. I remember having problems. So, I said to Mario—let's attend marriage sessions in the Church, it may help. He never wanted. Then, I got closer to the church, but Mario kept coming late home . . . sometimes he did not bother to come at all. I remember being upset all the time because of that.

But, doesn't the Christian Church support a family headed by the husband? Yes, you are right. The Church teaches us that the husband is the head of the family. But, I don't necessarily agree on this. Let me tell you why. A person, who is considered the head of the family, has to live by example. That means not making me angry because he does not come home. Perhaps, he is having an affair and I don't even know about it.

So, you [the researcher] tell me what kind of respect he deserves! Mario also is very cynical. He tells me, how come you don't cook for me anymore? I said to him, how come? You still coming home at four in the morning, please! So, don't expect me to wake early to cook you a meal and do your laundry! We don't live anymore at those times in which women were submissive and quiet, not anymore! Even as a religious person, I am a modern woman!

CONCLUSION

In this chapter, I delved closely into gender as an organizing principle of rural and urban community life in the LRGV. I found that a Mexican male-dominated environment substantially influences gender relations. This is not to say that the U.S. ideology of gender arrangements does not reach the Valley; it does. However, it appears to be more associated with urban areas than rural communities, perhaps because women's working and educational opportunities are greater in urban places.

By contrast, I discovered that the urban and egalitarian Mexican notion of gender barely permeated the border. Because most urban residents—who have migrated from other Mexican States to work in maquiladoras and other industries—do not have established meaningful links (like family) in the LRGV, the exchange of egalitarian ideas between urban Tamaulipas and the LRGV seems to be nonexistent, or at least minimal. In addition, the gendered exchange of ideas and values between rural settings across the river hampers the flow of more urban and progressive arrangements to the region.

Thus far, the argument is negative. To make this point is to imply that those women who live in the Valley conform to submissive—if not passive—gendered codes of behavior. I found, however, that many women vigorously resist this oppressively gendered order. They do so by following strategies based on the options that are available to them. While working and educational opportunities empower women to contest a male-dominated urban environment, women from rural towns often have to leave these places because of their limited resources—just as Anzaldúa (2007) did during the 1980s. Meanwhile, the women who stay have to face labor, educational, and religious constraints that undermine their positions within the family and at the community level.

Schooling in Capitalist America

by Samuel Bowles and Herbert Gintis

Education and Inequality

Universal education is the power, which is destined to overthrow every species of hierarchy. It is destined to remove all artificial inequality and leave the natural inequalities to find their true level. With the artificial inequalities of caste, rank, title, blood, birth, race, color, sex, etc., will fall nearly all the oppression, abuse, prejudice, enmity, and injustice, that humanity is now subject to.

Lester Frank Ward, *Education* c. 1872

A review of educational history hardly supports the optimistic pronouncements of liberal educational theory. The politics of education are better understood in terms of the need for social control in an unequal and rapidly changing economic order. The founders of the modern U.S. school system understood that the capitalist economy produces great extremes of wealth and poverty, of social elevation and degradation. Horace Mann and other school reformers of the antebellum period knew well the seamy side of the burgeoning industrial and urban centers. "Here," wrote Henry Barnard, the first state superintendent of education in both Connecticut and Rhode Island, and later to become the first U.S. Commissioner of Education, "the wealth, enterprise and professional talent of the state are concentrated . . . but here also are poverty, ignorance, profligacy and irreligion, and a classification of society as broad and deep as ever divided the plebeian and patrician of ancient Rome."[1] They lived in a world in which, to use de Tocqueville's words, ". . . small aristocratic societies . . . are formed by some manufacturers in the midst of the immense democracy of our age [in which] . . . some men are opulent and a multitude . . . are wretchedly poor."[2] The rapid rise of the factory system, particularly in New England, was celebrated by the early school reformers; yet, the alarming transition from a relatively simple rural society to a highly stratified industrial economy could not be ignored. They shared the fears that de Tocqueville had expressed following his visit to the United States in 1831:

> When a work man is unceasingly and exclusively engaged in the fabrication of one thing, he ultimately does his work with singular dexterity; but at the same time he loses the general faculty of applying his mind to the direction of the work. . . . [While] the science of manufacture lowers the class of workmen, it raises the class of masters. . . . [If] ever a permanent inequality of conditions . . . again penetrates into the world, it may be predicted that this is the gate by which they will enter.[3]

While deeply committed to the emerging industrial order, the far-sighted school reformers of the mid-nineteenth century understood the explosive potential of the glaring inequalities of factory life. Deploring the widening of social divisions and fearing increasing unrest, Mann, Barnard, and others proposed educational expansion and reform. In his Fifth Report as Secretary of the Massachusetts Board of Education, Horace Mann wrote:

> Education, then beyond all other devices of human origin, is the great equalizer of the conditions of men—the balance wheel of the social machinery. . . . It does better than to disarm the poor of their hostility toward the rich; it prevents being poor.[4]

Mann and his followers appeared to be at least as interested in disarming the poor as in preventing poverty. They saw in the spread of universal and free education a means of alleviating social distress without redistributing wealth and power or altering the broad outlines of the economic system. Education, it seems, had almost magical powers.

> The main idea set forth in the creeds of some political reformers, or revolutionizers, is, that some people are poor because others are rich. This idea supposed a fixed amount of property in the community . . . and the problem presented for solution is, how to transfer a portion of this property from those who are supposed to have too much to those who feel and know that they have too little. At this point, both their theory and their expectation of reform stop. But

the beneficient power of education would not be exhausted, even though it should peaceably abolish all the miseries that spring from the coexistence, side by side of enormous wealth, and squalid want. It has a higher function. Beyond the power of diffusing old wealth, it has the prerogative of creating new.[5]

The early educators viewed the poor as the foreign element that they were. Mill hands were recruited throughout New England, often disrupting the small towns in which textile and other rapidly growing industries had located. Following the Irish potato famine of the 1840s, thousands of Irish workers settled in the cities and towns of the northeastern United States. Schooling was seen as a means of integrating this "uncouth and dangerous" element into the social fabric of American life. The inferiority of the foreigner was taken for granted. The editors of the influential *Massachusetts Teacher*, a leader in the educational reform movement, writing in 1851, saw ". . . the increasing influx of foreigners . . ." as a moral and social problem:

> Will it, like the muddy Missouri, as it pours its waters into the clear Mississippi and contaminates the whole united mass, spread ignorance and vice, crime and disease, through our native population?

If . . . we can by any means purify this foreign people, enlighten their ignorance and bring them up to our level, we shall perform a work of true and perfect charity, blessing the giver and receiver in equal measure. . . .

With the old not much can be done; but with their children, the great remedy is *education*. The rising generation must be taught as our own children are taught. We say *must be* because in many cases this can only be accomplished by coercion.[6]

Since the mid-nineteenth century the dual objectives of educational reformers— equality of opportunity and social control—have been intermingled, the merger of these two threads sometimes so nearly complete that it becomes impossible to distinguish between the two. Schooling has been at once something done for the poor and to the poor.

The basic assumptions which underlay this comingling helps explain the educational reform movement's social legacy. First, educational reformers did not question the fundamental economic institutions of capitalism: Capitalist ownership and control of the means of production and dependent wage labor were taken for granted. In fact, education was to help preserve and extend the capitalist order. The function of the school system was to accommodate workers to its most rapid possible development. Second, it was assumed that people (often classes of people or "races") are differentially equipped by nature or social origins to occupy the varied economic and social levels in the class structure. By providing equal opportunity, the school system was to elevate the masses, guiding them sensibly and fairly to the manifold political, social, and economic roles of adult life.

Jefferson's educational thought strikingly illustrates this perspective. In 1779, he proposed a two-track educational system which would prepare individuals for adulthood in one of the two classes of society: the "laboring and the learned."[7] Even children of the laboring class would qualify for leadership. Scholarships would allow " . . . those persons whom nature hath endowed with genius and virtue . . ." to " . . . be rendered by liberal education worthy to receive and able to guard the sacred deposit of the rights and liberties of their fellow citizens."[8] Such a system, Jefferson asserted, would succeed in " . . . raking a few geniuses from the rubbish."[9] Jefferson's two-tiered educational plan presents in stark relief the outlines and motivation for the stratified structure of U.S. education which has endured up to the present. At the top, there is the highly selective aristocratic tradition, the elite university training future leaders. At the base is mass education for all, dedicated to uplift and control. The two traditions have always coexisted although their meeting point has drifted upward over the years, as mass education has spread upward from elementary school through high school, and now up to the post-high-school level.

Though schooling was consciously molded to reflect the class structure, education was seen as a means of enhancing wealth and morality which would work to the advantage of all. Horace Mann, in his 1842 report to the State Board of Education, reproduced this comment by a Massachusetts industrialist:

> The great majority always have been and probably always will be comparatively poor, while a few will possess the greatest share of this world's goods. And it is a wise provision of Providence which connects so intimately, and as I think so indissolubly, the greatest good of the many with the highest interests in the few.[10]

Much of the content of education over the past century and a half can only be construed as an unvarnished attempt to persuade the "many" to make the best of the inevitable.

The unequal contest between social control and social justice is evident in the total functioning of U.S. education. The system as it stands today provides eloquent testimony to the ability of the well-to-do to perpetuate in the name of equality of opportunity an arrangement which consistently yields to themselves disproportional advantages, while thwarting the aspirations and needs of the working people of the United States. However grating this judgment may sound to the ears of the undaunted optimist, it is by no means excessive in light of the massive statistical data on inequality in the United States. Let us look at the contemporary evidence.

We may begin with the basic issue of inequalities in years of schooling. As can be seen in figure 20.1, the number of years of schooling attained by an individual is strongly associated

FIGURE 20.1 ▷

Educational Attainments Are Strongly Dependent on Social Background Even for People of Similar Childhood I.Q.s

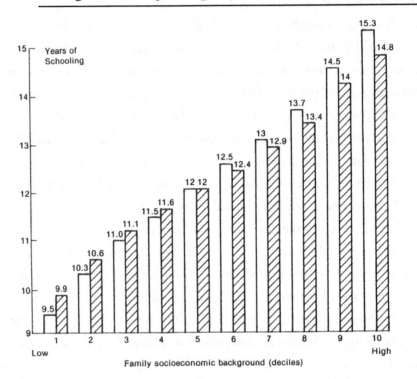

Notes: For each socioeconomic group, the left-hand bar indicates the estimated average number of years of schooling attained by all men from that group. The right-hand bar indicates the estimated average number of years of schooling attained by men with IQ scores equal to the average for the entire sample. The sample refers to "non-Negro" men of "non-farm" backgrounds, aged 35–44 years in 1962.17 source: Samuel Bowles and Valerie Nelson, "The 'Inheritance of IQ.' and the Intergenerational Transmission of Economic Inequality," *The Review of Economics and Statistics*, Vol. LVI, No. 1, February 1974. Reprinted by permission of the President and Fellows of Harvard College.

with parental socioeconomic status. This figure presents the estimated distribution of years of schooling attained by individuals of varying socioeconomic backgrounds. If we define socio-economic background by a weighted sum of income, occupation, and educational level of the parents, a child from the ninetieth percentile may expect, on the average, five more years of schooling than a child in the tenth percentile.[11]

A word about our use of statistics is in order. Most of the statistical calculations which we will present have been published with full documentation in academic journals. We provide some of the relevant technical information in our footnotes and Appendix. However, those interested in gaining a more detailed understanding of our data and methods are urged to consult our more technical articles.

The data, most of which was collected by the U.S. Census Current Population Survey in 1962, refers to "non-Negro" males, aged 25–64 years, from "non-farm" background in the experienced labor force.[12] We have chosen a sample of white males because the most complete statistics are available for this group. Moreover, if inequality for white males can be documented, the proposition is merely strengthened when sexual and racial differences are taken into account.

Additional census data dramatize one aspect of educational inequalities: the relationship between family income and college attendance. Even among those who had graduated from high school in the early 1960s, children of families earning less than $3,000 per year were over six times as likely *not* to attend college as were the children of families earning over $15,000.[13] Moreover, children from less well-off families are *both* less likely to have graduated from high school and more likely to attend inexpensive, two-year community colleges rather than a four-year B.A. program if they do make it to college.[14]

Not surprisingly, the results of schooling differ greatly for children of different social backgrounds. Most easily measured, but of limited importance, are differences in scholastic achievement. If we measure the output of schooling by scores on nationally standardized achievement tests, children whose parents were themselves highly educated outperform the children of parents with less education by a wide margin. Data collected for the U.S. Office of Education Survey of Educational Opportunity reveal, for example, that among white high school seniors, those whose parents were in the top education decile were, on the average, well over three grade levels in measured scholastic achievement ahead of those whose parents were in the bottom decile.[15]

Given these differences in scholastic achievement, inequalities in years of schooling among individuals of different social backgrounds are to be expected. Thus one might be tempted to argue that the close dependence of years of schooling attained on background displayed in the left-hand bars of Figure 20.1 is simply a reflection of unequal intellectual abilities, or that inequalities in college attendance are the consequences of differing levels of scholastic achievement in high school and do not reflect any additional social class inequalities peculiar to the process of college admission.

This view, so comforting to the admissions personnel in our elite universities, is unsupported by the data, some of which is presented in Figure 20.1. The right-hand bars of Figure 20.1 indicate that even among children with identical IQ test scores at ages six and eight, those with rich, well-educated, high-status parents could expect a much higher level of schooling than those with less-favored origins. Indeed, the closeness of the left-hand and right-hand bars in Figure 2–1 shows that only a small portion of the observed social class differences in educational attainment is related to IQ differences across social classes.[16] The dependence of education attained on background is almost as strong for individuals with the same IQ as for all individuals. Thus, while Figure 20.1 indicates that an individual in the ninetieth percentile in social class background is likely to receive five more years of education than an individual in the tenth percentile; it also indicated that he is likely to receive 4.25 more years schooling than an individual from the tenth percentile with the same IQ. Similar results are obtained when we look specifically at access to college education for students with the same measured IQ. Project Talent data indicates that for "high ability" students (top 25 percent as measured by a composite of tests of "general aptitude"), those of high socioeconomic background (top 25 percent as measured by a composite of family income, parents' education, and occupation) are nearly twice as likely to attend college than students of low socioeconomic background (bottom 25 percent). For "low ability" students (bottom 25 percent), those of high social background are more than four times as likely to attend college as are their low social background counterparts.[18]

Inequality in years of schooling is, of course, only symptomatic of broader inequalities in the educational system. Not only do less well-off children go to school for fewer years, they are treated with less attention (or more precisely, less benevolent attention) when they are there. These broader inequalities are not easily measured. Some show up in statistics on the different levels of expenditure for the education of children of different socioeconomic backgrounds. Taking account of the inequality in financial resources for each year in school and the inequality in years of schooling obtained, Jencks estimated that a child whose parents were in the top fifth of the income distribution receives roughly twice the educational resources in dollar terms as does a child whose parents are in the bottom fifth.[19]

The social class inequalities in our school system, then, are too evident to be denied. Defenders of the educational system are forced back on the assertion that things are getting better; the inequalities of the past were far worse. And, indeed, there can be no doubt that some of the inequalities of the past have been mitigated. Yet new inequalities have apparently developed to take their place, for the available historical evidence lends little support to the idea that our schools are on the road to equality of educational opportunity. For example, data from a recent U.S. Census survey reported in Spady indicate that graduation from college has become no less dependent on one's social background. This is true despite the fact that high-school graduation is becoming increasingly equal across social classes.[20] Additional data confirm this impression. The statistical association (coefficient of correlation) between parents' social status and years

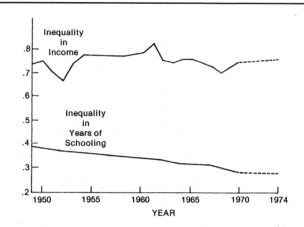

Notes: The upper line shows the trend over time in the degree of inequality of income, as measured by the standard deviation of the natural logarithm of annual income of males aged twenty-five or older. The lower line shows the trend over time in the degree of inequality of years of schooling, as measured by the coefficient of variation (the standard deviation divided by the mean) of the years of schooling attained by males aged twenty-five and older. Data for 1970 to 1974 are estimates based on U.S. Census data.

Source: Barry Chiswick and Jacob Mincer, "Time Series Changes in Personal Income Inequality in the U.S.," *Journal of Political Economy*, Vol. 80, No. 3, Part II (May–June 1972).

of education attained by individuals who completed their schooling three or four decades ago is virtually identical to the same correlation for individuals who terminated their schooling in recent years.[21] On balance, the available data suggest that the number of years of school attained by a child depends upon family background as much in the recent period as it did fifty years ago.

Thus, we have empirical reasons for doubting the egalitarian impact of schooling. But what of those cases when education has been equalized? What has been the effect? We will investigate three cases: the historical decline in the inequality among individuals in years of school attained, the explicitly compensatory educational programs of the War on Poverty, and the narrowing of the black/white gap in average years of schooling attained.

Although family background has lost none of its influence on how far one gets up the educational ladder, the historical rise in the minimum legal school-leaving age has narrowed the distance between the top and bottom rungs. Inequality of educational attainments has fallen steadily and substantially over the past three decades.[22] And has this led to a parallel equalization of the distribution of income? Look at Figure 20.2. The reduction in the inequality of years of schooling has not been matched by an equalization of the U.S. income distribution.[23] In fact, a recent U.S. Labor Department study indicates that as far as labor earnings (wages and salaries) are concerned, the trend since World War II has been unmistakenly away from equality. And it is precisely inequality in labor earnings which is the target of the proponents of egalitarian school reforms.[24] But does the absence of an overall trend toward income equality mask an equalizing thrust of schooling that was offset by other disequalizing tendencies? Perhaps, but Jacob Mincer and Barry Chiswick of the National Bureau of Economic Research, in a study of the determinants of inequality in the United States, concluded that the significant reduction in schooling differences among white male adults would have had the effect—even if operating in isolation—of reducing income inequality by a negligible amount.[25]

Next, consider that group of explicitly egalitarian educational programs brought together in the War on Poverty. In a systematic economic survey of these programs, Thomas Ribich concludes that with very few exceptions, the economic payoff to compensatory education is low.[26] So low, in fact, that in a majority of cases studied, direct transfers of income to the poor would have accomplished considerably more equalization than the educational programs in question. The major RAND Corporation study by Averch came to the same conclusion.

Lastly, consider racial inequalities. In 1940, most black male workers (but a minority of whites) earned their livelihoods in the South, by far the poorest region; the education gap between nonwhites and whites was 3.3 years (38 percent of median white education).[27] By 1972, blacks had moved to more affluent parts of the country, and the education gap was reduced to 18 percent (4 percent for young men aged 25–34 years).[28] Richard Freeman has shown that this narrowing of the education gap would have virtually achieved black/white income equality had blacks received the same benefits from education as whites.[29] Yet the income gap has not closed substantially: The income gap for young men is 30 percent, despite an education gap of only 4 percent.[30] Clearly as blacks have moved toward educational (and regional) parity with whites, other mechanisms—such as entrapment in center-city ghettos, the suburbanization of jobs, and perhaps increasing segmentation of labor markets—have intensified to maintain a more-or-less constant degree of racial income inequality. Blacks certainly suffer from educational inequality, but the root of their exploitation lies outside of education, in a system of economic power and privilege in which racial distinctions play an important role.

The same must be concluded of inequality of economic opportunity between men and women. Sexual inequality persists despite the fact that women achieve a level of schooling (measured in years) equivalent to men.

We conclude that U.S. education is highly unequal, the chances of attaining much or little schooling being substantially dependent on one's race and parents' economic level. Moreover, where there is a discernible trend toward a more equal educational system—as in the narrowing of the black education deficit, for example—the impact on the structure of economic opportunity is minimal at best. As we shall presently see, the record of the U.S. school system as a promoter of full human development is no more encouraging.

Education and Personal Development: The Long Shadow of Work

Every child born into the world should be looked upon by society as so much raw material to be manufactured. Its quality is to be tested. It is the business of society, as an intelligent economist, to make the best of it.

— Lester Frank Ward, *Education, c.* 1872

It is not obvious why the U.S. educational system should be the way it is. Since the interpersonal relationships it fosters are so antithetical to the norms of freedom and equality prevalent in American society, the school system can hardly be viewed as a logical extension of our cultural heritage. If neither technological necessity nor the bungling mindlessness of educators explain the quality of the educational encounter, what does?

Reference to the educational system's legitimation function does not take us far toward enlightenment. For the formal, objective, and cognitively oriented aspects of schooling capture only a fragment of the day-to-day social relationships of the educational encounter. To approach an answer, we must consider schools in the light of the social relationships of economic life. In this chapter, we suggest that major aspects of educational organization replicate the relationships of dominance and subordinancy in the economic sphere. The correspondence between the social relation of schooling and work accounts for the ability of the educational system to produce an amenable and fragmented labor force. The experience of schooling, and not merely the content of formal learning, is central to this process.

In our view, it is pointless to ask if the net effect of U.S. education is to promote equality or inequality, repression or liberation. These issues pale into insignificance before the major fact: The educational system is an integral element in the reproduction of the prevailing class structure of society. The educational system certainly has a life of its own, but the experience of work and the nature of the class structure are the bases upon which educational values are formed, social justice assessed, the realm of the possible delineated in people's consciousness, and the social relations of the educational encounter historically transformed.

In short, and to return to a persistent theme of this book, the educational system's task of integrating young people into adult work roles constrains the types of personal development which it can foster in ways that are antithetical to the fulfillment of its personal developmental function.

Reproducing Consciousness

> . . . children guessed (but only a few
> and down they forgot as up they grew
> autumn winter spring summer). . . .
> e e cummings, 1940

Economic life exhibits a complex and relatively stable pattern of power and property relationships. The perpetuation of these social relationships, even over relatively short periods, is by no means automatic. As with a living organism, stability in the economic sphere is the result of explicit mechanisms constituted to maintain and extend the dominant patterns of power and privilege. We call the sum total of these mechanisms and their actions the reproduction process.

Amidst the sundry social relations experienced in daily life, a few stand out as central to our analysis of education. These are precisely the social relationships which are necessary to the security of capitalist profits and the stability of the capitalist division of labor. They include the patterns of dominance and subordinacy in the production process, the distribution of ownership of productive resources, and the degrees of social distance and solidarity among various fragments of the working population—men and women, blacks and whites, and white- and blue-collar workers, to mention some of the most salient.

What are the mechanisms of reproduction of these aspects of the social relations of production in the United States? To an extent, stability is embodied in law and backed by the coercive power of the state. Our jails are filled with individuals who have operated outside the framework of the private-ownership market system. The modern urban police force as well as the National Guard originated, in large part, in response to the fear of social upheaval evoked by militant labor action. Legal sanction, within the framework of the laws of private property, also channels the actions of groups (e.g., unions) into conformity with dominant power relationships. Similarly, force is used to stabilize the division of labor and its rewards within an enterprise: Dissenting workers are subject to dismissal and directors failing to conform to "capitalist rationality" will be replaced.

But to attribute reproduction to force alone borders on the absurd. Under normal conditions, the effectiveness of coercion depends at the very least on the inability or unwillingness of those subjected to it to join together in opposing it. Laws generally considered illegitimate tend to lose their coercive power, and undisguised force too frequently applied tends to be self-defeating. The consolidation and extension of capitalism has engendered struggles of furious intensity. Yet instances of force deployed against a united and active opposition are sporadic and have usually given way to détente in one form or another through a combination of compromise, structural change, and ideological accommodation. Thus it is clear that the consciousness of workers— beliefs, values, self-concepts, types of solidarity and fragmentation, as well as modes of personal behavior and development—are integral to the perpetuation, validation, and smooth operation of economic institutions. The reproduction of the social relations of production depends on the reproduction of consciousness.

Under what conditions will individuals accept the pattern of social relationships that frame their lives? Believing that the long-term development of the existing system holds the prospect of fulfilling their needs, individuals and groups might actively embrace these social relationships. Failing this, and lacking a vision of an alternative that might significantly improve their situation, they might fatalistically accept their condition. Even with such a vision they might passively submit to the framework of economic life and seek individual solutions to social problems if they believe that the possibilities for realizing change are remote. The issue of the reproduction of consciousness enters each of these assessments.

The economic system will be embraced when, first, the perceived needs of individuals are congruent with the types of satisfaction the economic system can objectively provide. While perceived needs may be, in part, biologically determined, for the most part needs arise through the aggregate experiences of individuals in the society. Thus the social relations of production are reproduced in part through a harmony between the needs which the social system generates and the means at its disposal for satisfying these needs.

Second, the view that fundamental social change is not feasible, unoperational, and utopian is normally supported by a complex web of ideological perspectives deeply embedded in the cultural and scientific life of the community and reflected in the consciousness of its members. But fostering the "consciousness of inevitability" is not the office of the cultural system alone.

There must also exist mechanisms that systematically thwart the spontaneous development of social experiences that would contradict these beliefs.

Belief in the futility of organizing for fundamental social change is further facilitated by social distinctions which fragment the conditions of life for subordinate classes. The strategy of "divide and conquer" has enabled dominant classes to maintain their power since the dawn of civilization. Once again, the splintered consciousness of a subordinate class is not the product of cultural phenomena alone, but must be reproduced through the experiences of daily life.

Consciousness develops through the individual's direct perception of and participation in social life.[31] Indeed, everyday experience itself often acts as an inertial stabilizing force. For instance, when the working population is effectively stratified, individual needs and self-concepts develop in a correspondingly fragmented manner. Youth of different racial, sexual, ethnic, or economic characteristics directly perceive the economic positions and prerogatives of "their kind of people." By adjusting their aspiration accordingly, they not only reproduce stratification on the level of personal consciousness, but bring their needs into (at least partial) harmony with the fragmented conditions of economic life. Similarly, individuals tend to channel the development of their personal powers—cognitive, emotional, physical, aesthetic, and spiritual—in directions where they will have an opportunity to exercise them. Thus the alienated character of work, for example, leads people to guide their creative potentials to areas outside of economic activity: consumption, travel, sexuality, and family life. So needs and need-satisfaction again tend to fall into congruence and alienated labor is reproduced on the level of personal consciousness.[32]

But this congruence is continually disrupted. For the satisfaction of needs gives rise to new needs. These new needs derive from the logic of personal development as well as from the evolving structure of material life, and in turn undercut the reproduction of consciousness. For this reason the reproduction of consciousness cannot be the simple unintended by-product of social experience. Rather, social relationships must be consciously organized to facilitate the reproduction of consciousness.

Take, for instance, the organization of the capitalist enterprise. Power relations and hiring criteria within the enterprise are organized so as to reproduce the workers' self-concepts, the legitimacy of their assignments within the hierarchy, a sense of the technological inevitability of the hierarchical division of labor itself, and the social distance among groups of workers in the organization. Indeed, while token gestures towards workers' self-management may be a successful motivational gimmick, any delegation of real power to workers becomes a threat to profits because it tends to undermine patterns of consciousness compatible with capitalist control. By generating new needs and possibilities, by demonstrating the feasibility of a more thoroughgoing economic democracy, by increasing worker solidarity, an integrated and politically conscious program of worker involvement in decision-making may undermine the power structure of the enterprise. Management will accede to such changes only under extreme duress of worker rebellion and rapidly disintegrating morale, if at all.

But the reproduction of consciousness cannot be insured by these direct mechanisms alone. The initiation of youth into the economic system is further facilitated by a series of institutions, including the family and the educational system, that are more immediately related to the formation of personality and consciousness. Education works primarily through the institutional relations to which students are subjected. Thus schooling fosters and rewards the development of certain capacities and the expression of certain needs, while thwarting and penalizing others. Through these institutional relationships, the educational system tailors the self-concepts, aspirations, and social class identifications of individuals to the requirements of the social division of labor.

The extent to which the educational system actually accomplishes these objectives varies considerably from one period to the next. We shall see in later chapters that recurrently through U.S. history these reproduction mechanisms have failed, sometimes quite spectacularly. In most periods—and the present is certainly no exception—efforts to use the schools to reproduce and extend capitalist production relations have been countered both by the internal dynamic of the educational system and by popular opposition.

What aspects of the educational system allow it to serve these various functions? We shall suggest in the next section that the educational system's ability to reproduce the consciousness of workers lies in a straight-forward correspondence principle: For the past century at least, schooling has contributed to the reproduction of the social relations of production largely through the correspondence between school and class structure.

Upon the slightest reflection, this assertion is hardly surprising. All major institutions in a "stable" social system will direct personal development in a direction compatible with its reproduction. Of course, this is not, in itself, a critique of capitalism or of U.S. education. In any conceivable society, individuals are forced to develop their capacities in one direction or another. The idea of a social system which merely allows people to develop freely according to their "inner natures" is quite unthinkable, since human nature only acquires a concrete form through the interaction of the physical world and preestablished social relationships.

Our critique of education and other aspects of human development in the United States fully recognizes the necessity of some form of socialization. The critical question is: What for? In the United States the human development experience is dominated by an undemocratic, irrational, and exploitative economic structure. Young people have no recourse from the requirements of the system but a life of poverty, dependence, and economic insecurity. Our critique, not surprisingly, centers on the structure of jobs. In the U.S. economy work has become a fact of life to which individuals must by and large submit and over which they have no control. Like the weather, work "happens" to people. A liberated, participatory, democratic, and creative alternative can hardly be imagined, much less experienced. Work under capitalism is an alienated activity.

To reproduce the social relations of production, the educational system must try to teach people to be properly subordinate and render them sufficiently fragmented in consciousness to preclude their getting together to shape their own material existence. The forms of consciousness and behavior fostered by the educational system must themselves be alienated, in the sense that they conform neither to the dictates of technology in the struggle with nature, nor to the inherent developmental capacities of individuals, but rather to the needs of the capitalist class. It is the prerogatives of capital and the imperatives of profit, not human capacities and technical realities, which render U.S. schooling what it is. This is our charge.

ENDNOTES

1. Henry Barnard, *Papers for the Teacher: 2nd Series* (New York: F. C. Brownell, 1866), pp. 293–310.

2. Alexis de Tocqueville, as quoted in Jeremy Brecher, *Strike!* (San Francisco: Straight Arrow Books, 1972), pp. xi, xii.

3. *Ibid.*, 3. p. 172.

4. Horace Mann as quoted in Michael Katz, ed., *School Reform Past and Present* (Boston: Little Brown and Company, 1971), p. 141.

5. *Ibid.*, p. 145.

6. *The Massachusetts Teacher* (October 1851), quoted in Katz (1971), *loc. cit.,* pp. 169–170.

7. David Tyack, *Turning Points in American Educational History* (Waltham, Mass.: Blaisdell, 1967), p. 89.

8. *Ibid.*, p. 109.

9. *Ibid.*, p. 89.

10. Mann, quoted in Katz (1971), *loc. cit.,* p. 147.

11. This calculation is based on data reported in full in Samuel Bowles and Valerie Nelson, "The 'Inheritance of IQ' and the Intergenerational Transmission of Economic Inequality," *The Review of Economics and Statistics,* Vol. LVI, No. 1, February 1974. It refers to non-Negro males from non-farm backgrounds, aged 35–44 years. The zero-order correlation coefficient between socioeconomic background and years of schooling was estimated at 0.646. The estimated standard deviation of years of schooling was 3.02. The results for other age groups are similar.

12. See Appendix A, footnote 14, in Chapter 4 and the following sources: Bowles and Nelson (1974), *op. cit.;* Peter Blau and Otis D. Duncan, *The American Occupational Structure* (New York: John Wiley, 1967); Otis D. Duncan, D. C. Featherman, and Beverly Duncan, *Socioeconomic Background and Occupational Achievement,*

Final Report, Project No. S-0074 (EO-191) (Washington, D.C.: Department of Health, Education and Welfare, Office of Education, 1968); Samuel Bowles, "Schooling and Inequality from Generation to Generation," *The Journal of Political Economy,* Vol. 80, No. 3, Part II, May-June 1972.

13. These figures refer to individuals who were high-school seniors in October, 1965, and who subsequently graduated from high school. College attendance refers to both two- and four-year institutions. Family income is for the twelve months preceding October 1965. Data is drawn from U.S. Bureau of the Census, *Current Population Reports,* Series P-60, No. 183, May 1969.

14. For further evidence, see U.S. Bureau of the Census (1969), *op. cit.;* and Jerome Karabel, "Community Colleges and Social Stratification," *Harvard Educational Review,* Vol. 424, No. 42, November 1972.

15. Calculation based on data in James S. Coleman *et al., Equality of Educational Opportunity* (Washington, D.C.: U.S. Government Printing Office, 1966), and Bowles and Gintis (1972), *loc. cit.*

16. The data relating to IQ are from a 1966 survey of veterans by the National Opinion Research Center; and from N. Bayley and E. S. Schaefer, "Correlations of Maternal and Child Behaviors with the Development of Mental Ability: Data from the Berkeley Growth Study," *Monographs of Social Research in Child Development,* 29, 6 (1964).

17. This figure is based on data reported in full in our Appendix A and in Bowles and Nelson (1974), *op. cit.* The left-hand bars of each pair were calculated using the estimated correlation coefficient between socioeconomic background and education of 0.65. The results for other age groups were similar: 0.64 for ages 25–34 and 44–54, and 0.60 for ages 55–64 years. The right-hand bars were calculated from the normalized regression coefficient on socioeconomic background from an equation using background and early childhood IQ to predict years of schooling, which was estimated at 0.54. The results for other age groups were similar: 0.54 for ages 25–34 and 45–54, and 0.48 for ages 55–64.

18. Socioeconomic background is defined as normalized sum of father's education, father's occupational status, and parents' income. The mean and standard deviation of years of schooling were estimated at 11.95 and 3.02, respectively.

19. Based on a large sample of U.S. high-school students as reported in: John C. Flannagan and William W. Cooley, *Project Talent, One Year Follow-up Study,* Cooperative Research Project, No. 2333, University of Pittsburgh: School of Education, 1966.

20. Christopher Jencks *et al., Inequality: A Reassessment of the Effects of Family and Schooling in America* (New York: Basic Books, 1972), p. 48.

21. William L. Spady, "Educational Mobility and Access: Growth and Paradoxes," in *American Journal of Sociology,* Vol. 73, No. 3, November 1967; and Blau and Duncan, *op. cit.* (1967). More recent data support the evidence of no trend toward equality. See U.S. Bureau of Census (1969), *op. cit.*

22. Blau and Duncan (1967), *op. cit.* See the reported correlations in Appendix A.

23. We estimate the coefficient of variation of years of schooling at about 4.3 in 1940 (relying on Barry Chiswick and Jacob Mincer, "Time Series Changes in Personal Income Inequality in the U.S.," *Journal of Political Economy,* Vol. 80, No. 3, Part II [May–June 1972], Table 4 for the standard deviation of schooling and the Decennial Census for the mean), and at 2.95 in 1969 (relying on Chiswick and Mincer [1972], Table B10).

24. Calculated from Table B1 and Table B10 in Chiswick and Mincer (1972), *op. cit.*

25. Peter Henle "Exploring the Distribution of Earned Income," *Monthly Labor Review,* Vol. 95, No. 12, December 1972. Inequalities in income (profit, rent interest, and transfer payments plus labor earnings) may also have increased if the unmeasured income from capital gains and other tax shelters for the rich are taken into account. See Jerry Cromwell, "Income Inequalities, Discrimination and Uneven Development," unpublished Ph.D. dissertation, Harvard University, May 1974.

26. Chiswick and Mincer (1972), *loc. cit.*

27. Thomas I. Ribich, *Education and Poverty* (Washington, D.C.: Brookings Institution, 1968).

28. United States Bureau of the Census, *Current Population Reports,* Series P-60, October 1970, Table 75, p. 368.

29. *Ibid.* (November 1972), Table 1, p. 14.

30. Michael Reich, *Racial Discrimination and the Distribution of Income,* Ph.D. dissertation, Harvard University, May 1973.

31. Herbert Gintis, "Welfare Criteria with Endogenous Preferences: The Economics of Education," *International Economic Review,* June 1974; Alfred Schutz and Thomas Luckmann, *The Structure of the Life-World* (Evanston, Illinois: Northwestern University Press, 1973); and Peter L. Berger and Thomas Luckmann, *The Social Construction of Reality: A Treatise in the Sociology of Knowledge* (Garden City, L.I., N.Y.: Doubleday and Co., 1966).

32. For an extended treatment of these issues, see Herbert Gintis, "Alienation and Power," in *The Review of Radical Political Economics,* Vol. 4, No. 5, Fall 1972.

The Empowerment of The Arts

AN INSTRUMENTAL CASE STUDY IN THE SETTLEMENT HOUSE MOVEMENT

by Dawn Tawwater

In modern society, art and creative activity are usually viewed as a luxury afforded to those with a surplus of money and time. But what if art is more than a luxury? What if the act of creating art could be used to liberate groups marginalized in American society? Access to creative and artistic programs is limited for the poor, a problem that reflects the class system in the United States. Based on dominant societal ideology, creative display and what is considered "true" art is often regarded as special and unique to a select group of individuals creating a commodification of culture. Interestingly, however, this often exclusionary process of classifying artwork has not been altogether successful in diminishing the creative processes in areas and among populations with limited resources. Rather, it seems that creating art may be one of the rare human activities that can supersede the social construction of class systems.

Some sociological research has focused on the issue of creativity and artistic display. Some theorists, beginning with Karl Marx and Fredrick Engels (1845–46), see creativity as particularly human and as crucial to the labor process. A more contemporary theorist, Pierre Bourdieu views art and creativity as an important cultural component passed from one generation to the next. Other than these examples, however, sociologists have made little effort to address the role of art and creativity in human development and general well-being. This is an unfortunate oversight, given that art is consistently found throughout all stages of civilization, and among all walks of people, regardless of resource availability. Thus, there is reason to investigate the role and the meaning of creativity to individuals and groups.

In what follows, I will briefly review existing sociological literature and research along these lines and discuss where it falls short in fully appreciating the pervasiveness of human creativity and its relationship to individual empowerment. I will theoretically consider our understanding of the importance of creativity, drawing from the long-neglected theory of the American Settlement House Movement. I will also draw from the work of postmodernists who introduce art as a source of knowledge and empowerment rather than a luxury. This theoretical development is then followed by a qualitative exploration that introduces the narratives from individuals who have been engaged in creative programs. Lastly, I will discuss ways in which these findings can be used to inform current sociological thought and future research endeavors.

Sociological Theory

Sociological theory has considered the issue of creativity as related to the larger theoretical concepts of labor and culture. Labor theorists have regarded the creative autonomy of the craftsperson as central to theory. Karl Marx wrote of the "human potential" in one of his early works, *The German Ideology* (1845–46). The human potential referred to what Marx believed was the final evolutionary stage in the development of the social and individual lives of human beings (Ritzer, 1992).

Marx placed the process by which one becomes a human being (species being) in productive labor. To do so, one must engage fully and artfully in the creation of material culture, political culture, and ideological culture. By material culture, Marx meant food, shelter, clothing, and other utilitarian goods. By political culture, Marx meant full and informed participation in basic decisions in all the social institutions in which humans must live out their lives. In ideological culture, Marx included art, music, drama, poetry, literature, religion, and even science itself.

In his treatise on alienated labor, Marx noted that, in capitalism, the more one works, the less the worker has.

> Labour produces works of wonder for the rich, but nakedness for the worker. It produces palaces, but only hovels for the worker; it produces beauty but cripples the worker; it replaces

labour with machines but throws part of the working class back to a barbaric labour and turns the other part into machines. It produces culture, but also imbecility and cretinism for the worker. (1944)

Marx believed art was an essential element in human potential and therefore, in many "forms of human development" (1845–46). Marx associated art with the happiness and well-being of humans. With this happiness came increased productivity in the labor force and higher levels of cohesion in society (1845–46). Marx's proclamation for creativity/art was not related to the contemporary concerns about "talent," but rested in the unique experience found in the "process."

> The exclusive concentration of artistic talent in particular individuals, and it's suppression in the broad mass which is bound up with this, is a consequence of division of labour. If, even in certain social conditions, everyone was an excellent painter, that would not at all exclude the possibility of each of them being also and original painter, so that here too the difference between "human" and "unique" labour amounts to sheer nonsense. (1845–46)

Pierre Bourdieu, a labor/culture theorist, coined the term "cultural capital" to extend traditional labor-/class-based theory with the neglected benefits of the class found in all forms of culture, including art. Like class theory, "high culture," or access to and assumed appreciation for art, music, and drama, is passed from generation to generation, creating a cultural monopoly on concepts such as high art. Art, along with other cultural properties, becomes a form of symbolic power (Bourdieu, 1984). This symbolic power is the "power of consecration and revelation" and is used to structure class-based social rules (Bourdieu, 1984). This commodification of culture extorts art and seeks to control or ignore the utility of art as something besides a possession (Noonan, 1996).

Creativity

Art, and the work of creative people, is defined for the purpose of this paper as an act that serves to engage the imagination, trained or untrained; various forms such as written, visual, and musical arts are all included. In her book *Why Art?* Daniels writes, "The number of paintings or sculptures created in a society does not insure a better quality of life or a better world. Rather, it is the visual awareness of an artistic society brought about the understanding of the language of the art that opens the eyes of the people" (1978). Art has been used to bring action and awareness to almost every social issue in our world today (Daniels, 1978; Brett, 1986), yet it is still regarded by most as a form of leisure rather than as a legitimate form of expression.

In periods of overwhelming historical change, groups of "ordinary" people have sometimes reached for art as a means to express the experiences they are going through. Without artistic training, and using whatever materials are to hand, they have nevertheless produced intensely moving images. (Brett, 1986)

Theoretical concepts like those found in the work of Marx and Bourdieu have been treated as peripheral rather than given the weight of consideration they deserve. Yet art and creative works have pervaded all societies across time. We do not ask why art exists, because it simply always has. The legitimation of art by authorities (e.g., curators, critics) and the socially powerful has resulted in distinguishing the "true" artist from the "amateur." Regardless, art exists in all societies whether they are primitive or modern (Daniels, 1978). In any urban area in America, you can drive through neighborhoods and see art defiant of social constructions (e.g., graffiti); even without legitimation, art continues to exist. Art and creative works have been the tool by which many of the oppressed in society communicate the realities of their experiences. "The rawness of art is somehow tied up with the newness of the experience—and with the act of standing up for oneself, even though powerless." (Brett, 1986, p. 15)

Settlement House Theory

Jane Addams is known as the mother of the American settlement house movement (Deegan, 1990). The model for the emergence of settlements, Toynbee Hall, was established in 1884 by Canon Samuel Barnett (Berry, 1986). Barnett based his London settlement on three principles: (1) each person has the capacity to grow and the right to enjoy "the best"; (2) evolutionary rather than revolutionary change would be effective; and (3) the welfare of the nation as well as its neighborhoods was dependent on personal communication across the barriers of economic and social classes (Berry, 1986).

> The patriotism of the modern state must be based not upon a consciousness of homogeneity, but upon a respect for variation, not upon inherited memory, but upon refined imagination. . . .. It is always easy for democracy which insists upon writing its own programs to shut out imagination, to distrust sentiment and to make short work of recreation. It takes something like a united faith and collective energy to insist that these great human gifts shall be given the sort of expression which will develop in the arts. (Addams, 1899)

The American Settlement house movement officially began in 1886 with the establishment of the University Settlement in New York (Berry, 1986). Jane Addams and Ellen Gates Starr would follow with the founding in 1889 of Hull-House in Chicago (Deegan, 1990). Addams and Starr conceived of Hull-House after a visit to Toynbee Hall, but it differed in its establishment. Hull-House was predominantly women, it was less religious, and it emphasized an equal relationship between the staff and the neighborhood residents (Deegan, 1990). In 1893, Ellen Gates Starr authored a paper for the publication *Hull-House Maps and Papers*, entitled "Art and Labor" (Residents of the Hull-House, 1893). In the paper, Starr spoke to questions about whether art should be perpetuated "under conditions so hopeless" as those found in the working-class district of Chicago and other urban areas. She replied that "only by the re-creation of a source of art" can there be reparations to the community (Residents of the Hull-House, 1893). Starr believed that producing art fed the suffering, "hungering individual soul." Her passionate response arose from her work context. Surrounded by factories, Hull-House served primarily immigrants working in the exploitative conditions that dominated Chicago's inner city (Deegan, 1990). Similar to Marx, Starr viewed the work of the immigrants as oppressive in that they had no creative control over the product they made (Residents of the Hull-House, 1893). Starr called it the "fatal mistake of modern civilization" that we:

> Believed we could force me (sic) to live without beauty in their own lives and still compel them to make for us the beautiful things in which we have denied them any part. (Residents of the Hull-House, 1893)

In essence, lack of access to creativity fostered alienation (Marx & Engels, 1845–46). Addams shared a similar view in "A Function of the Social Settlement," (1899), but introduced the idea of art as a form of activity grounded in relaying meaning. Addams was a critical pragmatist; her position was stronger philosophically than practically. Exploring art in relation to the condition of the working class in America, she wrote, "the chief characteristic of art lies in freeing the individual from a sense of separation and isolation in his emotional experience." Addams believed that there were some qualities to life that could not be verbalized and that the "deed often reveals when the idea does not, just as art makes us understand and feel what might be incomprehensible and inexpressible" (1899). With Addams' explanation, the importance of art then to the underclass becomes more understandable. Art facilitates meaning and creates "voice" for those without equal access to legitimate avenues for democratic participation.

Contemporary settlement philosophy varies from city to city, but much of the original philosophy is still intact. John Sunami, the artist who designed a staircase and sculpture for the Southside Settlement House in Columbus, Ohio, distributed a handout, titled "Ideals in Steel," at the 1996 Annual Meeting of the United Neighborhood Centers of America about the experience.

Especially with the recent atmosphere of cultural censure and funding cutbacks, it takes courage, as well as vision and sensitivity for a social agency to say that art is more than just a decoration and entertainment, in that it provides a valuable fundamental experience that enriches and defines the reality of our lives and communities. (1996)

Settlement house theory, and more specifically the perspectives of Addams and Starr, has already shown that theory can be used in practice. Addams helped found hundreds of settlements around the United States before her death in 1935 (Deegan, 1988). Among the many accomplishments of Hull-House was the establishment of the first theater in the United States, the first painting loan program in Chicago, and the first free art exhibit program in Chicago (Addams, 1910). Today, many settlements carry on Addams' commitment to the arts. The struggle of settlement house programs is to integrate theory with activities to liberate participants in those settlement programs.

A Postmodern Interpretation

Postmodern critique is a loose body of thought/criticism which holds that all knowledge processes are richly informed by personal aims and cultural world views. All knowledge processes, including modern scientific theories, are constructed in and for a given socio-cultural life world; thus social theory may best be seen as a subjective narrative or text which legitimates existing or desired social relationships. Modern science talk privileges objectivity, rationality, power, control, inequality and hierarchy. Postmodern sociologist deconstruct each theory and each social practice by locating it in its larger socio-historical context in order to reveal the human hand and the group interests which shape the course of self-understanding of women, minorities and others. The political point from postmodernism is to enable women and others now excluded from such truth-claims to make and assert truth-claims which empower and honor different, more uncertain social-life worlds. (Young, 1995)

Postmodern critique is generally viewed to be nihilistic in that it challenges all claims of universal truth in science and universal standards in art. However, there are affirmative dimensions in postmodern sensibility. From the last sentence in the passage by Young, one can see that a distinctly postmodern approach to art does not rob it of its richness and human potential. Rather, such an approach insists only that excluded groups have access to the means by which to engage their artistic sensibility and use it in the construction of a social life-world that makes sense to them. Doing so helps them participate in every social institution in which they find themselves.

The utility of extending artistic voice to the disenfranchised can result in expressing the undefined angst so commonly attributed to conditions experienced by the underclass and extending to all groups regardless of age, race, gender, and sexual orientation.

> The world makes its impress on a child and man alike, and art can be the vehicle for the expression of deep feeling at any age. The things we feel, the things we do, the things we touch, all add to our impressions. We need to express our deepest feelings and in the process, these feelings are further sensitized. We grow and develop our potentialities as we reveal these impressions through art. (Addams, 1910)

The benefits of this are substantiated in the research I have done for the purpose of this paper. In her work *The Reenchantment of Art*, Suzy Gablik (1991) says that art can be used as "compassionate action" that arises when we empower others rather than merely seek to impose our own images upon the world. She writes,

> Most of us see art as we have been taught, as a tradition in which individuals and individual art works are the basic elements. Maintaining a deeply connected relationship with society is not how the myth of aesthetic freedom has been conceptualized in the modernist vision.

The commodification of art must be deconstructed and redistributed to acknowledge the basic right that all people share. The empowerment experienced through art, whether it be painting, drama, music, or any other form, requires that we look at art differently, not as limited to a few with "talent."

> We must take cognizance of the art medium as means of 'getting to' an individual, to probe into his (sic) personality, and use this as a basis toward understanding the various personalities displayed through art expression. We are trying to unify people, help them to understand each other, help them to find their true niche in life; there is no better common denominator than a rich art program. (Powers, 1952)

This can be done only by questioning the construction of the "consumerist imperatives of this culture" and opening the doors to a more empathic art (Gablik, 1991). Postmodernism is the tool for reawakening art as a tool of empowerment.

RESEARCH APPROACH

Research for this study followed the instrumental case study model. Robert Stake defines and instrumental case study as "a particular case being examined to provide insight into an issue of refinement of theory" (1995). Field research was conducted at the Southside Settlement

House, 310 Ennis Avenue, Columbus, Ohio, from August 9 to August 24, 1996. Included in the data are interviews, participant observation, photographs, and the collection of non-reactive data.

Site selection was based on the Southside Settlement philosophy, which stressed the role of creativity as an important human activity (Erlandson et al., 1993). Southside, established in 1898, has consistently offered individuals in the neighborhood it services creative programs in art, drama, and literature (Berry, 1986). This setting enabled me to examine the effects of creative programs on individuals living in urban areas where access to creative resources has been, and continues to be, scarce.

The collected data were carefully coded using a combination of grounded theory and a postmodern lens (Strauss & Corbin, 1990; Rosenau, 1992; Denzin, 1994). Grounded theory is based on allowing the experiences and perceptions of individuals to be recorded by the researcher without expectations for the findings. The researcher looked at the data for common themes that may indicate similarities in experience. The postmodern strategy "looks to feelings, personal experience, empathy, emotion, intuition, subjective judgment, imagination, as well as diverse forms of creativity and play" (Rosenau, 1992). A postmodern lens avoids grand generalizations as part of the goal of academic research, but instead seeks to represent the individual character participating in social life. The avoidance of generalization is achieved in the following analysis by focusing only on the local narrative of clients of Southside Settlement and with an avoidance of statements of truth. Truth statements are what postmodernists see as voices of authority that espouse an objective reality. Postmodernism condemns the economic and cultural benefits of truth statements and strives for an inter-subjective approach to social thought.

LOCAL NARRATIVES

Interviews are presented in the following section as narratives. A postmodern approach suggests that I not present information as universal truth, but as the experiences or "local narratives" of individuals who are now or have been involved in creative programs at Southside Settlement House (Rosenau, 1992). Multiple narratives and similarities in experience may be presented; however, this form of presentation is not intended to imply anything other than simplicity of form. Clients of the settlement house described various ways the art programs had impacted their lives. I found three general areas in which such impact was most illustrated. These areas are creative, social, and financial effects.

Creative Effects

Several clients expressed ways in which they were affected by access to creative resources. One client explained to me that learning to sew at the settlement helped to build her self-esteem:

> I just felt good that I can make something for myself. I can say I made this. Being proud you know. Showing them I could create something, make something, take some material and make something out of it. I enjoyed that, I enjoyed the sewing classes.

All of those interviewed showed different levels of pride about their work, but it was my feeling that the "levels" were attributable to individual perceptions of social interaction appropriateness. Some were quite open in sharing emotions; others were not. A client who was asked what was most valuable to her about the art programs relayed, "I don't know. I think it has a lot to do with my self-esteem, it does. It gives me a good feeling about myself. It makes me feel like I'm doing something." Many times, self-esteem was more visible in the statement not directly related to the subject. For example, one client saw an American Indian headdress she liked while installing windows in a home; she asked the owner permission to write down the bead pattern used in the headdress and then, as she says, "I went home and made one." This kind of initiative and confidence also existed in the ceramics class at the settlement. During my participation in the ceramics program, another client began making molds of more simplistic pieces and using them piecemeal, or cutting them up to create whole new pieces or add to another mold (e.g., putting a handle on a vase, transforming it into a pitcher). He was praised frequently for his ingenuity by settlement staff and clients; his usual response to a compliment was to show other pieces he had done.

An emergent theme found in the data was the use of art programs as a tool to relax. Two of the clients interviewed had been clinically diagnosed with nervous disorders and credited their work with creative programs as significant in their recovery. One client began attending art classes during recovery from agoraphobia. When asked how the art class helped him, he responded:

> Well it gets my mind off from myself. You know, if I'm thinking on myself, my nerves, see, I've had three, what do you call it? Three depressive breakdowns or three nervous breakdowns, and uh, by doing something like this that I enjoy doing, it helps me to keep my mind off myself and relaxes me. And uh, I know that just this year and a half that I've been here I've made more progress in the last year and have than I have in the last ten years to overcome my nervous condition.

Similarly, another client described her creative work as a source "to calm her nerves." Both of these clients referred to the focus and concentration required for their artistic work as relaxing. The other clients interviewed also described the use of art as easing stress. When asked why she was involved in ceramics, one client stated, "I do them for relaxation. I just drift off into another world of painting the pieces I've made; it's just relaxing." One client stated that as an adolescent she learned through the Settlement how to use visualization when writing poetry to escape the problems she had.

> Well, when I wrote my poetry I would think about something, someplace I wanted to go. . . . I'd just visualize in my mind that I would be sitting by a river bank, or a stream of water, and in my mind I visualize it and then describe in prose what I saw in my mind, how I felt I was there on that green grass.

In part, some clients attributed the relaxation not just to the process of art and creative work, but stated plainly that with the presence of the art programs they could escape loneliness.

Several clients attributed a sense of autonomy and self-expression to the artwork they did. One client described how participating in ceramics made her feel autonomous:

> I love making the different things, the dolls, the animals, then going home and using my own creative imagination with the way I wasn't to paint it. It's not like I'm doing this the way somebody else wants me to do it, I'm doing this the way my mind tells me to do it, you know?

Another form of expression was found among clients with experience in the drama and literature programs. Clients felt that the use of drama helped them gain confidence by putting them in the position to speak publicly with emotion, while writing allowed for a more individual or personal expression. "I think that ah, perhaps that I learned to express myself in poetry or literature, and the background I had in the dramatics helped me to face the public." Various individual perceptions and feelings are attributed to client participation in creative programs. However, common to almost all of the participants was the feeling they would not have been involved in art/creative programs without access to the free programs offered by the Settlement House. One client said without the free programs, "I couldn't afford to do it. I doubt anyone could do it, and have the facilities to do it."

Financial Effects

Among the clients interviewed, all but one had disability or social security as their only source of income, resulting in very little economic freedom and a significant amount of free time. One client, in talking about the ceramics class, said, "Oh something like this I believe would give anyone, you know, it gives them some place to go and something to do after you get there." The combined importance of filling time and relaxation is illustrated when one client responded to the possibility of the arts programs' losing their funding; she said, "They better not, because a lot of people need them because it calms people's nerves and it gives them some place to go; it brings their spirits up. . .if it wasn't for this I'd go nuts." In spite of not being able to afford art classes, clients did benefit financially from artwork. Personal financial gain occurred when participants would sell the art they made. One client talked about how her artwork at the Settlement helped her with her financial difficulties.

> Well, it's, in a way, it's good, because like me, I'm on a fixed income. And if you make the stuff and people like it they're gonna buy it and then you can live a little bit longer I think. Because then you got, you put some of your money in groceries, you put some of it, like I made a blanket and I raffled it off here, and I needed to pay two or three bills and I made enough money to pay those bills off. If helps you know, if you need, if you're in a bind it helps.

Once clients are comfortable with the sale of their artwork, the work itself illustrates how creativity can be born of necessity. Another form of financial gain occurred when participants sold their artwork to financially benefit the Settlement House. For example, a client said she had donated quilts to raise money to buy two new vans for the Settlement. She believed she would benefit from the purchase because the Settlement House would assist her and others in getting around, saving them from expenses related to other forms of transportation.

Clients received additional financial assistance by using their artwork as gifts for family and friends. Again, many of the clients expressed the belief that they would not be able to afford gift giving on many occasions without the art that they produced. When I asked one client what his friends and family thought of the gifts he gave them, he relayed,

> Oh! They think they're beautiful. You know they really act, seem to appreciate, you know. Yesterday as my youngest sister's birthday and I gave her a great big frog you know, and she, she love it! And I give, down where I live there's a lot of elderly people you know, and I give them pieces. . . . Oh it makes me feel great.

The social and individual significance of being able to give gifts appeared to greatly reduce feelings of deprivation for the clients. For example, almost everyone can relate to the shame and frustration associated with not being able to participate in holiday gift giving. For the poor, that shame and frustration can be a consistent feeling.

Social Effects

Clients described the use and refinement of social skills that were usually employed in dual roles where clients play both the counselor and the counseled. One client made the following comment when I asked her what skills she had learned during her involvement with the group art programs.

Learning to communicate with others, I learned that because everybody's different you know. Good friends, friendships. It helped me to learn to communicate with other people you know . . . . I mean you're not gonna be around your family all the time you know. You've got to get out there on your own, you know. And I think learning, going to organizations and learning different things about what you're going to face I think it's important. I really do.

Another client said that friends she makes in the Settlement art classes help her relax as well as feel understood. She commented on her painting, "You can come in and relax and you can talk while you're doing it and if you got any problems like I said, it's like a big family. You can just meet somebody and you can just talk to them, talk about anything and they will listen."

Several of the clients shared an inter-generational relationship with the Settlement. It was not unusual, for instance, to find grandmothers, mothers, and daughters involved in the same programs over time. One client had been asked by Settlement staff to participate in restoring a piece of mosaic tile art her mother, who is now deceased, had made. Another client became melancholy as she remembered activities she had attended with her mother; the following is a description of one:

> We use to have big dinners down there and when the Methodist ladies would come in we would, the mothers would cook the big dinners in this dining room; they had nice china, nice silver; it was real elaborate, the kids, the teenagers and whatever, would be the young waitresses. That was a big deal.

Organizing benefits for the settlement is one example of the potentially marketable leadership skills developed by participants in art programs. One client had never been involved in any community art program before the ceramics group at the Settlement, yet after six months of participation, he was asked to direct it. When I asked about his experience, he told me about his first official act of leadership:

> When I first took over the ceramics group here, you know I've become the leader of it, they were using a lot of profane language, you know. I mean it was just all over the place . . . . So I talked to my boss about it and he gave me the, you know, the authority, I guess or something. I put the rules up on that yellow paper there (gestures toward the wall), and that tells the people not to have any profanity. And uh, it's been a lot better since then.

All forms of leadership described by clients were facilitated by the Settlement House. For example, clients frequently developed the confidence and skills within art programs to act as teachers and to assist the Settlement staff and other clients in their art work. Clients took on responsibility for other programs or shared their artistic experience to maintain and restore art that had been displayed in the Settlement for years and was now in need of preserving. For the Settlement House clients, artistic skill has influenced them in ways useful to socially based self-development. As a result, clients have been successful in developing leadership skills, in enhancing interpersonal communication skills, and in facilitating inter-generational family relationships.

CONCLUSIONS

Early theorists like Karl Marx believed that creative autonomy was so important to individual and social well-being that they criticized governments for not recognizing it. Pierre Bourdieu said art is like society in that, regardless of how hard you try to be objective and stand at a distance, there is, as there is in art, an "ineffable" quality, or something uniquely subjective.

Jane Addams, while still invisible in most sociology curricula, forged one of the most socially significant centers for work with the poor in the history of our nation with Hull-House. Primary to the success of Hull-House was its commitment to the arts. In *Twenty Years at Hull-House*, Addams questioned why we, as a society, do not recognize the importance of the arts: "Why do we permit the waste of this most precious human faculty, this consummate possession of civilization? When we fail to provide the vessel in which it may be treasured, it runs out upon the ground and is irretrievably lost" (Addams, 1910, p. 383).

A postmodern lens gives us the language and the tools to deconstruct modern ideas about art and to look toward freeing the individual to reclaim art as "voice." The postmodern emphasis on activity meets naturally with the theory and practice of art programs found in settlements like that at Southside. The importance of the revelation of postmodernism is evident in the experiences of the clients at Southside Settlement. Postmodernism distinguishes traditional forms of voice held in the privileged status of the author from the public voice of the common people (Rosenau, 1992). I found that art had the potential to empower people creatively, socially, and, perhaps to some extent, financially in the unrestricted art and creative programs found in the Southside neighborhood. Indeed, if the creative process is so pervasive, might art and creativity be a means for liberating the individual? Perhaps then, artistic/creative activity can empower individuals and societies by meeting basic human needs. Through meeting their needs, art might thus serve as a liberating force.

Over the last decade, monumental governmental cuts at the local, state, and federal levels have left many children and adults without access to art/creative programs. I believe the work done at Southside Settlement House illustrates a bond between the individual and a creative process. Furthermore, I believe, for all those interviewed, this bond facilitated some positive social results. The findings here suggest that it might benefit sociological theory to further investigate art and creativity as a central rather than a peripheral subject. In addition, I think, for progressive sociology, the subject matter is unusually fitted for the aim of bringing the development of theory and the implementation of practice into synthesis. Future sociological research should include consideration of art as essential in people's lives. Such research should take into consideration the role of stratification in defining art, as well as determining who has access to the making of art. Such research on art might also consider that those who have been disenfranchised from art making have nonetheless engaged in creative work. In the creative work, the art of the disenfranchised is a bounty of social issues ripe for study like questions of public art versus activist art, how art builds solidarity, and how art can give social voice to otherwise marginalized groups/individuals. As we have seen from this limited sample of individual narratives, art and creative work can have powerful individual and group effects.

REFERENCES

Addams, Jane. (1899). A function of the social settlement. Paper presented to the American Academy of Political and Social Science.

Addams, Jane. (1910). *Twenty years at Hull-House.* New York: The Macmillan Company.

Berry, Margaret E. (1986). *One hundred years on urban frontiers: The settlement movement 1886–1986.* Cleveland: United Neighborhood Centers of America.

Berry, Margaret E. (1996). *Neighborhood needs and the settlement movement: Responses to changing times.* Presented at the 1996 Biennial National Conference of United Neighborhood Centers of America, Inc.

Brett. Guy. (1986). *Through our own eyes: Popular art and modern history.* Philadelphia: New Society Publishers.

Cook, Charles. (1952). Creative arts and the settlements. Paper presented at the 37th Annual Meeting of the National Federation of Settlements and Neighborhood Centers. New York, 1953.

Daniels, Florence Margaret. (1978). *Why art?* Chicago: Nelson-Hall Inc.

Deegan, Mary Jo. (1988). *Jane Addams and the men of the Chicago School.* New Brunswick, NJ: Transaction Publishers.

Denzin, Norman K., & Yvonna S. Lincoln (Eds.). (1994). *Handbook of qualitative research.* Thousand Oaks, CA: Sage Publications, Inc.

Erlandson, David A., Edward L. Harris, Barbara L. Skipper, & Steve D. Allen. (1991). *Doing naturalistic inquiry.* Newbury Park, CA: Sage Publications, Inc.

Gablik, Suzy. (1991). *The reenchantment of art.* New York: Thames & Hudson Inc.

Johnson, Mary Ann (Ed.). (1989). *The many faces of Hull-House: The photographs of Wallace Kirkland.* Chicago: University of Illinois Press.

Lasch, Christopher (Ed.). (1965). *The social thought of Jane Addams.* New York: The Bobbs-Merrill Company, Inc.

Marx, Karl, & Fredrick Engels. (1939) *The German ideology.* New York: International Publishers.

Marx, Karl. (1964). *The economic & philosophic manuscripts of 1844.* New York: International Publishers.

Noonan, Sean. (1996). Recuperation Debord: From fetishism to the spectacle a contribution to commodification theory. Presented in partial fulfillment of the masters of arts degree, department of sociology, Kansas State University.

Oakeley, Hilda D. (1923). *History and progress.* London: The Gresham Press.

Powers, Maxwell. (1952). The arts in life. Paper presented at the 37th Annual Conference of The National Federation of Settlements and Neighborhood Centers. New York,November, 1953.

Residents of the Hull-House. (1970). *Hull-House maps and papers.* New York: Arno Press.

Rosenau, Pauline Marie. (1992). *Postmodernism and the social sciences: Insights, inroads andintrusions.* Princeton, NJ: Princeton University Press.

Spradley, James P. (1980). *Participant observation.* Orlando, FL: Holt, Rinehart and Winston, Inc.

Stake, Robert E. (1995). *The art of case study research.* Thousand Oaks, CA: Sage Publications, Inc.

Webb, Eugene J., Donald T. Campbell, Richard D. Schwartz, Lee Sechrest, & Janet B. Grove. (1981). *Non-reactive measures in the social sciences.* Boston: Houghton Mifflin Company.

Yarbrough, James. (1995). Postmodern science: Methods for progressive humanism. Paper presented in meeting of the Red Feather Institute for Progressive Sociology at Texas Woman's University, Denton, TX.

Young, T. R. (1991). Deconstructing constructionism: Social problems theory in a postmodern modality. Paper prepared for the Red Feather Institute for Advanced Studies in Sociology as part of the Transforming Sociology Series. Weidman, MI.

Young, T. R. (1996). *The Red Feather dictionary.* Weidman, MI: Red Feather Institute forAdvanced Studies in Sociology.

SOCIAL OPPRESSION

An Existential Look at Homelessness

by Phillip K. Tompkins

The cover of the September 2000 issue of the *Denver Voice*:

> The *Voice* remembers
>
> Donald Dyer
>
> 1948–1999
>
> George "Billy" Worth
>
> 1936–1999
>
> Melvin "Fuzzy" Washington
>
> 1952–1999
>
> Milo Harris
>
> 1947–1999
>
> Kenneth Rapp
>
> 1956–1999
>
> Joe Mendoza
>
> 1949–1999
>
> Harry J. Redden, Jr.
>
> 1950–1999
>
> Mark Warren Davis
>
> 1956–2000

The last name on the list was a new one. Davis was found burned to death by a fire in an open camp, and although the police didn't regard it as a murder, the *Voice* wasn't so sure. In my mind there were still six cases to be solved, getting colder all the time.

And so was the weather. I quote my field notes for Friday, September 22, 2000. "I woke up several times early this morning, the first day of autumn. It was dark when I pulled back the blinds and saw the dark, wet city as a scene from the film *Blade Runner*. The temperature had dropped to 38F during the night; it was 41F and raining as I drove to the St. Francis Center at about 7:15. Some of the guests were miserable when they entered the building, pulling off plastic bags they had used as raincoats. We have few Asian guests, but that day a Korean man still wore his plastic bag when he came in the clothing room in the afternoon, looking for dry clothing."

In conversations with guests that day, I asked, "Did you keep dry last night?" Some said they had gone into a shelter; many others slept out but managed to keep fairly dry, under a bridge, in one case, in a van in another. It would rain all day, and I began to worry about their health. When I walked out of the showers at 9:00, I shouldn't have been so surprised by how many people were in the great room. I was the only worker in mail/ storage, and the guests were impatient with the long lines as well as being wet and cold. One man, for example, wanted to open his bag in the storage room, take some clothes out, and put some others in. I told him he had to take his bag into the other room so that I could help people waiting in line. "This is too much," he said.

I nodded at a man standing in line with his bag waiting to put it back on a storage shelf. As he started walking into the storage room, a man asked, "Why did you let him cut in front of us?"

"I'm sorry," I said, "were you here before he was?"

Nods.

But my apology seemed to help. Later, when the man brought his bag back, he said, "You're the man."

It was still raining when I turned on the windshield wipers to drive home at 2:30. Later I dropped in at the bar in Gallagher's Restaurant in our building. I wrote at the end of the notes for the day: "Never have been so physically and psychologically aware of the transition from one season to another."

Two weeks later, Friday, October 6, 2000, it was twenty-eight degrees at 7:30 as I drove to the shelter, the windshield wipers dealing with the drizzle. *They must be miserable.* At the 2:00 discussion after another tough, demanding day, I said, "This must be the hardest time of year for homeless people, autumn, the transition between the summer and winter." Tom and Jean nodded. I continued, "Today and September 22, the first day of fall, were cold and rainy and made our guests miserable." The group agreed. T. S. Eliot wrote that April is the cruelest month, and although that may be true for flowers, I suspect he never lived on the streets in October.

Scratch notes on my work slip record "longest line ever for clothing slips"; the thirty-five people who got clothing between 9:00 and 10:00 constituted a "record," according to our experienced coordinator Mike.

A man gave me trouble all day and walked back into the showers later in the day to announce, "I'll kill the motherfucker who stole my shirt." After he left, a discussion broke out about his remark. At least two men said they would never steal from another homeless man "because they work too hard for what little they have."

"I'd steal from a corporation but not from a man," said a third man while dressing, comfortable with the idea of stealing from the corporate powers that be, artificial persons, but not a real one.

A week later we anticipated it would be a wild and crazy day because it was Friday the thirteenth, with the moon in its full phase. I was troublesome, complaining because we no longer did the salt ritual. I had come to take pleasure participating in it. But at the end of the day, Carla said it had been a quiet one, with only 333 guests admitted, a low number for the season.

An article about time had appeared in the August 2000 issue of the *Voice* under the byline of Elberta, no last name, a regular writer for the tabloid who clearly knew the street people well. She wrote that the quality of time is affected by the schedules of the institutions that affect the homeless people—when they open and close. Those institutions are missions, soup kitchens, libraries, senior centers, and beer joints. The crucial point of the monthly cycle is what she called "mother's day"—the first day of the month, when Supplemental Security Income (SSI), Veterans Administration (VA), and welfare checks arrived in the mail. According to Elberta, even those who don't get checks on the first are excited because others who do get them have promised to treat their friends, and some intend to roll a drunk who cashed one, a perfect contrast to those who would steal from a corporation but not from a real person.

Weather is the major survival factor in the seasonal cycle, autumn bringing unpredictability and winter true hardship. But summer is more dangerous because of the risk of being rolled or attacked. Thanksgiving, Christmas, and Easter "evoke sadness and bitterness," despite the gala holiday meals. Elberta quoted a Christmas lunch patron as saying, "No, I didn't see my people—my children. I had nothing to give them. I don't want them to see how I was living."[1]

Homeless folks often talk about "killin' time." Although she didn't quote Orwell's observation that poverty annihilates time, Elberta came close and even surpassed the other writer with these words:

> Only those new to street life talk of the future as a progression from the past. When concrete goals are spoken, it is often of plans to travel elsewhere. Goals become associated with space rather than time; the hope becomes that a new location may make a difference in the knowledge that a "new time" will never come. Therefore, when some speak of goals, it is often in terms of going someplace else, like another state or relocating to another area across town on RTD [the local bus service].[2]

In these brilliant observations, she even explains the wanderlust and the fever of the tramps and wanderers, the thrill of going somewhere else, someplace new.

A guest named Karl gave me a seminar in hawking newspapers, seemingly enjoying it as much as I. He got the rhythm of stopping when a new guest approached me, picking up again where he had left off. Hawkers don't pay for the newspapers. The *Rocky Mountain News* and the *Denver Post* give them away. Karl sold the *Post* and had a "lock" on a spot in a suburb, Parker, Colorado, on private property owned by King Soopers, a supermarket grocery chain in Denver. He made $1.25 per paper and total sales over the weekend were $100. The conversation moved from mail/storage to the showers, and I learned he charged twenty-five cents per paper on weekdays, fifty cents on the weekend, so his customers were generous with tips. People in Parker travel on business so much, Karl hypothesized, that they didn't subscribe to the papers, relying on him and other hawkers when they were in town.

Karl understood the economics of newspapers and hawking them. Competition was fierce between the two newspapers. The companies gave the papers to the hawkers without charge in order to increase circulation. Circulation figures determine the fees the advertisers pay. Karl said that when his ankle and foot got better, he would go back to his job as a truck driver.

Another man in the showers joined the seminar. He agreed with Karl's numbers, saying if a hawker who worked weekdays as well as weekends could do quite well.

"Well enough to pay for housing?"

He paused to reflect on the question.

"Enough to pay," he nodded, "if I chose to live that way."

"Then you must choose to live another way."

Again he paused, and his smile turned into speech.

"Yesterday I went to a casino in Central City and lost. Lost a lot." Now I was nodding. I wished him a good weekend.

"Thanks."

Later, the two newspapers would sign a joint operating agreement, in which the *News* would publish the only paper on Saturday—with an editorial page for the other paper—and the *Post* would return the favor on Sunday, minimizing the competition between the two newspapers and eliminating the need for weekend hawkers, drying up a significant source of income for our guests.

Casey is a tall, slender African American man with some gray hair beginning to show on his well-cropped head. His speech is refined, his manner courteous and a bit dramatic at times. He had a limp when I walked him to get his storage bag. I didn't ask, but he let me know, "I got hit by a bus." He was retreating from someone who was beating him up when he backed into a bus.

Mike gave him a job so that he could earn a clothing slip, and while mopping near mail/storage within earshot of three volunteers, Casey gave this speech:

I can't seem to get out of this state of homelessness. I try, and yet I can't get out. I stopped smoking crack, but it doesn't get any better. I'm going to start smoking crack again.

We three volunteers spoke at once:

"No," said Liesl.

"No," said Jan.

"No," said Phil.

He sat down next to Jan, a retired schoolteacher who volunteers more than one day a week, and she counseled him at length.

Maybe we do try to fix them at times.

In the clothing room, an African American man was trying to find clothes that could constitute the uniform required for his job doing food preparation at St. Joseph's Hospital.

"Are you going to be able to find your own place?"

"I'm trying. I hope so. I lost my wife, lost my way, lost everything, but I'm trying to make it back."

"You can do it."

"Thank you." Our eyes locked for a long, transcendent moment. I later wrote, "That is why I work here."

I spent an hour and fifteen minutes editing Tom's message for the SFC newsletter. I complained to my superiors that we had a private-business mentality, boasting about growth, more and more guests and services offered to them. A *decline* in customers would be the best measure of our success.

The Affordable Housing Study Group invited a city planner to address us. After talking Denver housing history, new issues, and city efforts, we had a question-and-answer period. I thought the speaker was defensive on behalf of the Webb administration. I later stated my conclusion to two members of the study group: "We are losing ground on all fronts." Both men agreed with me.

On a Friday in November 2000, a cold day in Denver, I was responsible for cleaning the showers after many, many men had used them. Larry, a fellow volunteer, came in at 12:45 to help me for fifteen minutes, and there were still a lot of men in the room, delaying us from spraying with disinfectant. One man in particular I asked to finish his shower, dress, and leave.

He showered too long. Larry picked up a red plastic bag and threw it in the trash. I threw other trash in on top of it. When I finally got the man to come out of the showers, I noticed there were red spots all over his body, concentrated mainly on his legs. He walked over to Larry and screamed, "What did you do with my clothes?" The red sack was a biohazard bag with the man's clothing in it. We were able to retrieve the clothes for him. He was in considerable discomfort, shaking and picking at the red sores on his legs.

Our coordinator came in to check on him. Mike had sent the man in for a shower two hours earlier and got too busy to check on him. He gently urged the man to put his clothes on so that we could finish spraying.

"But the lice are dead and I'm picking them out."

The man volunteered to help us clean. Mike gently urged him to hurry with his clothes. The man began rapidly clawing his legs. Even after he got dressed he rubbed his legs and feet. Mike had said he had scabies, but the man said it was lice.

"What do you have?"

"Oh," he shouted at me, "now you're going to talk to me."

I felt bad for the man who showered too long, wishing I could do something to relieve his agony. He told me he slept outdoors and got a case of lice. I couldn't understand everything he said because of his spasms. I apologized to him, lamely saying I had not understood his problem. Mike also apologized and later told me privately that there were some mental illness issues in this case.

November 2000 was a period in which numbers became important. On Friday the seventeenth I wrote down the intake numbers on the calendar for the previous two weeks of the month, the second coldest period in recorded history for Denver. The range was from 381 to 520. The highest numbers are on Monday because the center is closed on Saturday and open only half a day on Sunday. The number for the preceding Friday, November 10, was 482, a high number. We volunteers joked about earning our pay. Mike had explained to me the previous week that cold days put more pressure on the organization because the guests spent more time in the building.

On the shortest day of the year, December 22, 2000, I was pleasantly surprised by the mood of the men in the showers. It was, after all, three days before Christmas, the first day of winter, and they were in good humor. The weather no doubt helped. We had blue skies, a warming sun that would bring us to a high of fifty. A middle-aged black man smiled when I asked him what he needed.

"A shower," he answered.

He attracted an audience as he talked and undressed, folding his pants in cadence with his speech. He sat down and looked across the room at me again, saying, "You must wonder why I am a man of joy."

"Yes, why are you a man of joy?"

"I've known Jesus since I was a boy, when I was nine years old." A heavy Hispanic man putting on his clothes near the tile bench nodded and encouraged the speaker.

"The problems I have are of my own making," he said, and as he paused, the men around him became more attentive.

"The burdens he gives me are slight; the burdens I have created for myself are staggering."

Other men were asking me for this and that so I couldn't follow all the soliloquy, but I had seen a bottle of Brut on our lunch table and assumed it was a Christmas present for our guests. After Jean verified my assumption, I took it with me to the showers.

"I've got some smellgood," I announced, and they came running. I poured it in their cupped palms, sternly cautioning them, "Don't drink it," reveling in the laughter of the men. One man winced as he slapped it on his cheeks.

"Does it burn your face?"

"No, I've got cracks in my hands."

He showed me the cracks. He was a mason by trade, and the bricks and mortar had dried his skin to the point of splitting open.

I began to say "Merry Christmas" to each man as he left the facilities, and most returned the wish, some simply saying, "Thanks," all of this making for a warm hour in the showers.

At lunch I fell into a conversation with Joe Brzozowski. We were becoming good friends and would become regular golf partners. SFC would emerge as a topic of conversation on the golf course or over a coke, beer, or glass of wine at the nineteenth hole. In response to a question at the morning sharing discussion, I had said that I thought our guests had a longer "now" than we did. Joe said he had been thinking about my comment, and he said that our sense of community at SFC made Friday so special that he looked forward to it, and that Friday at the shelter was one long "now," in that he didn't look forward to something in the future. I thought back to a remark he had made a couple of Fridays earlier, something to the effect of how much he "loved this place." I had similar feelings and, in fact, was sad that Cecil had to cut back his hours, leaving at 11:00 instead of 2:00 because of a problem with his neck that made standing for long periods difficult. Cecil was our mentor, a wise and good man. But then we would still have him for three hours each Friday. I wrote about the day that SFC had become part of my identity, a "we," a reference group, a community-of-salvation-in-this-world.

"Lance Armstrong" came into the shelter looking for warm clothing. He said he planned to ride his bicycle to Buffalo, Wyoming, even though it was early January. He had tried to do it the previous week but was stopped short of Casper, Wyoming, by a roadblock. He pitched his tent in weather so cold his drinking water froze, so cold he couldn't get to sleep.

The next entry in my field notes is dated Friday, January 21, 2001, even though it was actually written the next morning, Saturday the twenty-second. Elaine and I had taken a whirlwind trip to Italy with Larry Browning, a friend and professor at the University of Texas, and his wife, Vickie Hoch, an experienced traveler with United Airlines who was our informal tour leader. After seeing Sorrento and the Amalfi Coast, we wound up in the medieval city of Assisi, where we bought a print of *S. Francesco,* a fresco by Giovanni Cimabue in the lower basilica. We had it framed, and Craig, our handyman, hung it in a place of prominence, a central place on the wall behind the mail/storage desk.

I had missed a week because of a bad cold but was assigned to clean the showers. Joe said he should have been assigned to do it, that there should be a rule saying that a volunteer shouldn't have to do that duty after an illness. I suggested to Joe that we should form a union. He smiled. I suggested calling it the Amalgamated Homeless Shelter Volunteers of America, AHSVA for short. He smiled. In that moment was born a movement of solidarity unprecedented—to my knowledge—in the history of homeless shelters.

"They," or "management," were asking us to do more and more, to work harder and harder. Mike said we had set a record for the previous month. Tom confirmed it, saying we had 12,400 guests in December. We had averaged 10,000 per month during the previous year. When I asked for probable causes, Tom said cold weather and fewer day-labor jobs. The recent census of homeless people in the Denver metropolitan area came up with the number seven thousand.

On a Friday in March 2001, Lou, a regular guest, decided to take a pair of cotton pants from the clothing room, even though he said they looked like "joint" clothes. The others in the room broke out in laughter, but I was stumped, not understanding the humor. I pressed Lou for an explanation, and he supplied a verbal equation for me: *Joint* meant *pen,* the second term being an abbreviation for *penitentiary.* They all watched my reaction. I started laughing, and they joined me in appreciation of clothing as stigma.

The Lance Armstrong of the Homeless World forgot to take his meds, had an epileptic seizure, and wound up in the hospital. When I first saw him after that, he was reading an article about eating out.

"Do you eat at restaurants?"

"Yes," he said, giving the name of a Chinese restaurant near the hotel where he had a room.

"They made me pay before I ate when I first went there. Now I can pay after I eat." He paused, adding, "And after someone stole my bike, they gave me a new one, uh, a new used one."

"Some people are good, aren't they?" I asked.

"Yes—when they know you."

Lance changed the subject, saying his brother-in-law had told him that more people were losing their place to live.

"Why?" I asked, wondering what a brain-damaged, epileptic super-athlete would have as an answer.

"Because there are too many people and too few places to live in Denver. Only the people with a lot of money can afford a place to live." He paused. "That doesn't sound right." I couldn't disagree.

I ate lunch, as usual, from 11:15 to 12:00. A city police officer the center hired for security ate with us, a rare event. Quite naturally I inquired about the murders. He said he knew little about them but did know enough, however, to say the newspaper reports got it all *wrong*. The men hadn't been decapitated. They had been bludgeoned to death, to the point that their heads no longer existed, no trace of them. He also said I might not be able to get any information out of the department because the cases were still under investigation.

I went on talking with the others at the lunch. Joe and I resumed our playful discourse about forming a union of volunteers. The staff members began to make jokes about it. Everyone seems to enjoy the irony of volunteers organizing themselves into a union in an organization they loved and identified with, and the irony that they didn't have wages and benefits to bargain about.

How long did it take for me to connect the officer's remarks about the murdered homeless men, including Joe Mendoza, with the victim of Jack, the killer in the Colorado State Mental Hospital? I cannot say. The crimes were separated in time by forty-three years or more. Eventually I did see the similarity. The victims were beaten to death in such a way that they appeared to be decapitated. There was speculation in newspaper accounts that the heads had been eaten by wild animals, but that was later denied. There were no heads left after the bludgeoning killings in Denver, just as the mechanic's head on the Western Slope had been vaporized. What kind of person or persons could commit such atrocities? Could it be a group of highly identified kids who fit the criminal capital model? Was it a virulent killer of the kind Athens described? Or could it be a genuinely crazy person like the man I knew in Pueblo in 1956. By the way, I wondered, *Was he released during deinstitutionalization? Was he still alive? Would the police ever catch the killer or killers?*

Mary Hupp, the community minister for and head of the Capitol Hill United Ministries, invited me to give a thirty-minute speech at the annual dinner and meeting of CHUM on February 22, 2001. I was more nervous than usual anticipating the occasion because I'd never addressed an audience of ministers; the title of the speech was "An Existential Look at Homelessness."

I began talking about my experience at the St. Francis Center, moving on to the statistics, emphasizing the steady increase in the numbers of guests at the shelter and the numbers of people counted in the point-in-time studies. The number of homeless persons in Denver had increased by 33 percent during my tenure as a volunteer.

I talked about the reading I'd been doing—the social science research, literature, and theology. I admitted trying to find answers in the work of Martin Heidegger, the German Existential philosopher. His work had inspired me to think of homelessness in new ways.

I began with his idea of *Geworfenheit*,[3] translated as "thrownness." I gestured several times at the audience, pretending to throw a baseball in several directions. All of us experience thrownness, I said, not just the misfits. We don't throw ourselves; we are thrown. We are thrown into the midst of other beings. We don't come to rest; we stay "in the throw." In everyday language: "I like to think of thrownness in the concrete way we become human beings. We come into the world without having been asked if we wanted to enter it, without any say about the time, place, our parents, gender, race, or social capital." I tried to describe the trajectory of our thrownness.

Having been thrown, I continued, we have to fall. Falling was a way of saying that we are lost, lost in a crowd of other beings. What is relevant about our thrownness and our falling is that *we are all homeless beings*. We do not "reside."

According to Heidegger, we are driven to seek some sort of homecoming (he seemed to think doing philosophy was the best way to seek a homecoming), though we never achieve a true homecoming. We are stricken with homesickness. The audience seemed to be convinced by these ideas; at the least, my hearers were taking them seriously.

If we are all homeless and homesick, I asked, what is the difference between those of us who are comfortable in our homes and those who are sleeping on the South Platte River on a February night? What does the ordinary use of the word *homeless* now mean? Here I recalled the mole people of New York City as described by Jennifer Toth in her book *The Mole People: Life in the Tunnels beneath New York City*. When I first read the book, I had doubts as to whether an attractive young woman could descend three stories, armed only with a can of Mace, into the city under the ground. But I voluntarily set aside my critical predispositions when I saw the photographs of mole people in their environment.

I also found several passages in the book useful for my Existential project, including this statement: "Most tunnel dwellers prefer to be called 'houseless' rather than 'homeless.'"[4] This was the distinction I asked my audience of ministers to accept. All of us are homeless and homesick, but the guests at the St. Francis Center are different from us only by being *houseless*. Houselessness is a condition or state we can do something about.

I told the audience I had never ended a speech with a prayer before, but that night I wanted to do so with a petition I had found in the book about the mole people. More than a dozen people who lived in the abandoned train tunnel heard a young woman's screams on a freezing December night. She was in labor. A young Hispanic man named Juan who worked at McDonald's during the day said they should pray:

> Dear Lord, please deliver us this baby safely. His parents are good people. He's done nothin' bad, Lord. He's jus' a baby. He don't mean no disrespect being born underground. We'll take care of him when he's with us. Just deliver him and his mama safely, Lord, and we'll take care of the rest. Amen.[5]

"The Little Rock of the North"

RACE, GENDER, CLASS, AND THE CONSEQUENCES OF MASS INCARCERATION

by Susan Starr Sered and Maureen Norton-Hawk

[Black] women actually experience various forms of violence as layers of degradation that have a cumulative negative effect on their lives, resulting in systematic subordination.

—Beth E. Richie, *Arrested Justice* (2012)

Despite differences created by historical era, age, social class, sexual orientation, skin color, or ethnicity, the legacy of struggle against the violence that permeates U.S. social structures is a common thread binding African-American women.

—Patricia Hill Collins, *Black Feminist Thought* (2000)

When Anasia walks into the drop-in center, a few of the more timid women show a sudden need to leave for a cigarette, a bathroom run, or a vague appointment. Younger women may jump up to steer her to the most comfortable chair in the room, where she plops down with a thump and a groan. A heavy-set black woman in her late thirties, Anasia walks with a limp, listing to one side like a boat missing a rudder. Known for her street smarts and her quick temper, she is proud to have done whatever she needed to do to survive, and is not reticent when talking about shoplifting, selling drugs, or using other people to get what she needs. Many of the project participants prefer to shield us from direct knowledge of their illegal activities. In contrast, shortly after we first met Anasia, she stopped by our office asking if we had a plastic bag we could give her. "I picked up a couple of things and they are making my pockets looked stuffed," she explained in a nonchalant tone of voice as she pulled out four bottles of men's shampoo that she had just stolen from a store across the street.

***

Chaos is Anasia's word of choice for describing her family, her neighborhood, and her life. As a child, she and her siblings bounced between the house of their functioning but alcoholic mother and their father, an "abuser and serial cheater." Outside the house, things were no better. "I was moving from school to school, from place to place—it was crazy. When we first moved [to the Boston housing projects]," Anasia recalls, "it was more white people than black people; there were only like five black people, so they used to stone our house and write 'Get out nigger' on the doors and windows and stuff. And stuff like that, take our bikes, and stuff like that . . . I mean, we weathered the storm and we got through that, and then it got mixed."

During the 1970s when Anasia was growing up, Boston earned the nickname the "Little Rock of the North." In 1974, federal district court judge Arthur Garrity, Jr. found the Boston School Committee (the city's board of education) guilty of enforcing segregation in its schools. As a result, a mandated program of busing white students to predominantly black schools and black students to predominantly white schools was instituted. In retrospect this attempt at desegregation was modest in size. At the time, however, fights and riots broke out at South Boston High, Hyde Park High, and Charlestown High in opposition to busing. Within the first twenty-six days of the school year, there were over 140 arrests and reports of sixty-nine treatable injuries (Formisano 1991, p. 80). The tenacity of black parents determined to send their children to better schools reflects both personal courage and the abominable state of the segregated black schools of the time. Jonathan Kozol (1985), who taught in a school in Boston's primarily black Roxbury neighborhood in 1964, documented peeling paint, lack of textbooks, underqualified teachers, and overcrowded classrooms. Even more damning, he wrote, "the slave-master and black child feeling was prevalent" (p. 41).

Anasia recalls that school was a struggle for her. "It wasn't going real well. I mean every time I'd make friends, we was up and moving, leaving, going somewhere else, and then I had to make friends all over again and it was like chaos. Constant chaos . . . . One of my friends was smoking weed at that age [twelve], so [I started smoking] in order to fit in." Kicked out of the regular public school, she "started going to whatever they call the school for bad people." She dropped out when she was sixteen, "and I didn't have to go no more." No one seemed to make an effort to bring her back in to school.

Anasia's first boyfriend was a drug dealer, "so I no longer had to pay for [crack cocaine]. I always had it, right there." With her boyfriend she had two children. Reluctant to leave her crack supplier, Anasia frequently turned to her mother for support when her children's father hurt her or when he went to jail. "When I had my oldest son, immediately my mother took him because my mother said, 'I'd be damned if he beat my grandson.' " Her mother remained the primary caregiver of her elder son; her sister the primary caregiver of the younger. "I just went off . . . into the world. Doing what I wanted to do, constantly going to jail. I would only call my mother when I went to jail so she could send me some canteen money." Over the years Anasia has had other boyfriends, who "did the same things I did. Stole, went to jail. Bad boys, all of them."

Intersections of Race and Gender, Part 1

In chapter 1 we describe gender overdetermination as a social process in which femaleness is always made relevant, in which diverse social attributes are explained in terms of physical gender, in which gender trumps personhood. Parallel processes (though not parallel content) describe the persistent salience of race and racism in America (Bonilla-Silva 2013). For black women like Anasia, these potent social processes intersect: she is never "only" a woman or "only" African American. Both gender and race shape her engagements with family, community, employers, doctors, welfare institutions, and the correctional system.[1]

Like Francesca, nearly all of the white project participants narrated a path to pain, homelessness, and criminalization that revolved around childhood sexual abuse followed by PTSD and drug use. As their lives spiraled downward, many of the white women were cut off by their natal families for reasons ranging from well-intentioned "tough love," meant to bring the daughter to her senses, to exasperation, fear, and shame. In the words of one white parent we talked to, "She grew up with everything, but she acts like she comes from the ghetto."

Most of the black women in the Boston group grew up in "respectable" poor families; they may have lived in the housing projects, but their parents worked and managed to scrape by. While some of the black women were sexually abused as children, most recalled growing up in supportive households and continued to maintain positive relationships with their families (see Richie 1996). Even Anasia, whose father molested her, felt that her mother had always been there for her. Though disappointed when Anasia, as she puts it, "messes up," her mother would never consider *not* helping her out. According to the family ethos, Anasia explained, you help and protect other family members when they are in trouble. Indeed, Anasia's family has remained mutually supportive—providing one another a place to stay, taking care of one another's children, making efforts to keep one another safe, and helping one another deal with government agencies. Her eldest son, now in his twenties, has become her protector. "He smokes weed . . . . That's one thing I never hid from my oldest son. Like when I was getting high and he was younger, he knew, you know what I'm saying? I would tell him . . . . And I think he respects me more because of that." Over the past few years her son has taken on the responsibility to come and get her when she runs into trouble in a crack house. "My son takes care of me. He will go to the crack house with me and make sure I get out of there. He doesn't use, but watches out for me. People are scared of him and they know they shouldn't mess with him."

For the black women we met, far more than for the white women, it was the outside world more than the domestic one that set them onto a path of suffering. Vanessa was raised by warm and loving parents in the 1960s in a segregated black neighborhood where much of the housing was contaminated with high levels of lead. As a result of childhood lead poisoning, she struggles with reading, memory, and an array of other cognitive challenges. Mary, a black woman in her early fifties, explains that she and some other black students would be passed to the next grade in school even if they couldn't read, because they were needed on the track team. Given no remedial help (though plenty of track team coaching), Mary finished high school unable to fill out job application forms.

While most of the white women eagerly share psychologically framed narratives tracing their drug use to trauma, Anasia expresses little interest in picking apart her intrapsychic motivations. "There is no particular reason—I just do it. I seem to be doing good [not using drugs] and then just get bored or just give up . . . . It doesn't make any sense. I just decide to do it." In contrast to the white women, nearly all of the black women became involved with drugs "because it was everywhere." Mary began smoking crack in her late twenties because "it was always around in those days." (She stopped using shortly after we met her when, after many years of waiting, she received stable housing in a calm and well-maintained building for senior citizens.) Vanessa, a black woman who describes herself as "slow" both in terms of her abilities when she was in school and her social life, started using crack at age thirty-seven, "because I was trying to follow everyone else, be like everyone else." Now in her forties, she wants to stop using ("I'm tired"), but finds that living in what she calls a "drug-infested neighborhood" makes it hard to step away from crack. For black women far more than for white women, subpar schools, racially discriminatory hiring practices, and segregated and impoverished neighborhoods present insurmountable challenges to building the kinds of lives they wish for. As Tonya, a black woman who happens to be one of Anasia's former drug dealers explains, "As soon as you [a potential employer] see me, you don't think 'maybe she has skills.' They just have stereotypes—'ghetto black.'"

Racial Segregation and Mass Incarceration

Anasia, like many other women of color, grew up in a segregated community that had been systematically excluded from the economic and social opportunities of the late twentieth and early twenty-first centuries (Lipsitz 2012). Throughout the last decades of the twentieth century and into the twenty-first, deindustrialization—the closing down of manufacturing jobs—has disproportionately impacted African Americans (Costa Vargas 2006). By the second decade of the new millennium one-quarter of African Americans lived on incomes below the federal poverty level (FPL, which in 2013 was an annual income of $11,490 for a single person and $23,550 for a family of four). This rate is twice that of white Americans living below the FPL (Macartney, Bishaw, & Fontenot 2013). Nationally, black women experience higher poverty rates than either white women or black men (Ezeala-Harrison 2010).

Historian George Lipsitz (2012) draws particular attention to the deleterious effects of race-based housing segregation. White flight to the suburbs, lax or nonexistent enforcement of fair housing laws, redlining, predatory lending, exclusionary zoning, real estate steering, and refusing to rent or sell to members of targeted groups, all produce and intensify racially segregated housing patterns.[2] Housing segregation promotes the concentration of poverty in neighborhoods inhabited largely by blacks and Latinos. Concentrations of poverty, in turn, propel inequalities in resources and services. Poor minority neighborhoods are characterized by underfunded schools, inadequate health care services, lack of reasonably priced nutritious food, overcrowding, air and noise pollution from factories and mass transit hubs, and crumbling buildings (Williams and Mohammed 2009; Osypuk and Acevedo-Garcia 2010). Rates of lead poisoning are higher in poor and black neighborhoods (Bullard 1994); in New York, a black child is 8.5 times more likely than a white child to be exposed to lead poisoning (Hanley 2008). Recent statistical research shows that while black youth continue to be arrested at rates substantially higher than those of their white peers, crime rates among black youth began to fall vis-à-vis white youth when, in the wake of removal of lead from gasoline in 1988–1991, the difference in rates of elevated lead levels fell from six times higher for black children to "only" three times higher (Nevin 2013).

***

By the time Anasia was a teenager, both unemployment and the crack epidemic had begun to sweep through inner-city neighborhoods, and her two older brothers were incarcerated for drug involvement. "Crack was a marketing innovation" of the mid-1980s (Reinarman and Levine 1997). Powder cocaine, which had been around for decades, was expensive. But processed into the more powerful smokable form of crack cocaine, the drug could be sold on the street in small quantities to residents of impoverished inner-city neighborhoods. This marketing innovation succeeded, in part because of the availability of a huge workforce of unemployed young people ready to take jobs in the new, neighborhood-based business of crack preparation and sales (Reinarman and Levine 1997). This was an unemployed workforce that, as discussed in chapter 2, had been created by neoliberal "trickle down" policies, incentives to move factories overseas, and disinvestment from working-class communities.

Although the so-called War on Drugs was launched well before the crack cocaine innovation (see chapter 7), it has resulted in unprecedented rates of imprisonment in black communities. George Lipsitz argues that mandatory sentencing, harsher sentences for crack cocaine than for powder cocaine possession, more severe penalties for minor crimes, and "stop and frisk" policies "emerged as part of a counterrevolution against the democratic and egalitarian reforms of the mid-twentieth century that made more rights available to more people—as a result of the civil rights movement. This counterrevolution has used moral panics about crime as an ideological tool to reduce the number of rights-bearing citizens, to stigmatize members of aggrieved social groups, and to prevent workers from bargaining freely over wages and working conditions by rendering them displaceable, disposable, and deportable" (Lipsitz 2012). Mass incarceration is thus "linked to goals of maintaining inequality, scapegoating marginalized groups, and promoting economic benefit for social, political, and corporal elites" (Richie 2012, p. 21).

In the propaganda of the War on Drugs, the human face of both the victims and the dealers are disproportionately black or brown. Judith Scully (2002) traces public comments made by President George H. W. Bush, a central figure during a key period of the War on Drugs, in which he declared—and journalists reiterated—that the drug problem in America is most severe in public housing projects (a euphemism for the black community). Bush's own drug policy director, William J. Bennett, acknowledged that this was not the case; that the typical drug user is a white male who graduated from high school, is employed, and does not live in the inner city. "Consistent with this philosophy," however, Scully notes, "the nation's war on drugs has focused almost exclusively on low-level dealers and users in African-American neighborhoods. Police find drugs in these communities because that is where they look for them. Had they pointed the war at college campuses, it is likely that American jails would now be filled overwhelmingly with white university students who are both using and selling drugs" (2002, p. 59).

Black Americans are far more likely than white Americans to be incarcerated. Nationally, in December 2012, 463 out of every 100,00 white men; 2,841 out of every 100,000 black men; and 1,158 out of every 100,000 Hispanic men were incarcerated. The numbers for women, while smaller, reflect the same racial profile: .49 per 100,000 white women; 115 per 100,000 black women; and 64 per 100,000 Hispanic women are incarcerated (Carson & Golinelli 2013). Racial inequalities within the correctional system start early. African American girls are less likely to be diverted from the criminal system into educational or therapeutic programs; they receive the least amount of lenient treatment for offenses; and they are half as likely as female white youth to have the charges against them dismissed (American Bar Association & National Bar Association 2001).[3]

Anasia

Once Anasia had finished the program at the halfway house where she had been living when we first met her, she moved into what is called a sober house (in this case, overpriced rooms rented to "recovering addicts"). For Anasia, a woman who prided herself on her neatly cut short hair, nicely pressed jeans, and well-groomed appearance, the sober house was "chaos." It was actually more of a "crack house." Anasia explained: "[I] just lived there and got high. It is a disgusting place. You never know if a bullet is going to come through the wall. It is one street away from last week's murders. I was on that street earlier in the evening. Now I just make sure I go to the next street. All that goes on there is drug stuff. People get real touchy when you are messing with their money and there is a lot of money to be made." After the crack house, "I was staying at my sisters for a while, but she was shooting drugs, and I had to get away from all that. It's a mess."

Without access to a decent education or to social networks of people working in good jobs, Anasia's employment options were limited. Throughout her adult life, Anasia moved between shoplifting and prostitution, and legal jobs in stores and nursing homes. A few years after we first met her, a white friend helped her get a job as a home health aide for a physically disabled woman who needed a great deal of lifting. The job paid $11.60 an hour, with no benefits. Anasia quit the job when her employer called her "nigger." We have never seen Anasia as angry as she was the day she told us about this. "If she did not like the way I was working, that would be one thing. No one calls me a nigger." The woman apologized and asked her to come back, but Anasia had no interest in "wiping the behind" of an overt racist.

A year or so after the home health aide incident, she worked at a department store until she was caught stealing. But in truth, Anasia confided, she would not have lasted much longer in the job anyway. With arthritis in both hips and both knees, she has trouble walking and standing. "Arthritis from too many burglaries, too much running from the police, too much jumping out windows, and too much drug use." Doctors have told her she needs to have surgery, but she can't afford not to work, so she keeps delaying the surgery. In the meantime, any legal jobs she can get involve lifting heavy people or boxes, exacerbating her health challenges. Nonlegal sources of income, of course, increase her risk of being arrested; each arrest adds to her criminal record, further constraining her job options and further locking her into the caste of the ill and afflicted.

Racist attitudes and practices take a toll. Nationally, among blacks, infant mortality rates are higher and adult life expectancy is lower than for whites at all levels of income and education. Death rates among African Americans are higher than among white Americans for most of the fifteen leading causes of death; this disparity has persisted over time, and in some aspects (most notably infant mortality) has widened (Williams & Mohammed 2009; CDC 2011; MacDorman & Mathews 2011). Blacks are also more likely than whites to live with chronic pain (Massoglia 2008b). Anasia's experience as a home health aide to a racist client helps explain these disparities. Not only are her hips, knees, and back worn down by years of lifting heavy patients, but her sense of being in the world is worn down by the insults, fears, indignities, and worries of living with racism. For Anasia, as for millions of Americans, both the material conditions of poverty and the stress of persistent discrimination damage the cardiovascular and immune systems, weakening the body's ability to fight off disease and sometimes leading to unhealthy behaviors such as smoking in order to manage the pain and stress (Braveman et al. 2010; Olshansky et al. 2012; Pascoe & Richman 2009; Williams & Mohammed 2009). Given the disproportionate rates of incarcerating Americans of color, it is worth emphasizing that the health status of blacks relative to whites has worsened during the period of mass incarceration (Sabol 2011).

Intersections of Race and Gender, Part 2

Throughout American history black women's bodies—and especially their sexuality—have been targeted for control, exploitation, and assault. Under slavery white men literally owned black women's bodies; a slave woman's children did not belong to her, and rape of a black slave by a white "owner" was not considered a crime. To the contrary, it was an integral component of the master-slave relationship both in terms of producing more slaves to work the land and in terms of enforcing gender and racial hierarchies (Roberts 1997). In the twentieth-century, myths about black women's hypersexuality were used to justify involuntary sterilization and medical experimentation (Roberts 1997). As we discuss in chapter 2, late-twentieth-century and early-twenty-first-century welfare policy as articulated in the Personal Responsibility and Work Opportunity Act institutionalizes thinly disguised ideas that poor and black women do not control their fertility properly and so need to be regulated via policies such family caps on welfare eligibility. By the end of the twentieth century the myth of "crack babies" born to irresponsible black mothers ("crack whores") captured the American imagination and was driven by media reports predicting that the United States would shortly face an unprecedented crisis of babies who, due to prenatal cocaine exposure, would be born with terrible cognitive impairments that would require lifelong support from the state. The feared "crack babies" never materialized; studies show that use of crack by pregnant women actually did not give rise to predicted developmental and other disabilities in the infants born to these women (Hallam Hurt, cited in FitzGerald 2013). Yet these ideas continue to drive public beliefs and policies.

Except during the height of the "crack baby" moral panic, greater attention has been given to the mass incarceration of black men than of black women, both within the black community and in the white-dominated media. While black men are portrayed as "gangstas" and "gangbangers," black women are cast as "welfare queens." In reality, the white women of our project tended to use far more social services than did the black women. Still, we occasionally heard a white woman make thinly veiled racist comments about "those people" who "cheat the system and collect welfare and drive Cadillacs." Though derogatory (implying welfare fraud and low-level criminality), the term *welfare queen* also suggests that the state helps black women and even that it has generously stepped in and filled the shoes of black husbands and fathers who are too unreliable to care for their own families. Casting the state as savior of black women, of course, obscures the reality that in urban black neighborhoods affected by mass incarceration, large numbers of men exit prison to find that their criminal records bar them from ever obtaining employment in the legal economy and that they are permanently unable to afford stable housing or to support their families.

As Lipsitz explains (2012, p. 68), "Black women and Latinas endure injustices on their own, but they also suffer from the neighborhood race effects and collateral consequences of the mass incarceration of black and Latino men." Mass incarceration disrupts gender balances in ways that may allow the smaller number of men remaining in the community to exert greater power in their relationships with women, including the power to demand multiple sexual partners (Thomas & Torrone, 2006).[4] The consequences for black women are multifaceted. Drawn into what Beth Richie (2012, p. 36) calls the "trap of loyalty," black women live with the obligation to buffer their families from the impact of racism in the public sphere; pressure to live up to expectations that they as black women will better withstand abuse and mistreatment than other people; and acceptance of community rhetoric that claims that black women are in a more privileged position than black men.

Anasia's experiences with men during the years we have known her attest to these challenges. One day, over a cheeseburger and Pepsi, she told us that she had started going out with Jack. "He is a really nice guy," she said. "He is a Reverend! He used drugs when he was younger, then went to prison for a long time. He is very smart, and went to school and everything. He has been drug free a long time." Anasia continued to sing Jack's praises for another year or so. Then, over another cheeseburger and Pepsi, she announced that she was done with Jack. "He was screwing around. I don't need that." For a few months Anasia did not hear from Jack. And then she reported, "Jack just got out of jail. I don't know what he was in for. I want nothing to do with him. It was all lies anyway. I am done with him. He called yesterday, and I told him I was done with him. He didn't seem to believe it."

A year or so later Anasia became involved with another man. Before long she let us know, "My new boyfriend is in the hospital. He was beaten up and has broken ribs and cuts on his head. I sure can pick 'em, can't I? He drinks and gets drunk and picked a fight with a guy. He won that one, but then some of the guy's friends jumped him and beat him up. Now his family wants to come and get the guys who beat him up." This feud put Anasia in danger. Black women, in particular, suffer from assaults that are extensions of hostility between men (Richie 2012, p. 38).

In her own way, Anasia has explained to us that immersion of large numbers of black men in hypermasculine prison environments exacerbates sexual violence both inside and outside of prison. Indeed, studies show that communities with high rates of unemployed, insecurely housed, and formerly incarcerated residents tend to suffer high rates of street violence, increasing the chances that women and girls will be sexually assaulted (Coker et al. 2011). Beth Richie (2012, esp. p. 43) documents particularly high rates of sexual violence, including remarkably brutal forms of violence (multiple perpetrators, use of weapons or objects) carried out against black women by black men. And data indicate that while mandatory arrest policies for domestic violence may sometimes serve as a deterrent for men who feel that they have something to lose by being incarcerated, men with little to lose, socially and economically, often become more violent in response to arrest (Mills 2003). Coming full circle, black women are disproportionately likely to be evicted from their housing by landlords in the wake of calling the police to intervene in situations of domestic violence (Desmond & Valdez 2012).

Four years after first meeting Anasia, we asked her how she feels her life has been affected by her childhood experiences of racism in the Boston housing projects.

> Yes, there was a lot of people who hated blacks and would pick on me, but I don't think being black was what made a difference in my life. There is a lot of racism, and not all blacks end up like me. I made my own choices—bad choices—but they were my own. Yes, I guess some of the schools that I went to until I quit could have been better, but again, not everyone that went to that school ended up in prison. I just made my own path. What is interesting is that my best friends have almost always been white. Even in the housing project, my best friend was white. Even now my best friend is white. I don't really see them as white, but as who they are. I guess I do have some prejudices, like against Puerto Ricans. Where my mom lives is now all Puerto Rican. Since they have moved in, the place has really gone downhill.
>
> There is still a lot of racism, but you just deal with it, you live with it. Like when Obama was inaugurated, only the black women [in the rehabilitation facility where we first met her] watched it on the TV. One of the other black women saw that all the white women in the house had left the room. Later one of the white women said, "Hey, we should have something for St Patrick's Day," and I thought they sure didn't make a suggestion for Martin Luther King Day. It is there and it's everywhere, but you just keep on . . . you notice, but what are you going to do? If I had said anything about MLK, that woman would not have understood . . . . I don't think the police are racist . . . . At least with me. There are probably some who are. But they know me very well. All the police in town know me. I did the crime and I got caught. When they arrest me, they know me. The last time they simply said, "It is time to come in, Anasia," and I knew. It wasn't like they were targeting me but more like they knew I was playing fast and loose way too often, and it was time for me to stop it. The same with the courts. They have given me many, many chances. I once stayed clean for over two years and then used again, and then they give me another chance.

Whether Anasia truly believes what she told us about race or whether she told us what she believed we wanted to hear,[5] it is clear that she is well versed in the popular American script that attributes suffering to one's own bad choices and character defects. Even when acknowledging that racism is "everywhere," the example she offers has to do with the ignorance of a couple of homeless, marginalized white women regarding a particular individual—Martin Luther King, Jr. The police, in contrast, she described as not racially biased—a description that begs explanation in light of well-known practices of racial profiling and the obvious overrepresentation of black men and women in jails and prisons.

For the women in this project, gender typically seems to trump race. Race is not institutionally labeled in the way that gender is. Prisons, homeless shelters, and rehabilitation programs are not officially racially segregated, but they are officially gender segregated. Being a victim of gendered violence is a recognized status both in the correctional system and in the social welfare and therapeutic systems; being a victim of racism is not. Gendered explanations for women's misery are preached and drilled in the many facilities and programs in which women serve time. Racial explanations, if mentioned at all, are likely dismissed as "playing the race card."

Like Anasia, few of the project women—black or white—make much reference to race or racism. Melanie, a white woman who has been both a longtime client and, recently, a caseworker on the institutional circuit, mused that in her experience, "in the system, race doesn't really matter. What matters is shady cops who make women do things [have sex] with them or they turn them in." Perhaps, as Michelle Alexander (2012) points out, the supposed race neutrality of the War on Drugs makes it hard for society to see the racism that drives disparities in rates of arrest and punishment. Perhaps we Americans want to believe that racism (like other attitudes underlying hate crimes) denotes individual "bad" behavior rather than policies and attitudes that are core aspects of our history and social structure. Because racism is deeply embedded in American culture, it persists in institutions even when individuals do not profess racist attitudes (Williams & Mohammed 2009). Perhaps people such as Anasia and Melanie grow up in circumstances in which racism is so much a part of the air they breathe that they come to take it for granted, and it becomes hard to see as a distinct and nameable phenomenon.

Tonya, who was raised in a middle-class black family, is the only project participant who consistently offered race-based observations and interpretations. When we asked her why, in her opinion, other women seem tuned out to racism, she mulled the question over and replied that men's prisons are very racially divided but women's prisons are not. After giving examples of the race-based gangs and violence in men's prisons, Tonya explained that in women's prisons, "everyone is involved with everyone else, except for some of the Spanish-speaking women who keep to themselves." While racial tensions pop up from time to time, they rarely if ever resemble the overt racial hostility and violence that are characteristic of men's prisons. On another occasion we chatted with Tonya about race and mass incarceration. Her response echoed mainstream public discourse: black men are overincarcerated, not black women. While black men are seen as racial victims of mass incarcerations, the criminalization of black women tends to be ignored.

In real life, race and gender identities are never separate. Anasia is always both a black person and a woman, and the lived experiences of her blackness are gendered as much as her lived experiences as a woman are racialized. These two identities are mutually constitutive and structured in dominance.[6] The fact is that Anasia is more likely to be arrested and incarcerated than her white female counterparts, *and* she is more likely than her black male counterparts to be sexually assaulted and to be sent to so-called therapeutic programs in which she is taught that her problems lie within her own "victim mentality." Certainly at this point in her life Anasia feels that changing her own behavior seems more possible than changing racist beliefs, practices, and policies over which she has little control.

The neoliberal doctrine of personal responsibility that is drilled and drilled again in both correctional and therapeutic institutions serves to obscure racism and other structural causes of suffering from public consciousness. It seems to us that the valorization of personal responsibility in and of itself indexes culturally persistent racist images of dark-skinned people as "lazy" and "childlike" (Gilens 1999). Put differently, the language of personal responsibility has come to stand in for explicit references to race in an era in which we, as a society, would like to believe that we have put our history of racism behind us. Our cultural taboo on using the "*N*-word" or making explicitly racist comments does not mean that institutionalized racism has disappeared. To the contrary, in this age of mass incarceration, the structural manifestations of racism have escalated. As is disproportionately the case for black Americans, Anasia received a substandard education in a neighborhood with substandard apartment buildings housing a population that suffered from high rates of illness and incarceration. Because these systems feed and reinforce each other, there were few opportunities for Anasia to avoid a fate shaped by racism. Anasia couldn't catch a break, not because she dodged personal responsibility for making good choices, but because the systemic forces that constrain her choices are so very strong.

ENDNOTES

1. Any race-based patterns that we identify among the women in this project must be understood in the broader context of overall higher rates of arrest and incarceration among African Americans vis-à-vis white Americans, despite research consistently showing that rates of drug abuse among whites are actually higher than among African Americans (L. T. Wu et al. 2011; Alexander 2012). Because the police as well as the courts seem slower to arrest and incarcerate white women, those white women who do end up in prison tend to be more troubled over longer periods of time than the black women.

2. Municipalities, counties, and states routinely ignore their legal obligations to affirmatively foster fair housing. As a consequence, even middle-class black families face barriers in moving away from poor and troubled neighborhoods (Lipsitz 2012).

3. In the first decade of the twenty-first century, for the first time in nearly forty years, there was a decline in the number of African Americans in prison—particularly African American women—and a steep rise in the number of white women going to prison. Among Hispanics the number of women imprisoned rose, and the number of men declined slightly (Mauer 2013).

4. This dynamic is, of course, exacerbated by broader social norms regarding racially segregated dating and family relationships. In particular, black women experience race-based exclusion from dating white men.

5. We are aware that women often told us what they thought we wanted to hear, and we believe that to be especially true in how black women spoke about race to us or in our presence. All of our interactions were shaped by the inequalities between the project women and us in power, status, class, and access to resources, and we are especially cognizant of the complexities of the racial dynamics and history of racism in the relationships between white researchers and black research subjects.

6. We thank George Lipsitz for this insight and wording.

Rural Poverty

THE GREAT RECESSION, RISING UNEMPLOYMENT, AND THE UNDER-UTILIZED SAFETY NET

by Jennifer Sherman

Jennifer Sherman, "Rural Poverty: The Great Recession, Rising Unemployment, and the Under-Utilized Safety Net," *Rural America In a Globalizing World*, ed. Conner Bailey, Leif Jensen and Elizabeth Ransom, pp. 523-539. Copyright © 2014 by West Virginia University Press. Reprinted with permission.

Introduction

In the first decade of the 2000s, rural America, like the rest of the United States, saw its fortunes rise and then fall on the wave of the Great Recession (Grusky, Western, and Wimer 2011), while it continued to struggle with ongoing issues including deindustrialization and the decline of manufacturing and many resource-based industries (Anderson and Weng 2011; Hamilton et al. 2008; Smith and Tickamyer 2011). As in previous decades, poverty has been a persistent problem throughout much of rural America, and overall nonmetropolitan[1] poverty rates have continued to be higher than metropolitan rates throughout the 2000s (Lichter and Graefe 2011, 28; Jensen, Mattingly, and Bean 2011; Farrigan 2010). Rural poverty rates fell in the 1990s, but began rising again in the 2000s, particularly since the 2008 recession and the resulting increase in unemployment (Jensen, Mattingly, and Bean 2011). By the end of the decade nonmetropolitan unemployment rates, which have long been higher than metropolitan rates, reached high levels not seen in more than twenty-five years—9.8 percent in 2009, versus 8.7 percent in metropolitan areas (McBride and Kemper 2009). In 2010, the overall nonmetropolitan poverty rate was 16.5 percent, compared to the metropolitan rate of 14.9 percent. Rural children had even higher poverty rates, at 24.4 percent versus the metropolitan rate of 21.6 percent (USDA Economic Research Service 2011).

Children growing up in poverty not only suffer in the short term, but "are less likely to become the productive adult workers, capable parents, and involved citizens," thus contributing to the future disadvantage of rural areas as well (O'Hare 2009, 3).

Poverty is not evenly distributed across rural America, however, and continues to be particularly severe and persistent in the South and West (Farrigan 2010), and to hit rural minority populations the hardest (Anderson and Weng 2011; Kandel et al. 2011; Lichter and Graefe 2011). Nonmetropolitan poverty rates at the end of the decade were over 30 percent for blacks and Native Americans, and 29.5 percent for Hispanics, versus 13.1 percent for whites (USDA Economic Research Service 2011). Factors contributing to rural poverty include economic and industrial restructuring, falling real wages, and increased unemployment, due to both the recession and larger global forces. The continued growth of neo-liberal ideologies and policies since the 1980s has been partly responsible for increasing "out-sourcing, privatization, and the growth of part-time and contingent employment" (Clawson and Clawson 1999, 101), and the weakening of worker protections and labor unions (Crow and Albo 2005), all of which have negatively impacted rural American workers and contributed to job losses and falling wages and benefits.

Rural poverty is exacerbated by migration patterns, including the out-migration of young, advantaged, and educated adults from rural communities and the in-migration of low-income populations, often in search of jobs, affordable housing, or lower costs of living (Carr and Kefalas 2009; Crowley, Lichter, and Qian 2006; Lichter and Graefe 2011;). The abilities of families to cope with and survive poverty are impacted by the specific cultural norms and community histories of rural places, which often influence the choices and options available within the context of small, isolated, and often tightly knit communities (Brown and Lichter 2004; Lichter and Graefe 2011; Nelson 2005; Pickering et al. 2006; Sherman 2006; 2009; Tickamyer and Henderson 2011). Academic researchers frequently focus on the structural causes of poverty, including policies, economic shifts, labor markets, and racism (Schiller 2007). However, cultural understandings throughout much of the rural United States, heavily influenced by neoliberal ideologies, tend to portray poverty as an individual shortcoming, thus adding social stigma to the challenges faced by the rural poor (Sherman and Sage 2011; Sherman 2006; 2009). In this chapter, I will examine the causes of and contributors to rural poverty in the 2000s. I will also discuss some of the outcomes of current rural poverty trends, focusing on the impacts of poverty on rural American families and their strategies for survival.

Industrial Restructuring, Employment, and Poverty

Nonmetropolitan poverty rates have been higher than metropolitan rates since the 1960s, when the official US poverty measure was first developed. The bulk of persistent poverty counties in the United States have been, and continue to be, nonmetropolitan (Farrigan 2010). Despite its disproportionate share of US poverty, rural poverty tends to be understudied, and thus both its causes and its dynamics are poorly understood. While many of the main causes of poverty, including deindustrialization, job loss, legacies of racism and discrimination, and lack of educational opportunities, are similar across diverse settings, the impacts and meanings of poverty are often distinct in rural America. In non-metropolitan America, it has long been common for poor families to include at least one working adult (Shapiro 1989), and the rural poor are more likely to be working than the urban poor (Anderson and Weng 2011). They are also less likely than the metropolitan poor to rely on cash aid, even when they qualify for it (Brown and Lichter 2004; Jensen et al. 2011; Lichter and Graefe 2011; Sherman 2006; 2009). The realities of rural poverty contrast sharply with the common stereotypes of the poor as lazy, immoral, and dependent on "entitlements" (Hays 2003).

In order to understand rural poverty, it is thus important to begin by looking at the labor markets and economies of rural places. According to Pickering et al. (2006, 1), many rural American adults struggle to find or keep jobs, "because local formal economies and labor markets are generally weak, systems of education are poor, transportation is difficult, child care is hard to come by, and levels of human capital are extremely low." Rural America is of course not monolithic, and includes different types of communities with different economic prospects. Hamilton et al. (2008) argue that recent social and economic trends have resulted in the formation of distinct types of rural places, each with a different set of economic trajectories and conditions. These ideal types of rural communities lie on a spectrum, from amenity-rich communities seeing growth in tourism-related industries and in-migration by affluent professionals and retirees, to chronically poor communities with depleted resources, "dysfunctional services, inadequate infrastructure, and ineffective or corrupt leadership" (Hamilton et al. 2008, 6). In the middle are communities with declining resources, many of which have seen their fortunes and economies shrink further over the past decade as the recession increased the pace of industrial losses. Throughout rural America, the last decade has seen the forces of globalization and deindustrialization continue to replace "good jobs" with "bad" ones (Nelson and Smith 1999), as the service sector has come to replace manufacturing and resource-based industries as the main source of employment in most rural American communities (Brown and Schafft 2011; Hamilton et al. 2008; Lichter and Graefe 2011; Smith and Tickamyer 2011).

The growth of the service sector relative to manufacturing and resource-based industries has been one of the largest contributors to working poverty in rural America (Lichter and Graefe 2011; Jensen and Jensen 2011). Other sectors have declined for multiple reasons, most importantly global competition in the form of lower prices or wages overseas. The success of the neoliberal agenda has resulted in decreasing trade restrictions throughout the world and the widespread belief that such deregulation is necessary for capitalist enterprises to flourish (Clawson and Clawson 1999). Loosening regulations have allowed companies to shift manufacturing to less-developed nations where labor and raw materials are cheaper. Much natural resource extraction has also been moved to other countries, where labor and materials are less expensive and environmental regulation weaker. Even agriculture has not been immune to the forces of globalization, as the industry continues to consolidate into fewer and larger farms, due in large degree to national and international policies that favor corporate farming and the globalization of farm commodity markets (Lichter and Graefe 2011). Although these trends predate the recession, the economic downturn hastened the pace of job losses in these industries.

As manufacturing and resource-based jobs have dried up across the rural United States, they have been replaced mostly by service-sector jobs that are more difficult to outsource. However, unlike the work that they often replace, service-sector jobs by and large do not pay living wages, provide full-time employment, or come with benefits such as health care. They are also rarely unionized, thus allowing employers to erode worker protections and other gains made by manufacturing workers over the previous century. The growing popularity of neo-liberal doctrines has provided employers with a favorable political environment in which to push for policies that further weaken unions (Albo 2009). Union density in the United States peaked at nearly 32 percent in 1955, but since the early 1980s, "union density declined precipitously, falling to 13.5 percent in 2001" (Crow and Albo 2005, 16). Much of this loss of union power is associated with the growth of the service sector (Albo 2009; Clawson and Clawson 1999; Crow and Albo 2005). While the service sector has grown throughout the United States, the lack of diversity in rural labor markets and economies often means that when a local industry declines, there are few other sources of employment outside of service jobs, and fewer chances for displaced workers to find new jobs that pay as well as those they lost. Compared to metropolitan workers, workers in nonmetropolitan communities are more likely to be concentrated in low-wage service jobs (Brown and Schafft 2011), which contributes heavily to the lower average wages and higher working poverty in rural areas compared to urban and suburban workers (Smith and Tickamyer 2011; Lichter and Graefe 2011).

Deindustrialization and the growth of the service sector have also contributed to changes in the gender makeup of the rural workforce. As Sachs discusses in the framing chapter to this section, rural job losses during the economic downturn have tended to impact men more heavily than women, because men held a disproportionate share of the lost jobs (Jensen and Jensen 2011). This can be particularly difficult for men because rural cultural norms frequently construct masculinity around work in specific types of manual labor (Sherman 2006; 2009), exemplified by the land-based industries upon which a particular community's economy is centered. When jobs in these industries disappear, rural men often struggle to remain in the workforce, as the service sector jobs that remain represent losses both in terms of income and in terms of acceptability and masculinity. Many service sector jobs, including those in care-based industries but also many retail positions, tend to be seen as more appropriate for women, and thus as emasculating for many rural men. To take such jobs can add a level of shame and a loss of both masculine identity and self-esteem for men whose lives have been spent in a traditionally masculine local industry. Thus, many rural men's own cultural norms make it difficult for them to accept jobs in service and care-work industries (Sherman 2009). The result is that many rural communities have experienced not only losses of income, but also changes in the gendered nature of work as deindustrialization occurs.

Even in communities with more traditional and conservative cultural norms, in which men are expected to be the main breadwinners and women the homemakers, it is often the case that women will take on part-time work in service jobs before men will accept feminized positions (Nelson and Smith 1999; Sherman 2009; Smith 2011). Evidence of these trends is seen in the rural workforce participation rates, which are lower for rural men than urban men (Hamilton et al. 2008; Jensen and Jensen 2011; Mattingly, Smith, and Bean 2011). These differences have persisted through the recession, even though unemployment has risen sharply in urban America (McBride and Kemper 2009). Meanwhile, rural women's employment rose until about 2000, and then began declining into the recession along with men's (Smith 2011), but their contributions still grew as a share of total family earnings, particularly since the recession (Smith 2011).

These changes in the gender structures of rural labor markets have several implications that can add to the problems poor rural families face. The emotional struggles that unemployment can create for rural men whose identities have long been tied to their roles as workers and bread-winners can negatively impact families in multiple ways that threaten the stability of romantic partnerships (Sherman 2009). This may contribute to marital instability and the growth of single parenting that is associated with poverty in rural communities (Hamilton et al. 2008).

In addition, women's jobs generally tend to be poorly paid relative to men's, and thus the rise in female workforce participation has not been sufficient to make up for the lost male income. Particularly when women are relied on as the main or sole breadwinners, families are more likely to experience poverty and low incomes, and increased reliance on women workers has contributed to the growth of rural poverty (Anderson and Weng 2011; Lichter and Graefe 2011). Given the strain that male job loss puts on families, the recession and continued deindustrialization will likely contribute to even more households relying on women's incomes, putting more rural families at risk for working poverty.

These employment trends, which have been ongoing for decades but were exacerbated by the recession, suggest that rural populations will likely continue to experience hardships into the next decade. Although by 2010 experts believed that the recession had peaked (Grusky et al. 2011), there has not yet been significant recovery in rural America. Research from previous recessions suggests that rural employment may be slower to recover than that in urban and suburban places (Parker, Kusmin, and Marre 2010), and thus it may be years before we see sufficient economic growth and development to replace significant numbers of living wage jobs in rural areas. As I have illustrated in this section, there are not enough jobs to go around, and the work opportunities that do exist are increasingly failing to protect rural families from poverty. Furthermore, changes in the gendered nature of work will continue to influence rural families in new ways, and more research is needed to fully understand their long-term impacts on the structures and survival strategies of rural families.

Regional Differences, Migration, and the Exacerbation of Rural Poverty

Although deindustrialization and its results have been contributing to high unemployment and poverty throughout rural America during the last decade, the severity of problems varies by region and race or ethnic group. Poverty rates tend to be lower in the rural Midwest and Northeast because of the relative stability of the farm economy and the growth of high-tech industries in these regions (Anderson and Weng 2011). Rural communities in the South and West, on the other hand, tend to have the highest poverty rates, and wages and incomes tend to be lowest, particularly for African Americans, Native Americans, and Hispanics (Anderson and Weng 2011). These two regions also have the highest concentrations of minority groups, whose poverty tends to be both persistent and concentrated (Lichter and Graefe 2011). Poverty is an enduring problem for minority populations because their education levels tend to be lower and their unemployment rates tend to be higher (Jensen and Jensen 2011; Kandel et al. 2011; Smith 2011), due to both the dynamics of regional labor markets and the enduring effects of racism that continue to disadvantage minority groups relative to whites. Regional differences in rural poverty rates are due to a complex combination of factors that includes the specific economies of different communities and population dynamics that cause some rural places to have greater or lesser concentrations of people whose race and/or lack of education put them at a disadvantage in the workforce.

Migration patterns and population dynamics have also exacerbated poverty in many rural American communities by contributing to the lack of workers with necessary levels of human capital. Rural communities are often hurt by the out-migration of more advantaged young adults in search of educational and employment opportunities elsewhere, known as the "brain-drain" phenomenon (Carr and Kefalas 2009). Rural areas have experienced slower growth than the rest of the United States—2.9 percent growth in rural counties versus 9.1 percent in the country as a whole between 2000 and 2009—due in large part to the loss of young adults (Gallardo 2010a; 2010b). The brain-drain problem tends to disproportionately impact those communities that are already the most disadvantaged, where lack of employment, education, and training opportunities leave young adults with little chance of finding decent long-term work close to home. The worse off the economy and labor market of a community, the more likely it is to lose its more talented and ambitious young adults. This phenomenon means that many of the most impoverished rural communities are further disadvantaged in that their remaining residents tend to be older and less educated, and their labor pools lack younger and better educated and trained workers. During the past decade, out-migration and brain drain have been particularly severe problems for declining and poor rural communities (Carr and Kefalas 2009; Hamilton et al. 2008).

At the same time, over the past decade in-migration into poor rural communities has often failed to improve their residents' fortunes substantially. Although in some rural communities in-migrants are welcomed for their potential to counteract the impacts of out-migration and brain drain, newcomers frequently differ substantially from the more advantaged residents who have left (Clark 2012). Often in-migrants to poor rural communities are poor themselves, drawn to struggling communities in search of low-cost housing and living (Clark 2012; Sherman 2009). These new low-income residents can be a drain on existing resources, including local schools and social services (Sherman and Sage 2011). Many long-time residents also complain that recent in-migrants, particularly those who are poor, are less likely to actively participate in the community (Sherman and Sage 2011; Sherman 2009), leaving rural communities with growing social problems but declining capacities for addressing them.

Many rural communities, particularly in the Southwest and West, have also attracted substantial numbers of recent immigrants from Latin America and Mexico in search of jobs in agriculture, food processing, construction, and other industries (Crowley et al. 2006; Crowley and Lichter 2009; Lichter and Graefe 2011; Schmalzbauer 2011). As Sachs notes in the introductory chapter to this section, these trends have been accelerated by NAFTA and its negative impacts on Mexican workers. Although they may be attracted to rural communities for the same lifestyle reasons that appeal to both long-standing residents and non-Hispanic newcomers,[2] Latino immigrants are frequently treated as unwelcome outsiders (Crowley and Lichter 2009; Schmalzbauer 2011; Sherman 2009). Often coming with low education levels and cultural and linguistic barriers that set them apart from long-time community residents, these recent immigrants also may contribute to declines in community cohesion, as many long-term residents are reluctant to accept the culturally distinct newcomers (Crowley et al. 2006; Crowley and Lichter 2009). They are also frequently blamed for strains on local services, although researchers have found little evidence that the growth in rural immigrant populations is directly correlated with increased demands on services (Crowley and Lichter 2009). Their propensity for working does not protect immigrant populations from poverty, however, as they are preferred for the lowest paid jobs such as agriculture and service, further contributing to rural working poverty (Crowley et al. 2006). Researchers have expressed concern that the influx of poor immigrants may be turning some rural communities into "rural ghettos," "that impede rather than promote incorporation into American society" (see also Crowley et al. 2006; Lichter and Graefe 2011, 36).

With regard to in- and out-migration, there is still much left unknown, particularly with regard to the long-term impacts of immigrant settlements in rural communities. It is also important to note that with regard to this issue the method of inquiry can influence findings, as rural residents in ethnographic studies have long been found to overstate the negative impacts of in-migration, as well as the degree to which their home communities are attracting low-income newcomers (Crowley and Lichter 2009; Fitchen 1991; Sherman 2009). While there is strong evidence that in- and out-migration trends are exacerbating the poverty of many of the most disadvantaged rural places, and are further contributing to the persistent and concentrated poverty of rural minority groups (Crowley et al. 2006), much additional research is necessary to improve our understandings of the impacts of recent demographic changes.

Surviving Poverty in Rural America

The result of all of the trends discussed above is that many rural families are living close to or below the poverty line and face growing challenges to meeting their own basic needs. Living in poverty is difficult regardless of the setting, but rural communities offer unique barriers to, as well as opportunities for, coping with poverty. When the formal labor market fails to provide either enough jobs or enough income for families to survive, they are faced with a set of tough choices, among them formal aid from government and charitable sources; reliance on social networks including friends, family, and community; and informal work activities that either bring in extra (unreported) income or provide for other basic needs such as food or fuel (Brown and Lichter 2004; Lichter and Graefe 2011; Nelson 2005; Sherman 2006; 2009; Tickamyer and Henderson 2011). The degree to which poor rural families rely on different survival strategies varies according to their circumstances, including local cultural norms and values; size and relative isolation of their communities; available social networks; and constraints of time, knowledge, and physical ability. As I will illustrate in this section, despite the belief in many rural communities that poor in-migrants choose rural settings for the relative ease they provide to those living on restricted incomes, in many ways rural communities come with more challenges and fewer acceptable survival strategies for coping with poverty than do urban communities.

It is often assumed that the poor rely heavily on Temporary Aid to Needy Families (TANF, also known as welfare) in order to survive, and in the United States there is much concern about poor families becoming "dependent" on this aid, which many believe undermines work ethics and moral values (Hays 2003; Sherman 2009). As discussed above, rural poor families are more likely to be working than are non-rural poor families. However, even when they are not working, poor rural families face many barriers to TANF receipt, making them less likely to rely on this form of aid even when they are in need of it. TANF rates are lower in rural areas than in urban (Brown and Lichter 2004; Lichter and Graefe 2011), and have fallen precipitously since welfare reform in 1996 (Jensen et al. 2011). Jensen et al. (2011, 1) find that even the recession has not significantly increased the rate of rural welfare receipt, and "in 2009, just over 11 percent of poor rural families reported receiving any income from TANF, as compared to nearly 14 percent of poor urban families." Thus in rural areas TANF provides less of a safety net for poor families than in other parts of the United States.

The reasons for the lower rural rates of TANF receipt are manifold and difficult to pinpoint. Several researchers have looked in depth at the impact of welfare reform in rural areas, particularly with regard to work requirements in places with very tight labor markets. They find that welfare reform has made the receipt of aid difficult for families in these types of communities, where fulfilling work requirements often requires long commutes to places with jobs. Commutes can be a serious hardship for poor rural families, who often do not have reliable vehicles, and who frequently live in areas without adequate public transportation (Parisi et al. 2011). However, there is evidence that in the past decade there has been greater workforce participation by rural women alongside falling TANF receipt rates, which suggests that TANF's new restrictions may have succeeded to some degree in pushing poor rural women off of aid and into the labor force (Tickamyer and Henderson 2011). Other researchers question whether welfare reform really had much of an impact on rural populations at all however, arguing that even before TANF, welfare generally was inadequate and used "only temporarily to deal with short-term emergencies" (Pickering et al. 2006, 4). Nonetheless, there is some consensus that welfare reform has made it more difficult for rural families to receive and stay on this form of aid, and that the new requirements have resulted in more sanctions and fewer opportunities for education and job training than were available under the previous program (Pickering et al. 2006).

In addition to the bureaucratic and structural constraints to welfare receipt in rural communities, there is also evidence that cultural norms and social stigma play important roles in discouraging rural families from seeking out this form of aid (Brown and Lichter 2004; Lichter and Graefe 2011; Sherman 2006; 2009). Rural cultural norms often stress the importance of hard work, self-sufficiency, and independence (Nelson 2005; Nelson and Smith 1999; Sherman 2006; 2009). Because of welfare's association with laziness, dependency, and moral degeneracy—the antithesis of these values—rural welfare recipients are often judged as undeserving and immoral by others in their communities. High social cohesion and lack of anonymity in rural communities can exacerbate this stigma and its impacts on poor residents, who often refuse this form of aid in order to avoid judgment by community members and exclusion from social networks (Sherman 2006; 2009). The degree to which this stigma applies to other forms of need-based government aid appears to vary by community and cultural norms, as well as by time period. While some research has found a similar tendency for rural families to avoid food stamps in order to minimize stigma (Sherman 2009), there is evidence that Supplemental Nutrition Assistance Program (SNAP, the current version of food stamps) rates have been rising in rural areas since the recession (Bean 2011).

While TANF and SNAP are often highly stigmatized in rural communities, other government aid programs, with either stricter eligibility requirements or clearer ties to prior or current work activity, seem to be preferred. Because of its obvious connection to previous work, aid in the form of unemployment insurance appears to come with less stigma in rural communities, particularly when jobs are scarce or a major local employer suddenly shuts down. In these cases, recipients often see the aid as "earned" or "deserved," and portray themselves as distinctly different from the undeserving recipients of welfare (Sherman 2006; 2009). Disability assistance in the form of Supplemental Security Income (SSI) also is preferred to welfare in many rural communities, often because of the perceived connections between disabilities and prior work activities in dangerous local industries (Pickering et al. 2006; Sherman 2006; 2009). While also less stigmatized because of its tie to labor market activity, the Earned Income Tax Credit is underutilized in rural areas compared to urban (Parisi et al. 2011).

For rural poor families who want to avoid the stigma of welfare and food stamps but do not qualify for less stigmatized forms of aid, options for survival are limited in rural areas. Resources like food banks and homeless shelters are often minimal (or non-existent) in rural communities, as are other types of private, nonprofit support for struggling individuals and families (Whitley 2013). On the other hand, many rural communities offer numerous options for enterprising individuals to enhance their subsistence through informal work and self-provisioning activities such as hunting, fishing, cutting or gathering wood, and growing gardens. Many researchers have noted rural poor families' heavy reliance on these sorts of informal activities as sources of income, as well as well-developed systems of barter with friends, family, and neighbors (Lichter and Graefe 2011; Nelson 2005; Sherman 2006; 2009; Tickamyer and Henderson 2011). Unlike public sources of aid, self-provisioning activities are generally socially and culturally prized in rural communities, and many people who are not poor also engage in significant amounts of informal work as sports or hobbies, or simply as part of a rural lifestyle (Sherman 2006; 2009). These types of informal self-provisioning activities can greatly enhance rural poor families' subsistence while simultaneously helping them to maintain self-respect and social standing within their communities.

Yet, informal work activities are not equally available to all rural poor families, and can be particularly difficult for the elderly and disabled, those who lack social ties, or single parents with young children (Whitley 2013). Nelson (2005) notes that the ability to engage in self-provisioning activities is gendered, and that most of these activities are generally done by men, not women, in rural communities. She finds that single mothers by and large do not engage in self-provisioning activities, despite their disproportionate likelihood of poverty, because they lack skills, time, energy, and help with childcare (Nelson 2005). Left with fewer options for informal subsistence activities, single mothers are more likely to rely heavily on their social networks, which often can create additional stress as they work to manage obligations and avoid conflict (Nelson 2005). The ability to mobilize social networks for support can also be dependent on the level of local community cohesion and an individual's or family's history and social standing, and in some tightly knit communities those who are seen as less morally upstanding are less likely to receive informal help from family and community (Sherman and Sage 2011; Sherman 2006). Unfortunately, often the deepest social divisions are found in the poorest communities, leading to lack of cooperation and support for those at the bottom of the social hierarchy (Hamilton et al. 2008; Sherman 2009). Thus, reliance on both self-provisioning and social networks is generally more common among those poor rural residents who are relatively better off in terms of health, family structure, and social integration. Poor individuals and families who lack these types of advantages are left with few survival options besides the stigma and bureaucratic hurdles of the formal safety net. Receipt of formal aid, which seldom provides enough for poor families' survival, also serves to further diminish their moral worth in the eyes of the larger communities in which recipients reside, and thus often leads to even greater social isolation, which can diminish their options for coping with poverty even further.

Beyond the safety net are illegal activities, which are also often highly stigmatized and generally understudied in the rural context. While it has long been understood that production of certain illegal substances, most notably marijuana and methamphetamines, is common in rural areas (Donnermeyer and Tunnell 2007), their role in the economies of struggling rural communities has rarely been studied, in contrast with the substantial body of literature that investigates illegal activities in urban settings. Most existing rural research on illegal substances has focused on use and abuse rather than production and sales, and thus little is known about the role that illegal drugs play as income generation strategies for the rural poor, despite the high prevalence of both production and use in poor rural communities (Lambert, Gale, and Hartley 2008). With the decriminalization of marijuana in several Western states, there is evidence that this industry is seeing a resurgence in its economic importance to rural communities (Semuels 2009). Meanwhile, growing concern about methamphetamine production and its impact on rural communities (Donnermeyer and Tunnell 2007; Lambert et al. 2008) also begs for more research. Given the sluggishness of the economic recovery, particularly in rural areas (Parker et al. 2010), informal and illegal activities will likely continue to play an important role in the survival strategies of poor rural families, and more research is needed into the social and economic repercussions of illegal drug activity in rural America.

Conclusions

While the 1990s brought hope and some reduction in poverty rates to many rural communities, the first decade of the 2000s has brought renewed struggles and hardships. Poverty has risen again throughout rural America, and persists in many places that have long experienced high poverty and unemployment, as well as lack of infrastructure, educational opportunities, and resources. As in previous decades, rural minorities and single parents are disproportionately likely to be poor and often have fewer resources available for coping with poverty. Given the depth of the recession and its exacerbation of ongoing deindustrialization and globalization trends, it is likely that these problems will not resolve themselves quickly in rural communities. Future research is needed to continue to explore the impact of the recession on rural communities, as well as to expand our knowledge of emerging issues, such as immigrant settlement in rural communities and the growth of rural drug trades and gang activities.

Blanket solutions to the causes and effects of rural poverty are hard to come by, although for many communities investment into economic development and social support would likely help. It is clear that today many rural families need more resources and better options for surviving without sufficient income, and thus investments into both public and private sources of aid are vital. However, as we look past the current crisis into its future recovery, it is important to think about investing into the infrastructure and resources of rural communities in ways that will go beyond short-term solutions to immediate needs. Hamilton et al. (2008) argue that most rural communities would benefit from improvements in telecommunications technology and infrastructure, greater access to affordable health care, better educational facilities and opportunities for both children and adults, improved and expanded public transportation, more affordable housing, and jobs that offer living wages. All of these policies have in common that they will be beneficial to both the working poor and the unemployed poor, and most importantly, to the nonpoor as well. Universality of policies appears to be key to their acceptance by both communities and policymakers, particularly in the current political and economic climate in which the poor are seen as individually responsible for their own poverty, and redistribution policies are widely vilified for undermining economic growth, job creation, and individual work ethics.

As the recession drags on and its recovery is barely perceptible, political agendas across the nation have retrenched rather than questioned the neoliberal agenda, and focused on cutting costs and services, particularly "entitlements" for the poor. As I discussed in the previous section, the rural poor are already using less than their share of publicly available resources, and if the current focus on cutting these programs continues it is likely that the rural safety net will shrink further. Yet it is also clear that in rural America there is even less social acceptance for the stigmatized safety net than in the rest of the nation, and that the best way to protect vulnerable rural families given the current cultural and political climate may be to include them in the larger agenda of rural economic health, rather than treat them as a separate group whose interests are unique from those of their larger communities. While it may not be possible to break down popular stereotypes and images of the poor, we may have more success if we stop thinking of those who live below the (rather arbitrary) poverty line as being fundamentally different from those who hover above it. Investing in the larger economies and infrastructures of rural communities will likely provide more opportunities for better lives for rural Americans, both above and below the poverty line, and eventually contribute to reversing the high rates of poverty in rural America.

Endnotes

1. Throughout this chapter, I use the terms *rural/nonmetropolitan* and *urban/metropolitan/non-rural* interchangeably, although technically these are somewhat different measures. For detailed information about how rurality is being measured, please see the original sources of data.

2. Schmalzbauer (2011) notes that many of her Latino immigrant subjects in rural Montana chose the location because they felt that rural communities exemplified more traditional gender and family values. This echoes sentiments from long-time white residents in my own rural California case study (Sherman 2009), who similarly describe their rural community as safer and morally superior to urban communities in terms of family values. However, these white subjects also associate Latino immigrants with drugs, gangs, and violence, and resist in-migration by minorities into their mostly white community (Sherman 2009).

References

Albo, Gregory. January 2009. "The Crisis of Neoliberalism and the Impasse of the Union Movement." *Development Dialogue* 51: 119–31.

Anderson, Cynthia D., and Chih-Yuan Weng. 2011. "Regional Variation of Women in Low-Wage Work across Rural Communities." In *Economic Restructuring and Family Well-Being in Rural America*, ed. Kristin E. Smith and Ann R. Tickamyer, 215–30. University Park: The Pennsylvania State University Press.

Bean, Jessica A. 2011. *Reliance on Supplemental Nutrition Assistance Program Continued to Rise Post-Recession*. New Hampshire: Carsey Institute.

Brown, David L., and Kai A. Schafft. 2011. *Rural People and Communities in the 21st Century*. Malden, MA: Polity Press.

Brown, J. Brian, and Daniel T. Lichter. 2004. "Poverty, Welfare, and the Livelihood Strategies of Nonmetropolitan Single Mothers." *Rural Sociology* 69 (2): 282–301.

Carr, Patrick J., and Maria J. Kefalas. 2009. *Hollowing out the Middle: The Rural Brain Drain and What It Means for America*. Boston: Beacon Press.

Clark, Sherri Lawson. 2012. "In Search of Housing: Urban Families in Rural Contexts." *Rural Sociology* 77 (1): 110–34.

Clawson, Dan, and Mary Ann Clawson. 1999. "What Has Happened to the US Labor Movement? Union Decline and Renewal." *Annual Review of Sociology* 25 (1): 95–119.

Crow, Dan, and Gregory Albo. 2005. "Neo-liberalism, NAFTA, and the State of the North American Labour Movements." *Just Labour* 6/7 (Autumn): 12–22.

Crowley, Martha, and Daniel T. Lichter. 2009. "Social Disorganization in New Latino Destinations?" *Rural Sociology* 74 (4): 573–604.

Crowley, Martha, Daniel T. Lichter, and Zhenchao Qian. 2006. "Beyond Gateway Cities: Economic Restructuring and Poverty among Mexican Immigrant Families and Children." *Family Relations* 55 (3): 345–60. http://dx.doi.org/10.1111/j.1741-3729.2006.00407.x.

Donnermeyer, Joseph F., and Ken Tunnell. 2007. "In Our Own Backyard: Methamphetamine Manufacturing, Trafficking, and Abuse in Rural America." *Rural Realities* 2 (2): 1–12.

Farrigan, Tracey. 2010. "Rural Income, Poverty, and Welfare: Poverty Geography." ERS/USDA Briefing Room. Accessed 20 June 2011. http://www.ers.usda.gov/topics/rural-economy-population/rural-poverty-well-being.aspx.

Fitchen, Janet M. 1991. *Endangered Spaces, Enduring Places: Change, Identity, and Survival in Rural America*. Boulder: Westview Press.

Gallardo, Roberto. 2010a. "Rural America in the 2000s: Age." *Daily Yonder*, 21 July. http://www.dailyyonder.com/age-test/2010/07/20/2849.

Gallardo, Roberto. 2010b. "Rural America in the 2000s: Population." *Daily Yonder*, 14 July. http://www.dailyyonder.com/rural-america-2000s-population/2010/07/12/2834.

Grusky, David B., Bruce Western, and Christopher Wimer, eds. 2011. *The Great Recession*. New York: Russell Sage Foundation.

Hamilton, Lawrence C., Leslie R. Hamilton, Cynthia M. Duncan, and Chris R. Colocousis. 2008. "Place Matters: Challenges and Opportunities in Four Rural Americas." *Carsey Institute Reports on Rural America* 1 (4): 2–32.

Hays, Sharon. 2003. *Flat Broke with Children: Women in the Age of Welfare Reform*. Oxford: Oxford University Press.

Jensen, Leif, and Eric B. Jensen. 2011. "Employment Hardship among Rural Men." In *Economic Restructuring and Family Well-Being in Rural America*, ed. Kristin E. Smith and Ann R. Tickamyer, 40–59. University Park: The Pennsylvania State University Press.

Jensen, Leif, Marybeth J. Mattingly, and Jessica A. Bean. 2011. *TANF in Rural America Informing Re-authorization*. New Hampshire: Carsey Institute.

Kandel, William, Jamila Henderson, Heather Koball, and Randy Capps. 2011. "Moving up in Rural America: Economic Attainment of Nonmetro Latino Immigrants." *Rural Sociology* 76 (1): 101–28.

Lambert, David, John A. Gale, and David Hartley. Summer 2008. "Substance Abuse by Youth and Young Adults in Rural America." *Journal of Rural Health* 24 (3): 221–28.

Lichter, Daniel T., and Deboarah Roempke Graefe. 2011. "Rural Economic Restructuring: Implications for Children, Youth, and Families." In *Economic Restructuring and Family Well-Being in Rural America*, ed. Kristin E. Smith and Ann R. Tickamyer, 25–39. University Park: The Pennsylvania State University Press.

Mattingly, Marybeth J., Kristin E. Smith, and Jessica A. Bean. 2011. *Unemployment in the Great Recession: Single Parents and Men Hit Hard*. New Hampshire: Carsey Institute.

McBride, Timothy, and Leah Kemper. 2009. "Impact of the Recession on Rural America: Rising Unemployment Leading to More Uninsured in 2009." RUPRI Center for Rural Health Policy Analysis. Accessed 1 December 2011. http://www.public-health.uiowa.edu/rupri/publications/policybriefs/2009/b2009-6%20Rising%20Unemployment%20Leading%20to%20More%20Uninsured.pdf.

Nelson, Margaret K. 2005. *The Social Economy of Single Motherhood: Raising Children in Rural America*. New York: Routledge.

Nelson, Margaret K., and Joan Smith. 1999. *Working Hard and Making Do: Surviving in Small Town America*. Berkeley: University of California Press.

O'Hare, William P. 2009. "The Forgotten Fifth: Child Poverty in Rural America." New Hampshire: Carsey Institute. Accessed 11 July 2013. http://www.carseyinstitute.unh.edu/publications/Report-OHare-ForgottenFifth.pdf.

Parisi, Domenico, Steven Michael Grice, Guangqing Chi, and Jed Pressgrove. 2011. "Poverty, Work, and the Local Environment: TANF and EITC." In *Economic Restructuring and Family Well-Being in Rural America*, ed. Kristin E. Smith and Ann R. Tickamyer, 320–35. University Park: The Pennsylvania State University Press.

Parker, Timothy S., Lorin D. Kusmin, and Alexander W. Marre. 2010. "Economic Recovery: Lessons Learned from Previous Recessions." United States Department of Agriculture Economic Research Service. Accessed 2 December 2011. http://www.ers.usda.gov/amber-waves/prior-issues-(through-2003).aspx#march20100toc.

Pickering, Kathleen, Mark H. Harvey, Gene F. Summers, and David Mushinkski. 2006. *Welfare Reform in Persistent Rural Poverty: Dreams, Disenchantments, and Diversity. University*. University Park: The Pennsylvania State University Press.

Schiller, Bradley R. 2007. *The Economics of Poverty and Discrimination*. 10th ed. New Jersey: Prentice Hall.

Schmalzbauer, Leah. 2011. "'Doing Gender,' Ensuring Survival: Mexican Migration and Economic Crisis in the Rural Mountain West." *Rural Sociology* 76 (4): 441–60.

Semuels, Alana. 2009. "Marijuana Growers Upend Hard-Luck California Town." *Los Angeles Times*, 1 November. http://articles.latimes.com/2009/nov/01/business/fi-dope-county1.

Shapiro, Isaac. 1989. "Laboring for Less: Working but Poor in Rural America." Washington, DC: Center on Budget and Policy Priorities.

Sherman, Jennifer. 2006. "Coping with Rural Poverty: Economic Survival and Moral Capital in Rural America." *Social Forces* 85 (2): 891–913. http://dx.doi.org/10.1353/sof.2007.0026.

Sherman, Jennifer. 2009. *Those Who Work, Those Who Don't: Poverty, Morality, and Family in Rural America*. Minneapolis: University of Minnesota Press.

Sherman, Jennifer, and Rayna Sage. 2011. "'Sending off All Your Good Treasures': Rural Schools, Brain-Drain, and Community Survival in the Wake of Economic Collapse." *Journal of Research in Rural Education* 26 (11): 1–14.

Smith, Kristin E. 2011. "Changing Roles: Women and Work in Rural America." In *Economic Restructuring and Family Well-Being in Rural America*, ed. Kristin E. Smith and Ann R. Tickamyer, 60–81. University Park: The Pennsylvania State University Press.

Smith, Kristin E., and Ann R. Tickamyer, eds. 2011. *Economic Restructuring and Family Well-Being in Rural America*. University Park: The Pennsylvania State University Press.

Tickamyer, Ann R., and Debra A. Henderson. 2011. "Livelihood Practices in the Shadow of Welfare Reform." In *Economic Restructuring and Family Well-Being in Rural America*, ed. Kristin E. Smith and Ann R. Tickamyer, 294–319. University Park: The Pennsylvania State University Press.

USDA Economic Research Service. 2011. "ERS/USDA Briefing Room—Rural Income, Poverty, and Welfare: Poverty Demographics." Accessed 30 May 2012. http://www.ers.usda.gov/topics/rural-economy-population/rural-poverty-well-being.aspx.

Whitley, Sarah. 2013. "Changing Times in Rural America: Food Assistance and Food Insecurity in Food Deserts." *Journal of Family Social Work* 16 (1): 36–52.

Going Public

DOING THE SOCIOLOGY THAT HAD NO NAME

by Patricia Hill Collins

For years, I have been doing a kind of sociology that had no name. With hindsight, the path that I have been on seems clear and consistent. In the early 1970s, as a teacher and community organizer within the community schools movement, I did some of my best sociology, all without publishing one word. For six years, I honed the craft of translating the powerful ideas of my college education so that I might share them with my elementary school students, their families, my fellow teachers, and community members. My sociological career also illustrates how the tensions of moving through sociology as a discipline as well as engaging numerous constituencies outside sociology shaped my scholarship. This impetus to think both inside and outside the American sociological box enabled me to survive within the discipline. Early on, I recognized that I needed to create space to breathe within prevailing sociological norms and practices. I wrote "Learning from the Outsider Within: The Sociological Significance of Black Feminist Thought" to create space for myself as an individual, yet that article simultaneously generated dialogues with a broad range of nonsociologists (Collins 1986). Similarly, writing *Black Feminist Thought* (Collins 2000) for social theorists, for sociologists, for feminists, and for ordinary people—in particular, African American women whose lives I hoped to influence—was an exercise in the energy that it takes to engage multiple audiences within one text. When colleagues tell me how much the ideas in that one book have traveled, I realize the importance of connecting scholarship to broader audiences. With hindsight, I see how important my years spent working in the community schools movement have been to my subsequent sociological career.

Over the years, my personal engagement in speaking with multiracial, multiethnic audiences from many social class backgrounds, citizenship categories, genders, sexualities, and ages has taught me much. As a professor, discussing my ideas with diverse groups at colleges, universities, community centers, academic conferences, and social activist arenas has improved my scholarship. Take, for example, how different audiences engaged the ideas in *Black Sexual Politics* (Collins 2004). Writing a book is one thing—talking with different groups of people about what I had written was an entirely different experience. My generic lecture title, "Introduction to *Black Sexual Politics*," fails to capture the wide range of talks that I actually delivered. The African American community residents in Tulsa, Oklahoma, who came out to their local public library to hear the version of the talk that I prepared for them had different reactions than the college students and faculty on the beautiful campus of the University of California, Santa Barbara, who encountered the same ideas, yet in a vastly different format. At times, I had to fall back on pedagogical skills honed during my days teaching seventh- and eighth-grade students, the case when I addressed a lively group of African American and Latino high school students in Louisville, Kentucky. How different their reactions were to the ideas in *Black Sexual Politics* than those of the audience at the feminist bookstore in Cambridge, Massachusetts. The list goes on. I realize how diverse American society is, let alone how rich the tapestry of global cultures and experiences outside U.S. borders. Writing for and speaking with multiple publics has been challenging, but also worthwhile.

Despite this history, I initially found Michael Burawoy's ideas about public sociology unnerving (this volume). I certainly like Burawoy's model and think that it interjects a much-needed breath of fresh air into some increasingly stale sociological debates. At the same time, I'm not completely comfortable with it. Apparently, I had been *doing* public sociology without even knowing it. Moreover, I was not alone. Despite my inability to classify them as public sociologists, many other sociologists had also made the decision to "go public."

On the one hand, I should be happy that the type of sociological practice that has so long preoccupied me is now gaining recognition. What has long been "out" now has a rare invitation to attend the party within American sociology, which has not been particularly inclined to changing its ways. Most certainly individual sociologists have been at the forefront of many progressive issues, yet they do not constitute the center of the discipline of American sociology. On the other hand, I question whether this new visibility for public sociology is inherently good for practitioners of public sociology as well as for public sociology itself. What are the potential challenges that accompany Burawoy's gutsy move?

WHAT'S IN A NAME?

One challenge facing public sociology concerns the way in which naming it will help or hurt its practitioners. Is naming public sociology inherently beneficial? Most people assume that institutionalizing public sociology will be a good thing. Naming public sociology should help legitimate it within the discipline. Perhaps. Yet as mental patients, escaped slaves, runaway brides, and prisoners remind us, institutionalization need not be good for everyone. It all depends on where you stand. Once a set of practices is named, and thereby placed in its classificatory cell within an institution, those practices can become even more difficult to do. In this spirit, I wonder how discussions about public sociology will assist sociologists who currently practice public sociology? We assume that naming will elevate the status of current practitioners, but it may instead install a permanent and recognizable underclass that now carries the stigmatized name of public sociology. Stated differently, will doing public sociology emerge as a new form of tracking within the discipline?

As an ideal type, public sociology seems glamorous. Yet who actually does this kind of sociology? Current practitioners of public sociology are typically not housed in premier institutions, nor do many of them come from privileged groups. I suggest that individuals who are most likely to commit to public sociology have had experiences that provide them with a distinctive view of social inequality. African Americans, Latinos, new immigrant groups, women, working-class and poor people, lesbian, gay, bisexual, and transgendered (LGBT) people, and others who remain penalized within American society and their allies may gravitate toward a sociology that promises to address social issues that affect the public. If not predisposed before entering sociology, individuals from these groups and their allies may develop a public sociology perspective as a result of their sociological graduate training.

Many graduate students choose sociology because they are attracted to the vision of an until-now-unnamed public sociology that they encounter in their undergraduate classrooms. Most do not enter graduate programs to become professional or policy sociologists. For many, graduate training resembles a shell game—they look under one shell for the public sociology prize that they anticipated; yet when they pick up the shell, nothing is there. The real prizes, they are told, lie under the remaining three shells of professional, policy, and, to a lesser extent, critical sociology. They are pressured to choose among types of sociology and to leave behind the idealism of public sociology and the "you'll-never-get-a-job-if-you-keep-that-up" stance of critical sociology. Fortunately, my graduate training differed. I was encouraged to be an independent thinker, and I took my professors at their word. My own path within sociology certainly reflects this predisposition to focus on the recursive relationship between doing and naming.

I often wonder how I managed to carve a path for myself by doing a sociology that had no name. For me, this is not a new question, but rather one that has shaped my entire career. Being an African American woman in overwhelmingly white and male settings, as well as carrying my working-class background into situations that routinely privilege the cultural (and actual) capital of middle-class families, has been frustrating yet immensely helpful. I am used to not belonging, to being stared at as the one who must introduce myself to yet another sociological clique at the American Sociological Association (ASA) in order to put my colleagues at ease. Because I belong to groups that garner less value within American society, I hold ideas about democracy, social justice, color blindness, feminism, and a long list of social practices that differ from those of the mainstream. I stand in a different relationship to power relations, and as a result, I hold a distinctive standpoint on those relations. Being committed to principles that are larger than myself has not been easy. I am the one who has been denied jobs for which I am qualified because I do not do the kind of sociology that is valued. Doing public sociology either will make you strong or might kill you. Would naming the kind of sociology that I have been doing have made these struggles any easier?

Perhaps. Yet at the same time, being classified under the banner of public sociology may foster a kind of sociological ghettoization, primarily because those who gravitate toward public sociology may already hold subordinate status within the discipline itself. Public sociology can thus become a convenient tool for getting African Americans, Latinos, women, community college teachers, and the like to do the service work of the profession, this time not just spreading sociology's mission to students, or serving on endless committees because their "perspective" should be represented, but also by explaining sociology to multiple publics. In this endeavor, would time remain to "do" public sociology in its most robust form? Or would a legitimated public sociology be reduced to a service arm of the discipline, with the "real" sociology of professional sociology still holding sway? Is public sociology a "sociology of and for the Others," namely, all those people who cannot make it within other ideal types of sociology? If so, then the irony of having those who have struggled so mightily to become sociologists serve as the public face of sociology, with the sociological center remaining intact, becomes especially poignant.

Beyond this issue of how legitimating public sociology via naming it might not necessarily help its current practitioners, the act of naming might also shift the very mission of this kind of sociology. I envision the spirit of public sociology as resembling historian Robin D. G. Kelley's notion of a "radical imagination"; or the tenets of "magical realism" invoked by Lani Guinier and Gerald Torres as part of their project to transcend the limits of current thinking about race and democracy; or even sociology's own C. Wright Mills's clarion call for a new "sociological imagination" (Kelley 2002; Guinier and Torres 2002; Mills 1959). In my own work, I draw upon these ideas via the concept of visionary pragmatism within African American women's oppositional knowledge, a creative tension that links visions for a better society and pragmatic strategies of how to bring it about (Collins 2000).

Public sociology resembles these activities. It constitutes a constellation of oppositional knowledges and practices. If American society were just and fair, if the American public were fed, clothed, housed, educated, employed, and healthy, there would be no need for public sociology. Its very existence speaks to the need to *oppose* social injustice yet also to be proactive in creating a democratic and just public sphere. Naming public sociology strives to enhance the stature of these oppositional knowledges and practices by carving out spaces within the boundaries of an established discipline in ways that legitimate the public sociology that already exists and, perhaps, catalyze more. Naming aspires to redefine public sociology as no longer being a subordinated, submerged way of doing sociology and seeks to elevate its stature.

Yet, in the American context, making the shift from outsider to insider knowledge may change the ethos of public sociology. Ironically, despite good intentions, naming public sociology may step on existing land mines of defining the purpose and practices of oppositional knowledge as well as the social location of insiders and outsiders who produce such knowledge. Naming public sociology, and thereby opening the doors to the valid question of defining its distinguishing features, can catalyze endless debates about boundary making. A subtle shift can easily be made from doing an unnamed, messy, and thus incorrigible public sociology to talking about public sociology in ways that shrink its possibilities. Public sociology can easily become yet another fad, a nugget of commodified knowledge that privileged sociologists can play at just as a cat toys with a mouse. What comforting procrastination—one remains ethically honorable by paying lip service to public sociology while never having to take a stand by actually doing it. I can see it now—legions of dissertations analyzing the contributions and failures of public sociology versus dissertations that *do* public sociology. Better yet, what would the "Introduction to Public Sociology" course look like? Which sociological worthies would make the cut to be included on the required reading list and which would be left outside to stare at a closed door?

WHAT'S IN *THIS* NAME?

Another challenge confronting public sociology concerns its chosen name. Is this a good time for the discipline of sociology to claim the term *public*? Is this the best name for this work, even as we persist in doing it? After over two decades of sustained assault on public institutions in the United States, throwing in one's lot with the sinking ship of anything "public" may seem suicidal. Let's just paint a big target on sociology, some professional and policy sociologists could argue; sociology will become viewed as a field for losers.

In the United States, the privatization of public power seems ubiquitous (Guinier and Torres 2002). In the 1980s and 1990s, social policies dramatically reconfigured the meaning of *public* generally and the social welfare state as the quintessential public institution. Current efforts to privatize hospitals, sanitation services, schools, and other public services and attempts to develop a more private-sector, entrepreneurial spirit in others by underfunding them—public radio, public television, subcontracting specific services via competitive bidding—illustrate this abandonment and derogation of anything public. Deteriorating schools, health care services, roads, bridges, and public transportation, resulting from public failure to fund public institutions, speak to the erosion and accompanying devaluation of anything deemed "public." In this context, *public* becomes reconfigured as anything of poor quality, marked by a lack of control and privacy—all characteristics associated with poverty. This slippage between lack of privacy, poor quality, and poverty affects the changing meaning of *public*.

Much of this push toward privatization in the United States has covert yet powerful racial undertones. When African Americans and Latinos among others gained expanded rights, individuals and groups with power increasingly abandoned public institutions. Take, for example, the legacy of the 1954 *Brown* decision that outlawed racial segregation in public education. Thurgood Marshall, Derrick Bell, and other civil rights activists had no way to anticipate how a new color-blind racism would effectively stonewall school integration initiatives. The early trickle away from public schools by middle-class white parents who founded private white academies so that their children need not attend racially integrated public schools opened the floodgates of white flight from public institutions of all sorts. Public schools, public health, public transportation, and public libraries are all now devalued in the face of market-based policies that say "privatization will shield you from rubbing elbows with the public." These new social relations signal a distinct reversal—the public sphere becomes a curiously confined yet visible location that increases the value of private services and privacy itself. Public places become devalued spaces containing Latinos, poor people, African Americans, the homeless, and anyone else who cannot afford to escape. In this context, privacy signals safety; control over one's home, family, and community space; and racial homogeneity—all qualities that can be purchased if one can afford them. This version of privatization dovetails with Lani Guinier and Gerald Torres's notion of the privatization of power. If private spaces are better, then shouldn't private entities run the public itself?

In this political context, naming this sociology *public* sociology inherits this history and these social issues. What does it mean for sociology to claim to be for and about the public at this historic moment? Will this be perceived as sociology for the dispossessed, the displaced, and the disadvantaged? Despite Burawoy's efforts to generate much-needed dialogue that is designed to reinvigorate sociology, I suspect that those currently privileged within professional, critical, and/ or policy sociology will express far less enthusiasm for an increased emphasis on public sociology than the internal integrity of doing public sociology might suggest. Following public sociology into the realm of the public raises too many uncomfortable questions about the discipline of sociology's merit, value, purpose within contemporary American society. Currently, the term *public* invokes neither populist nor democratic sensibilities. Rather, it means *popular* (as in popular versus high culture) and, more ominously, inferior. Let the diverse public in and your discipline suffers. Let public sociology in and your scholarship deteriorates. Is sociology ready for that?

I certainly hope so. The social justice sensibilities of public sociology constitute one of its defining features. Caring about the public, seeing all of the others not as devalued entities that one must "mentor" or "help" but rather as potential partners for the betterment of society itself provides a core vision or ethos for this kind of work. People want ideas that matter both to them and within society itself. Public sociology suggests a recursive relationship between those inside the profession and people who are engaged in efforts to understand and challenge prevailing social inequalities that now characterize an increasingly devalued public. In this regard, if public sociology is unprepared to jump into the controversies that surround the term *public,* then this may not be the best name for it.

CAN WE ALL GET ALONG?

A third distinctive challenge confronts public sociology in the United States. Now that public sociology has a name, when it comes to its relationship with professional, critical, and policy sociology, I wonder, can we all get along? American sociologists familiar with the circumstances that catalyzed the 1992 riots in Los Angeles might remember these words from motorist Rodney King. King's videotaped beating by members of the Los Angeles police department was shown around the world. The court decision that exonerated the police also catalyzed several days of rioting, when Angelenos burned down entire city blocks because they couldn't envision living in Los Angeles the way it was. The media loved to broadcast King's query, "Can we get along?" His plea reified American assumptions that talking things through will yield a fair solution for everyone, that better evidence yields stronger public policy, and that if we just put our heads together and let rational minds prevail, we should be able to solve this mess.

However, can it ever be this simple? I have great difficulty imagining a mahogany conference table with representatives of the Los Angeles police force, African American, Latino, and Korean grassroots community groups, mayoral staff, the Los Angeles chamber of commerce, church folks, representatives of the Justice for Janitors and Bus Riders unions, and other members of the Los Angeles community putting aside their differences with an "oops-let's-try-this-again" mentality. Most of us would recognize that the historical power relations in Los Angeles that created many of these groups in the first place make such a scenario unbelievable. The groups themselves are involved in a continually shifting mosaic of hierarchical relationships with one another—sometimes they operate as friends, other times as enemies, and often they have little knowledge of what the others are actually doing. Despite my incredulity about such a meeting, if it did occur, at least the people around that conference table would recognize that the knowledge they brought to the mahogany conference table grew directly from the power relations that got them there. They would know that they could not achieve a new vision for Los Angeles without taking power differentials among themselves into account, let alone among those segments of the public that did not get invited to the meeting.

I wonder whether sociologists would have the same sensibility, if they even saw the need for such a meeting in the first place. Burawoy's four-cell typology gives the impression of parallelism among professional, policy, critical, and public sociology, yet it is important to reiterate that Burawoy proposes a Weberian *ideal-type* framework. These four types have never been nor are they expected to be equal to one another. Therein lies the problem. Unless sociology itself expands (the old Reagan policy of creating a bigger pie so that public sociology can cut a piece), creating space for public sociology means taking away from the space of the other three. Will they move over to make room at the mahogany table? Or do professional, policy, and critical sociology see public sociology as the interloper in a game of musical chairs?—because they occupied the three subdisciplinary seats when the music stopped, poor public sociology is left permanently standing.

This is the rub—in the U.S. context in the post–World War II period, professional and policy sociology have exercised imperial authority within American sociology in ways that obscure public sociology. One would think that critical sociology resists these impulses, but when it comes to the privatization of power, practitioners of critical sociology promise more than they deliver. Critical sociology often talks a good game, yet when it comes to the types of institutional change required to let in sufficient numbers of the unruly public, the intellectual blinders of many progressive sociologists keep them from delivering the goods. For example, the ideas of color blindness and gender neutrality that underpin conservative agendas of the Right seem eerily similar to arguments on the left that race and gender-based identity politics basically destroyed a progressive, class-based politics. They too long for a color blindness and gender neutrality that will uphold a class-based agenda. Yet this failure to engage race and gender as a route to rethinking social class has limited critical sociology's contributions as a vibrant force within American society. Just as it took Hurricane Katrina in 2005 to jolt the American public into seeing the realities of race and class in the United States, so too were critical sociologists caught off guard.

As the sociological pie shrinks, in large part because the demonization of the public outside sociology occurs via race- and gender-based bashing of large segments of the American population, fighting over crumbs within the discipline mimics behaviors that are as American as apple pie. Professional and policy sociology have well-established constituencies and do make important contributions. Critical sociology may have long contested the ideas of professional and policy sociology, yet it too has its well-established constituencies who can be just as resistant to a fully actualized public sociology as their well-heeled counterparts. Why should any of these three ideal sociological types cede territory to the upstart of public sociology, especially one that may contain disproportionate numbers of less desirable people? Given the derogation of anything public in the American setting, public sociology faces an uphill battle in finding its place at the sociological table.

WHY DO PUBLIC SOCIOLOGY?

Given these challenges, why would anyone willingly choose public sociology? When I've shared Michael Burawoy's typology of professional, policy, critical, and public sociology as four ideal types of sociology with some of my students, or even simply summarized its ideas, their eyes light up. There's the aha factor at work—"Public sociology is the kind of sociology we want to do," they proclaim. They resonate with the name *public sociology*. Wishing to belong to something bigger than themselves, they know implicitly that doing public sociology constitutes intellectual labor placed in service to broader ethical principles. They are drawn to the concept of a reenergized public where every individual truly does count. By positioning itself in solidarity with ethical principles of democracy, fairness, and social justice, public sociology seemingly offers a path away from provincial careerism and back toward the sociological imaginations that many students felt they needed to check at the graduate school door.

Yet the inevitable questions that come next speak to their pragmatic concerns. "Where do I go to study it? Do the top sociology programs offer a degree in it? Can I get a job doing it?" they query. Moving quickly through the preliminaries and homing in on the promises of mentoring and role modeling, they shift to the next set of questions: "How did you come to do public sociology?" they ask. "You appear to be successful. Can you teach me how to become a public sociologist?"

I don't fault the students. Their questions stem from the disjuncture between one set of promises within American sociology to place the tools of sociology in service to solving social problems and actual sociological practices that must attend to the realities of car loans and mortgage payments. Unlike students of the past, contemporary students are much more cognizant of the fact that the bill will come due one day. So they feel pressured to choose wisely. Professional and policy sociology may position them to better pay off their student loans—what can critical sociology deliver, or worse yet, public sociology? They confront the contradiction of wishing to garner the moral capital of supporting social justice initiatives without taking personal risks such as having articles rejected from top journals or being denied their dream job. Can one truly work for social justice from the comfort of a cushy job with tenure? Derrick Bell labels this impetus "ethical ambition" and offers reassurances to his readers that it is possible to be ethical and successful at the same time (Bell 2002). I sincerely hope that he is right, but I also know that the vast majority of people who actually do public sociology receive few perks and even less praise.

I suspect that people work at public sociology for very much the same reasons that some individuals become dancers, actresses, singers, painters, or poets—training for their craft may be part of their passion, but they would find a way to dance, act, sing, paint, or write even if no one paid them. The ardor of artists provides a template for the passion for social justice that many sociologists bring to their intellectual work. American pragmatism and its grand entrepreneurial spirit strive to stamp out this passion for justice, raising the question of whether there is even any room for public sociology sensibilities within American sociology anymore. Yet visitors from other national sociological traditions at the 2004 ASA meeting on public sociology remind us that public sociology not only exists but also holds a much larger place in their sociological vision than it does in the United States. It may be more difficult to see public sociology here, in the center of a major world power, but the stakes are too high not to.

When I look back and try to map my involvement in public sociology, I realize that, as with love, I found it in unlikely places. For example, I love social theory—no secret there. But with hindsight, I recognize that the reason that I so appreciated early sociological theorists is that they all seemed to be doing public sociology, or at least that is the way I was introduced to their work. Despite our current efforts to objectify, deify, freeze, and squeeze Karl Marx, Max Weber, Georg Simmel, Émile Durkheim, W. E. B. DuBois, and other classical social theorists into ossified boxes of their "most important contributions that you will need to know in order to get a job," I read the works of these theorists as public sociology. I remain inspired by their commitment to bring the tools of sociology to bear on the important issues of their time. The public need not have been their direct audience—given literacy rates of the late nineteenth and early twentieth centuries, few could read their work—yet so much of what they did was on behalf of bettering the public. They talked to one another because they wanted to understand and better society.

Contemporary American sociology has moved away from this kind of energy and excitement. Yet because public sociology demands that we consider the major issues of the day and that we bring tools of sociological analysis and empirical research to bear on them, it promises to breathe new life into sociological theory as well as the discipline overall. Despite the challenges facing public sociology, as well as the difficulties that I have encountered in my career doing it, I would choose it all over again. At this point in my career, what we call it matters less to me than knowing that I am not alone in choosing this path.

REFERENCES

Bell, Derrick. 2002. *Ethical Ambition: Living a Life of Meaning and Worth.* New York: Bloomsbury.

Collins, Patricia Hill. 1986. "Learning from the Outsider Within: The Sociological Significance of Black Feminist Thought." *Social Problems* 33 (6): 14–32.

———. 2000. *Black Feminist Thought: Knowledge, Consciousness, and the Politics of Empowerment.* New York: Routledge.

———. 2004. *Black Sexual Politics: African Americans, Gender, and the New Racism.* New York: Routledge.

Guinier, Lani, and Gerald Torres. 2002. *The Miner's Canary: Enlisting Race, Resisting Power, Transforming Democracy.* Cambridge, MA: Harvard University Press.

Kelley, Robin D. G. 2002. *Freedom Dreams: The Black Radical Imagination.* Boston: Beacon.

Mills, C. Wright. 1959. *The Sociological Imagination.* New York: Oxford.

Solidarity

by Jeremy Brecher

As a young child I had listened over and over to a song with this refrain: " Solidarity forever, solidarity forever, solidarity forever, for the union makes us strong." But what is solidarity and where does it come from?

As the powerlessness of workers or indeed any individuals makes their position look less and less tenable, the psychology of "looking out for number one" becomes futile. The need to support others who in turn will support you can become evident, and a spirit of all-for-one and one-for-all can spread in a bond that is at once an intellectual recognition of necessity and an emotional feeling of unity. That bond is summed up in the hallowed labor movement adage, "An injury to one is an injury to all." That bond is worker solidarity.

The reason this sense of solidarity crystallizes so suddenly is the feeling that, as Paul Mattick, Jr., used to put it, "I will only make sacrifices for you when I can sense that you will grasp the need to make sacrifices for me." Such mutuality develops in a thousand miniature experiments taking place in the background of a mass strike—like the railroad blockade in Martinsburg in 1877 and the Briggs work stoppage in Detroit in 1929.

One result of this process is the sense of being part of a class. That is in some ways comparable to the sense of being part of a nation, but, I maintained, its source and result are different from those of nationalism. The common situation of workers is that individually they are powerless, but together they embody the entire productive force of society. Workers' solidarity reflects their discovery of this. It is rooted in the fact that in modern society individuals can gain control of the social forces that determine their lives only by cooperating. Thus "individualism" keeps the individual weak, while solidarity increases the individual's control over her or his life. Once the consciousness of this need for solidarity develops, it becomes impossible to say whether the motive for an act such as joining a sympathetic strike is altruistic or selfish, because the interest of the individual and the collective interest are no longer antagonistic; they have come to be the same. (*Strike!* was less forthright on the ways in which those who shared some interests in common might nonetheless have others that conflicted.)

Worker solidarity is a special case of what I would now call common preservation. It can be undermined, of course, by pursuit of the narrow self-interest that economists refer to as the "free rider problem"—the attempt to share in the benefits of joint action without sharing in its sacrifices. But that is often overcome by a shared understanding that cutting the other guy's throat ends up with everyone cutting their own throat; by the experience of benefit through mutual support; by a process that I would later come to call de-centering, which allows you to see yourself in others' shoes; and by a view of solidarity as a better way to live and act.

What Is Liberation Sociology?

by Richard A. Quantz

In the spring of 1845 one of the founders of the liberation social science tradition, the young Karl Marx, wrote that "the philosophers have only interpreted the world, in various ways; the point, however, is to change it."[1] Sociologists centrally concerned about human emancipation and liberation take this insight seriously. The point of liberation sociology is not just to research the social world but also to assist in changing it in the direction of expanded human rights, participatory democracy, and social justice.

Liberation sociology is concerned with alleviating or eliminating various social oppressions and with creating societies that are more just and egalitarian. An emancipatory sociology not only seeks sound scientific knowledge but also often takes sides with, and takes the outlook of, the oppressed and envisions an end to that oppression. It adopts what Gideon Sjoberg has called a *countersystem approach*. A countersystem analyst consciously tries to step outside her or his own society to better view and critically assess it. A countersystem perspective often envisions a society where people have empathetic compassion for human suffering and a real commitment to reducing that suffering. It envisions research and analysis relevant to everyday human problems, particularly those of the socially oppressed. The countersystem standard is broader than that of a particular society or nation-state. Using a strong human rights standard, such as the UN Universal Declaration of Human Rights, the liberation social scientist accents broader societal and international contexts and assesses existing social institutions against a vision of more humane social arrangements.[2]

The consequences of taking this standpoint are explored throughout this book. We are eclectic in our approach and influenced by Enlightenment, modernist, and postmodernist theorists. Neo-Marxist, feminist, and antiracist conceptions have had their impact on our thinking. Moreover, the liberation theology of Latin America and Africa and important developments in the way we think about the mind and the body—no longer a viable dichotomy—have also been influential.

We do not propose here another abstract or doctrinaire approach but rather an emancipatory way to practice good sociology. Taking sides with, and understanding the outlook of, the socially oppressed can have profound consequences for the stages of social research: on how we know what we know, on what we choose to research, on the nature of our scientific endeavor, on the methods we choose, and on the conclusions we can draw from research.

A sociologist's, or a social research team's, choice of what to study is consciously goal-oriented. This always subjective choice is not made in social isolation but according to personal and collective tastes and convictions and is often in response to enticements such as grant monies, career prestige, or job security. Thus, many sociologists choose to deeply research US society with an eye to changing it for the better, whereas others choose to narrowly research topics whose description or analysis is mainly sought by leading agents of the status quo. Some social scientists go into the field and critically examine the impact that powerful nation-states or large corporations have on people's everyday lives and provide that information to proponents of change, whereas others limit their research to less critical descriptions of the views or attitudes of the general population for an establishment funding agency. Some choose to dig deeply into a society's foundations, including its systems of social control and information distribution, whereas others choose to do only surface-level research that helps those who head dominant institutions perform their roles more successfully.

Some social science research emphasizes its policy relevance for those at the helm of the nation-state or corporations. In contrast, the research of liberation sociology is generally defined by its usefulness to those who are oppressed and struggling for their liberation. A contemporary example of a sociologist who exemplifies the liberation sociology message is Peyman Vahabzadeh from the University of Victoria in Canada. As a student in Iran, he supported the overthrow of the reviled Shah of Iran, who with US help deposed a *democratically* elected government. As a refugee, he found a new homeland in Canada.

Through it all, Vahabzadeh remained haunted by the fate of his fellow Iranians, including his brother, who survived one tyranny (the Shah) only to face another (the Ayatollahs). His brother was one among many murdered by Iran's leaders in the Islamic Republic.[3]

Presently, Vahabzadeh's research emphasizes the constitutive role of social movements in Iran. From the women's movement, to the student movement, to the workers' movements and trade unionism, to ethnic and environmental movements, he studies emerging secular politics. His path to liberation sociology makes clear an agonizing fact of society: the prevalence of violence in countless forms that coexists with innumerable injustices. He has dedicated his research, teaching, and activism to nonviolent alternatives for social change, while exposing systemic and frequently hidden forms of violence. But "most rewarding," for Vahabzadeh, "is training a new generation of activists."[4]

Radical phenomenology has become a guiding theory and method that informs Vahabzadeh's work on human collective action and social movements. A contemporary addition to the tradition of phenomenological sociology, radical phenomenology situates thinking and acting in epochal frames, presenting truth as temporal and conditioned by diverse periods and offering dissimilar and shifting possibilities for thinking and acting. Vahabzadeh reassesses democratic discourse, the notion of rights, liberal democratic regimes, time and epochs, oppression, and the practice of sociology itself.[5] As he told us,

> Radical phenomenology offers a glance into the epochal frames in which Truths become dominant and matters-of-fact. By showing that Truth has a temporal character and thus rises and falls, radical phenomenology cultivates an approach that is always in search of, and attuned to, the new. The new always reveals itself through action and as such the sobriety of the actors will decide the common future of humans and nonhumans in terms not imposed by regimes of truth.[6]

Another influential Iranian sociologist is Sarah Shari'ati Mazinani at the University of Tehran. She is a public intellectual and regular commentator on women's status and social justice. She is the daughter of Iranian liberation sociologist and theorist Ali Shari'ati—one of the most important Iranian intellectuals of the twentieth century. Shari'ati offered a liberationist reading of Shi'i Islam and is said to have influenced the younger generation that participated in the 1979 revolution. He supported the Algerian Front de Libération Nationale and had correspondences with Frantz Fanon and Jean-Paul Sartre.[7]

Like her father, Shari'ati Mazinani is a defender of social justice and insists that sociologists be interested in practical questions. Mohammad Amin Ghaneirad, a sociologist for the National Research Institute for Science Policy, an Iranian think tank, has explained Shari'ati Mazinani's position well. According to Ghaneirad, she endorses what some Iranian sociologists call "clinical sociology." Clinical sociology suggests that theory have an applied purpose, namely, to determine the most effective means for healing society. As Ghaneirad puts it, "The clinical sociologist enters the society and experiences various social phenomena and analyzes them with theoretical tools available to her/him rather than making judgments based on his/her theories from a distance."[8]

Commitments to alleviating human suffering or to peace, human rights, social justice, and real democracy, as evidenced in the research, teaching, and activism of Vahabzadeh and Shari'ati Mazinani, politicize the practice of sociology no more than the social science commitments that assert indifference and supposedly value-free methods or neutral knowledge.

One of the exciting developments over recent decades has been the emergence of an array of critical social theories in the humanities and social sciences. These include, among others, feminist theory, postmodern theory, queer theory, antiracist theory, and a variety of Marxist theories. Numerous sociologists have joined progressive social science organizations. Since the 1960s, critical social theory and research have frequently been published in books and certain social science journals.[9] As sociologist Berch Berberoglu has noted, "This new generation of critical scholars—envisioning a society without exploitation, oppression, and domination of one class, race, sex, or state by another—helped provide the tools for analysis for the critical study of social issues and social problems that confront contemporary capitalist society."[10]

In their research and analysis, most critical social analysts press for the liberation of human beings from oppressive social conditions. Most research the larger institutional contexts and macrostructures of oppression, domination, and exploitation and yet also view such structures as crashing into the everyday lives of human beings. The daily experiences of oppressed and subjugated peoples are a central focus and concern. Moreover, as a rule, critical social theorists do not focus only on the negative realities and consequences of oppression but often target issues and strategies of human liberation from that oppression. These theoretical frameworks generally see resistance to oppression and domination as beginning "at home, in people's everyday lives—sexuality, family roles, workplace."[11] These critical social thinkers support the agency and action of human beings in their own liberation.

Another Effort at Liberation Sociology: Using Sociology to Fight Contemporary Slavery

Social scientist Kevin Bales is another compelling example of a counter-system analyst committed to reducing human suffering. Locating few articles on modern-day slavery after completing an exhaustive review of thousands of articles, he established that no social scientist had conducted rigorous research on the topic. He decided to do something about it. "As a social scientist and a sociologist, I was thinking 'wow! There are millions of people in slavery'; [t]his is a very important thing to understand. This is an ancient form of social interaction and social control, which many believe had been eradicated . . . . So it was my curiosity and my sociological approach that drove me into the issue." Bales undertook a qualitative research project and traveled to meet slaves and slaveholders. "It had to be . . . qualitative," he explains, "as the crime was so hidden. I looked at the economics of slave-based businesses in different parts of the world. I tried to tease out the different dimensions of what was going on."[23]

His book *Disposable People: New Slavery in the Global Economy* is the result of his research. There he tells the disturbing story of a "new slavery," one linked to the global economy.[24] In 1999, the same year *Disposable People* first appeared in print, Bales teamed with Simon Pell, head of Arts for Labour in the United Kingdom, to establish a fund-raising and research consultancy. The progressive company raises money for environmental campaigns, human rights groups, medical charities, overseas development, and other charities and voluntary sector groups.[25] In 2000, together with others, Bales founded Free the Slaves, a nonprofit organization that works to "liberate slaves around the world, helps them rebuild their lives and researches real world solutions to eradicate slavery forever." Free the Slaves works both on the ground to liberate individuals from slavery and on policy initiatives to eliminate slavery worldwide.[26] During a recent talk, Bales explained, "Liberation, and more importantly all the work that comes after liberation, it's not an event, it's a process. It is about helping people to build lives of dignity, stability, economic autonomy, citizenship."[27]

As in other countersystem sociology projects, Bales's approach is coupled with a desire to change the world, to make a difference. Like the social scientists at Project Censored, Bales has engaged in an important type of liberation sociology, with a critical approach to research and analysis. Recently, Bales has further explained his motivations:

> We have to ask ourselves, are we willing to live in a world with slavery? If we don't take action we just leave ourselves open to having someone else jerk the strings that tie us to slavery in the products we buy and in our government policies. And yet, if there is one thing that every human being can agree on, I think it's that slavery should end.[28]

Sociology and Societal Betterment

The sociology of liberation is part of a long tradition that aims at both studying and rebuilding society. Auguste Comte, the French social philosopher who coined the word *sociology* in the nineteenth century, viewed the new science as laying bare the reality of society and thereby helping to transform it (see Chapter 2). Comte gave lectures in France on his "positive philosophy" (later called *positivism*). However, Comte was not a progressive philosopher. The new directions for societal change that he envisioned were rather protective of a certain societal status quo. In a draft of his book on the civil war in France, Karl Marx noted that Comte "was known to the Paris workers as the prophet of personal dictatorship in politics, capitalist rule in political economy, hierarchy in all spheres of human activity, even in science, the creator of a new catechism, a new Pope, and new saints to replace old ones."[29]

In the 1930s, in one of the first probing analyses of the social meaning of what sociologists were doing, Robert Lynd proposed that the knowledge produced by a critical sociology is required so that democracy can "continue to be the active guiding principle of our culture."[30] In his major book *Knowledge for What?* Lynd argued that sociology should focus on practical problems in need of societal reform. Operating with an interdisciplinary focus that questioned the building of self-perpetuating academic traditions, Lynd called for research oriented toward truly democratic principles.

In this book we, too, call for the practice of more emancipatory and liberation sociology, but we do not seek an end to all conventional sociological research linked to funding by the nation-state or by mainstream foundations. These latter research efforts often do generate valuable knowledge about the structure and reality of US society, such as in sociological research projects dealing with the corporate abandonment of central cities.[31] Nevertheless, many traditional social science projects directly or indirectly reinforce the oppressive structures of society, if only by not challenging those social structures with strong alternatives going beyond the limits of present-day elite-controlled US politics. We also call here for greater democratic access to social science knowledge, which some regard as a commodity that confers the power to control nature, to shape other human beings, and to improve ourselves. Knowledge is power, and some, like Michel Foucault, use the combined word phrase *power/knowledge* to describe the two aspects of the same phenomenon.[32]

Thus, we call for the reassertion of a sociological practice designed to empower ordinary people through social science research and knowledge. By having better access to critical sociological knowledge, people will be in a better position to understand their personal and familial troubles, make better sense of the world we live in, plan their individual and collective lives, and relate in egalitarian and democratic fashions to others within and outside their own nation-state. This includes being in a better position to struggle for individual and collective human rights. A broad-based democracy can be fully developed in our era only if key types of knowledge are made available to all, not just to those at the top of the socioeconomic pyramid and their professional servants.

We envision here much more egalitarian access to relevant scientific knowledge. We believe that a renewed social science commitment to human liberation and social justice—a shift to the "for whom" and "for what" relevance of social science research and writings—can significantly reshape the scientific practice and product that sociology and other social scientific disciplines regularly generate. As we have seen in the examples of Project Censored and of Bales's slavery project, a major aim of a countersystem research project is to raise both the researchers' and the people's consciousness of society's oppressive structures. A related goal is to stop, or significantly reduce, human oppression and suffering. As we will make clear in subsequent chapters, liberation sociology follows in the paths of early sociologists like Jane Addams and W. E. B. Du Bois, who connected sociological ideas to social activism, and of later sociologists like C. Wright Mills, who proposed that a sociological imagination allows people "to grasp what is going on in the world and to understand what is happening in themselves as minute points of the intersections of biography and history within society."[33]

Oppression: A Central Sociological Problem
Questioning Social Hierarchy

Liberation sociology is concerned with the oppression of various groups in society, including those who are poor or are discriminated against because of their physical appearance, alternative lifestyles, or orientations. Everyday life involves interaction, with most people coming into contact with others daily. Our relationships are shaped by societal structures and forces, including racism, patriarchy/sexism, heterosexism, class exploitation, and other processes of domination. Such societal forces are expressed in informal networks and formal bureaucratic organizations. Social scientists have long observed what the effects of these and other social forces are on people enmeshed in them—much in the way physicists infer the existence of the forces of gravity or electromagnetism.

Since early in the history of the discipline, progressive sociologists have questioned the major inequalities in the distribution of socioeconomic resources in societies where they have lived, as well as across the world. However, at least since the 1920s, mainstream sociology and other social sciences have too often tiptoed around major issues of elite power and coercion, especially in regard to class, racial, and gender oppression. In recent decades, when mainstream social scientists have examined power issues, they have often preferred to research legitimate power (sometimes called *authority*) rather than illegitimate power. In addition, they have substantially ignored the (mostly white male) ruling class at the helm of society. For example, most social scientists who have researched social class and social mobility in US society have limited themselves to social classes below the level of the very top elite.[34] Clearly, the social sciences sometimes play a traditional role in society. A glaring example is the once widely discussed book *The Bell Curve*, written by social scientists Richard Herrnstein and Charles Murray. This book, which has sold millions of copies, explicitly argues against the ideal of societal equality. By defending the meaningfulness of so-called intelligence test differentials (actually, learned-skills test differentials) between white and black and Latino students for US government educational policy, this social science book further attempts to legitimize racial inequality and discrimination.[35] As sociologist Alvin Gouldner once noted, social science has a "dialectical character and contains both repressive and liberative dimensions."[36]

In the United States, deeply critical analyses of power and hierarchy are resisted by most captains of industry, politicians, and mainstream intellectuals and by much of the general public. This country's traditionally white, male leadership resists such probing analyses because these will likely make more obvious the unfairness of the existing distribution of social positions and material and symbolic rewards. Since most leaders and much of the public do not ask for critical analyses of major power holders, it is easy for many social scientists to take the position that it is not their responsibility to research or correct the large-scale power and resource inequalities. In contrast, the sociology of liberation embraces concerns about this toxic social inequality and about the illegitimacy of the powers that be. It takes the additional step of choosing the societal processes and institutional arrangements that produce this deepening inequality as its central problem to study closely.

In this book we underscore the act of choosing what should be studied because this is a crucial decision in much social science practice. Injustice should be examined not just in its maldistribution of goods and services but also in the deep-lying social relations responsible for making that distribution possible. These social relations, among which oppressive power relations are a key part, are responsible for the way in which important societal goods are distributed. They determine whether individuals, families, and other groups are integrated into or excluded from society's decision-making processes. And they can shape the development of human identities and the sense of belonging and dignity. In the end, social justice is more than a question of redistribution of power, more than a matter of resolving within existing relations how goods are distributed. It is a matter of totally restructuring the larger framework of inegalitarian social relations for the greater human good.

As we have noted, important among the major social oppressions are racism, patriarchy/sexism, heterosexism, and class exploitation. Dorothy Smith has argued that mainstream sociology is linked to the dominant ideological apparatus of US society, which accounts for its historical emphasis mostly on research issues primarily of concern to white men. For the most part, mainstream sociology's themes are "organized by and articulate the perspectives of men—not as individuals . . . but as persons playing determinate parts in the social relations of this form of society."[37] For many decades, feminist sociologists and others representing subjugated groups have pressured social scientists to research the social world from the perspectives of the oppressed and to take their experiences seriously as a source of societal understanding and knowledge.

The common social science term *social system* is often laden with the assumption that societal arrangements are more or less harmonious and that change in one element brings about change in other elements and in the general organization of the system. Although some societal relations exhibit an equilibrating or harmonious character, many do not show any such character. Expropriation, exploitation, domination, and oppression are processes that produce and reproduce the way Western societies like the United States are hierarchically arranged. To characterize a social arrangement as a more or less static social system without explaining how it was initially created and how it is being reproduced takes for granted as immutable what we need to actively observe and change.

Many influential social scientists—particularly those who have the best-paying, most-stable jobs—have been white men, and if they wish, they can isolate themselves from the many severe consequences of social oppression. C. Wright Mills once noted that "most social scientists have had little or no sustained contacts with such sections of the community as have been insurgent; there is no left-wing press with which the average academic practitioner in the course of his career could come into mutually educative relations." Such isolation has had significant and negative impacts on both the social sciences and on society.[38]

What Is Social Oppression?

In a probing analysis, political scientist Iris Young suggested that oppression and domination are disabling constraints that affect the "institutional conditions necessary for the development and exercise of individual capacities and collective communication and cooperation." Domination involves "institutional conditions which inhibit or prevent people from participating in determining their actions or the conditions of their actions."[39] These constraints operate at various societal levels. For example, loving parents who routinely make important decisions without consulting their children when they are old enough to make their own choices disable them through their domination. In like fashion, benevolent dictators have disempowered the people whose good they have claimed to seek.

Oppression consists of "systematic institutional processes which prevent some people from learning and using satisfying and expansive skills in socially recognized settings or institutionalized social processes which inhibit people's ability to communicate with others or to express their feelings and perspective on social life in contexts where others can listen."[40] The persecution and killing of Jews and Roma ("Gypsies") in Nazi-dominated Europe, the exploitation of farm laborers in the United States, the pillage of indigenous people's lands in the name of progress, the enslavement of Africans in the Americas, and the sweatshops still found in US and other Western cities are major examples of societal oppression. Those who must work for much less pay on account of their class, race, ethnicity, sexual orientation, or gender status are thereby socially oppressed. Oppression also eliminates or reduces human dignity and the capacity to express oneself and participate in society as effectively as those who are more privileged.

The oppression of women has been a central issue of the current era. In her famous 1960s book *The Feminine Mystique*, Betty Friedan wrote of the troubled North American housewife, especially the white suburban housewife, as being in a state of recurring personal distress. Though most such women lived in enviable circumstances by international standards, they often felt cheated and suffered from numerous gendered afflictions that came to be known as "housewives' fatigue." Friedan did not write her book merely to engage the reader's sympathy but to show that these women were being prevented from self-realization through gendered oppression and cultural conspiracy; this "feminine mystique" framing led women to believe that their happiness lay only in the kitchen and nursery.[41] Friedan's analyses were part of the feminist resurgence of the 1960s. In the years that followed, her analysis was criticized for seriously neglecting the central concerns of working-class women and women of color, especially those who had long worked outside the home. Eventually, the concerns of many women became part of a complex women's liberation movement.[42]

Here we underscore the institutional and embedded character of contemporary societal oppression. In one sense, the term *oppression* does cover the tyranny that a despot or ruling group exercises over others.[43] For example, in twentieth-century Europe, numerous fascist and Communist regimes oppressed their peoples in political terms. Yet there are other forms of contemporary oppression that do not involve this overt tyranny but rather are embedded in social norms and beliefs extending over long periods of time. Another term for this is *hegemony*, or domination with "a velvet glove."[44] In today's forms of societal oppression, many individuals who contribute to maintaining and reproducing the various oppressions see themselves as merely doing their jobs and living out normal lives. If asked, they would reject the view that they could be agents of oppression. Our emphasis on broad social processes and long-term institutions allows us to understand the apparent paradoxes of a society's oppressed peoples sometimes contributing to their own victimization—and even turning into oppressors of yet others.

In the United States and other countries around the world, there are privileged groups and oppressed groups that differ in the goods, resources, and opportunities that these countries make available to their members and in the degree to which they participate in societal decision-making that affects lives. These differences are hard to deny, even though some might choose not to see their continuing reality. As sociologist W. E. B. Du Bois once noted, some groups are privileged *because* others are oppressed. For example, for long decades in the nineteenth and twentieth centuries, the extreme poverty and degradation in the African colonies of European nations was "a main cause of wealth and luxury in Europe. The results of this poverty were disease, ignorance, and crime. Yet these had to be represented as natural characteristics of backward peoples."[45] Centuries of colonial exploitation of African labor and land have long been omitted from numerous historical reviews of the realities of European prosperity and development. A similar situation exists for generations of white Americans, whose prosperity is deeply rooted in centuries of exploitation of the labor and land of African Americans, Native Americans, and other people of color in North American history. A similar argument can be made for the privileges of men in regard to the conditions of women. This historical background of the United States is too often ignored or downplayed in contemporary accounts of racial discrimination and other oppressions, especially in the mainstream media.

The heterogeneous society that is the now United States is clearly differentiated in terms of oppressed and privileged peoples. Thus, we wish to gain some distance from arguments built upon the assumption of a homogeneous "American public," as found in much Western sociology of culture. Too often the term *Americans* in the media and in scholarly writings actually means "white Americans," and little thought is given by the commentators to the fact that a large proportion of the population may not share the view or behavior attributed to those "Americans."[46] Political and academic viewpoints that attempt to pass themselves off as neutral, or that claim a national consensus, are often the viewpoints of the privileged.

The particular meanings attached to social differences—which make them seem natural, traditional, or necessary—are deeply embedded in our stock of tacit understandings and knowledge. A sociology of liberation often questions and uncovers the hidden aspects of these concrete, historically given social arrangements so that they can be better understood—and perhaps acted upon so that their oppression is undercut.

Humanization and Critical Consciousness

Increasing Humanization

One conceptual starting point for our endeavor is the human vocation, the calling to be fully human. Seldom stated in conventional social science, the initial assumptions of the researcher need to be made explicit, for they shape research much more than just in its methodological principles. The statement of underlying domain assumptions is an important means for preserving the integrity of research, a topic we examine in detail later.[47]

A contemporary example of a sociologist who makes initial assumptions explicit is Donatella della Porta, a professor at the European University Institute. Like many scholars of social movements before, she has both studied and participated in social movements. She explains:

> My entrance to university corresponded with a very tense moment in Italian politics, with political violence and state repression closing down spaces for movements. Although still sympathetic to the left-libertarian movements in general, I left active politics, but not politics as a focus of attention. In fact, I started to study social movements in 1981, while I was doing a Master's degree at the École des hautes études en sciences sociales (School for Advanced Studies in the Social Sciences) with Alain Touraine. Social movements remain a main focus in my work.[48]

In addition to social movements, presently della Porta's research concerns political violence, corruption, police behavior, and policies of public order. She has conducted investigations in Italy, France, Germany, and Spain. Currently she is director of the comparative research project Mobilizing for Democracy, which addresses the role of civic organizations in democratization processes, thereby bridging social science approaches to social movements and democracy. From a theoretical point of view, she addresses structural preconditions and actors' tactics, and the main focus is on recent democratization processes in European Union member and associated states. Reflecting on how her research has been shaped by more than methodological principles, della Porta explains:

> I think what helped me was that my parents—even if moderate in politics—were quite open-minded for Sicily, especially at that time. I could therefore develop autonomously. Cousins of my mother and her husband . . . were active members of Medicina Democratica, a social movement organization that worked on health issues, such as the effects of pollution. In my youth, they were for me a source of political and social inspiration.[49]

Brazilian educator Paulo Freire wrote that while human beings have the potential for humanization and dehumanization, their true vocation is only humanization. Injustice, exploitation, the violence of oppressors—and their denial and dissimulation in euphemisms and ideologies—generate and undergird dehumanization. Our humanity is affirmed in struggles to achieve freedom and social justice. Dehumanization marks and defines the oppressor as much as it torments the oppressed. Activist sociologist Onwubiko Agozino, whose work we examine in later chapters, echoes Freire's sentiments:

> I have always argued that oppression does not harm only the targeted group . . . slavery also harmed white men morally because they raped black women and then sold their own blood children into slavery as property; sexism harms men too because many men do not approximate the ideals of dominant hegemonic masculinity and because the women directly harmed are our sisters, daughters, friends, wives and mothers; and poverty is a problem for all because the rich cannot sleep safely knowing that the hungry man is an angry man.[50]

For Freire, the struggle to recover humanity is a struggle of the oppressed "to liberate themselves and their oppressors as well."[51] Oppressors who exploit and exclude by virtue of their power ordinarily cannot find the strength to liberate anyone. At best, they may soften their grip and may become gentler in exercise of power. In contrast, liberation sociology struggles to understand society well and then to disrupt the realities of oppression, the taken-for-granted, "natural" order that supports it and makes it possible.

Facing Challenges in Communities

In the United States, sociology originated as a field whose early practitioners were substantially committed to research for major social change. Among these were Jane Addams and W. E. B. Du Bois, whose work we examine in Chapters 3 and 4. Addams and Du Bois are examples of what Antonio Gramsci has called "organic intellectuals."[52] They are from or represent the oppressed sectors of society whose lived experience gives them an understanding superior to those intellectuals who come from highly advantaged sectors of society. Organic intellectuals work for liberation of their oppressed groups, often in local communities. For the first time, Addams and Du Bois brought into US social science the actual experiences, history, and culture of formerly excluded peoples. Not surprisingly, their research was aimed at improving the lives of the poor, the working class, immigrants, women, and Americans of color. Their progressive sociology sought mostly to better the lives of less powerful Americans, not to advance their careers or create a people-distancing social science discipline.

In later chapters we will observe that there is much interesting research linking community activists and social scientists in common efforts to understand various types of oppression and bring about social change. Some of this research is mainly evaluative; it attempts to assess the effectiveness of existing remedial programs. Another approach is broader and tries to collectively spell out community needs and how they might be addressed in new and innovative ways, and then works with people to help them deal with serious social problems. Such research is usually linked to community-defined goals.

Take the example of an organization called Project South: Institute for the Elimination of Poverty and Genocide, based in Atlanta, Georgia. This organization incorporates sociological research into education and organizing projects. An activist organization shaped in part by sociologists, it engages in workshops, action-research projects, and popular education projects across the country. Workshops are organized by and for community activists and activist scholars and are designed to help them better comprehend problems such as health care and the criminal "injustice" system. Project South's action-research efforts pull together teams of grassroots activists and social scientists to develop materials for popular education and community organizing. One project has gathered oral histories and statistical data to describe socioeconomic conditions in Georgia's communities and to discover what impact political campaign funds have had on these areas. Low-income neighborhoods in several cities have been part of the project, and in each case the findings have been put into videos and pamphlets for use in workshops and for community organizing. Project South researchers begin the process of community discussion by conducting at least one local workshop to examine the research findings and often work with community leaders. Project South has also developed other projects, such as the Grassroots Popular Education Project, which is a resource-building program for grassroots organizations, and the Leadership Development Initiative, a development program for low-income grassroots leaders in Georgia.[53]

In 2007 the first ever US "Social Forum" took place in Atlanta under Project South auspices. Project South organized this forum over two years of intense efforts. Some 15,000 people, young and old, men and women, participated in many workshops spread over the city. After the 2007 Social Forum, and after working with other activist groups, Project South set up the Southern Movement Assembly. The purpose of this organization is to groom grassroots leaders, especially youth leaders, and to support progressive grassroots organizations in the Southern states. The goal is to regenerate a twenty-first-century freedom movement for the South's many underserved communities. Included in this effort is a strong accent on a National Student Bill of Rights. The forum's major themes have included Gulf Coast reconstruction in the post-Katrina era;

persisting US imperialism, invasions, militarism, and oppressive prison systems; indigenous people's issues; immigrant rights; liberating people from gender and sexuality discrimination; and workers' rights in a global economy.[54]

Significantly, several sociologists have been active in this organization, two of whom we can mention briefly. One is Jerome W. Scott, who once served as the director of Project South. Growing up in working-class Detroit, Scott "lived the reality of its poverty-stricken neighborhoods."[55] He is an organic intellectual whose sociological ideas have been honed by experience. After serving in Vietnam, Scott took courses at Lawrence Technical College but left for a job in an auto plant. There he participated in the League of Revolutionary Black Workers, a workers' group that pressed unions and management for more racial integration in auto plants. He became part of groups of workers and scholars studying sociopolitical theory, including that of Marx, Du Bois, and Malcolm X, in the context of building movements for change. This provided an important part of his broad sociological and political education. As he has noted to us, "From both my lived experience and theory I developed an understanding of society rooted in class analysis and social struggle, as the larger historical and institutional context of white supremacy, male privilege, and US global domination."[56] Moving to Atlanta in the 1970s, he began work on social justice issues. Soon he was working with community activists and activist sociologists and helped to found Project South. He also became involved in the American Sociological Association and the Association of Black Sociologists.[57]

An activist sociologist, Scott has coauthored articles and book chapters on US history, globalization and the electronic revolution, race and class issues, and people's movements for social change. He has noted current challenges facing sociologists: "Today, as globalization in the electronic age sweeps the world, liberation sociology is being transformed; and those of us who are engaged are building bridges to the emerging bottom-up movement for global justice and equality. For me, liberation sociology is an essential part of the larger project of human liberation."[58]

Another sociologist active for a time in Project South is Walda Katz-Fishman, who once served as chair of the board of Project South. In a communication to us, she noted that her activism is rooted in her background. Growing up in the South, she saw her parents active in the civil rights movement, civic and Jewish organizations, and the Democratic Party. At an early age, she became aware of racial, class, and gender inequalities, "but did not have a framework for truly understanding the world, a clear vision, or a strategy for how to change it."[59] After graduating from college, she attended graduate school at Wayne State University, where she became educated in a working-class perspective and Marxist interpretations of society. "From that point on," she reported, "I was always developing my historical materialist world-view and participating in many activist arenas—from scholar activism among professional groups to anticapitalist movements building in multiracial and multiclass organizations, often with women in the leadership."[60]

Moving to Washington, DC, in 1970, Katz-Fishman took a teaching position at Howard University. She continued developing her liberation sociology ideas and has taught many students about ideas and strategies of societal transformation. Like Scott, she has worked as an educator who uses her research on class, racial, and gender inequality to help grassroots organizations working for social justice. Katz-Fishman views her sociological education and research work as a crucial background and constant resource for her community activism: "To me sociology is a key to understanding social history and society—its past, its present, and its future, that is, what it is becoming. It offers me the tools for theoretically understanding the world and for practically transforming the world. But I have done and continue to do this within the collective process of study and movement building."[61]

More recently, Katz-Fishman and Scott have moved on from Project South to other group organizing projects, including some that focus on global social issues and movements. They have participated in the US Social Forum National Planning Committee as representatives of the League of Revolutionaries for a New America. They also continue to focus on educational curricula and programs to build progressive people's movements. As Katz-Fishman has recently stated, we "conduct movement schools for liberatory transformation with Move to Amend, a national organization working to end corporate personhood; the Green Party, an independent political party committed to economic justice, peoples' democracy, and ecological sustainability; and the Wayside Center for Popular Education in the DC and Virginia area."[62]

Listening to the People

At its best, social action research involves a willingness of both community participants and social science researchers to listen carefully and democratically to each other. Historically, some community-based research has involved social scientists who were not seriously interested in listening to community residents. For example, one group of experienced action researchers, sociologists at Loyola University in Chicago, has noted that too often social science researchers have come in, gathered community data, and left without giving anything back to the community.[63] In such settings, one problem is getting researchers and local community activists to listen well to one other and communicate without jargon.

Although some mainstream social scientists may see it as "too subjective," good collaborative research with community residents can be as carefully done and meaningful as other social research (see Chapter 4). From the community point of view, good social science research provides people with solid ideas about the depth of their problems and about how change strategies can be more effective. All social science research is pervaded by the perspectives of the researchers and of those funding or supporting the research. No research is conducted without underlying assumptions or without linkages to the structures of power and inequality in society. Francis Moore Lappé has noted that "each of us carries within us a worldview, a set of assumptions about how the world works—what some call a paradigm—that forms the very questions we allow ourselves to ask and determines our views of future possibilities."[64]

Teaching Liberation Sociology

In the United States and other parts of the world, sociology is an academic discipline, with its teachings being part of the mainstream curriculum in institutions of higher education and sometimes in high schools. Much of what is published and read within the disciplinary boundaries of these institutions is written by academicians. We should pay particular attention to the teaching of sociology because the sociology taught in high schools, colleges, and universities is, or can be, practiced in everyday life—as a way for individuals and small groups to examine the societal conditions in which they live and the consequences of individual and collective actions.

Teaching the sociology of liberation typically involves a process of creation of awareness, what Paulo Freire has called "conscientization"—a pedagogy of how oppressed people struggling for liberation can free themselves. It refers to "learning to perceive social, political, and economic contradictions, and to take action against the oppressive elements of reality."[65] The sociology of liberation is not just a sociology that discusses liberation; it is a sociology that can show or facilitate the way to it. A famous educator, Freire discovered that his pupils learned how to read and write better when language details were associated with acquisition of a critical consciousness. Learning how to read and the process of education in general were thus projects of human liberation.

Freire contrasts radicalization, the aim of his pedagogical method, with the more typical political sectarianism. Whereas radicalization nourished by a critical spirit is creative, "sectarianism, fed by fanaticism, is always castrating."[66] Radicalization literally means going to the *root* of things, a process that in Freire's experience involves "ever greater engagement in the effort to transform concrete, objective reality." Political sectarianism of the right or the left, because it is usually "mythicizing and irrational," can create a wrongheaded image of social reality and a sense of futility in changing that reality.[67] This distinction between radicalization and sectarianism is vital to a viable sociology of liberation. As we see it, the goal of liberation sociology is not to replace one dominant mythology with another but to contribute substantially to the freedom of human beings to think critically about society and to liberate themselves from dominant reality-distorting mythologies.

Consider this contemporary example. Alia Tyner-Mullings, professor of sociology and founding member at the New Community College at the City University of New York, connects the theoretical perspective of Freire with the teaching and learning styles of teachers and students at Central Park East Secondary School, a public alternative high school in Harlem (New York) that successfully serves predominantly low-income students. She has examined some of the ways the Freirean model has worked within the public school system and considers the challenges in implementing it. An article published in *Schools: Studies in Education*, based on research conducted on former students of the high school, concludes that while much of the Freirean model has been used successfully there—especially those aspects that focus on relationships inside the school—critical questions remain about the implementation of Freire's curricular recommendations.[68] Tyner-Mullings was once a student there and invites all who read her work to contemplate the potential of alternative educational models to deliver quality education to low-income students otherwise underserved by public schools.

Consider another contemporary example. Tim Woods, who teaches at Manchester Community College in New Hampshire, expects his students to bring their communities into the classroom. Service-learning is a requirement in most of his courses.

> One of the great opportunities about teaching sociology in a community college is that nearly all of the students are genuinely enmeshed in the community while simultaneously attending classes . . . . Bringing the community into the classroom feels natural under these circumstances. In fact, expecting students to leave their social backgrounds, personal troubles, family issues, and job worries at the door is nearly impossible. Rather, the goal of teaching becomes connecting the classroom to the community to strengthen both.[69]

While Woods and his students are involved in a range of community issues, his students' commitment and engagement toward ending homelessness stands out. For instance, one student stayed after class to visit with him about the troubles he was having studying. The student was a veteran and, while motivated toward educational success, could not find time to study. After several days of the student staying after class, he finally admitted that he was living in a homeless shelter. He wanted to study but could not find any free time or quiet space in the shelter to do so.[70]

Trying to assist this one student and walking with him (sometimes literally) to learn the story of homeless vets, Woods and his students started on the path toward homeless advocacy. With the college's help and collaboration with community members, the Manchester Initiative for Supportive Housing was created. They utilized the strength of each community member, including students, to advocate in their town for more supportive housing. Meanwhile, students were reading social science books like Elliot Liebow's *Tell Them Who I Am* and John McKnight and Peter Block's *The Abundant Community*. Most importantly, they were connecting class readings to their community, both in writing and in actions they were involved in during the course. For example, students successfully invited community leaders to class discussions on homelessness and housing. Community members and students decided to host a public forum at the college to advocate for the building of supportive community housing in the community. Some students took on the task of media coordination, while others invited local residents. Students who had their own band wrote a song about homelessness and started the conference by debuting the song.[71]

All of this community collaboration eventually resulted in the construction of new housing apartments in the community. Students reportedly view the housing with pride, knowing that they played an important role. Additionally, they have discovered strong connections within their community and realized the power of those connections to help others and themselves.[72]

The activist social scientist Karl Marx once wrote that he did not seek to anticipate the world for all time to come but to engage in relentless criticism of existing reality. This does not mean hurling distorted or undocumented critiques at the way other people act or think. In our view, liberation sociologists should stay deeply connected to empirical reality, with what they can discover about the daily experience of the members of a society, including global society. A full empirical understanding of a society like the United States leads to the knowledge that it, and especially its social hierarchies, is systematically structured in the wrong way for full human self-realization. In the nineteenth century, Marx carefully studied the concrete realities of Western capitalism and came to the savvy conclusion that the logic of modern capitalistic societies "made injustice, alienation, and exploitation inevitabilities rather than contingencies."[73]

Without this empirical connection to everyday life and its constraints, there is no viable sociology. For liberation sociology, this connection between the empirical reality that sociologists study and sociologists' subjectivity—personal commitments, social biases, and existential coefficients of all sorts—is part of an ongoing dialectical and reflective process. Indeed, subjectivity usually provides the impetus to explore the social world.

Liberation sociology thus does not seek to establish certainty for all time, as some sociologists have tried to do. Practitioners of liberation sociology study current societal realities so they and others can better transform them. Thus, much new knowledge is tied to the transformations that such social science study and research bring about, to the remedial practices that are paired to what field researchers find in their work. They are not afraid of ordinary people or participating with others in the search for knowledge. The liberation sociologist is not afraid of becoming an activist-researcher committed to an oppressed people's history or to fight on their side of human history. The critical consciousness at the heart of liberation sociology is self-reflective and part of an interactive learning process. Reflective decisions about studying a societal problem and about methods for its analysis are acts of judgment and are made possible only by previous experience listening to and communicating well with other human beings.[74]

What Type of Society Will We Have?

Taking Sides with the Oppressed

If sociology is to become a stronger intellectual framework for people struggling for liberation from the structures and mystiques of domination, then sociologists need to decide on the type of sociology they will practice and whose interests they will serve. All sociologists, like all other social scientists, make personal choices as to the problems they are going to devote their energies to, the terms in which they will cast research questions, and the research methods they will utilize. They do not make such choices in a social vacuum but typically as they struggle to provide for themselves and their families.

The noncommittal attitude of much sociology and other social science today—usually formulated as scientific detachment, objectivity, or value freedom—is too often a cover-up for the accommodation the research has made with dominant group interests. Mainstream sociology, like other intellectual endeavors, is part of the political, social, and psychological status quo. To ignore or deny the political, social, and psychological standpoints of our own sociological thinking and discipline is to make sure that the latter will stay rooted in a deeply troubled status quo. W. E. B. Du Bois provided an eloquent examination of the social forces at play in the decision to take sides with the oppressed: "The educated and cultured of the world, the well born and well bred, and even the deeply pious and philanthropic" cannot escape the contradiction that they "receive their training and comfort and luxury, the ministrations of delicate beauty and sensibility, on condition that they neither inquire [too closely] into the real source of their income and the methods of distribution nor interfere with the legal props which rest on a pitiful human foundation of writhing white and yellow and brown and black bodies."[75]

In our view, social science researchers should make every effort to do honest and open research work and to minimize as best they can the intrusion of unstated assumptions that can distort that research. We support "objectivity" in this sense, although we recognize that this task is not an easy one since the mainstream accent on "objectivity" is often part of an argument to coerce research into a certain conventional mode. Indeed, it is frequently the countersystem sociologists who have the greatest ability to be objective and socially truthful because they critically analyze and demystify established interpretations of oppressive social arrangements. According to Sandra Harding, the truly democratic values that legitimate critical analysis of established structures from the viewpoint of the dispossessed "tend to increase the objectivity of the results of research."[76] As the social sciences become more diverse in terms of who does social science, these fields embrace a broader array of human perspectives and knowledge, and more critical questions are raised about traditional perspectives and hidden societal realities. In addition, by regularly bringing in the social and historical contexts of social science, one can increase its objectivity by reducing its parochialism. Democracy-enhancing practices can only improve science, whereas democracy-reducing practices—the traditional practices of much natural and social science—can only limit science.

One of sociology's great contributions to modern thought is that at its best it encourages us to think critically about the socially patterned nature of the world around us. Early European sociologists like Max Weber and Emile Durkheim researched, and wrote insightfully about, broad societal forces such as industrialization, bureaucratization, and urbanization. Yet these are not the only processes that characterize the modern period in Western societies. The differentiating processes of exploitation, social discrimination, and oppression also distinguish the modern period.

These latter realities were perhaps best understood by other early sociologists such as Jane Addams, Charlotte Perkins Gilman, W. E. B. Du Bois, and Ida B. Wells-Barnett. All of them analyzed issues of discrimination and exploitation in their efforts to understand US society.[77] Experiencing social oppression firsthand, these white women and black men and women sociologists saw what most white men at the time could not—that major "social difference is the first consequence of modern society and, thus, the more reasonable first principle of sociology."[78] A relevant sociology must be grounded in the studied realization of the extent to which US society, as well as other societies, are founded in social differentiation, inequality, and oppression.

Taking an Overt Moral Stance

The flight from serious discussion of issues of morality and ethics in social science must be ended. Beyond a desire for a deeper understanding of exploitation and oppression, liberation sociology takes an overt moral stance, which includes identification and empathy with the victims of oppression and a calling for and working toward their liberation from misery and inequality.

Sociology can liberate when it applies its humanistic concern and empathetic reasoning to solving the everyday problems afflicting human beings. In this book we advocate a broad human rights standard for social research, affirm the value of humanization, and call for maximizing human self-realization and achievement. One starting place for a broad human rights standard, which has international resonance, is the United Nations' Universal Declaration of Human Rights. This international agreement stipulates in Article 1 that "all human beings are born free and equal in dignity and rights" and in Article 7 that "all are equal before the law and are entitled without any discrimination to equal protection of the law." Article 8 further asserts: "Everyone has the right to an effective remedy . . . for acts violating the fundamental rights," and Article 25 states that these rights extend to everyday life: "Everyone has the right to a standard of living adequate for the health and well-being of himself and his family, including food, clothing, housing."[79] From this influential international human rights perspective, no one can be expected to take care of their family and civic responsibilities without adequate daily sustenance and freedom from intrusive oppressions (see Chapter 9). We believe that this commitment to broad human rights and freedoms should be the starting point for much sociological research and analysis. Interestingly, the American Sociological Association now has a research section explicitly on human rights, one in which both social science specialists and interested practitioners can exchange ideas about research and practice.

An important example of sociological analysis interweaving with moral concerns is liberation theology, a powerful tradition among Catholic activists in numerous postcolonial countries, especially in South and Central America. For some time now, liberation theology has drawn in part on sociological writings, and, in turn, liberation theology has influenced the thinking of progressive sociologists, including ourselves. Stan Bailey, a former priest and sociologist, made this cogent comment on an early draft of this book:

I am an ex-priest trained in liberation theology in Córdoba, Argentina, where I spent nearly a decade working with oppressed communities. As a priest, what kept me going was the perspective of solidarity with the poor, and doing theology from the bottom up—being a voice for those denied a voice. Now, to hear the same terms being used to indicate a certain type of sociological praxis is gratifying . . . . We reduce the world to our disciplines with their internal rules and regulations, and their authorities who determine the true path. Don't we realize the futility of our intellectual conclusions for most of the world's population living in subhuman conditions? Our "ivory towers" distort our visions and move us along in the justification of the powerful.[80]

Liberation theology emerged in Latin America in response to the inadequacy of doctrinaire European theology for Catholic priests doing pastoral work among the poor and politically disenfranchised. In 1968 liberation theology came to the world's attention as a result of the second meeting of the Latin American Bishops' Council in Colombia. At that meeting Father Gustavo Gutierrez, "the father of liberation theology,"[81] and others called for new church initiatives to meet the economic and social justice needs of the poor in Latin America. As a result, these Catholic bishops declared that the Catholic Church should have a "preferential option for the poor," the liberation theology phrase for taking sides with the oppressed. This movement was criticized by Catholic Popes John Paul and Benedict, but more recently, Pope Francis has accented the importance of serving the poor and has met informally with Father Gutierrez. As we discuss in Chapter 8, while Francis has distanced himself from the liberation theology movement, he has included some elements of its philosophies in his speeches.[82]

Looking beneath the Surface

In ancient Roman myth, the giant Cacus lived in a cave and once stole some oxen from Hercules, then dragged them backward into his cave. When Hercules came seeking his cattle, he saw tracks that appeared to indicate that the cattle had gone out of the cave, and he was initially deceived. All too often, modern social science analysts are like the puzzled Hercules. They note the shape of the cave and count the number and direction of the footprints but do not dig deeper into the social realities that their observations often represent.83 Indeed, several social science commentators have noted that if social life were only what it seemed to be on its surface, there would be no need for social science.

Too much mainstream analysis of US society, economy, and politics reflects a status-quo ideology that denies or hides many of this society's most serious "distorting contradictions."[84] One of the tragedies of any society is the failure of its people and leaders to understand the real social problems confronting them. For example, today modern capitalism seems to be riding high, with many mainstream analysts, business leaders, and academics singing its praises. Indeed, there is a general denial that the mechanisms and machinations of modern capitalism are creating very serious social and economic troubles for the billions of residents of planet Earth.

The United States appears to be on a path of continuing social conflicts, of accentuated economic and other inequalities, and of environmental degradation shaped by such trends as global warming and the deterioration of air and water. The social contradictions of contemporary capitalism are becoming ever more evident to those who attend to the empirical data. Clearly, there is no historical reason to expect the system of capitalism to last forever. The failures of other societal systems, such as the demise of state communism in Eastern Europe, have received far more academic and media attention than the continuing crises of US and global capitalism. Politicians' debates over cutting social programs, over job losses, and over trends in Social Security and Medicare have often been conducted with little sustained reference to the growing income and wealth inequalities underlying capitalistic societies like the United States. Today, most large US corporations are part of a global market system and have periodically directed many of their profit-making activities to low-wage areas overseas as they close US plants and eliminate many decent-paying jobs. Although many US corporations have made very good profits, their economic "advances" have frequently come at great cost to US workers and their families. In the United States the real wages of a majority of ordinary workers are lower today than they were a few decades ago, a situation that has forced many to take on extra jobs or put more family members to work.[85] The so-called free market is celebrated by mainstream analysts as the solution for social and economic problems overseas at the same time that it is creating recurring serious economic problems and severe environmental problems for workers and their families across the globe.

The increasing inequalities of income and wealth have often been rationalized by an array of US politicians, media commentators, and intellectuals. Most societies are controlled substantially by elites who take overt and covert actions to shape society in terms of their group interests. The oppressing classes and the bureaucratic organizations they control hide many of their exploitative operations from the public and do not wish for social scientists to do research on systems of oppression they create or uphold. In analyzing society, liberation sociologists typically try to dig beneath these overt rationalizations and everyday fictions. Major tasks for critical social scientists are to ascertain the larger social framework around such elite actions, and how the actions arose or developed. At its best, sociology provides a useful collection of interpretive concepts and methods, and it relies on actual field observations, interviews, experimentation, and comparison to reach critical conclusions about conditions in society.

Conclusion

Throughout this book, we have asked the hard questions, "Social science for what purpose?" and "Social science for whom?" In proposing a liberation sociology, we give a strong humanistic, democratic, and progressive-activist answer to these questions. Liberation sociology can be a tool to increase the human ability to understand deep societal realities, to engage in dialogue with others, and to increase democratic participation in the production and use of knowledge. Making oppression more visible and forcing public discussions of it are essential. C. Wright Mills put it thus: "It is the political task of the social scientist . . . continually to translate personal troubles into public issues, and public issues into the terms of their human meaning for a variety of individuals."[113] A critical, committed sociology can help those who are powerless to become more powerful. It can give voice to those who are oppressed and voiceless. For example, it can help women and people of color to understand better where and how sexism and racism operate and suggest useful countermeasures. Or it can help white male workers who join right-wing supremacist groups to understand why they feel alienated and why reactionary ideologies play into the hands of their own class oppressors.

Well-established research methodologies, including face-to-face interviews and social surveys, can be coupled with newer approaches such as Dorothy Smith's institutional ethnographies of US schools.[114] For Smith, field ethnography means more than observation and interviewing; it means a commitment to finding out how a social entity really works in its practices and everyday relationships. Discovering social facts can thus involve a diversity of social science methods. For example, some researchers have made good use of the diaries and other materials left by the victims of the German Nazi Holocaust to get a sense of everyday realities of extreme oppression and genocide. In South Africa, new methods were pioneered by that country's Truth and Reconciliation Commission, which has looked into the atrocities of the old apartheid system. They sought out the voices of the survivors of this violent oppression in order to air the truth about its horrors and allow the country to better face its future with its eyes wide open. Similarly in Chile, after Augusto Pinochet's dictatorship (1974–1990), a special national committee investigated and assembled data on the civil rights abuses of that brutal regime with the hope of bringing about societal openness and eventual reconciliation.

The ultimate measure of the value of social science knowledge is not some type of academic propositional theory building but whether that knowledge sharpens our understanding of society and helps to build a more just and democratic society. Liberation sociology seeks to stimulate debate in the field of sociology and in the larger society over what humane societal arrangements would look like and how they could be implemented. To bring change, powerless human beings must be empowered. Liberation sociology can provide probing research that supports the struggles of the oppressed against classist, racist, sexist, heterosexist, and other authoritarian types of oppression. Liberation sociology is oriented toward people acting to change oppressive conditions. Karl Marx once wrote that people "make their own history, but they do not make it just as they please; they do not make it under circumstances chosen by themselves, but under circumstances directly encountered, given and transmitted from the past."[115] C. Wright Mills noted a qualification to this: "Men are free to make history, but some men are much freer than others. Such freedom requires access to the means of decisions and of power by which history may now be made."[116]

Both Marx and Mills recognize that people are acting agents and actually can and do make or remake their history. A former secretary general of the United Nations, Dag Hammarskjöld, put it this way: "We are not permitted to choose the frame of our destiny. But what we put in it is ours."[117] Each member of this society is a part of the systems of oppression, for no one can escape and all are part of the struggle to maintain or remove these systems. But we can choose which side to be on.

Endnotes

1. Karl Marx, *Theses on Feuerbach*, reprinted in Karl Marx and Frederick Engels, *Selected Works, vol. 2* (Moscow: Foreign Languages Publishing House, 1962), p. 405.

2. See Gideon Sjoberg and Leonard D. Cain, "Negative Values, Counter-system Models, and the Analysis of Social Systems," in *Institutions and Social Exchange: The Sociologies of Talcott Parsons and George C. Homan*, ed. Herman Turk and Richard L. Simpson (Indianapolis: Bobbs-Merrill, 1971), pp. 212–229; and Ted R. Vaughan, "The Crisis in Contemporary American Sociology: A Critique of the Discipline's Dominant Paradigm," in *A Critique of Contemporary American Sociology* (New York: General Hall, 1993), pp. 42–47.

3. Hawthorn, "Unrest in Iran Nothing New to Professor," *Globe and Mail,* www.theglobeandmail.com/news/british-columbia/unrest-in-iran-nothing-new-to -professor/article4276608/ (retrieved February 23, 2014).

4. Peyman Vahabzadeh, email communication to authors, February 2014. Used with permission.

5. Ibid.

6. Ibid.

7. Ibid.

8. Mohammad Amin Ghaneirad, "A Critical Review of the Iranian Attempts at the Development of Alternative Sociologies," www.ios.sinica.edu.tw/cna /download/proceedings/20.Ghaneirad.Iran.pdf (retrieved February 23, 2014), p. 58.

9. It is now called *Critical Sociology*.

10. Berch Berberoglu, "Introduction," in *Critical Perspectives in Sociology*, ed. Berch Berberoglu (Dubuque, Iowa: Kendall/Hunt, 1991), p. xiv.

11. Ben Agger, *Critical Social Theories: An Introduction* (Boulder: Westview, 1998), p. 5.

12. "Some Comments About Project Censored and Sociology," personal communication from Carl Jensen, July 13, 1996, p. 1.

13. Ibid.

14. Ibid.

15. Carl Jensen and Project Censored, eds., *Censored: The News That Didn't Make the News and Why* (New York: Seven Stories Press, 1996), p. 35.

16. Project Censored, "Signs of an Emerging Police State," Project Censored, www.projectcensored.org/1-signs-of-an-emerging-police-state (retrieved December 22, 2013).

17. Project Censored, "Fukushima Nuclear Disaster Worse than Anticipated," www.projectcensored.org/3-fukushima-nuclear-disaster-worse-than-anticipated (retrieved December 22, 2013).

18. Walter Cronkite, "Let the Chips Fall Where They May," in *Censored: The News That Didn't Make the News and Why*, p. 25.

19. Ibid., p. 27.

20. Peter Phillips, "Media Censorship and a Free Press in America," *Censored Alert* (newsletter), Director's Column, Spring 1998.

21. Quoted in Jensen and Project Censored, *Censored: The News That Didn't Make the News and Why*, p. 32.

22. Phillips, "Media Censorship and a Free Press in America."

23. Jamie Panzarella, "Kevin Bales: Using Sociology to Fight Slavery," *ASA Footnotes*, vol. 40, no. 3, published March 2012, www.asanet.org/footnotes/mar12/app_soc.html#sthash.z61MYra7.dpuf (retrieved 19 December 2013).

24. "Kevin Bales," www.kevinbales.net/books.html (retrieved December 19, 2013).

25. Panzarella, "Kevin Bales: Using Sociology to Fight Slavery."

26. "Free the Slaves," www.freetheslaves.net (retrieved December 19, 2013).

27. Kevin Bales, "How to Combat Modern Slavery," TED Talks (filmed February 2010, posted March 2010), www.ted.com/talks/kevin_bales_how_to_combat_modern_slavery.html (retrieved December 19, 2013).

28. Panzarella, "Kevin Bales: Using Sociology to Fight Slavery."

29. Quoted in Frank E. Manuel and Fritzie P. Manuel, *Utopian Thought in the Western World* (Cambridge: Harvard University Press, 1979), p. 717.

30. Robert S. Lynd, *Knowledge for What?: The Place of Social Science in American Culture* (New York: Grove Press, 1964), p. 215.

31. William J. Wilson, *When Work Disappears: The World of the New Urban Poor* (New York: Knopf, 1996).

32. See Michel Foucault, *Power/Knowledge* (New York: Pantheon, 1980), p. 98. 33. C. Wright Mills, *The Sociological Imagination* (New York: Oxford University Press, 1959), p. 7. Some liberation sociologists have paid a substantial price.

33. C. Wright Mills, for example, never was promoted to the rank of full professor.

34. David L. Featherman and Robert M. Hauser, *Opportunity and Change* (New York: Academic Press, 1978).

35. Richard J. Herrnstein and Charles Murray, *The Bell Curve: Intelligence and Class Structure in American Life* (New York: Free Press, 1994); see Hernán Vera, Joe R. Feagin, and Andrew Gordon, "Superior Intellect? A Sincere Fiction of the White Self," *Journal of Negro Education* 64, 3 (Summer 1995): 295–306.

36. Alvin Gouldner, *The Coming Crisis of Western Sociology* (New York: Basic Books, 1970), p. 12.

37. Dorothy Smith, *The Everyday World as Problematic: A Feminist Sociology* (Boston: Northeastern University Press, 1987), p. 56.

38. Mills, *The Sociological Imagination*, p. 99.

39. Iris M. Young, *Justice and the Politics of Difference* (Princeton: Princeton University Press, 1990), pp. 38–39.

40. Ibid., p. 38.

41. 41. Betty Friedan, *The Feminine Mystique* (New York: Dell, 1963), p. 306.

42. Ibid., p. 40.

43. Ibid., pp. 40–42.

44. Mary R. Jackman, *The Velvet Glove: Paternalism and Conflict in Gender, Class, and Race Relations* (Berkeley: University of California Press, 1994).

45. W. E. B. Du Bois, *The World and Africa* (New York: International Publishers, 1965 [1946]), p. 37.

46. For evidence on this, see Joe R. Feagin, *Racist America: Roots, Current Realities, and Future Reparations* (New York: Routledge, 2000).

47. See Gunnar Myrdal, *Objectivity in Social Research* (New York: Pantheon Books, 1969).

48. Donatella della Porta, email communication to authors, February 2014. Used with permission.

49. Ibid.

50. Onwubiko Agozino, email communication to authors, January 2014. Used with permission.

51. Paulo Freire, *Pedagogy of the Oppressed* (New York: Continuum, 1995), p. 26.

52. Antonio Gramsci, *Letters from Prison*, trans. Lynne Lawner (New York: Harper and Row, 1973), pp. 43–44, 183–185.

53. Walda Katz-Fishman and Jerome Scott, personal communication, November 2000; and www.wideopen.igc.org/projectsouth/indexl.html (retrieved Nov. 16, 2000).

54. This paragraph draws heavily on an updating email communication from Walda Katz-Fishman, December 31, 2013. Used with permission.

55. Jerome W. Scott, personal communication, November 2000.

56. Ibid.

57. Ibid.

58. Ibid.

59. Walda Katz-Fishman, email communication to authors, November 2000.

60. Ibid.

61. Ibid.

62. This paragraph draws heavily on an updating email communication from Walda Katz-Fishman, December 31, 2013. Used with permission.

63. Philip Nyden, Anne Figert, Mark Shibley, and Darryl Burrows, "University-Community Collaborative Research: Adding Chairs at the Research Table," in *Building Community: Social Science in Action*, ed. Philip Nyden, Anne Figert, Mark Shibley, and Darryl Burrows (Thousand Oaks, CA: Pine Forge Press, 1997), p. 7.

64. Quoted in Sidney Liebes, Elisabet Sahtouris, and Brian Swimme, *A Walk Through Time: From Stardust to Us* (New York: Wiley, 1998), p. 204.

65. Translator's note in Freire, *Pedagogy of the Oppressed*, p. 17.

66. Freire, *Pedagogy of the Oppressed*, p. 19.

67. Ibid.

68. Alia R. Tyner-Mullings, "Central Park East Secondary School," *Schools: Studies in Education* 9 (September 2012): 227–245.

69. Tim Woods, email communication, February 10, 2014. Used with permission.

70. Ibid.

71. Ibid.

72. Ibid.

73. Sheldon S. Wolin, "Political Theory as a Vocation," *American Political Science Review* 63 (1969): 1080.

74. Karl Mannheim, *Ideology and Utopia* (New York: Harcourt, Brace and World, 1969), pp. 4–5.

75. W. E. B. Du Bois, "'To the World': Manifesto of the Second Pan-African Congress," in *W.E.B. Du ̇ Bois Pamphlets and Leaflets*, compiled by Herbert Aptheker (White Plains, NY: Krauss-Thompson, 1986), as quoted by Leigh Bin-ford, *The El Mozote Massacre* (Tucson: University of Arizona Press, 1996), p. 201.

76. Sandra Harding, "Introduction," in *The "Racial" Economy of Science: Toward a Democratic Future* (Bloomington: Indiana University Press, 1993), p. 18.

77. See Charles Lemert, *Sociology after the Crisis* (Boulder: Westview, 1995), pp. 117–118.

78. Ibid., p. 118.

79. For international human rights documents, see Department of Public Information, United Nations, *The United Nations and Human Rights, 1945–1995* (New York: United Nations, 1995), pp. 33–225.

80. Stan Bailey, email communication, spring 1996.

81. Jaime Weinman, "Pope Francis: The unlikeliest liberal hero?" *Maclean's*, www2.macleans.ca/2014/01/08/ cafeteria-catholics (retrieved February 7, 2014).

82. Ibid.

83. See Bertell Ollman, *Alienation: Marx's Conception of Man in Capitalist Society*, 2nd ed. (Cambridge: Cambridge University Press, 1976), pp. 227–228.

84. Ibid., p. 16.

85. Karin Kamp, "By the Numbers: The Incredibly Shrinking American Middle Class" (September 20, 2013), Moyers and Company, http://billmoyers.com /2013/09/20/by-the-numbers-the-incredibly-shrinking-american-middle-class/ (retrieved February 28, 2014).

86. Frances F. Piven and Richard A. Cloward, *Regulating the Poor* (New York: Pantheon Books, 1971).

87. Brian Stelter, "Spotlight From Glenn Beck Brings a CUNY Professor Threats," www.nytimes.com/2011/01/22/ business/media/22beck.html (retrieved February 17, 2014).

88. Frances Fox Piven. *Who's Afraid of Frances Fox Piven?: The Essential Writings of the Professor Glenn Beck Loves to Hate* (New York: New Press, 2011).

89. Gunnar Myrdal, *An American Dilemma* (New York: McGraw-Hill, [1944] 1964); and Leo Grebler, Joan W. Moore, and Ralph G. Guzman, *The Mexican-American People* (New York: Free Press, 1970).

90. Cheri Jo Pascoe, *Dude, You're a Fag: Masculinity and Sexuality in High School* (Berkeley: University of California Press, 2011).

91. Gouldner, *The Coming Crisis in Western Sociology*, p. 86.

92. Dorothy Ross, *The Origins of American Social Science* (New York: Cam-bridge University Press, 1991); see also Donald N. Levine, *Visions of the Sociological Tradition* (Chicago: University of Chicago Press, 1995), p. 79.

93. Levine, *Visions of the Sociological Tradition*, p. 80.

94. Harding, "Introduction," p. 17.

95. Jennifer Schuessler, "Academia Occupied by Occupy," www.nytimes.com/2012/05/01/books/academia-becomes-occupied-with-occupy-movement.html?partner=rssnyt&emc=rss (retrieved February 10, 2014).

96. Alex S. Vitale, "Rule of Law vs. the Forces of Order," *Occupied Wall Street Journal*, http://occupiedmedia.us/2011/10/rule-of-law/ (retrieved February 23, 2014).

97. Howard Becker, "Whose Side Are We On?" *Social Problems* 14 (1967): 241, 243.

98. Henry A. Giroux, *Teachers as Intellectuals: Toward a Critical Pedagogy of Learning* (Granby, MA: Bergin and Garvey, 1988), pp. 40–45 and passim; and Abigail A. Fuller, "Academics and Social Transformation: The Radical Movement in Sociology, 1967–1975," PhD dissertation, University of Colorado Boulder, 1995, pp. 10–11.

99. Christopher G. A. Bryant, *Positivism in Social Theory and Research* (New York: St. Martin's Press, 1985), p. 133; on "abstracted empiricism," see Mills, *The Sociological Imagination*, chapter 3.

100. L. L. Bernard, "The Teaching of Sociology in the U.S.," *American Journal of Sociology* 15 (October 1909): 196. His italics. The sexist phrasing of this comment is particularly important given the fact that many of the early founders were women sociologists, most of whom were also progressive activists.

101. Fuller, "Academics and Social Transformation," p. 11.

102. On misunderstandings of physical science, see Paul Feyerabend, *Against Method* (London: Verson, 1975), p. 19.

103. Bryant, *Positivism in Social Theory and Research*, p. 142.

104. Wolin, "Political Theory as a Vocation," p. 1064.

105. Thomas Kuhn, *The Structure of Scientific Revolutions* (Chicago: University of Chicago Press, 1962), pp. 165–166.

106. Gouldner, *The Coming Crisis in Western Sociology*, p. 441.

107. Ben Agger, *Public Sociology: From Social Facts to Literary Acts*, 2nd ed. (Lanham, MD: Rowman and Littlefield, 2007).

108. Michael Burawoy, "For Public Sociology," *American Sociological Review* 70 (February 2005): 4–28.

109. Ibid., pp. 9–11.

110. Agger, *Public Sociology*, p. 274. See also p. 269. Personal communication with Ben Agger, December 26, 2013. See also Ben Agger, *Critical Social Theories*, 3rd ed. (New York: Oxford University Press, 2013).

111. Burawoy, "For Public Sociology," p. 24,

112. Ibid., p. 25. See also pp. 21–24.

113. Mills, *The Sociological Imagination*, p. 187.

114. Smith, *The Everyday World as Problematic*, pp. 157–167.

115. Karl Marx, *The Eighteenth Brumaire of Louis Bonaparte*, in *Karl Marx and Frederick Engels, Selected Works* (London: Lawrence and Wishart, 1968), p. 97.

116. Mills, *The Sociological Imagination*, p. 181.

117. Quoted in Alfred M. Lee, *Sociology for the People: Toward a Caring Profession* (Syracuse: Syracuse University Press, 1988), p. 57.

Freedom and Security

by Judith Blau and Alberto Moncada

Civil and political rights are often juxtaposed with economic and social rights, but that is not because they rest on different principles. Indeed, they rest on the same identical principles, and they are enshrined as mutually interdependent and reinforcing rights in the 1948 Universal Declaration of Human Rights. It was the United States that made this crisp distinction, favoring civil and political rights and dismissing economic, social, and cultural rights. This was not always the case. In fact, President Franklin Delano Roosevelt in his 1944 State of the Union Address proposed "An Economic Bill of Rights" that fully embraced economic and social rights (see Blau and Moncada 2006; Sunstein 2004). Although he died shortly afterward and his proposal never made it out of congressional committees, the fact that he could propose it to the nation suggests that Americans were favorably disposed to the idea that rights were indivisible and that people's freedoms depended on such indivisibility and coherence. The Great Depression and war years had taken a great toll on all Americans, and besides that there were strong feelings of solidarity.

The cold war changed all this, basically by politicizing human rights. The ideological message was that Americans had unique freedoms, including the freedoms of consumption, employment, competition, entrepreneurship, and capitalist freedoms, whereas the socialist system was one of tyranny, oppression, and the denial of freedom. To enforce this contrast, children had to hide under their desks at school, in closets at home, and to pray for agnostic Russian souls. The House Committee on Un-American Activities, chaired by Senator Joseph McCarthy, embarked on a fierce witch-hunt, accusing authors, filmmakers, artists, teachers, and others of being communists, and finally broadening its net to accuse government bureaucrats and military officers. McCarthy was finally forced to resign in infamy, but the lasting legacy of this period—the cold war—was the sharp break between, on the one hand, freedoms—civil and political rights—and on the other hand, security—economic and social rights. Capitalism was a "moral" system for "moral" Americans, and it rested on assumptions about freedoms, eschewing assumptions about rights.

The Europeans, our practical, but hardly our ideological, allies, did not see the world exactly in these same terms. Beginning in the postwar decade, they started implementing varieties of welfare plans ("social democracies"), providing their citizens with economic security, codetermination in the workplace, housing rights, pension plans, assistance with education, health care, and labor protections. Whereas Americans were led to believe that market freedoms and political freedoms were cut of one cloth, Europeans felt that personal freedoms were best achieved when people were buffered from the excesses and rawness of capitalism.

The Indivisibility of Rights

The human rights perspective does not abstract people according to their functional roles in the polity and economy, but rather grants persons freedoms and self-determination and recognizes their integral social, economic, and cultural needs and their social, economic, and collective responsibilities. Thus, among the consequences of acting in terms of rights it enlarges the spaces for cooperation and collaboration, encourages new projects that enhance popular democracy and economic fairness, and allows people and groups to contribute in ways that are consistent with their distinctive interests, capabilities, and strengths.

Economic and social rights, political and civil rights, environmental rights, and cultural rights are thus indivisible and interdependent, making up an integral set of rights that ensures full equality and underscores each person's self-determining agency and the responsibilities they have to others. Aside from the responsibilities that people have in their communities to ensure equality of rights, human rights accompany the obligation, often met by states, to protect vulnerable groups and individuals.

There is, for example, an emphasis on the rights of children, the elderly, and the disabled. In principle there is no distinction either between human rights provisions and humanitarian laws, but because crimes against humanity, war crimes, apartheid, and genocide are such atrocious violations they are handled within their own distinct legal framework. The point to be made here is that human rights compose a coherent and unified logic, and because human rights advance human security they also advance human freedom, which no competitive economic system possibly can do.

American Freedom as Creation Myth

Almost all societies have creation myths. The Aztecs believe that Coatlique was first impregnated by an obsidian knife and gave birth to Coyolxanuhqui, goddess of the moon, and to a group of male offspring, who became the stars. In the Navaho creation myth, First Man ('Altsé Hastiin) and First Woman ('Altsé 'Asdzáá) were two of the beings from the First or Black World. First Man was made in the east from the meeting of the white and black clouds. First Woman was made in the west from the joining of the yellow and blue clouds. It might be said that the functional equivalent of a creation myth for the white settlers in America and for subsequent generations was the story about freedom and liberty. Americans return to it time after time, when recounting their war of independence from Great Britain, conquering the frontier, stories about the struggles of immigrants, landing a man on the moon, America's entrepreneurial spirit, the American inventor, and the embodiment of individual courage and personal initiative. It is a tradition to be proud of, and people around the world admire Americans, partly because this love of freedom accompanies equalitarian and anti-authoritarian attitudes.

When cold war politicians, like McCarthy, pitched an appeal to Americans, they used two code words—freedom and liberty. When one of his fiercest opponents, Senator Margaret Chase Smith, drafted a declaration, dated June 1, 1950, she used the strongest language one could use in America, and fighting fire with fire, she said, "basic principles of Americanism— are the right to criticize, the right to hold unpopular beliefs, the right to protest, and the right of independent thought." For our purposes, the American creation myth that embraces freedom and other virtues is drawn upon by all sides—left, center, right, prowar, antiwar, procapitalism, and anticapitalism. This freedom myth mobilizes as nothing else possibly can in America.

When Americans are stressed, as they were after September 11, recalling the creation myth is comforting, as George W. Bush instinctively knew, and what he told Americans was, "They want to take our freedom away from us. Americans love freedom. They don't have freedom. Oh, and by the way, Go shopping." Bush's statements put down on paper look ludicrous, but his oral argument after September 11 seemed to have made a lot of sense to Americans. The air was aflutter with American flags—cars, houses, highway overpasses, buildings, fishing boats, and bicycles. As if to say, "No, they can't take my freedoms away from me."

Freedom and Security

When it became known that the U.S.-led invasion of Iraq was carried out under false pretenses and that Saddam Hussein did not have weapons of mass destruction (as Bush had known all along), Bush's high ratings in opinion polls began to drop. But none so far in the Senate has been brave enough to issue a declaration against him as Margaret Chase Smith did in 1950 against Joseph McCarthy. But then, it still might happen. We suspect that the case would have to be made on the basis of America's Creation Myth that Bush is threatening the freedoms of Americans. This was the heart of Chase's message to the Senate.

We have argued that freedom and independence are so salient that for Americans to support virtually anything, it needs to be consistent with their creation myth. Smith knew this. So did Franklin Delano Roosevelt, who, when proposing the Second Bill of Rights, stated that "necessitous men are not free." He knew that his audience cherished freedom, and he also knew that in 1944 they would be thinking of the difficult years of the Great Depression. But we can update this because we live in different times. Globalization threatens the security of everyone on the planet. Multinationals close operations without warning, leaving massive numbers of unemployed behind, and free trade practices have created huge inequalities around the world. These days America's bridges collapse because there are precious few funds for infrastructural maintenance and repair. There is virtually no housing aid for the homeless in America, and when the homeless become ill, they often do not get medical treatment. Bit by bit, Americans are losing their security, and the loss of security is also the loss of freedom

Countries around the world are revising their constitutions to ensure greater security for their populations, and as the accompanying discussions and documents make clear, these revisions are largely in response to globalization and to some extent, to the threats posed by pending environmental catastrophes. These constitutional reforms go far to advance the welfare and security of citizens, and none impairs the freedoms of citizens. When a state constitution is revised, most typically the revision includes provisions for human rights (including labor rights, health care rights, protections against discrimination, and so forth), provisions that will promote greater democracy, and often provisions that will bolster cultural social pluralism. The U.S. Constitution is the oldest in the world—nothing to be proud of. Were the U.S. Constitution revised to encompass the full complement of rights, Americans would newly discover they have their freedoms.

References

Blau, Judith, and Alberto Moncada 2006. *Justice in the U.S.: Human Rights and the U.S. Constitution.* Lanham, MD: Rowman and Littlefield.

Sunstein, Cass R, 2004. *The Second Bill of Rights: FDR's Unfinished Revolution and Why We Need It More Than Ever.* New York: Basic Books.

CPSIA information can be obtained
at www.ICGtesting.com
Printed in the USA
LVOW03s1429041116

511689LV00006B/223/P